Applications of
Inductive Logic

Applications of Inductive Logic

Proceedings of a Conference
at The Queen's College, Oxford,
21–24 August 1978

Edited by
L. JONATHAN COHEN and
MARY HESSE

CLARENDON PRESS · OXFORD
1980

Oxford University Press, Walton Street, Oxford OX2 6DP

OXFORD LONDON GLASGOW
NEW YORK TORONTO MELBOURNE WELLINGTON
KUALA LUMPUR SINGAPORE JAKARTA HONG KONG TOKYO
DELHI BOMBAY CALCUTTA MADRAS KARACHI
NAIROBI DAR ES SALAAM CAPE TOWN

Published in the United States by
Oxford University Press,
New York

Printed in Great Britain by The Pitman Press, Bath

Applications of inductive logic.
  1. Induction (Logic) – Congresses
  I. Cohen, Laurence Jonathan
  II. Hesse, Mary
  161   BC91   79–41126
  ISBN 0-19-824584-X

Contents

Introduction

The past two decades of work in philosophy of science have been exceptionally lively and fruitful; but, compared with some other topics, the problems of inductive logic have not been in the forefront of attention. Three sorts of reason may be suggested for this.

1. The Carnapian era in confirmation theory left a host of purely technical problems for inductive logic. Similarly, the statistical and decision-theoretic methods, which increasingly replaced attempts at purely logical interpretations of probabilistic induction, have been elaborated in immense technical detail, and frequently in applications to problems which do not seem central to the philosophy of scientific inference. As a result there has been plenty of demanding and intellectually rewarding work for inductive logicians to do, without their having to return to the philosophical issues that ultimately motivate their enquiry.

2. A most important positive influence counting against inductive logic as a viable philosophical enterprise has, of course, been the philosophy of Popper and his successors, represented in this Conference in almost pure form by David Miller's paper. Not only has Popper himself, in his own analysis of science, rejected the concept of inductive reasoning in favour of standard patterns of deduction, but he has also received powerful support for this rejection from some reflective scientists, who have announced that their methods are not in fact Baconian (a concept not always clearly explained), but are hypothetico-deductive and falsificationist.

3. Within Popper's own school, and independently among philosophically-minded historians of science such as Kuhn, there has arisen a new emphasis on the claim that concrete examples from the history of science provide the laboratory, as it were, for testing theories of scientific inference and explanation. Most of these studies have also purported not to find any 'inductive logic' in their case histories, and some have purported not to find the hypothetico-deductive method either. The upshot has been a quite powerful movement towards relativism and scepticism regarding the justifiability of scientific inference, and an emphasis on the infinite variety of actual procedures involved in science, with respect to which all idealizations or systematizations of the reasoning process may be presented as pernicious distortions.

These relativist and sceptical extremes, however, have not failed to provoke their expectable backlash. Fearful of the collapse of all orderly criteria for scientific knowledge, some philosophers have interpreted the situation as the inevitable legacy of Hume and positivism, and have reintroduced hard concepts of causality, necessity, realism, and theoretical frameworks, with the aid of which they make short work of the problem of induction as such, at the cost, of course, of raising again all the traditional philosophical puzzles about causality and necessity that flowed from Kant's reply to Hume. This Kantian turn in recent philosophy of induction has undoubtedly been a fruitful one for much needed reinterpretations of the problem, and several examples of it are to be found among the papers that follow. Indeed it may perhaps be said that in the present state of the game, discussions of induction are polarized between the heirs of the empiricists and the rationalists: those who espouse contingency, correlations, finiteness, and concrete examplars, versus those who espouse necessity, causality, lawlikeness, universality, and theoreticity. Almost all the papers in the present volume exhibit unresolved controversies in this area; controversies that have not perhaps yet been openly and explicitly joined. Compared with this issue, the older polarizations of methodology versus logic, confirmation versus acceptance, objective versus subjective probability, probabilistic versus non-probabilistic theories of inductive support, and even normative versus psychological premisses for induction, are either seen to be negotiable, or else take on new significance as essentially rationalist versus empiricist issues.

The current task for inductive logic therefore seems to be to respond both to Popperian objections, and to relativism and scepticism with regard to scientific rationality. It can do this in broadly two ways: either by showing itself more adequate to deal with the theoretical aspects of science and with causal modalities, or by exploring the consequences of a more modest role relating to the pragmatics of science and its applications in action. These approaches are not necessarily contradictory, and both are exemplified in the papers that follow.

In planning the programme of the Conference, we had in mind two negative and two positive aims. First, we wanted to exclude purely technical developments of one or other system of inductive or statistical logic, in favour of a more profound exchange of views between proponents of different schools regarding their philosophical premisses. Secondly, we wanted to exclude purely historical and sceptical accounts of scientific cases without any attempt at philosophical reflection or rational generalization. In the event it proved easier to satisfy the second negative aim than the first, and it may be that a little more detailed attention to historical cases would have been beneficial, especially as there are not many occasions on which historians of science are brought into close personal contact with inductive logicians.

Positively, our first aim was to relate the current state of inductive logic to underlying issues in the philosophy of science, especially in the light of its recent comparative isolation for the reasons just outlined. Secondly, we wanted to represent a wide variety of applications of inductive logic. Applications to statistical inference, economic prediction, experimental design, ethical, legal, and linguistic theories, and to artificial intelligence are all touched upon in the papers, and the need for further work in relating them to more traditional types of inductive logic is documented.

With regard to the papers themselves, the philosophical problems addressed may be summarized by asking four questions:

1. Do we need to *accept as true* any propositions in science, and if so, what is our justification for so doing?

2. Is scientific inference primarily *enumerative* or *eliminative*, and in particular how do either of these traditional methods apply to scientific *theories*?

3. Does scientific inference require *metaphysical concepts* of causality, necessity, etc., and what is the relation between these and more modest conceptions of induction as only local or as concerned with particular things rather than with universal laws?

4. What is the relation between the *biological, psychological, and computer sciences of reasoning* on the one hand and *normative studies* on the other?

We will outline the topics of the papers under these four headings, and we have printed the papers in the corresponding order.

1. *Acceptance*

Several papers turn explicitly or implicitly on the question of how far induction needs a theory of acceptance. Levi presents a detailed analysis and comparison of various theories of acceptance, raising in particular the problems of how new knowledge can accrue consistently to an accepted knowledge corpus, given that deductive closure is satisfied, and that evidence exhibits *dissonance*, that is, different parts of the evidence may warrant conflicting conclusions. He is explicitly concerned with what he calls a 'normative account of belief and decision making', rather than with specific applications, although he allows that different types of application may require different types of acceptance rules. Teller takes up this point, and objects to a certain inflexibility inherent in Levi's approach: for example, he cannot at present accommodate the contraction of a knowledge corpus by rejecting previously accepted propositions, and he neglects utilities other than epistemic utilities. Teller proposes a simpler Bayesian criterion of acceptance: accept if and only if there is high probability relative to all options having a non-zero chance of occurring, and at least one of those options has been tested for. This criterion, however, does not allow us to maintain requirements of consistency and deductive closure for the accepted corpus.

Conversely, Rosenkrantz's paper is an argument for a Bayesian theory of support without acceptance rules, applied in three areas of inference which require different procedures, namely, theorizing, hypothesis-partition problems, and practical decision-making under uncertainty. With regard to theorizing, Rosenkrantz argues for an index of support that unifies the apparently conflicting requirements of comprehensiveness and accuracy on the one hand, and simplicity on the other, illustrating his thesis from the Copernicus–Ptolemy dispute. Kyburg replies that *every* type of inductive inference requires the acceptance or rejection of *some* propositions, if only those reporting the results of some experiments. Inductive logic, in his view, is just the attempt to justify such acceptance by means of a coherent system of rules. Moreover, inductive logic construed this way influences experimental design in non-trivial ways depending on whether it emphasizes hypothesis testing and rejection rules, or maximal expectation and acceptance rules.

At first sight Miller's defence of Popper's anti-inductivism does not appear to be a direct contribution to the debate about acceptance, but as responded to by Lehrer, and in the subsequent discussion, the chief focus of the criticisms directed against Popper becomes his inability to deal with the acceptance of anything as *knowledge*. In terms of the acceptance debate, *anything* must apparently be accepted in Popper's and Miller's knowledge corpus, except perhaps anything that has been falsified as contradicting accepted observation. Which of all the remaining mutually contradictory hypotheses are we to act upon and why?

2. Enumerative and Eliminative Induction, and Theories

Questions about what can be presupposed, or accepted, come up again in Cohen's and Hesse's papers. Cohen describes his 'method of relevant variables' as an eliminative form of inductive support, and argues that the logic underlying this is appropriate not only for scientific laws which require a concept of causal modality, but also for the logic of inference to legal rules from precedents, and to the meaning of a word from the contexts of its use. He then seeks to determine a quite general characterization of the type of reasoning to which this logic applies. The crucial feature of all such reasoning turns out to be that it concerns non-additive gradations of provability in incomplete deductive systems. In his reply Burks argues that this kind of eliminative and causal logic for science rests upon lower levels of inductive inference which are themselves enumerative, and that those enumerative inferences are required to justify the assumptions of relevance required in Cohen's theory. With the aid of conceptions drawn from computer design he sketches a theory of *complexity* and *hierarchy* in terms of which a computer formalization of levels of inductive inference as a model of human performance could in principle be developed.

Hesse also espouses enumerative induction as the most primitive form of scientific inference, both for low-level generalizations and for theories. She argues that the failure of transitivity for confirmation, and the absence of adequate criteria of acceptance for theories, means that confirmation of theoretical predictions, like that of next instances, ought to be understood in terms of enumerative induction and the concept of exchangeability. She also argues that Cohen's paradigm experiments for his method of relevant variables can be reinterpreted in terms of enumerative induction and Pascalian probability if his experimental presuppositions are brought to light. In his reply, Niiniluoto describes how the problems of universality, transitivity, and prediction from theories can be resolved within a Hintikka-type confirmation theory, together with an index of 'reliability' which effectively requires accepting some theories as part of the background information.

3. *Causal Powers and Particularity*

The two sessions introduced by the papers of Giere and Shoemaker, though very different in subject matter and philosophical tradition, were both primarily concerned with very similar questions, namely, what kind of causal modality, if any, needs to be presupposed in scientific inference? Giere argues for indulgence towards the notion of causal necessity with regard to deterministic systems, and towards the notion of propensity with regard to statistical systems, since only thus can counterfactual inferences be accounted for. But at the same

time Giere's theory refers to particular systems and finite populations, not universal generalizations. He defines a notion of the
'causal effectiveness of a given factor for a given effect in a given
population', and shows how this explicates certain accepted methods
of testing – for example randomization. In his reply Dorling accepts
Giere's finitism and his use of counterfactuals, but rejects the
non-Humean analysis of counterfactuals, replacing it by an analysis
either in terms of possible worlds without metaphysical overtones,
or in terms of personalist degrees of belief that will differ as
between accidental correlations and putative laws. He uses personalist arguments also to explicate the semantics of statistical
hypotheses as *belief*-conditional, rather than truth-conditional, and
explains how personalist beliefs can nevertheless be objective.

In contrasting style, Shoemaker develops a metaphysical theory of
causal powers to distinguish 'genuine' from 'mere Cambridge' properties (e.g., 'green' from 'grue'). He argues that the related concepts
of causality, genuineness, projectibility, lawlikeness, and so on, must
be interdefinable and irreducible to non-modal concepts, and that
the justification of induction is a relatively trivial consequence of our
best explanations in terms of accepted hypotheses and causal laws.
Swinburne does not dissent from the metaphysics, but objects to
Shoemaker's strong thesis that all genuine properties are potentialities for causal powers. This, he argues, is circular and not
required for the weaker thesis that projectibility must be justified by
causal laws.

4. *Sciences of Reasoning versus Normative Logic*

Seventeen years ago Ernest Nagel wrote in his Introduction to the
proceedings of a similar conference on Induction,[1] that most investigations of the biological, psychological, etc. conditions for inductive behaviour are 'undoubtedly irrelevant to the formal and normative issues' of the subject of induction. Perhaps one of the most
striking differences between philosophical moods then and now is
the greater tolerance extended by philosophers to such scientific
studies of non-demonstrative reasoning, and their increasing introduction into discussions about the problems of inductive logic.
These themes are, as noted above, pursued in Burks's paper. They
also form the subject matter of the session introduced by Winograd,
who outlines some current research in computer simulation of
extended inference modes which are not formalizable in standard

[1] *Induction: Some Current Issues*, ed. H. E. Kyburg and E. Nagel, 1963, p. xiii.

truth-theoretic or recursive terms. He and Boden both emphasize the need to presuppose theoretical frameworks in investigating artificial intelligence and in explaining the results of psychological experiments, and both may be said therefore to follow the current Kantian turn away from Hume.

The concluding session addressed by Adler and Bogdan points up some morals and describes some unfinished business. Is the project of inductive logic a 'progressive research programme'? Adler considers that it is, if the moves to 'local induction' and subjectivism can be shown still to be relevant to epistemological problems, and to objectivity and the growth of knowledge. Bogdan adds that the turn from 'logic' to 'methodology' and to the conceptualization of world models are both foreshadowed by Carnap, and are both currently fruitful types of inductive investigation.

In the two-centuries old debate between Hume and Kant, there is no doubt that the consensus of philosophy of science now favours Kant. All, from Popper to the enumerative inductivists, agree that there is no science without presuppositions – presuppositions that are not wholly validated by current empirical evidence. But as between different identifications and interpretations of these presuppositions there is much room for controversy. Are they genetically innate, to be explained by natural selection processes? This would not seem to account for presuppositions specific to advanced scientific theories, which can hardly have had survival value. Are they metaphysical analytic propositions? It seems unlikely that they are analytic of rationality as such, since they seem to be subject to social and cultural change, and to be specific to particular periods in the history of science. Are they the presuppositions of any natural language whatever? This seems too strong for the same reasons. Are they socially or culturally induced? If so, it is difficult to understand how they have inductive force in the empirical world. Are they just the consequences of the accumulated knowledge corpus of all human empirical experience? But this is patently circular. To take an example from two topics raised at the Conference, it would be interesting to have a closer confrontation between the relatively analytic elements of artificial intelligence, on the one hand, and the metaphysical analytic put forward by many philosophers in their accounts of causal modalities, on the other. For example there is surely a potential conflict between Winograd's claim that circular and holistic definitions of a 'family resemblance' type can be modelled in context-dependent systems, and Shoemaker's fear that there can be no account of sense and reference in a language without the whole apparatus of causal powers, essential properties, and universal laws. This is just one of the fruitful questions that may profit from greater collaboration between such widely different approaches to inductive logic. We hope the Conference did something to facilitate much more collaboration of this kind.

The record of the Conference would obviously be defective if it included no account of the discussions which followed delivery of the main papers and to which over half of the time of the Conference was in fact devoted. But we have not found it easy to regulate either the number or the length of the comments that participants in those discussions have contributed. We are very glad to have been able to include so much, but we are also sorry that we have not been able to include a lot more. We have not excluded any subsequently written-up material that has reached us, but we are conscious that much else of value was said.

It should be added that in planning the conference we wished to make it both international and broadly representative of different schools of opinion and age-groups, and yet small enough to facilitate vigorous discussion. We are fully conscious that there are many other important contributors in this area whom we could otherwise have invited.

In making our arrangements we profited from consultation with a small advisory committee, composed of Professors Ilkka Niiniluoto, Wesley Salmon, and Richard Wojcicki. We take this opportunity to thank them most cordially for their co-operation, though we ourselves take sole responsibility for all the actual decisions.

Finally we have to record our deep gratitude to the grant-giving bodies whose generosity made the Conference possible. These were the Alfred P. Sloan Foundation, the Fritz Thyssen Stiftung, and the International Union for History and Philosophy of Science (Division of Logic, Methodology, and Philosophy of Science).

LJC
MBH

1

Acceptance as a Basis for Induction

§1. ISAAC LEVI
Potential Surprise: its Role in Inference and Decision-Making

G. L. S. Shackle published *Expectation in Economics* in 1949.[1] That essay introduces potential surprise in determining the expectations controlling decision-making in general and the decisions of investors and other agents in the market-place in particular.

In this paper, I shall attempt to do the following:

(i) Reformulate an account of Shackle's theory of potential surprise along lines similar to those I first followed in 1966.

(ii) Explain the application of this account of potential surprise I suggested in *Gambling with Truth*.[2]

(iii) Outline Shackle's decision theory and the role of potential surprise in that theory and evaluate Shackle's theory from the vantage point of the decision theory I favour.

(iv) Compare Shackle's theory of potential surprise with L. J. Cohen's measures of inductive support and inductive probability[3] and G. Shafer's belief and support functions.[4]

My aim will be to show that Shackle's ideas merit serious attention from philosophers but that the domain of application of greatest interest is not the one he intended.

1. Credal States

At time *t*, I suppose that ideally situated agent X is in a cognitive state representable by a *corpus of knowledge* $K_{X,t}$ and a *credal state* $B_{X,t}$.[5]

X's corpus of knowledge (expressible in regimented language L) is representable by a set of sentences in L containing all logical truths, set-theoretical truths, and any other items expressible in L

---

[1] G. L. S. Shackle, *Expectations in Economics* (1949, 2nd ed. 1952). A more recent account is found in G. L. S. Shackle, *Decision, Order and Time in Human Affairs*, (1961, 2nd ed. 1969).

[2] I. Levi, *Gambling with Truth* (1967), chs. VIII and IX. An earlier account is found in I. Levi, 'On Potential Surprise', *Ratio* 8 (1966), pp. 107–29 and a more recent discussion is found in 'Potential Surprise in the Context of Inquiry', in *Uncertainty and Expectation in Economics: Essays in Honor of G. L. S. Shackle*, ed. by C. F. Carter and J. L. Ford (1972), pp. 213–36.

[3] L. J. Cohen, *The Implications of Induction* (1970) and *The Probable and the Provable* (1977).

[4] G. Shafer, *A Mathematical Theory of Evidence* (1976).

[5] For further details, see I. Levi, 'On Indeterminate Probabilities', *J. Phil.* 71 (1974), pp. 391–418; 'Acceptance Revisited', in *Local Induction*, ed. by R. Bogdan (1976), pp. 1–71; and 'Direct Inference', *J. Phil.* 74 (1977), pp. 5–29.

consigned to an incorrigible uncorpus *UK*. In addition to containing *UK*, the corpus is deductively closed.

X's corpus serves as *X*'s standard for serious possibility at time *t*. *h* is seriously possible according to *X* at *t* if and only if *h* is consistent with *X*'s corpus at *t*.

X's credal state at *t* is representable by a set of functions each member of which is of the form $Q(h; e)$ where both *h* and *e* are in *L* and *e* is consistent with *X*'s corpus at *t*. The set $B_{X,t}$ is non-empty; each *Q*-function in $B_{X,t}$ obeys the requirements of the calculus of probabilities relative to $K_{X,t}$; and $B_{X,t}$ satisfies a convexity requirement.

Strict Bayesians insist that *X*'s credal state should contain exactly one *Q*-function. Sometimes they will acknowledge that *X* will find it difficult to determine what his *Q*-function is. However, an ideally rational agent will be committed to exactly one such function.

B. O. Koopman, I. J. Good, C. A. B. Smith, and H. E. Kyburg[6] all abandoned strict Bayesianism in favour of an approach allowing credal states representable by the largest sets of *Q*-functions compatible with specifications of upper and lower probabilities for sentences in *L*.

More recently, A. P. Dempster has investigated a more restricted class of credal states but one still broader than that allowed by strict Bayesians.[7]

According to such *intervalist* views, credal states can be represented by specifying a lower probability function $Q(h; e)$; for the upper probability $\bar{Q}(h; e)$ should equal $1 - Q(h; e)$. Given the identification of $Q(h; e)$, intervalists recommend adopting as credal state the largest convex set of *Q*-functions obeying the calculus of probabilities and agreeing with $Q(h; e)$ and $\bar{Q}(h; e)$. If the only credal states allowed are of this kind, specifying lower probabilities suffices as a complete characterization of the credal state.

I have argued elsewhere[8] that we should not be so restrictive, but should permit several non-empty convex sets of *Q*-functions – obeying the requirements of the calculus of probabilities and com-

---

[6] B. O. Koopman, 'The Bases of Probability', *BAMS* 46, (1940), pp. 763–74; I. J. Good, 'Subjective Probability as a Measure of a Non-measurable Set', *Logic, Methodology and Philosophy of Science*, ed. by P. Suppes, E. Nagel, and A. Tarski (1965), pp. 319–29; C. A. B. Smith, 'Consistency in Statistical Inference and Decision' (with discussion), *J. Roy. Stat. Soc.* B XXIII (1961), pp. 1–25; H. E. Kyburg, *Probability and the Logic of Rational Belief* (1961).

[7] A. P. Dempster, 'Upper and Lower Probabilities Induced by a Multivalued Mapping', *Ann. Math. Stat.* 38 (1967), pp. 325–39.

[8] I. Levi, 'On Indeterminate Probabilities', pp. 407–8 and 416–17.

patible with the same interval-valued specifications – to be credal states.

The point is of some importance.

Strict Bayesians have thought that degrees of belief could be represented by unique Q-functions representing the credal states of rational agents. Those who have doubted the strict Bayesian doctrine have not despaired of proposing numerical representations of degrees of belief. Intervalists can represent credal states by lower probability functions. As has been known for a long time, these lower probability functions do not behave like probability measures. I am not familiar with anyone who has suggested in print that such lower probability measures be interpreted as degrees of belief. However, G. Shafer has proposed measures of degrees of belief which he explicitly acknowledges to have the same formal properties as Dempster's measures of lower probability. As will be explained later, Shafer appears to interpret Dempster's formalism differently from how Dempster intended.

In any case, such interpretations of lower probabilities as degrees of belief are precluded by my approach according to which a lower probability function cannot characterize X's credal state completely.

2. *Degrees of Belief and Disbelief*

Strict Bayesians sometimes regard the Q-function representing X's credal state as measuring degrees of belief in various hypotheses. I noted how intervalists could (but in practice do not) represent degrees of belief by lower credal probability functions.

The interesting point to notice is that neither representation captures what appears to be the conception of degree of belief and degree of disbelief which is dominant presystematically.

In presystematic discourse, to say that X believes that h to a positive degree is to assert that X believes that h. To claim that X disbelieves that h to a positive degree implies that X disbelieves that h (i.e., believes $\sim h$). Finally, when X believes that h to a 0 degree and disbelieves that h to a 0 degree, he suspends judgement as to the truth of h.

On this understanding, X assigns maximum degrees of belief to hypotheses when he is certain of their truth so that they belong to his corpus. However, he can assign minimum 0 degree of belief to a hypothesis even though he is not certain that it is false. Similarly, X may assign a positive degree of belief to h even when he is not certain that h is true.

No function obeying the requirements of the calculus of probabilities can represent such degrees of belief. Consequently, strict

Bayesian conceptions of degrees of belief are automatically violated.

Unlike lower probability functions, measures of the sort under consideration are *acceptance-based*. They presuppose that in addition to what X accepts as evidence in his corpus $K_{X,t}$, X accepts as true additional hypotheses whose falsity is consistent with $K_{X,t}$. Recall that X's corpus of knowledge or evidence consists of all hypotheses X is committed to accepting as certainly true and not possibly false – i.e., to accepting as evidential in subsequent deliberations and enquiries. If X assigns a positive degree of belief to h even though he is not certain that h is true, X must accept h (i.e., in some sense, believe that h) even though he does not accept h as evidence at the time.

Shackle's measure of potential surprise is intended by him as a measure of degrees of disbelief in an acceptance- (or rejection-) based sense.[9]

3. *Four Kinds of Ignorance*

To elaborate on the distinctions just made, it may be helpful to explain four different senses in which X may be said to be ignorant concerning rival hypotheses.

X is *modally ignorant* concerning $h_1, h_2, \ldots, h_n$ if and only if each of the h_i's is consistent with $K_{X,t}$ and $K_{X,t}$ entails that at least and at most one of the h_i's is true. In that event, all of these hypotheses are serious possibilities according to X at t and he is not certain as to which of them is true.

Given a set U of hypotheses concerning which X is modally ignorant at t, X is *Laplace ignorant* concerning the elements of U if and only if every Q-function in $B_{X,t}$ satisfies the condition that $Q(h_i) = Q(h_j)$ for every h_i and h_j in U. (For simplicity, I consider only finite U.)

X is *probabilistically ignorant* with respect to U if and only if every Q-distribution over the elements of U is represented in $B_{X,t}$ (with the implication that $Q(h_i) = 0$ for every h_i in U).

Given a set U of hypotheses with respect to which X is modally ignorant, X is *modally ignorant in the extreme* concerning the members of U if and only if no disjunction of a proper subset of elements of U is accepted as true without being accepted as evidence. That is to say, no disjunction of a proper subset of U is assigned a positive acceptance-based degree of belief and no such disjunction is assigned a positive degree of disbelief (i.e., of potential surprise).

[9] G. L. S. Shackle, *Decision, Order and Time in Human Affairs*, ch. IX.

Modal ignorance is presupposed by the other three kinds of ignorance. Laplace ignorance is the plaything of strict Bayesians. Those unencumbered by the dogmas of strict Bayesianism are not likely to take it seriously. Conceptions of probabilistic ignorance are discussed by Smith, Kyburg and Dempster. Extreme modal ignorance is discussed by Shackle and, so it appears, by Shafer.[10]

Thus, we have an abundance of conceptions of ignorance. Are they in competition with one another? Or do they possess different uses in enquiry and deliberation? Answers to these questions go hand in glove with clarification of the conceptions of credal state and acceptance-based measures of degrees of belief.

4. Caution-Dependent Acceptance-Rules

Let K be X's corpus of evidence (I omit subscripts whenever convenient). I suppose K is deductively closed, contains the urcorpus UK and is consistent.

U is a set of hypotheses with respect to which X is modally ignorant. $D(U)$ is the set of hypotheses equivalent given K to disjunctions of subsets of elements of U.

Let R_k be an acceptance-rule relative to K and U. It specifies the set of elements of $D(U)$ which are merely accepted.

Suppose that R_k belongs to a family of such rules indexed by values of k ranging from a maximum (which I shall fix at 1) to a minimum (set at 0). The family of rules is *caution-dependent* if and only if for every g in $D(U)$ there is a value $k(g)$ of k such that $k(g) = 0$ if g is inconsistent with K and otherwise $k(g)$ is the maximum value of k for which R_k fails to reject g (i.e., fails to recommend acceptance of $\sim g$) and where g is unrejected for all smaller values of k.

To illustrate, suppose U consists of a null hypothesis H_0 and its rival H_1 where both are simple statistical hypotheses. Suppose the rule is to pick a significance level and pick a test so that the power is maximized. If a sample point falls in the critical region, reject H_0 and otherwise reject nothing. Let the significance level range from 50 per cent to 0 per cent. The resulting family of rules specifies for

---

[10] G. Shafer, *A Mathematical Theory of Evidence*, pp. 22–4. K. Arrow and L. Hurwicz take note of Shackle's conception of extreme modal ignorance in 'Decision Making under Ignorance', *Uncertainty and Expectation in Economics: Essays in Honor of G. L. S. Shackle*, ed. by C. F. Carter and J. L. Ford, pp. 1–11. They appear to confuse it with probabilistic ignorance. Shafer may be doing the same thing. I claim that probabilistic ignorance implies modal ignorance in the extreme sense but not conversely. I discuss the four kinds of ignorance in 'Four Types of Ignorance', *Social Research* 44 (1977), pp. 745–56.

each outcome of experiment what the set of accepted hypotheses will be and does so in a manner satisfying requirements of caution-dependence. I do not endorse this rule but pending later discussion, it can serve to illustrate the idea.

Given a caution-dependent family of acceptance-rules, a corpus K, an ultimate partition U, and set of hypotheses $D(U)$, $b(h) =$ the degree of belief that $h = d(\sim h) =$ the degree of disbelief that $\sim h$.

$$b(h) = d(\sim h) = 1 - k(\sim h).$$

When $b(h)$ is equal to 0, h is not accepted according to any of the rules in the caution-dependent family. It is in this sense that it is not accepted as true. If $b(h) > 0$, h is accepted according to all rules for which $k > k(\sim h) = 1 \sim b(h)$.

Thus, if we are given the values of the belief function $b(h)$ for all h in $D(U)$, we can recover the result of applying the caution-dependent family of acceptance-rules through the equation $k(h) = 1 - d(h) = 1 - b(\sim h)$.

The parameter k for the caution-dependent family of acceptance-rules represents the degree of boldness (or degree of caution) entailed in using R_k. The higher the value of k, the bolder the rule. X's degree of belief is positive if there is some sufficiently high level of boldness at which h is accepted ($\sim h$ is rejected) according to rules in the family.

Neither Shackle, Shafer, nor Cohen explicitly introduce caution-dependent rules to explicate their ideas of belief and disbelief (or inductive probability in Cohen's case). However, any acceptance-based measure of degrees of belief may be seen to generate results of employing members of a sequence of caution-dependent acceptance-rules. In this sense, all these authors are tacitly committed to such rules.

The connection between acceptance-based degrees of belief and caution-dependent families of acceptance-rules is a useful one; for any clue we might find as to the intended meaning and application of acceptance based on degrees of belief may shed light on the corresponding notion of acceptance. Conversely any clarity we may have regarding acceptance may illuminate our understanding of degrees of belief.

5. Cogency

Let MK_k be the set of sentences in $D(U)$ accepted according to R_k where R_k is a member of a caution-dependent family of acceptance-rules.

R_k is *feebly cogent* if and only if it satisfies the following conditions:

(1) K is deductively closed and consistent and MK_k contains K.

(2) If $\sim h$ is in K, h is not in MK_k.

(3) If h is in MK_k, so are all logical consequences of K and h.

R_k is *piecemeal cogent* if and only if it is feebly cogent and satisfies the following:

(4) If h is in MK_k, $\sim h$ is not in MK_k.

R_k is *deductively cogent* if and only if it is piecemeal cogent and satisfies the following:

(3*) MK_k is deductively closed.

We can show that measures of degrees of belief derived from a caution-dependent family of acceptance-rules must satisfy the following theorems.

If the family of rules is feebly cogent,

B1: If $k \vdash \sim g$, $b(g) = 0$ and $d(g) = 1$.

B2: If $K \vdash g$, $b(g) = 1$ and $d(g) = 0$.

B3: If $K, h \vdash g$, $b(h) \leqslant b(g)$ and $d(\sim h) \leqslant d(\sim g)$.

If the family is piecemeal cogent as well,

B4: Given a set of elements of $D(U)$ exclusive and exhaustive relative to K, at most one member of the set bears positive b-value and at most one member of the set of negations of members of the set bears positive d-value.

If, in addition, the caution-dependent family is deductively cogent, B3 and B4 may be strengthened as follows:

B3*: $b(h \,\&\, g) = \min(b(h), b(g))$ and $d(hvg) = \min(d(h), d(g))$.

B4*: Given the set of exclusive and exhaustive alternatives relative to K specified in B4, at least one member bears 0 d-value and the negation of at least one member bears 0 b-value. B4 continues to hold.

6. Potential Surprise

Shackle imposes conditions B1, B2, B3*, and B4* on d-functions – i.e., measures of potential surprise.[11] I propose interpreting Shackle

[11] G. L. S. Shackle, *Decision, Order and Time in Human Affairs*, ch. X, especially axioms (2), (4), (6), and (9). Axiom (1) does not conform precisely to my characterization of degrees of belief. (See also p. 73.) However, the characterization on p. 71 does conform to mine. I suspect Shackle considers two senses of 'belief'. Degrees of belief in the sense in which $b(h) = d(\sim h)$ and a belief state for h represented by the pair $(d(h), d(\sim h))$.

as being committed by implication to families of deductively cogent and caution-dependent acceptance-rules. I offered this interpretation of Shackle's view in 1966 and, setting minor adjustments to one side, see no reason to change the proposal today.

Why should acceptance-rules be deductively cogent? Alternatively, why should potential surprise conform to Shackle's requirements? I believe presystematic precedent strongly supports this view. X's degree of belief that h & g should equal the smallest of $b(h)$ and $b(g)$ as Shackle's theory requires. This idea is so intuitively compelling that instructors offering popular discussions of probability as a measure of degree of belief must go to some lengths to overwhelm qualms concerning the multiplication theorem.

But intuition is not decisive here. Whether probabilities are degrees of belief or not, credal probabilities have a useful role to play in deliberation and enquiry. Given X's credal state and some decision problem confronting him, X should restrict his choice of an option to members of that subset of feasible options bearing maximum expected utility relative to computations of expected utility employing some Q-function from X's credal state. That is to say, either X should restrict his choice of this set of E-admissible options or find some way of deferring choice between E-admissible options pending further deliberation.

I do not care to argue the matter here; but I have no doubt strict Bayesians are mistaken in requiring rational agents to adopt credal states representable by single Q-functions. Even so, indeterminate appraisals of hypotheses with respect to credal probability play a critical role in the evaluation of the admissibility of hypotheses.

The challenge is to find a use for measures of potential surprise and cognate measures of degrees of belief which have some important use in deliberation and enquiry.

There are two reasons for this:

(1) Bayesians have been sceptical of inductive acceptance-rules. By implication they must be sceptical of acceptance-based measures of degrees of belief and disbelief (potential surprise). They challenge those who are friends of acceptance to identify a use for acceptance-rules.

(2) Friends of acceptance disagree among themselves concerning the properties acceptance should have; and such disagreements are not likely to be resolved by an appeal to intuition. I suggest that a more promising avenue of attack is to consider the intended applications of acceptance-rules.

In my opinion there is a useful sense of acceptance which argues decisively in favour of acceptance-rules (for that sense of acceptance) satisfying requirements of deductive cogency.

Suppose X seeks to revise his body of knowledge K via induction by adding new information supplying an answer to some question. Adoption of the answer should result in a shift from K to a new corpus K^* which is consistent and closed. K^* should be obtained from K by adding some hypothesis in $D(U)$ and forming the deductive closure.

The deductive closure requirement on the corpus of knowledge or evidence is an expression of the function of X's corpus as a standard for serious possibility and the idea that, when we ignore limitations on X's capacity for making computations and on his memory, his standard should be represented by the set of all hypotheses whose falsity is not seriously possible according to X's point of view.

Prior to adopting a potential answer to his question and changing his corpus, X might contemplate the inductive expansion strategies recommended by various rules for inductive expansion which differ from one another in the way members of a family of caution-dependent acceptance-rules do. He can identify the optimal expansion strategy according to each rule R_k in the family.

Some hypotheses will not be added to K no matter what value of the parameter k is used. Others will be added for some values of k but not for others. Thus, relative to X's initial corpus K, X can evaluate hypotheses in $D(U)$ by specifying those rules licensing their addition to the body of evidence and those rules which fail to license their addition. In this manner, both a b-function and a d-function can be defined.

To decide which hypotheses to add to K involves determining a level of boldness k and accepting all hypotheses into the evidence which are licensed by the rule with that value of the index k. *But to fix on a value of k is equivalent to determining how high the acceptance-based degree of belief relative to K should be before a hypothesis may be added to K and become evidence in its own right.* To do this is tantamount to determining whether enquiry into the truth-value of the hypothesis h ought to continue or the matter settled by adding h (or $\sim h$) to the body of evidence.

This is the understanding of the matter I had in *Gambling with Truth*.[12] But on that understanding, it is plain that the caution-dependent family of acceptance-rules should be deductively cogent;

[12] I. Levi, *Gambling with Truth*, chs. VIII and IX. See also I. Levi, 'Potential Surprise in the Context of Inquiry', pp. 213–36. In those essays, I suggest that surprise and belief-measures capture an aspect of Keynes's conception of weight of argument. The reader should check those references for elaboration.

for the purpose of such a family of rules is to evaluate in a preliminary manner various potential expansion strategies leading to the revision of the corpus of knowledge. Given the function of a body of knowledge as a standard for serious possibility, the deductive cogency requirement becomes compelling.

Thus, if it is ever legitimate to revise a corpus of knowledge (understood as a standard for serious possibility) via inductive expansion, there is room for the conception of potential surprise to play a useful role in the evaluation of expansion strategies. Moreover, the measures of potential surprise to be employed should have the formal properties Shackle claimed they should have.

Can plausible caution-dependent and deductively cogent acceptance-rules be constructed? I shall suggest two candidates. The first is derived from a proposal of I. Hacking's[13] which eschews appeal to probability in favour of likelihood in deciding which elements of U to reject.

> *Hacking$_k$:* Let the elements of U be simple chance hypotheses and let K consist of background knowledge b, data e concerning the outcome of an experiment and the deductive consequences thereof. The likelihoods of all elements of U on e are given. h^* bears maximum likelihood relative to e and h_i is another element of U. h_i is rejected ($\sim h_i$ accepted) if and only if $L(h_i; e)/L(h^*; e) < k$. g in $D(U)$ is accepted if and only if g is equivalent to the disjunction of elements of a subset of U such that all elements of U not in that set are rejected.

Hacking$_k$ is deductively cogent and caution-dependent. One can define b-functions and d-functions relative to Hacking$_k$. Thus, one need not appeal explicitly to probability measures in determining degrees of potential surprise that have the desired formal properties. Whether such rules are otherwise adequate is, of course, another story.

On the other hand, there is no obstacle to using credal probability to determine surprise. I myself favour caution-dependent families of deductively cogent rules which are based on credal probability in the following manner:

> *Levi$_k$:* Let the credal state be B and consider all unconditional Q-distributions over elements of U allowed by B. Let $\mathfrak{M}$ be

---

[13] I. Hacking, *The Logic of Statistical Inference* (1965), pp. 89–91. Rule B on p. 115 of I. Levi, 'On Potential Surprise', is an alternative likelihood-based rule. Hacking's suggestion and mine were proposed quite independently of one another.

another convex set of probability distributions (called M-distributions) over elements of U. These are the information-determining probability functions. Reject h_i in U if and only if for every Q-function in B and M-function in $\mathfrak{M}$, $Q(h_i) < kM(h_i)$. Accept g in $D(U)$ if and only if $\sim g$ is equivalent given K to a disjunction of rejected elements of U.

In both *Gambling with Truth* and 'Information and Inference',[14] I took B and $\mathfrak{M}$ to be single-membered. In *Gambling with Truth*, I required the single M-function to assign equal values to all elements of U. This last requirement was abandoned in 'Information and Inference' and now that I have constructed an alternative to strict Bayesian dogma, I no longer assume that B and $\mathfrak{M}$ are single-membered. Yet, the more general Levi_k provides a deductively cogent acceptance-rule for each value of k. Measures of potential surprise satisfying Shackle's requirements can be constructed relative to these rules.

7. Deviation from Deductive Cogency

According to a widely held view, h should be accepted relative to corpus K if and only if the credal probability that h relative to K is sufficiently high. I suspect this view is based on a confusion of credal probability with acceptance-based degrees of belief (b-measure); for if the acceptance-based degree of belief is sufficiently high and other contextual factors are right, h should be added to X's corpus via induction.

Be that as it may, many authors insist that high probability is sufficient for acceptance and H. E. Kyburg has generalized this view to apply to cases where credal probability goes indeterminate by insisting that the lower probability $Q(h)$ be sufficiently high.[15]

$Kyburg_k$: Let $m = k/2$ where k, as usual, ranges from 0 to 1. Accept g in $D(U)$ if and only if $Q(g) > 1 - m$. Reject g in $D(U)$ if and only if $1 - Q(\sim g) = \bar{Q}(g) < m$.

Consider the set of acceptance-rules obtained by modifying $Kyburg_k$ through equating m with k so that m ranges from 0 to 1. This too is a probability-based and caution-dependent set of acceptance-rules. I shall call it $Shafer_k$.

According to $Shafer_k$, $b(h) = Q(h)$ and $d(h) = b(\sim h) = Q(\sim h) = 1 - \bar{Q}(h)$.[16]

[14] I. Levi, 'Information and Inference', *Synthèse* 17, 1967, pp. 369–91. Levi_k is first proposed in my 'Potential Surprise in the Context of Inquiry', p. 230.
[15] H. E. Kyburg, *Probability and the Logic of Rational Belief*.
[16] G. Shafer, *A Mathematical Theory of Evidence*, p. 43.

Thus, the measures of degrees of belief generated by Shafer$_k$ coincide with measures of lower credal probability. The family of acceptance-rules is feebly cogent and, hence the b-functions and d-functions are constrained to conform to B1, B2, and B3 but not necessarily B4, B3*, or B4*.

Kyburg has never introduced b-functions or d-functions generated by Kyburg$_k$. He has, however, endorsed rules from this family for acceptance. He has not intended his acceptance-rules as rules for the preliminary appraisal of potential strategies for inductive expansion of the evidential corpus as I have done.

Thus, it is entertainable that Kyburg and I do not disagree over issues of deductive closure as I once thought we did; for Kyburg's conception of acceptance and the function acceptance performs within his epistemological programme appears to be different from the function of mere acceptance within my framework.

Furthermore, a great many authors have thought of accepting a hypothesis as tantamount to assigning it a high credal probability. Kyburg has generalized the idea so that it applies in cases where credal states are not representable by unique Q-functions.

None the less, I find Kyburg's conception difficult to evaluate. If Kyburg meant by acceptance what I mean, he could not plausibly remain faithful to a high probability rule; for such a rule fails to be deductively cogent. On the other hand, if he does not mean what I mean by 'acceptance', what does he mean? Why should we not dispense with the notion of acceptance altogether and rest content with the corpus of knowledge (and the cognate notion of acceptance as evidence) and the credal state? Perhaps there is an answer other than one based on an appeal to intuition. Kyburg's intuitions and mine seem to clash so strongly here, I have not found appeal to either his intuitions or mine very helpful.

Unlike Kyburg, Shafer never discusses acceptance-rules explicitly; but he does investigate measures of degrees of belief or support and measures of degrees of disbelief. Moreover, his measures exhibit the formal properties of measures satisfying B1, B2, and B3 and, in addition, his b-functions are explicitly acknowledged by Shafer to be formally similar to lower probability functions.

Thus, *if* Shafer's b-functions are acceptance-based measures of degrees of belief, they are generated by the family Shafer$_k$. Indeed, Shafer's b-functions are determined by the family Shafer$_k$ for those cases where the credal states meet the requirements imposed by Dempster.

On this construal, the difficulties confronting Kyburg face Shafer along with some additional ones. *Shafer*$_k$ consists of acceptance-rules which are not even piecemeal cogent. Furthermore, although Kyburg's theory belongs to a tradition which considers high probability as warranting acceptance, Shafer's theory implies that any positive probability – no matter how low – warrants acceptance.

Both of these results are bizarre enough to render Shafer's idea difficult to swallow. One wonders here even more than in Kyburg's case why the talk of degrees of belief, disbelief, and support is not eliminated altogether in favour of representations in terms of the credal state with its upper and lower probabilities.

It is clear, however, that Shafer wants to resist that interpretation. He is quite anxious to acknowledge his debt to Dempster. Yet, he seeks a 'reinterpretation of Dempster's work, a reinterpretation that identifies his 'lower probabilities' as epistemic probabilities or degrees of belief, takes the rule for combining such degrees of belief as fundamental, and abandons the idea that they arise as lower bounds over classes of Bayesian probabilities'.[17]

Thus, Shafer wishes to retain Dempster's formalism but with a new interpretation. Moreover, Shafer does construe his 'epistemic probabilities' or 'degrees of belief' in a manner often suggesting an acceptance-based interpretation. If X assigns 0 degree of belief to h and also to $\sim h$, X is ignorant as to the truth of h and, in a sense in which X neither believes that h nor that $\sim h$ and has no warrant for believing either alternative. When X has evidence supporting h, Shafer seems to suggest that he has a warrant for believing that h to a positive degree.

Reading Shafer's idea as an effort to reinterpret Dempster's theory in terms of some acceptance-based conception of degrees of belief is reinforced by his brief discussion of L. J. Cohen's account of inductive support and Shackle's account of potential surprise.[18] He incorrectly identifies Cohen's measure of inductive support as satisfying B1, B2, B*3, and B*4 and correctly contends that Shackle's measures obey the same requirements.

Shafer contends that Shackle's measures are special cases of measures in the family he is studying. He has a name for them. They form the family of 'consonant' support functions. He complains that both Cohen and Shackle fail to take into account the phenomenon of dissonance.

It is easy to share the desire of these scholars to ban the appearance of conflict from our assessment of evidence and our allocation of belief. But in

[17] Ibid., p. ix.
[18] Ibid., pp. 223–6.

the light of what we have learned, the ambition of doing so must be deemed unrealistic. The occurrence of outright conflict in our evidence should and does discomfit us; it prompts us to reexamine both our evidence and the assumptions that underlie our frame of discernment with a view to removing that dissonance. But this effort does not always bear – at least not quickly. And using all the evidence means using evidence that is embarrassingly conflicting.[19]

An inspection of Shafer's examples of conflict or dissonance[20] reveal that what he has in mind are situations where X might have a corpus obtained by adding to the urcorpus the proposition e_1 & e_2 and forming the deductive closure. Relative to K_1, obtained by adding e_1 to UK and forming the closure, X is justified in accepting h and all its consequences. Relative to K_2, obtained by adding e_2, X is justified in accepting g contrary to h together with the consequences including $\sim h$.

e_1 and e_2 are not inconsistent with each other but they conflict in the sense that when taken separately they warrant incompatible conclusions.

This notion of conflict, which presupposes a conception of acceptance or warranted acceptance, is not itself embarrassing or difficult. Its presence need not prompt us to reexamine our evidence as Shafer suggests. Neither Cohen nor Shackle ever denied the presence of such conflict or dissonance in data.

Shafer thinks otherwise because he wishes his measures of degrees of belief or support to satisfy two demands: (i) they should be acceptance-based; and (ii) where the total evidence exhibits dissonance, all hypotheses receiving positive support from part of the evidence when taken by itself should be assigned positive support (and, hence, should be believed to a positive degree) when the evidence is pooled.[21]

Once this pair of requirements is insisted upon, dissonance does create trouble; for now two incompatible hypotheses must be positively believed and, hence, accepted whenever dissonance is present. Shackle would surely object to this and so would Kyburg. Even Shafer allows that such conflict would and should 'discomfit' us.

Shafer suggests that we should undertake efforts to remedy the

---

[19] Ibid., pp. 225–6.
[20] G. Shafer, *A Mathematical Theory of Evidence*. See examples 4.3 and 4.4 on pp. 84 and 85.
[21] In *A Mathematical Theory of Evidence*, ch. 4, G. Shafer assumes this for separable support-functions. Some qualification of no importance for the points under consideration in this discussion should be introduced to obtain Shafer's general theory. See ibid., chs. 7 and 9.

situation; but the conflict cannot be eliminated by adding new evidence but only by getting rid of some of the old. And Shafer does state that we should 'reexamine' dissonant evidence. The only thing which prevents getting rid of conflicting evidence is that our effort to do so does not always 'bear fruit' – whatever that means.

I submit it is a bizarre theory which implies that, whenever we have two bits of data e_1 and e_2 each of which supports contrary hypotheses when taken in isolation from each other, we should undertake efforts to remove one of the bits from our evidence!

To escape the predicament Shafer acknowledges himself to be in (without appreciating how troublesome it is for his theory) Shafer could surrender the idea that degrees of belief are acceptance-based; but this move can raise anew the problem of giving an interpretation different from Dempster's for Dempster's formalism.

The alternative is to give up (ii). To be sure, (ii) is part of an answer to an important question. If e_1 warrants positively believing that h when e_1 is the total evidence, and e_2 warrants believing that g when e_2 is the total evidence, and h and g are contraries, what attitude should X adopt when his total evidence is e_1 & e_2? This is one of the questions Shafer seeks to answer in discussing the problem of 'combining evidence'.[22]

My contention is that, whatever the correct solution of the problem may be, it is not to be found in recommending that rational men believe both hypotheses to a positive degree (as (ii) requires). e_1 & e_2 may warrant believing that h, or it may warrant believing that g, or it may warrant refusing to believe either. It cannot justify believing both h and g. In at least one important sense, recommending this is recommending inconsistency. I stop short of saying this because feebly cogent acceptance-rules still prevent believing that h & g even when h is believed and g is believed. To me that is small comfort, not be enhanced by euphemisms like 'dissonance'.

Thus, Shafer's claim that Shackle's theory is less general than his because it fails to acknowledge the phenomenon of dissonance is a

---

[22] Ibid., ch. 3. Both Shafer and I. Hacking ('Combined Evidence', in *Logical Theory and Semantical Analysis*, ed. by S. Stenlund, (1974), pp. 113–23) see their problem as one investigated by J. Bernoulli in *Ars Conjectandi*. I have read this book in German so that perhaps some nuance in the original has escaped me. But the discussion in part IV to which Shafer and Hacking allude suggests to me that they have both misread Bernoulli. Bernoulli is far from clear, but he is obviously concerned with situations where one can only in part satisfy the requirements fulfilled according to Huyghens' analysis (incorporated as part I of the *Ars Conjectandi*) and he is exploring ways and means to characterize indeterminate probability judgements which then ensue. This, however, is a construal of his own theory which Shafer disavows.

mare's nest of confusion. I do not think Shackle handled the question of combining evidence any more adequately than Shafer has; but at least his insistence on measures of belief and disbelief grounded on deductively cogent acceptance-rules exhibits a good grip on common sense lacking in Shafer's discussion.

8. *Combining Evidence.*

The source of Shafer's confusion seems to reside in his assumption that the b-distribution over the elements of $D(U)$ relative to e_1 & e_2 should be uniquely determined by (1) U relative to background knowledge, (2) the b-distribution over $D(U)$ relative to e_1, and (3) the b-distribution over $D(U)$ relative to e_2.

If Levi$_k$ is used to determine b-values, the b-function relative to e_1 & e_2 is determined by (a) the partition U, (b) the credal state relative to e_1 & e_2, and (c) the set $\mathfrak{M}$ of information determining M-functions.

Given (a) and the credal state relative to e_1, the credal state relative to e_1 & e_2 required by (b) may be obtained by a suitably formulated principle of conditionalization. From the system of M-functions relative to e_1, one can also compute the set $\mathfrak{M}$ relative to e_1 & e_2 required by (c).

But the b-distribution relative to e_1 & e_2 will not be uniquely determined by (1), (2), and (3).

To illustrate let U consist of h_1, h_2, and h_3. Let there be exactly one M-function assigning each element of U the value 1/3.

Case 1: The strictly Bayesian credal state relative to e_1 assigns the three elements of U the values 0.5, 0.4, 0.1 respectively. Relative to e_2 the assignment is 0.1, 0.1, 0.8 and relative to e_1 & e_2 it is 0.6, 0.3, 0.1. The three sets of d-values for elements of U are 0, 0, 0.7; 0.7, 0.7, 0; and 0, 0.1, 0.7.

Case 2: The credal states relative to e_1, e_2, and e_1 & e_2 are 0.45, 0.45, 0.1; 0.1, 0.1, 0.8; and 0.3, 0.6, 0.1. The corresponding triples of d-values are 0, 0, 0.7; 0.7, 0.7, 0; and 0.1, 0, 0.7.

The d-function for e_1 is the same in both cases as is the d-function for e_2. Yet the d-function for e_1 & e_2 in case 1 differs from that in case 2. Shafer's requirements are violated.

Of course, this result is obtained using Levi$_k$. But similar results could be obtained using Kyburg$_k$ or Hacking$_k$. We are capable, therefore, of constructing acceptance-rules which account for combining evidence but not in a manner meeting Shafer's requirements. Shafer nowhere explains why the principles for combining evidence should satisfy his requirements. Once we direct attention to the identification of acceptance-rules underlying acceptance-based measures of degrees of belief and disbelief, the temptation to embrace Shafer's requirements dissipates.

Like Shafer, Shackle also was concerned to account for the revision of surprise values with new data. This particular aspect of his theory has caused him more technical difficulty than any other ingredient in his account of potential surprise. He has had to modify the principles he used for revision of surprise to accomodate trenchant criticism. Shackle's revised approach requires considering surprise relative to e_1 & e_2 as a function of the surprise of h & e_2 relative to e_1 and the surprise of e_2 relative to e_1, and even this revised approach has been subject to what, in my opinion, is telling criticism.[23] On my reconstruction, Shackle's account can be no more satisfactory than Shafer's.

The source of Shackle's difficulty, like the source of Shafer's, is his failure to attend to the implications of dealing with acceptance-based notions of degrees of belief and disbelief and, in particular, his failure to attend to the way acceptance-rules control the question of revising b-values and d-values in the light of new data.

9. Decision-Making Under Uncertainty

X assumes he faces a decision-problem where he must choose at least and at most one option from the set α. He knows that at least and at most one hypothesis (state of nature) from the set Ω is true and that if he chooses $A_i \in \alpha$ when $h_j \in \Omega$ is true, o_{ij} is true.

Under these conditions, every Q-function in X's credal state B must meet the requirement that $Q(o_{ij}; A_i$ is chosen$) = Q(h_j; A_i$ is chosen$)$ for every i and j.

I shall discuss decision-problems of this kind where the states of nature are *credally* or *probabilistically* independent of the states of nature. That is to say, for every i and j, $Q(h_j; A_i$ is chosen$) = Q(h_i)$.

Suppose X evaluates the o_{ij}'s relative to his goals and values in terms of a utility function $u(o_{ij}) = u_{ij}$ unique up to a linear transformation.

$E(A_i/Q) =$ the *expected utility* of A_i according to the function Q in B and is equal to $\sum Q(h_j)u_{ij}$ where the sum is over all the h_j's in Ω.

A_i in α is *optimal* relative to Q in B if and only if $E(A_i/Q)$ is a maximum for all options in α. A_i is *E-admissible* relative to B for

---

[23] G. L. S. Shackle, *Decision, Order and Time in Human Affairs*, p. 80, axiom (7) and its variants. Also pp. 82–3 and ch. XXIV.

the decision-problem under consideration if and only if A_i is optimal relative to some Q in B.

The decision problem is, in the terminology of Luce and Raiffa's *Games and Decisions* a decision-problem *under risk* if and only if the credal state B contains exactly one Q-distribution over the states of nature in Ω. Luce and Raiffa contrast this kind of problem with decision making *under uncertainty*.[24] I suggest that this kind of problem may be represented as one where B allows all Q-distributions over the states of nature in Ω which satisfy the requirements of the calculus of probabilities.

We may also envisage decision-problems belonging to neither category. In such cases, the credal state allows some convex subset of the set of all distributions over Ω although the set is not a unit set.

Most writers concede that in decision-making under risk, all and only E-admissible options are admissible – i.e., legitimately chosen by rational X.

Difficulties arise, however, when the credal state fails to single out a unique Q-distribution. Those devoted to strict Bayesian doctrine insist that appearances are deceiving and that rational X should be (or even is) committed to a single-membered credal state at all times and is, therefore, always facing a decision-problem under risk. Others rightly question this dogma.

Typically only situations where the decision-problem is under uncertainty are considered although, in my view, intermediate cases are the most realistic ones. In decision-making under uncertainty, every feasible option is E-admissible unless dominated by some other feasible option. Consequently, efforts are made to discriminate among the E-admissible options by invoking some additional crieterion such as some variant of a minimax or maximin rule or the Hurwicz optimism–pessimism criterion.[25]

It has been customary to think of decision-making under risk and decision-making under uncertainty as being regulated by distinct decision theories. On the view I propose, this is not the case. In both kinds of decision-making, E-admissibility is taken to be necessary and not sufficient for admissibility. To be sure, most students of decision-making under risk regard E-admissibility as sufficient in that case for admissibility. I suggest amending that view. When two or more options are optimal with respect to expected utility, other criteria may be invoked to decide between them just as when, in

[24] R. D. Luce and H. Raiffa, *Games and Decisions* (1958), pp. 275–8.
[25] Ibid., pp. 278–86.

decision-making under uncertainty, other criteria are invoked to decide between the abundance of E-admissible options.

This simple modification in outlook yields several advantages.

(1) We have some hope of giving a unified account of decision-making where the same principles govern decision-making under risk and under uncertainty and without pretending that all decision-making is under risk.

(2) This general account extends in an obvious and natural way to the intermediate cases between risk and uncertainty.

(3) We can see the fallacy in some of the standard objections to decision-criteria such as maximin.

This last point is worth explaining. Advocates of maximin are alleged to be urging decision-makers to behave as if they are confronting a hostile nature in a 0-sum two-person game. That analogy may be useful for identifying formal similarities between decision making under uncertainty and 0-sum two-person games; but it can also be misleading. In decision-making under uncertainty, the decision-maker makes no assumption as to which state of nature is 'most likely' to be true. He has no definite view of the probabilities of the states of nature. He is probabilistically ignorant concerning the states of nature and, hence, is neither optimistic nor pessimistic.

In using maximin, X is not deciding on a new and more determinate credal state relative to which to maximize expected utility. Rather he is invoking a new criterion different from and supplementary to expected utility to decide between options which have already passed the test of expected utility. Because so many options have passed the test of expected utility, considerations additional to expected utility have to be invoked to decide between them. Maximiners invoke considerations of security. It is sheer confusion to suppose that when X chooses an E-admissible option which bears maximum security among all E-admissible options, he regards himself as modifying his credal state so that it is restricted to Q-distributions which render that particular option optimal.[26]

Some authors object to maximin because it ignores all but the worst possible outcomes of each option. This objection is symptomatic of the confusion just noted. All possible outcomes have been taken into account in assessing E-admissibility. But the appeal to expected utility has failed to discriminate finely enough and other criteria are being invoked. It is not surprising if these criteria take

[26] L. J. Savage (*The Foundations of Statistics* (1954), p. 206) seems to acknowledge this point.

other factors into account different from those invoked in appraising expected utility.

Several criteria have been proposed for decision-making under uncertainty which could be generalized in the manner I am suggesting and which could be defended against Bayesian question-begging in the manner I have indicated in the case of maximin. It is far from obvious which of these alternatives should be favoured. I have no decisive argument for my position but I think a carefully but weakly formulated maximin principle (or, better still, a leximin principle) is most suitable. The following familiar phenomenon may help motivate acceptance of this viewpoint.

I recall reading in the papers in the summer of 1973 that British bookmakers were prepared to offer odds of 2 to 1 that Nixon would not be impeached while offering 1 to 3 odds that he would be impeached. Assuming utility linear in money, this practice does not coincide with the Bayesian theory. Bayesians can explain the phenomenon away. Bookmakers are out for a profit and, in any case, utility is not linear in money.

There is another way to account for the spread in the odds. We might suppose that the bookmakers adopted a credal state assigning the hypothesis that Nixon will not be impeached a lower probability of 2/3 and an upper probability of 3/4. Assuming utility linear with money, a bet at 5 to 2 odds on Nixon's not being impeached would have been E-admissible among the pair of options consisting of offering the gamble and refusing to do so. So would refusing the gamble. The refusal to offer the odds derives from the fact that offering the gamble bears lower security than refusing to do so. The maximin solution is to refuse the gamble. On the other hand, for odds less than 2 to 1, the gamble is uniquely E-admissible. Even though refusing the gamble bears a higher security-level, the gamble is chosen. For similar reasons, a gamble on Nixon's being impeached would be accepted at odds lower than 1 to 3.

This rationalization of the behaviour is not the only one available as I have already acknowledged. But it is as cogent as the rival accounts and suggests a bias in favour of maximin as the criterion to use to arbitrate between E-admissible options. I offer it as an elementary illustration of behaviour in conformity with the theory I favour.

10. *Shackle's Decision-Theory*

Shackle has been interpreted as addressing the question of decision-making under uncertainty. Shackle is, indeed, investigating decision-problems where X's credal state contains more than one

Q-distribution over the states of nature. But if potential surprise is related to credence in the manner suggested by $Levi_k$, Shackle's proposals cover more than decision-making under uncertainty. According to $Levi_k$, if all Q-distributions conforming to the calculus of probabilities are in B, every state of nature in Ω bears 0 potential surprise. However, all states of nature can bear 0 potential surprise even when probabilistic ignorance does not obtain. Moreover, there are cases of partial indeterminacy where some states of nature bear positive surprise. Shackle clearly intends to cover some situations where some states of nature bear positive surprise. On my reconstruction, Shackle does intend to cover more than decision-making under uncertainty.

What Shackle fails to do, however, is to restrict the domain of applicability of his criteria to options which are E-admissible – i.e., which pass the test of expected utility. I have already registered my disagreement and shall not belabour the point any further. I shall proceed with this exposition under the assumption that credence is related to surprise via $Levi_k$ and that Shackle's decision-principles are designed to apply to E-admissible options.

In order to understand Shackle's decision-criterion,[27] we need a notion additional to potential surprise. I shall use a modification of Shackle's notion of an ascendancy function. Consider a real-valued function $A(x, y)$ where x ranges over the utility values u_{ij} and y ranges over the values of $d(h_j)$ or, more generally, over any pair (x, y) where x is a utility and y a surprise-value even though that pair is not realized in the agent's decision-matrix. $A(x, y)$ is the *ascendancy-value* X would assign to the utility x were it associated with potential surprise y.

The A-function represents an aspect of X's cognitive and valuational state additional to those aspects captured by the credal state, the utility-function and the assignment of degrees of potential surprise. To explain it further, we shall have to consider Shackle's conception of its role in decision-making. Before doing that, however, mention should be made of some very weak conditions imposed on A-functions.

Values of the A-function can be determined by reference to a designated number n, the range of utility-numbers, and a function $f(d)$ whose arguments are surprise-numbers from 0 to 1 and which is a strictly decreasing positive function of d such that $f(0) = 1$.

$$A(u, d) = f(d)u + n(1 - f(d)).$$

[27] For the mature account of Shackle's theory, see *Decision, Order and Time in Human Affairs*, part III.

Thus when $d = 0$, $A(u, d) = u$ and otherwise is a positive linear transformation of u (where the transformation depends on the value of d). If, instead of u, $u' = au + b$ is used as the utility-function, $n' = an + b$ and $A'(u', d) = aA(u, d) + b$.

The designated value n represents that utility such that for every pair of surprise-values d and d', $A(u, d) = A(u, d')$. Shackle regards n as the value (I, not he, call it utility) of a 'neutral' outcome. That is the value the agent X places on his circumstances from his viewpoint when reaching a decision. From X's viewpoint, utility-numbers greater than n represent values of situations which are improvements over his current situation as he sees it and utilities less than n represent situations worse than this.

The A-function is a sort of extended and modified utility function. It reduces the value of prospects bearing utility greater than n as they become more surprising and increases the values of prospects bearing utility less than n as they become less surprising.

Let A_i be E-admissible. For each o_{ij}, there is a definite utility u_{ij} and surprise value $d(h_j)$. Hence, for each o_{ij}, $A(u_{ij}, d(h_j))$ is defined. Let A_i be the least of these values and A_i be the greatest. Thus, with each E-admissible option, we can associate a pair of A-values $(A_i, \bar{A}_i)$.

We finally come to the last exogenous variable in Shackle's theory. Shackle assumes the agent has a 'gambler's indifference map' for such pairs of values. He makes no assumptions about the indifference curves except that they conform to the requirements for an ordering and obey usual convexity conditions.

Shackle then recommends that the agent pick that option (from the set of E-admissible options, so I am assuming) which is on the highest indifference curve (or one of those on a highest indifference curve).

Shortly after Shackle wrote *Expectation in Economics*, L. Hurwicz[28] proposed a criterion similar to Shackle's.

According to Hurwicz, for each (E-admissible) A_i, one should identify the value of utility u_i which is a minimum and the value $\bar{u}_i$ which is a maximum and plot indifference curves for pairs $(u_i, \bar{u}_i)$. Hurwicz assumed that the indifference curves are linear implying that there is some real number α between 0 and 1 such that an

[28] L. Hurwicz, *Optimality Criteria for Decision Making under Ignorance*, Cowles Commission Discussion Paper: Statistics #370 (1951) as summarized in R. D. Luce and H. Raiffa, *Games and Decisions*, pp. 282–4. The relation between Hurwicz and Shackle is discussed in S. A. Ozga, *Expectations in Economic Theory* (1965), pp. 269–72. In K. J. Arrow and L. Hurwicz, 'Decision Making under Ignorance', pp. 1–11, a weaker position closer to Shackle's is adopted.

option A_i is on the indifference curve characterized by $\alpha \bar{u}_i +$ $(1 - \alpha)u_i = r$. The agent should maximize r.

Hurwicz's proposal is a special case of Shackle's. If indifference curves for ascendancy pairs are linear and $f(d) = 1$ for all values of d rather than being a strictly decreasing function, Shackle's theory becomes Hurwicz's.

Moreover, in those cases where all states of nature bear 0 potential surprise, as they must in decision-making under uncertainty, A-values coincide with u-values. Given the linearity assumption on the indifference-map, Shackle's theory once more become Hurwicz's.

Hurwicz's theory was intended for decision-making under uncertainty. Shackle's theory preceded his by a few years and, moreover, is more general in several respects.

Maximin criteria are special cases of the Hurwicz's theory when $\alpha = 0$. This is so in Shackle's theory as well. However, the injunction is maximizing the minimum A-value rather than the minimum u-value. However, in cases where all states of nature bear 0 surprise, this difference disappears.

I have already registered my preference for some form of maximin (or, perhaps, leximin) criterion for the purpose of evaluating rival E-admissible options. I am inclined to think that there is no need to modify such criteria in order to take into account potential surprise and A-values.

I have no utterly decisive arguments against Shackle's decision-theory; but I suspect the strongest motivation for it derives from Shackle's view of potential surprise as serving as a rival to credal probability as a measure of uncertainty.

Now I readily concede that, as a rule, credal states will fail to be numerically determinate and, moreover, E-admissibility, in general, fails to be sufficient for admissibility. But decision-criteria such as Shackle's, if cogent at all, are to be invoked only after considerations of expected utility have failed to render a verdict. In resisting the dogmatism of Bayesianism, we should not ignore its insights.

If that is so, potential surprise should not be construed a rival to credal probability. Its function in decision-making – if it has such a function – should be understood differently from the functioning of credal probability in computing expectations.

But this is the rub! Shackle utilizes surprise measures in decision-making in a manner resembling the use of credal probability in computing expectations. An expected utility is a sum of products where each product is of a utility and a probability. Shackle avoids

using sums. But his decision-theory, in effect, introduces 'expectation elements' which are products of utilities and functions of
surprise-values. These are exactly what A-values are. These A-
values are ways of discounting utilities in terms of surprise just as
the more familiar expectation elements are ways of discounting
utilities in terms of probability.

But in testing for E-admissibility, such a discounting process has
been undertaken. I find it doubtful that we should discount a second
time using surprise rather than probability. I confess that my discomfort is nothing more than that – namely a sense of discomfort. I
have no decisive argument against Shackle's idea.

Whether my reservations are well taken or not, it has been shown
that the role of potential surprise in Shackle's decision-theory need
not be construed as rival to that of credal probability but as
supplementary. This in itself is a significant correction of what
appears to have been Shackle's own view of the matter.

Furthermore, even if Shackle's own proposed use of measures of
potential surprise in decision-theory is misguided, the concept of
potential surprise has other uses in connection with the appraisal of
rival potential answers being considered for addition via induction
to a body of knowledge.

Thus, there are at least two entertainable domains of application
for measures of potential surprise. Neither of these are rival to
applications of credal probability measures. Both types of application merit further consideration.

11. *Applications to Economics*

Shackle completed his doctoral dissertation in 1936 and published it
in 1938.[29] It indertook to provide a dynamic model for the business
cycle compatible with Keynesean ideas including the multiplier by
appealing to changes in investors' expectations. By Shackle's own
testimony, work on this idea provided some of the impetus for his
efforts to develop a theory of decision-making taking expectations
and uncertainties into account.[30]

I am unqualified to pass judgement on Shackle's ideas about the
business cycle. Although Shackle clearly was one of the early
proponents of a model of the business cycle to take Keynesian (and
neo-Wicksellian) ideas into account, this aspect of his work is rarely
discussed in the economics literature.

[29] G. L. S. Shackle, *Expectations, Investment and Income* (1938).
[30] See the introduction to the second edition of G. L. S. Shackle, *Expectations,
Investment and Income* (1968).

On the other hand, other elements of his work have been discussed. I refer, in particular, to his efforts to apply his account of decision-making to the problem of choosing investment portfolios. Once more neither space nor my qualifications warrant my discussing the technical particulars of his applications of his theory to problems of economics.

One point, however, is worth mentioning. I have already commented on the difficulties Shackle faced in providing an account of how surprise-values change in the light of new data. Yet, Shackle persisted in attempting to construct such an account. The reason seems to have been that he was concerned to provide an account of how changes in investors' expectations control developments in a business-cycle. He sought to do this by appealing to a surprise-based decision-theory of the sort we described together with a model of how surprise-values should change with changes in data.

Shackle emphatically denied that one could predict the behaviour of investors or explain their behaviour without reference to their cognitive attitudes and their desires. In every way he could, he emphasized the 'freedom' of such decision-makers.

Shackle did not preclude explanation of the behaviour of investors; but he did insist that adequate explanation required appeal to epistemic and affective attitudes. Indeed, to the extent that one could in advance make assumptions about the subjective states of economic agents, one could predict their behaviour.

Shackle thought of his decision-theory as a framework for such explanation and prediction. But the theory is not free of all normative components. Shackle disclaims the intention of constructing a theory of rational decision-making or rational belief and disbelief. But in developing his account of potential surprise, he defends some of the key conditions on surprise-functions by insisting that some ways of making assignments are 'logical' and others 'illogical'.

Shackle apparently sought a system of conditions on potential surprise which he thought men, if they are 'logical' would conform to. He also thought that men do conform to a good degree of approximation. He also thought men have ascendancy functions meeting his conditions and, at least implicitly, that they are committed to gambler's indifference-maps. But he left these factors relatively unstructured so that his apparatus would be flexible enough to model widely different kinds of behaviour.

Shackle is to be admired for his interest and concern for the application of his decision-theory. For my part, I have been more inclined to consider his ideas in the context of a normative account of belief and decision-making and shy away from dealing with explanatory or predictive applications. Shackle's emphasis on the importance of deliberation due to the circumstance of human freedom suggests that he would not be indifferent to this concern.

12. *Cohen on Inductive Support and Inductive Probability*

In his recent book, *The Probable and the Provable*, L. J. Cohen has introduced a measure of 'inductive probability' having the formal properties of Shackle-like measures of degrees of belief (*b*-functions).[31] Moreover, Cohen has followed my interpretation of Shackle-like measures as indices of weights of argument sufficient for the termination of enquiry and the addition of new information into evidence.

This pleasant agreement with my proposed reconstruction of Shackle's idea is enhanced by Cohen's contribution to the discussion. Cohen contends that inductive probability (*b*-value) has properties rendering it useful in clarifying certain kinds of reasoning in Anglo-American law. I regret to say that I lack the competence to make an independent judgement as to the merits of Cohen's proposals; but his discussion promises to extend the reach of Shackle's ideas to an important new domain.

There are some important differences between Cohen's approach to the application of Shackle's measures and my own. He seeks to restrict the domain of scientific applications of his measures of inductive probability (Shackle *b*-measures) in such a way as to render their use parasitic on applications of measures of inductive support he introduced in his earlier book, *The Implications of Induction*.[32] According to Cohen, establishing this link ties applications of inductive probability to the Baconian method of relevant variables in scientific inquiry.

Inductive support is the measure Shafer wrongly identified as a Shackle measure. I have not been able to construct a useful application for Cohen's idea of inductive support. I think the link he alleges to hold between inductive support and inductive probability in his sense is expendable and that Cohen's concern to retain the link has led him to restrict the scope of applicability of his measures of inductive probability unnecessarily. In saying this, I do not think I am rejecting the 'Baconian' emphasis on the need to control for relevant variables in well-designed experimentation.

Space does not permit greater elaboration on these comments

[31] L. J. Cohen, *The Probable and the Provable*, ch. 17
[32] Ibid., part III contains the views summarized in the subsequent discussion.

here. Further discussion will be found in a review article to appear in the *British Journal for the Philosophy of Science*.[33]

13. *Conclusion*

Contemporary literature on scientific enquiry contains an abundance of proposals for ways to appraise hypotheses. We have more measures of belief, support, corroboration, and the like than anyone can hope to take seriously. It is important to be able to identify the intended domains of application and the significance of the intended applications so that a clear idea can be had as to which measures have established worth and which still stand in need of vindication.

In my opinion, the contributions of G. L. S. Shackle to the study of non-additive measures of degrees of belief or support continue to be the most important ones in the literature. Shackle himself has suggested interesting applications; and there are others which he himself did not explicitly consider.

I do not mean to suggest that potential surprise should be assigned as central a place in the epistemic polity as the concept of credal probability or the more general notion of a credal state. We should not, however, let the verbal posturings of simplistic probabilism blind us to the virtues of Shackle's contribution.

[33] 'Support and Surprise: L. J. Cohen's View of Inductive Probability', *Brit. J. Phil. Sci.* 30 (1979) 279–92.

§2. PAUL TELLER
Zealous Acceptance

Levi seeks to treat acceptance and qualitative belief by first introducing a notion of belief relativized to a set of strongest possible answers to a question and then suggesting an unrelativized notion, acceptance relative to all 'serious questions'. I suggest following the same procedure developed in terms of what I take to be a more natural relativization: acting as if something is true. Developing this commonplace idea turns out to be a bit more involved than one might at first guess. I then introduce Zealous Acceptance, namely acceptance relative to all serious possible sets of options or alternative acts. I give 'serious' the specific interpretation of a set of possible options which has a non-negligible chance of actually occurring, with the result that Zealous Acceptance does not quite meet the conditions of consistency and deductive closure. But I argue that Zealous Acceptance none the less comes as close to meeting these conditions as one could sensibly require.

As Levi remarks, friends of acceptance disagree concerning the properties acceptance-rules should have, and in the foregoing paper he has nicely compared his own views with those of Shackle, Kyburg, Shafer, and Cohen. In particular he argues that Shackle's notion of potential surprise, when properly reinterpreted within his own system, corresponds to his notion of a degree of disbelief, and he suggests that these notions, together with his reconstruction of degrees of belief and measures of caution, have important applications in the expansion of a body of knowledge via induction.[1] Now, I am no friend of acceptance, and thus little surprised to find that I have nothing worth taking space to say about Levi's comparisons. Instead I plan to execute my assignment as commentator by taking a look at the applications for which Levi's system (and Shackle's, by Levi's implication) seems to be designed. In so doing, I will try to put some critical pressure on Levi's system, mainly by seeing whether some of his objectives can be achieved by what seems to me a natural application of the Bayesian framework.

I want to get under way by going over some of the ground rules for evaluating inductive logics. A few paragraphs are warranted here because inductive logicians sometimes forget these rules in the heat of critical discussion, with the result that arguments miss their mark. I hope that you will agree with these observations – I think Levi does – and if you do not, at least you will be advised of my methodological prejudices.

[1] Levi, p. 9 above.

Before theorizing sets in we work on problems using a stock of imprecise, pretheoretical concepts. This imprecision has a virtue of flexibility, but also severe limitations in the range and precision of problem-solutions which we can put forward. To solve more problems and to put forward more exact solutions we theorize, and in so doing we have to refine our pretheoretical conceptual tools. Different problems often call for different refinements, and the refinements often do not accurately reflect their pretheoretic precursors. Often refinement results in idealization, that is, introduction of conceptual tools which, when applied, do not approximate to all the facts within some known margin of error. Instead, they distort some of the facts in serious ways. As with refinements generally, different problems may call for different idealizations, each of which is suitable for some purposes but not for others. I mention this variation with problems because inductive logics are designed to deal with a wide range of problems. These include:

How does a reflective person change his beliefs?
How ought a reflective person change his beliefs?
How does a scientist change his beliefs?
How ought a scientist change his scientific beliefs?
How does a reflective person make choices?
How ought a reflective person make choices?

Some of these problem-areas may well divide. It is an assumption that the same normative principles which should guide a quality-control analyst should guide a theoretical physicist. The problems are of course connected. But again, it is an assumption that the same theory based on one set of idealizations, or even different theories based on the same idealizations, will be adequate to all these problem-areas.

These considerations indicate why it is in itself no objection to a system of inductive logic that it involves idealizations. Take the Bayesian idealization that agents have degrees of confidence described by a probability-function which describes perceived fair betting quotients. This idealization is a good one just in so far as it serves as a basis for coming to grips with an important range of problems. In particular, it is perfectly beside the point to remark on the obvious fact that real people rarely have such exact degrees of confidence. One might as well protest against the application of Newtonian dynamics expressed in terms of the idealization of point masses that there are no point masses. In many situations the idealization none the less serves extremely well. Similarly there is no sound objection to such idealizations that these conflict with certain presystematic conceptions. Levi forgets these facts when he concludes that 'strict Bayesians are mistaken in requiring rational agents to adopt credal states representable by single Q functions'.[2] At most objectors may point to a range of problems which can't be handled on the basis of an idealization such as point masses or exact Bayesian degrees of confidence. And of course advocates may err in thinking that because their favoured idealization is useful for certain problems it will provide a sound basis for handling others.

I have argued that concepts used in inductive logics do not have to accord with presystematic ideas. But of course one may want, among other things, to gain a clarified picture of the intuitive origins from which more exact theories arise. One can often do this, starting from idealized theories, by showing how to reconstruct presystematic conceptions under special circumstances. Again, modern physics provides many examples: consider the perceived non-relativity of simultaneity when velocity differences are small compared with that of light, and the classical behaviour of physical objects when actions are large compared to Planck's constant. I mention this because Levi seems very concerned that we stay in touch with our presystematic attitudes toward belief and induction, and I will try to show how some of these concerns can be met without requiring that we be tied down from the beginning by our pretheoretical ideas.

I take Levi to be concerned with two important applications throughout his many publications. First, he wants a system which will capture what he sees as our presystematic and qualitative use of 'believes'. In particular, he insists, 'presystematic precedent' dictates that any adequate reconstruction must satisfy a deductive cogency requirement of consistency and deductive closure. He calls this notion of belief 'acceptance as true', which he contrasts with the stronger notion of 'acceptance as evidence'. The stronger notion arises in the context of his second intended application, the characterization of conditions governing the alleged unqualified acceptance of propositions which we arrive at by induction (or observation) and then use within an expanded evidential basis for further investigations. On Levi's usage, we *use* a proposition as evidence when we appeal to it as a premiss in our practical or cognitive deliberations, and we *accept* a proposition as evidence when we are prepared to

[2] Levi, p. 8 above.

use it as evidence in any deliberations which might come up, in complete disregard of the risk of the proposition being false.[3]

For ease of reference, I will review the steps Levi takes towards these objectives. He characterizes an agent as having a deductively closed knowledge corpus, *K*, relativized to a person at a time. As Levi structures the problem, we should characterize acceptance-rules which, under suitable conditions, allow us to expand our body of knowledge. Levi's acceptance-rules characterize acceptance as true relative to a question, or more exactly relative to an 'ultimate partition', construed as a set of strongest candidate-answers to a question. The acceptance-rules are parameterized by an index of caution *k*, and a proposition is admitted into *K* only when it is accepted relative to a rule with the agent's chosen sufficiently stringent degree of caution. Finally, the degree of caution is used to develop a notion of degree of acceptance or belief (and a correlative notion of degree of disbelief corresponding to Shackle's degrees of surprise) such that the things believed to any positive degree satisfy the condition of deductive cogency.

No less than others, Levi's system involves many severe idealizations. As I have been at pains to remark, this is in itself no objection, but I want to mention some of the idealizations by way of getting a clearer fix on the system's limitations and its comparison with others.

The corpus *K* is itself an idealization. I do not mean here to question whether agents ever accept propositions as evidence (I will come back to this later). But surely we idealize when we require deductive closure and when we assume that there is a sharp distinction between what the agent does and does not accept as evidence.

Second, as Levi has so far developed his system, *K* can only grow. It follows immediately that his system cannot deal with the important problem of change of heart about what we once took to be evidential. Furthermore, Levi's overall attitude toward epistemology seems to me to leave little room for extending his system to take such matters into account. In 'Acceptance Revisited'[4] and 'Subjunctives, Dispositions, and Chances'[5] Levi addresses this question; but, as he has not dealt with it to my satisfaction, I would like to digress long enough to explain my reservations. The problem arises because

---

[3] See Levi's 'Acceptance Revisited', pp. 3–5, in *Local Induction*, ed. R. J. Bogdan (1976), pp. 1–71.

[4] op. cit.

[5] 'Subjunctives, Dispositions, and Chances', *Synthèse* 34 (1977), pp. 423–55.

of Levi's insistence (repeated frequently in 'Acceptance Revisited', pp. 3–5[6] and throughout) that the agent regards propositions in his corpus as certainly, infallibly true, to be used in whatever deliberations might come up, with personal probability of 1, in complete disregard of the possibility that such propositions might be false. The problem can be succinctly put by observing that consideration as to whether some proposition *H*, presently accepted as evidence, should after all be taken to be false, or perhaps just cast in doubt, is itself a deliberation. But, if all deliberations require that we accept *H* as certainly, infallibly true, deliberating as to the serious possibility that *H* is false does not seem to make much sense. Levi agrees that a move directly from accepting *H* as evidence to accepting not-*H* as evidence in one's corpus would be inconsistent with his attitude toward epistemology. But he seeks to defuse this objection by suggesting that such moves should be broken down into two steps.[7] In the first step one contracts the corpus, suspending qualitative judgement about *H*. Thus, he says one does not in this first deliberation consider accepting anything inconsistent with what is already accepted. Then in a second step one is free to consider accepting not-*H* or other propositions inconsistent with *H*.

But this response does not really meet the objection as I have stated it. Relative to the original corpus, one has a decisive objection to contracting: *H* is accepted as certainly, infallibly true. Relative to this, it is inconsistent to consider *H* as even possibly false. The objection can be put by observing that relative to the original corpus the agent accepts the proposition *H'*: '*H* is certainly true'. (Levi considers such metalinguistic propositions as being accepted within one's corpus,[8] though he does not specifically mention this one.) Thus in considering moving to a new corpus in which '*H* is possibly false' is accepted, the agent does, after all, consider accepting something inconsistent with his original corpus. The objection can also be put indirectly: Consider the practical issue of spending money on an experiment designed to collect evidence for or against *H*. Relative to a corpus in which *H* is accepted as evidence, one would have to regard such an experiment as pointless, certain to yield confirming results. An administrator of research funds would have uniformly to veto grant proposals designed to test hypotheses accepted in the administrator's corpus, no matter how good the proposal. May my proposals be protected from such a-Leviation of grant-administrators' workload!

In 'Subjunctives, Dispositions, and Chances',[9] Levi offers some further considerations which (he tells me) he believes to undercut the problems I see for contraction within his overall framework. But before discussing these considerations I need to mention a further related idealization. A corpus, K, washes out all evidential relations between the hypotheses it contains. First of all, for any H in a corpus, any possible evidence, E, which implies not-H is inconsistent with the corpus. For given that E implies not-H, H implies not-E and given the fact that corpora are deductively closed, not-E will be in the corpus. Thus one cannot even consider accepting evidence which conflicts with H. Nor can probabilistic arguments be used relative to the corpus, for all propositions in a corpus receive probability of 1. It follows that the probability of H on any evidence whatsoever is one and the likelihood function isn't even defined for competitors to H.

In 'Subjunctives, Dispositions, and Chances' Levi acknowledges that '[t]here is no basis for discriminating between items in [the agent's] corpus with respect to credal probability or evidential support'.[10] On what basis then can the agent select items for elimination from his corpus? Levi suggests that one look at the situation like this. Suppose that not-H is in the agent's corpus, so that $p(H) = 0$. But H is attractive in its informational promise, broadly construed. Then, '[even] though [H] is infallibly and certainly false for X [the agent] at t, he may wish to give it a hearing because of the informational value he imputes to it due to its explanatory virtues ... That is to say, X may have good reason to open his mind by suspending judgement between [H] and statements conflicting with it in [his corpus] in order to explore the question of the truth value of [H] without begging any questions'.[11] Furthermore in so doing, Levi argues, the agent is not accepting anything in his contracted corpus inconsistent with his original corpus. In particular, if 'It is impossible that H' is a truth-value bearer at all, it characterizes the agent's current epistemic state, it constitutes an assertion of epistemic modality relative to the agent's current corpus, and it should be taken as elliptical for 'H is impossible for the agent at t', which is consistent with 'H is possible

---

[9] op. cit.
[10] op. cit., p. 428.
[11] 'Subjunctives, Dispositions, and Chances', p. 427.

for the agent at t'', for some t' later that than t. The first quoted proposition is in the agent's corpus at t, the latter in his (now contracted) corpus at t', and thus the agent accepts nothing in his contracted corpus inconsistent with anything in the original corpus. (This argument is suggested in 'Subjunctives, Dispositions, and Chances'.[12] I have filled in a bit.)

I don't think that all this helps very much. To take the latter point first, in earlier writings, Levi explained, in part, what it means for an agent to accept a proposition into his corpus by saying that in so doing the agent comes to regard the proposition as certainly true and its negation as impossible. But now we are told that this modal talk is to be understood as an elliptical characterization of (one aspect of) the agent's current epistemic state which comes down to saying just what is and is not in the agent's corpus. Thus I acknowledge that Levi can avoid the problem of explicit contradiction for contraction, but only at the expense of robbing his frequent use of 'certain', 'impossible', and the like of any informative value in explaining to us what is involved in accepting a proposition into one's corpus. Of course, we still have Levi's second characterization of the nature of corpora: Items in a corpus are assigned credal probability of 1, which is taken to mean that the agent is committed to ignoring completely the possibility that such propositions might be false. But this continues to conflict with Levi's claim that one can sensibly suspend judgement about a proposition in one's corpus when one is seduced by the negated proposition's informational promise. Referring to the schematic example described one paragraph back, the agent can sensibly open himself to open-minded consideration of H only if he takes H to have *some* chance of being true, no matter what H's informational appeal. But since not-H is in his corpus, the agent takes $p(H) = 0$. I can press the point by putting it in terms of Levi's style of epistemic acts judged by Bayes's rule. Contracting will always result in some loss of information.[13] Levi suggests that sometimes '$\cdots$ the information value imputed to [H] due to its explanatory (or other informational) virtues renders giving it a hearing sufficient compensation for this loss'.[14] But on Levi's own terms, this can never happen. Since $p(\text{not-}H) = 1$, $p(H) = 0$, and (we may assume) the informational value of both H and not-H are finite, Bayes's rule will always describe such contemplated contracting epistemic acts as unreasonable. In sum, once one has

[12] Ibid., pp. 423–4.
[13] Ibid., p. 427.
[14] Ibid.

accepted something as evidence in Levi's sense one is stuck with it for good.

Levi idealizes in yet further respects. Surely his measure of caution is every bit as much idealized as personal probabilities. So too is relativization to an ultimate partition. I do recognize a pre-systematic notion of acceptance but I do not see it as relativized to a list of candidate answers to a question. Finally, we may mention, not a further idealization, but a relevant area of interest not treated in Levi's system. We do have an important pre-systematic notion of acceptance relative to a goal or choice situation. As I will make clear as we go along, I find that Levi has swept aside a promising approach by substituting a less comfortable intuitive notion for this one.

Beyond surveying Levi's idealizations, I want to make two further remarks about his system. Levi claims that his notion of 'acceptance-based' degree of belief and Shackle's correlative measure of potential surprise have important applications in connection with the appraisal of rival potential answers being considered for addition via induction to a body of knowledge.[15] I am less taken by the problem-solving power of these concepts. Acceptance-rules are Levi's real problem-solving tools, and deductive cogency is his central theoretical constraint. On my reading, the measures of belief serve as an aid to intuitive comparison of various acceptance-rules (much as Venn diagrams aid intuition in set theory) more than as basic theoretical machinery.

More importantly, I have reservations about Levi's second application. Levi wants to reconstruct a notion of unqualified acceptance as evidence, and not just as a description of actual practice but as prescriptive of reasonable change of opinion. I do agree that we speak pre-systematically in terms of a seemingly unrelativized notion of acceptance, but we must ask whether this feature should be preserved when we move to refine and strengthen our reflective procedures for improving reasonable opinions. The mere facts of pre-systematic prejudice do not show very much – we might as well argue against the relativity of motion on the grounds that in pre-systematic discourse we generally take motion to be absolute. Levi seems to be dominated by the pull of common talk in terms of unrelativized acceptance and belief. I am more affected by what is surely a contrary pull, the feeling that all of our empirical convictions are fallible and revisable, and that all of our considered

---

[15] Levi, p. 8f. above.

opinions, even so-called 'evidence', would be the more reasonable for reflecting this fallibility.

These considerations present a challenge: Can we develop a framework which acknowledges the uncertainty of all reasonable empirical opinion and yet deals with Levi's concerns for reconstructing our presystematic notion of qualitative belief and explaining how reasonable conviction gets used as evidence? Given Jeffrey's generalized notion of conditionalization, the Bayesian framework provides a natural approach to treating reasonable opinion subject to recognized fallibility at every empirical point. I propose to investigate the feasibility of applying this framework to deal with the other issues which Levi calls to our attention.

The obvious Bayesian move is to characterize qualitative belief as subjective belief greater than some fixed number. But, as Levi has argued in numerous places, this proposal falls prey to the lottery paradox. Levi's solution to the lottery paradox involves relativizing acceptance or belief to an ultimate partition of strongest-candidate answers to a question. (Indeed, all approaches to qualitative belief on probabilistic foundations seem to involve some such relativization.) Note, however, that this relativization causes *prima facie* tension in Levi's account, for ultimately Levi wants an unrelativized notion of acceptance into the corpus. Levi responds to this dilemma by stipulating that a proposition may be reasonably accepted as evidence in that unrelativized sense when it is accepted with such great confidence that it will be accepted relative to 'all questions recognized as serious ones'.[16]

However well this sort of move works for Levi's relativization (a question to which we shall return), we may hope that it will work as well for others, an important consideration since I find Levi's relativization unnatural in the extreme. Consider a short dialogue between L and T. There are two propositions, H_1 and H_2, which L regards as probabilistically independent. L's personal probabilities are $P(H_1) = P(H_2) = 0.99$. His degree of caution is $k = 0.03$ (values close to zero characterize high caution):

> T: Consider the question: is H_1 true or is it false? What do you accept?
>
> L: I accept H_1.
>
> T: (A moment later.) The question has changed as to whether H_1 & H_2, H_1 & $\bar{H}_2$, $\bar{H}_1$ & H_2 or $\bar{H}_1$ & $\bar{H}_2$ is true. But I would still like to know whether you accept H_1?

[16] I. Levi, *Gambling with Truth* (1967), p. 150.

If L is using Levi's principles, he must no longer accept H_1 relative to the new question, though his evidence has not changed. More striking examples can be given in which the agent must actually reject what he formerly accepted as a result of a change of question.[17]

Presystematic usage suggests a much more natural relativization, and one which in any case stands in need of explication. We talk freely about accepting an hypothesis as a basis for action. To accept an hypothesis in this sense is to act in a way which would be appropriate should the hypothesis be true. I go out without my umbrella, and in so doing act on the assumption that it won't rain. Or I decide to go ahead and build a not very expensive piece of experimental apparatus which will work only if a certain moderately well-confirmed theoretical statement is true. In so doing, I act as if this statement is true. I might not have if the apparatus cost more. Finally, Pascal argued that we should act as if God exists.

Levi refers to the implied proposal as one form of 'behaviouralism'.[18] He rejects it on the grounds that we have to account for some kind of unqualified acceptance of propositions as evidence, which, he asserts, cannot be done on the basis of acceptance relative to practical objectives.[19] But, as we have already remarked, Levi himself faces the problem of moving from a relativized notion to an unrelativized one, and we can appeal to a close analogue to his solution to this problem. Roughly, we will say that a proposition is accepted in the unqualified sense (or zealously accepted as I will henceforth say) just in case it is accepted relative to all sets of options which have a non-negligible chance of actually occurring. This approach recommends itself, not only by its more comfortable intuitive underpinnings, but by its greater generality, since it includes Levi's concerns with purely cognitive acceptance as a special case.

Many writers have mentioned acceptance as acting as if a proposition is true, but so far as I know, no one has tried to work out details. I would like to offer at least a start, showing how one may deal with certain questions that arise along the way, in particular how one may adapt essentially Levi's procedure for dealing with the Lottery Paradox. Consider a simple set of options, (A_1, A_2), including their decision matrix with respect to exhaustive alternative

---

[17] 'Acceptance Revisited', pp. 62–7.
[18] *Gambling with Truth*, p. 11.
[19] Ibid., p. 15.

hypotheses H_1 and H_2:

	0.4 H_1	0.6 H_2	
A_1	120	-50	18
A_2	-10	20	8

Here and henceforth, probabilities of hypotheses will be written directly above the hypotheses, the utility for an act A_i on the assumption that a hypothesis H_j is true will be written in the cell for act A_i and hypothesis H_j, and the expected utility for A_i will be written to the right of A_i's row. When we want to argue generally, the utility for act A_i on hypothesis H_j will be written 'u_{ij}' and the expected utility for act A_i will be written '$E(A_i)$'. By 'a set of options' I shall always mean all the information contained in the decision matrix and not just the relevant alternative acts. In this simple example, Bayes's rule prescribes act A_1, and in choosing act A_1 we say that the agent acts as if H_1 is true. Introducing some technical terminology, I will say that in choosing A_1 the agent accepts H_1 relative to the set of options (A_1, A_2).

Acceptance of H_1 relative to (A_1, A_2) here seems clearly right, but do we want to say this because $120 > -50$, suggesting a row-maximum rule, or because $120 > -10$, suggesting a column-maximum rule? Consider:

	H_1	H_2
A_1	20	80
A_2	-20	120

Here, if we use the row-maximum rule H_2 will be accepted whatever the probabilities. This seems wrong: the fact that the values in the H_2 column dominate the values in the H_1 column ('column dominance') should not dictate acceptance of H_2, for there may be relative advantage in choosing one act over the other depending on the probabilities and if act A_1 is chosen this may be seen as acting as if H_1 is true. To bring out this point, consider:

	H_1	H_2
A_1	20	-20
A_2	-20	20

Here, if $p(H_1) > p(H_2)$, act A_1 will have higher expected utility, and choosing act A_1 will count as acting as if H_1 is true on either the row- or column-maximum rule. Now suppose that I promise a bonus of 100 utility units if H_2 is true, whichever act is chosen. This gives the previous decision-matrix and does not change the difference in the expected utilities of the acts. Thus, offering such a bonus does not change which act is recommended, and it should likewise not change what it is the agent accepts relative to the set of options. In choosing, say, act A_1 over A_2, one is guided by relative expected advantage, that is, by which act holds the better expectation, not by the absolute value of expected gains; and if one chooses act A_1 over A_2 it is likewise the difference in possible gains available from choice among competing acts which induces us to say that one acts as if one of the hypotheses is true. In general, fixed rewards (or penalties) independent of which act is chosen, whether offered by a person or by nature, do not affect the decision-problem and should not affect judgements as to what the agent is said to accept relative to a set of competing options when he picks from among them.

In short, the phenomenon of column dominance is really a pseudo-phenomenon, and we can wash it out by using the fact that differences between expected utilities are not affected by adding an arbitrary constant to all the utilities in a column. We can always see the relevant differences in utilities more clearly if we column-normalize a decision-matrix, that is, subtract the average of utilities in a column from all entries in the column. Henceforth, I will often present decision matrices in column-normalized form. The column-normalized form of the one but last matrix is the last matrix, which still does not provide any basis for choosing between a row- and column-maximum rule.

We need to expand our stock of examples. Consider:

	H_1	H_2
A_1	10	20
A_2	-10	-20

Here A_1 dominates in the usual sense and will be picked no matter what the probabilities. But it seems clear that in so doing the agent does not act as if H_2 is true and H_1 is false (or the reverse), for he is better off with A_1 in either case. The row-maximum rule is wrong. Clearly we should say that the agent acts as if $H_1 \vee H_2$ is true and, qualitatively, he suspends judgement between them. This example shows us that in some cases an agent will act if a disjunction of some of the partitioning hypotheses is true and suggests the constraint on any acceptance-rule that dominance will always result in complete qualitative suspension of judgement.

But the column-maximum rule is not right either. Consider:

	0.49	0.45	0.01	0.05	
	H_1	H_2	H_3	H_4	
A_1	100	-60	200	-60	21
A_2	-300	260	-100	60	-28
A_3	200	-200	-100	0	7

A_1 has maximum expected utility, and the column-maximum rule dictates that the agent acts as if H_3 were true. This is surely wrong – if it is not already clear, consider a modification of the example in which H_3 has an even lower probability. We might want to say that the agent acts as if H_3 were true in choosing A_1 if its utility under act A_1 were so high that even after discounting for its low probability H_3's utility was large compared to other entries in the matrix. But as things are, the contribution to expected utility from the A_1–H_3 cell is only 2, as compared to contributions of approximately 50 and -25 from the first two cells in the first row, among others. In choosing among the acts for this matrix, attention largely focuses on H_1 and H_2.

To see what is going on in this case, we need to give a qualitative description of the application of Bayes's rule. In choosing act A_1, the agent is definitely not acting as if H_1 is true and the other hypotheses are false. Such an acceptance would be described by choosing act A_3 if by anything. Similarly, the agent is not acting as if H_2 were true, since such acceptance would dictate A_2 over A_1. Rather the agent is hedging his bets. In so far as his deliberations proceed by focusing largely on H_1 and H_2, as I suggested above, he acts as if H_1 or H_2 is true and he is qualitatively unsure which. Thus in choosing A_1 he is balancing possible gain against possible loss in recognition of his uncertainty as to whether H_1 or H_2 is true. Given that the most important considerations lead him to choose A_1 and that he will fare better choosing A_1 if H_3 is true than he would have under all other options, we do not want to say that he acts as if H_3 were false. But in choosing A_1 we do want to say that he acts as if H_4 is false, for if H_4 is true he will have lost more in choosing A_1 than he would have under any other alternative. Putting all these considerations together, we have a plausibility argument for the

Column-Minimum Rule:
If $E(A_i)$ is maximal, the agent should choose A_i. In so doing he acts as if H_j were false for all H_j such that the utility of H_j on act A_i is minimal in the H_j column. The agent acts as if the disjunction of the remaining hypotheses is true. Relative to the set of options, the agent accepts this disjunction, suspends qualitative judgement between the disjuncts, and rejects its negation.

We have made progress, but we are not done yet. Consider:

	H_1	H_2	H_3
A_0	0	0	0
A_1	2	-1	0
A_2	-1	2	0

The agent is offered a bet on the flip of a coin he regards as more likely to come up heads than tails. H_1 is 'heads comes up', H_2 is 'tails comes up', and H_3 is 'the bet is called off', of which there is a non-negligible chance. A_0 is to refrain from taking the bet, A_1 is to bet on heads, and A_2 is to bet on tails. As indicated in the matrix, the agent gets his money back in case of H_3. Given his attitude toward the coin, the agent chooses act A_1. Clearly, he acts as if H_2 is false, and does not act as if H_1 is false. But what about H_3? In this situation the agent is acting in clear cognizance of the possibility of the act being called off. In choosing A_1 he does nothing which suggests that he acts as if H_3 were false, since he will be no better or worse off if H_3 is true by choosing A_1 as opposed to A_0 or A_2. Thus he should be described as acting as if $H_1 \lor H_3$ is true. And the column-minimum rule should be modified by reading 'strict-minimum' where it now reads 'minimum'.

We have yet to deal with lottery-type situations. Consider a lottery described by

	H_1	H_2		$\cdots$		H_n
A_0	0	0		$\cdots$		0
A_1	+	−		$\cdots$		−
A_2	−	+		$\cdots$		−
$\cdot$	$\cdot$	$\cdot$				
$\cdot$	$\cdot$	$\cdot$				
$\cdot$	$\cdot$	$\cdot$				
A_n	−	−		$\cdots$		+

H_i is the hypothesis that ticket number i wins, and all H_i are equiprobable. To keep the example simple we suppose that the agent has the option of not buying a ticket or of buying exactly one. So the exhaustive set of options is given by A_0 (do not buy a ticket) and the A_i (buy ticket i), $1 \leq i \leq n$. We suppose that $E(A_i) = E(A_j) > E(A_0) = 0$, all $i, j \neq 0$. Bayes's rule recommends choosing one of the A_i, for any $i \neq 0$; in effect it recommends choosing randomly among A_1 through A_n. But in so doing, the agent is not acting as if H_i is true for the i he happens to settle on. Rather he acts as if the truth lies with some one of the hypotheses corresponding to the acts recommended for random choice, but he does not know which one. And the same sort of considerations would apply if a more limited subset of the acts take on maximum expected utility.

The obvious modification of the column-strict-minimum rule is to apply it to each act which receives maximum expected utility, and then disjoin the hypotheses thus selected to obtain the act accepted relative to the set of options. I bring all these considerations together now in the following formal definition:

Let $\{A_i\}_I$ be the exhaustive set of alternative acts and $\{H_j\}_J$ the relevant partitioning hypotheses. Let u_{ij} be the utility of A_i if H_j

is true and $E(A_i)$ the expected utility of A_i. Let

$$H^i_{rej} \equiv \bigvee_{j \in J_i} H_j, \qquad J_i = \left\{ j \mid u_{ij} = \underset{i' \in I}{\text{strict min }} u_{i'j} \right\}$$

$$H^i_{acc} \equiv \sim H^i_{rej} \equiv \bigvee_{j \in J - J_i} H_j$$

$$H_{acc} = \bigvee_{i \in I_{max}} H^i_{acc}, \qquad I_{max} = \left\{ i \mid E(A_i) = \underset{i' \in I}{\max} E(A_{i'}) \right\}$$

The Decision-Theoretic Acceptance-Rule:
The agent should choose randomly from among the A_i in $\{A_i\}_{I_{max}}$ and in so doing he acts as if H_{acc} is true. Thus relative to $\{A_i\}_I$ he should accept H_{acc} as strongest, he should suspend qualitative judgement between H_{acc}'s disjuncts and he should reject the negation of H_{acc}. He should also accept all propositions implied by H_{acc} and he should reject all propositions which imply the negation of H_{acc}.

The intent of 'accept as strongest' in this definition is just that H_{acc} is the strongest proposition which the agent is warranted in accepting relative to $\{A_i\}_I$. This, together with the addendum about accepting all propositions implied by H_{acc} is just Levi's strategy for guaranteeing consistency and deductive closure. Thus this rule satisfies Levi's requirement of deductive cogency.

The Decision-Theoretic Acceptance-Rule provides a good basic development of the intuition that our presystematic talk about acceptance can be reconstructed on the basis of our willingness to act as if certain propositions are true. The proposal could of course be developed further. For example, one may wish to take account of the fact that people do not have exact utility functions, and that even when small differences in utility can be noticed, they are in most situations reasonably ignored. One can easily reflect these facts in the definitions by relaxing the strict minima and the maxima requirements in the definitions of H^i_{rej} and H_{acc}. Thus we could substitute

$$\hat{H}^i_{rej} \equiv \bigvee_{j \in J_i} H_j, \qquad J_i = \left\{ j \mid u_{ij} \leq \underset{i' \in I}{\text{strict min }} u_{i'j} + \varepsilon \right\}$$

$$\hat{H}^i_{acc} \equiv \sim \hat{H}^i_{rej} \equiv \bigvee_{j \in J - J_i} H_j$$

$$\hat{H}_{acc} \equiv \bigvee_{i \in I_{max}} \hat{H}^i_{acc}, \qquad I_{max} = \left\{ i \mid E(A_i) \geq \underset{i' \in I}{\max} E(A_{i'}) - \delta \right\}$$

The exact values of ε and δ are stipulated to be 'small' but otherwise left undetermined. This is as it should be, because I am, after all, reconstructing a presystematic conception which is intrinsically vague. By leaving these values vaguely specified as 'small' I accurately reconstruct one aspect of the vagueness of the reconstructed notion.

Another further development follows upon residual tension between the column-strict-minimum rule and the column-maximum rule. I have worked with the strict-minimum rule, because the maximum rule gives clearly wrong results when one of the hypotheses has a much smaller probability than others. But in many cases in which probabilities are all comparable, the maximum rule gives appealing results. Also the maximum rule is clearly less 'cautious' in something like Levi's sense. This suggests describing a family of rules characterized by a Levi-style caution/boldness index, k, $0 \leqslant k \leqslant 1$. When $k = 0$ we would have the Decision-Theoretic Acceptance-Rule as I have presented it. When $k = 1$ we would have the same kind of rule based on column-maxima instead of column-strict-minima. This is still not quite right because of the mentioned tendency for a column-maximum style rule to give the wrong results when some hypothesis has markedly lower probability than some other. To the extent that such a situation arises, we want our rule to look more like a strict-minimum rule. All these considerations may be taken into account as follows. Let p_{max} be the maximum probability of the partitioning hypotheses, and p_{min} be the minimum probability. Let D_j be the difference between the minimum and maximum utility values in the jth column, that is, $D_j = \max_{i \in I} u_{ij} - \min_{i \in I} u_{ij}$. Then we adjust the minimum value referred to in the definition of H^i_{rej} by adding the quantity $k(p_{min}/p_{max})D_j$, yielding

$$H^i_{rej} \equiv \bigvee_{j \in J_i} H_j, \qquad J_i = \left\{ j \mid u_{ij} \leqslant \operatorname*{strict\,min}_{i' \in I} u_{i'j} + k(p_{min}/p_{max})D_j \right\}$$

Special cases actually require that k be limited to the range $0 \leqslant k < 1$, or, equivalently the '$\leqslant$' in the definition of J_i could be changed to '$<$' with k limited to $0 < k \leqslant 1$. Of course, one could consider other measures combining all the relevant factors revealed by our discussion, but I think we already have the means of describing presystematic intuition beyond refinements which it will support. As I have neither taste nor talent for formal flourish, I will leave further technical development to those who enjoy the sport.

I do however, need to make a number of further qualitative

comments about the Decision-Theoretic Acceptance-Rule and its comparison with Levi's work. I have been presenting the account prescriptively. The rule enjoins the agent to follow Bayes's rule, and thus derivatively to accept, relative to the presented set of options, those propositions described as accepted when Bayes's rule is followed. But the account also has descriptive application. It describes actual relative acceptance in so far as agents follow Bayes's rule (and the admittedly very stringent idealizations that it involves). More noteworthy, the account also provides the tools for describing relative acceptance when an agent violates Bayes's rule. When the agent chooses act A_i, without any randomization, he acts as if H^i_{acc} is true. A similar comment applies in case the agent randomizes in some way other than that recommended by Bayes's rule.

Both Levi and I indulge in extreme idealization in our reconstruction of the problem situation. Levi faces the question of how to assign his ultimate partitions, and the problem is pressing because the choice of partition has enormous repercussions in the application of his rules. Levi maintains that partitions result from choice of a relevant question and candidate-strongest answers to that question, but he gives no general discussion of how these choices are to be made. Indeed, he despairs: 'Perhaps some criterion of the legitimacy of questions is available, although this is doubtful'.[20] I have a similar problem, for I have been pretending that life simply hands us exhaustive sets of options. The best I can do is to plead (and it is a weak plea) that the problem of determining what set of options a given context makes available to an agent is not a special problem for my account, while Levi's corresponding problem is somewhat idiosyncratic. And in one further respect, the present account fares much better. Once the alternative acts of a set of options has been specified, one can apply a very precise prescription for selecting the partitioning hypotheses: Use the finest partition subject to the constraint that no column of utilities in the decision-matrix differs from another by a constant. This prescription works because when two columns differ by a constant, one does not affect the differences between the expected utilities by collapsing the columns, that is, by using the disjunction of the two collapsed hypotheses and using the utilities from either of the two columns, or their expected average.

Another point worth mentioning is that, on the present account, acceptance depends on utilities as well as probabilities. So far as I

[20] Ibid., p. 151.

am concerned, this is as it should be. When one acts as if something were true, expected gain importantly guides tacit acceptance. In any case, I share this utility-dependence with Levi and with some other accounts of qualitative acceptance. A particularly striking feature of this utility-dependence (again shared with Levi's account) arises in cases of relative acceptance of low probability hypotheses. This can happen when a low probability is none the less greater than other low probabilities, or when low probabilities are offset by very high utilities. Pascal's wager provides the obvious dramatization of this possibility. For a better example consider the agent who buys a lottery ticket which has a slightly higher payoff than the others or a slightly better chance of winning. Or we could recount an adventure story about a hero who acts on a long shot but his only hope for survival.

I have yet to deal with the topic of zealous acceptance, that is acceptance or belief which the agent regards as not being relative to any particular context or situation. As I have already remarked, Levi eliminates relativization from his account by appealing to acceptance relative to all questions the agent regards as serious. I will follow Levi's procedure, but before doing so we need to look more carefully at how, and how well, this strategy works for Levi. Levi's explicit characterization in *Gambling with Truth* stipulates that

When a given sentence is accepted as true with confidence great enough to settle the doubts of all but virtual skeptics relative to all questions recognized as serious ones, further evidence collection for the purpose of checking on that sentence seems pointless. Under such conditions, one would seem to be justified in accepting the sentence as evidence.[21]

But the rule which takes a proposition to be accepted as evidence if and only if it is accepted relative to all serious questions cannot be right. For example, Levi maintains that all of us accept as evidence the proposition that the Earth will not explode.[22] But this proposition is not accepted relative to the question of whether or not pulsars are rotating neutron stars. Clearly a sympathetic reading recasts Levi's rule to stipulate that a proposition is accepted as evidence if and only if it is accepted relative to all *relevant* questions. But what counts as relevant? Let us say that an ultimate partition which Levi uses to specify a question tests a proposition,

[21] Ibid., p. 150.
[22] 'Acceptance Revisited', p. 4.

H, if one of the partition's members implies *H*. (To simplify exposition in the following, I will use the term 'question' to cover the ultimate partition which Levi assumes to specify the relevant nature of a question, so that 'partitioning hypothesis of a question' refers to any one of the elements of the question's ultimate partition. This notion of a test provides at least one kind of relevance which we must take into account. For, consider any H_i which is one of the question's partitioning hypotheses and any *H* implied by H_i. If H_i is accepted relative to the question, then *H* is also accepted relative to the question. Consequently, if a question tests a proposition in the sense given, acceptance of the proposition relative to the question is possible, at least so far as the structure of the question goes before probabilities and utilities are taken into account.

If we analyze relevance in terms of tests, we might take the rule Levi needs to be that a proposition is accepted as evidence just in case it is accepted relative to all serious questions which test the proposition. We must amend this suggestion, however, because surely Levi would not want a proposition to be accepted as evidence by default because it happened not to be tested by any serious questions. Clearly we must add the existence requirement that the proposition actually be tested by at least one serious question. Altogether, in attempting to make out Levi's intention we may propose

The Weak-Evidential Acceptance-Rule:
A proposition is accepted as evidence by an agent just in case it is tested by at least one question the agent regards as serious and it is accepted by the agent relative to all questions, serious for him, which test the proposition.

This rule, however, does not yet put Levi clearly home, for it fails to meet his condition of adequacy, the deductive cogency requirement. Take consistency first. Suppose that there are only two serious questions, Q_1 and Q_2. Let H_1 and H_2 be two inconsistent propositions such that H_1 is tested by Q_1 but not by Q_2 and H_2 is tested by Q_2 but not by Q_1, and H_1 & H_2 is tested by neither question. In such a situation the weak evidential acceptance rule characterizes each of H_1 and H_2 as being accepted as evidence. This model is wholly unrealistic, of course; but it proves that the consistency of the rule cannot be proved without the aid of further assumptions. The same example (with or without the assumption that H_1 and H_2 are inconsistent) shows that two propositions may be accepted according to the rule while their conjunction is not accepted.

It should be obvious that at least part of the difficulty arises because the existence-condition can fail for a conjunction even though it is satisfied for both of the conjuncts. And the following argument shows that this problem constitutes the whole of the difficulty. Suppose that H_1 and H_2 are accepted according to the rule and that Q is a serious question which tests the conjunction H_1 & H_2. Since a test of a proposition tests anything implied by the proposition, Q tests H_1 and Q tests H_2, and since H_1 and H_2 are both assumed accepted by the rule, they are both accepted relative to Q. It follows that H_1 & H_2 is accepted relative to Q, by the same argument which Levi uses to show that his relative acceptance-rules satisfy the conjunction-condition. Consider that H which is accepted as strongest relative to Q. H implies H_1 and H implies H_2. So H implies H_1 & H_2, and since anything implied by H is accepted relative to Q, H_1 & H_2 is accepted relative to Q. Consequently, if H_1 and H_2 are both accepted by the rule, H_1 & H_2 is accepted relative to any serious question which tests it. In other words, if H_1 and H_2 are both accepted according to the rule, their conjunction is accepted by the rule unless it is not tested by any serious question. Also, if H_1 and H_2 are inconsistent, their conjunction is not tested by any question, since contradictions are never tested by any question, and in this sense the existence-condition also lies in the way of the consistency of the rule.

In as much as the existence-condition lies in the way of proving that the rule satisfies the deductive-cogency-condition, Levi clearly needs the following further assumption to prove deductive cogency:

The Principle of Combination of Serious Questions:
If there is a serious question which tests H_1 and a serious question which tests H_2 then there is a serious question which tests both H_1 and H_2.

(We do not need the stronger principle that the question mentioned in the consequent actually tests the conjunction H_1 & H_2, since if H_1 and H_2 are both accepted according to the weak evidential acceptance rule, this stronger required conclusion will follow from the combination principle as I have stated it.) This principle clearly suffices for proving deductive cogency, and as far as I can see it is also necessary. Unfortunately, this principle is not very plausible. Let H_1 be the proposition that chlorophyll is needed for photosynthesis, tested by the serious question of whether or not it is true. Let H_2 be the hypothesis that pulsars are rotating neutron stars, tested by the serious question of whether this is true. While one can easily concoct questions which test both H_1 and H_2, it seems highly implausible that such questions would ever count as serious.

Even if Levi could argue convincingly for the principle of combination of serious questions, the weak-evidential acceptance-rule faces another difficulty: A proposition accepted relative to all serious questions may none the less be rejected relative to some serious question which does not test it. This is because for Levi (as for my proposal) it suffices for rejection that a proposition imply a rejected partitioning hypothesis.[23] Such a circumstance certainly runs counter to the intuitive idea underlying acceptance as evidence, and so I would expect Levi to rule it out:

The Strong-Evidential Acceptance-Rule:
A proposition is accepted as evidence just in case it is accepted according to the weak rule and it is not rejected relative to any serious question.

The strong rule fares ever so slightly better than its weak counterpart with respect to consistency: There cannot be two mutually inconsistent propositions accepted according to the strong rule, but there can be three such, as long as they are pairwise consistent. One could guarantee consistency of the strong rule by invoking the principle of combination of serious questions, but even this principle will not ensure deductive closure. Even if H_1 and H_2 are accepted according to the strong rule, so that neither is rejected relative to any serious question, and even though their conjunction H_1 & H_2 is tested, the conjunction may be rejected relative to some question which does not test it. Some further restrictive principle seems to be called for. Not to burden further this already lengthy discussion, I will simply report that all my own efforts have turned up only proposals which all prove implausible on one ground or another. Indeed, we seem to be faced with a sort of qualitative analogue of the multiplication principle for probabilities. Although H_1 and H_2 may each be unrejected by every serious question, their conjunction is stronger, and thus may be rejected relative to some serious question which rejects neither H_1 nor H_2. I conjecture that this situation will occur

---

[23] Risto Hilpinen proves a proposition (CA2, p. 101 in *Rules of Acceptance and Inductive Logic*, Acta Philosophica Fennica, 1968) which appears to contradict this claim. However, his proof assumes that the proposition concerned is a member of or a disjunction of members of the ultimate partition of a question. Thus his proof does not apply to propositions which properly imply a rejected member of an ultimate partition, and such propositions must be taken to be rejected if the relativized acceptance-rules are to satisfy deductive closure and if the negation of something which is accepted always counts as rejected.

for any attempt to develop an unrelativized notion of qualitative acceptance on probabilistic foundations.

This conjecture certainly holds for de-relativization of acceptance relative to a set of options as developed in this paper. Following the spirit of Levi's strategy I will replace serious questions with 'serious' possible sets of options, where a possible set of options is said to be serious if there is a non-negligible chance of its actually arising. My account is vague in its vague appeal to 'non-negligible' chances. But, as with the last occurrence of vagueness in the account, the vagueness already occurs in the presystematic conception and so is appropriately left in the reconstruction. Using this interpretation of 'serious', I give exact analogues of the rules proposed for Levi's account:

The Weak Zealous-Acceptance-Rule:
A proposition is zealously accepted just in case it is tested by at least one serious possible set of options and it is accepted relative to all serious possible sets of options which test the proposition.

The Strong Zealous-Acceptance-Rule:
A proposition is zealously accepted just in case it is accepted according to the weak rule and it is not rejected relative to any serious possible set of options.

These rules fail to meet the deductive cogency requirement in exactly the way the rules proposed for Levi fail to meet it, and exactly the same comments about rejection of zealously accepted propositions apply. And given the probabilistic interpretation I have put on 'serious possible sets of options', there is not even partial relief to be had from the analogue of the principle of combination of serious questions. If two serious possible sets of options each have a small but non-negligible chance of occurring there may well be no way to combine the two sets into a third with a non-negligible chance of occurring. If the two sets are, crudely speaking, independent, the combined set may have as its chance of occurring only the product of the two already small chances of the two original sets, and this product may be completely negligible.

How bad is this failure of deductive cogency? I submit that both zealous-acceptance-rules come as close to satisfying deductive cogency as one could sensibly require and that at least the strong rule satisfies all sensible demands on rationality. (To streamline exposition I will henceforth take zealous acceptance to be acceptance according to the strong rule.) Consider possible failure of consistency: An inconsistent set of propositions can be zealously accepted, but only when there is no one serious possible set of options which tests all the members of the inconsistent set. Thus there will be no more than a negligible chance of a situation arising in which the inconsistency could be activated. As for failure of closure, consider first cases in which closure fails because there is no serious possible set of options which tests a conjunction of zealously accepted propositions. Then it simply does not matter whether or not the conjunction is accepted, again in the sense that there is no more than a negligible chance of any situation arising in which acceptance or failure to accept will make a difference. Or consider cases in which closure fails because of rejection of a conjunction of zealously-accepted propositions by a serious possible set of options which does not test the conjunction. Here again, failure of closure can have no practical repercussions, because the serious possible set of options relative to which the conjunction is rejected is not one in which the conjunction could figure as a basis of action.

Levi, I know, will not be satisfied. He will argue that when we focus on cognitive aims, putting practice aside, rationality demands full deductive cogency. But, if he does so argue, I feel he will be playing false to his theme of gambling with truth. To gamble with truth, in his sense, includes accepting the risk of error, and the sort of inconsistency which might strike a zealous acceptor is no more than run of the mill error. It does not permit the sort of cognitive catastrophe fear of which makes some insist on avoiding inconsistency at all costs. Although the strong zealous-acceptance-rule allows the possibility of zealously accepting an inconsistent *set* of propositions, the same problem that generates this possibility ensures that one will not zealously accept any one inconsistent proposition (or a set of inconsistent propositions used in any one argument) and thus inconsistency cannot be used by a zealous acceptor to justify any and all conclusions. In positive respects also, I feel that zealous acceptance covers Levi's concern with cognitive deliberation very adequately. Suppose we are taken by the game of gambling with truth and consider acts of accepting propositions for purely cognitive reasons, independently of practical concerns. Following Levi we consider acceptance decision-matrices filled in with epistemic utilities. Any such matrices with which we are seriously concerned will be among the serious possible set of options. So if H_1 and H_2 are zealously accepted and we also have any serious cognitive concern with their conjunction, an epistemic utility-matrix which tests the conjunction will be among the serious possible sets of options. Thus the existence-condition will be satisfied. If a conjunction of zealously accepted propositions fails to be zealously accepted only because it is rejected relative to a serious possible set of options which does not test it, and if we become cognitively concerned with this anomaly, we may expect that the cognitive concern will introduce new elements into the decision-theoretic situation, resulting in a decision-matrix which will translate the rejection of the conjunction into at least a non-acceptance of the conjunction relative to a new serious possible set of options which does test it. In fact, it seems plausible that such interplay of cognitive and practical concerns will in practice eliminate any difference in effect between the weak and strong zealous-acceptance-rules for all propositions with which we have any active cognitive concern. Similarly, as soon as one becomes concerned with an inconsistency which arises among one's zealously-accepted propositions, serious possible sets of options will arise which test for the source of the inconsistency, with widespread repercussions throughout one's zealous acceptance. No reasonable cognitive deliberator need come any closer to deductive cogency. Surely zealous acceptance is zealotry enough.

Before closing I would like to touch on Levi's aim of developing a notion of acceptance which would serve as a reconstruction of rational use of propositions as evidence. The present account gives a uniform treatment of reasonable use as evidence in case of zealous acceptance and in cases in which one reasonably uses a proposition as evidence in some situations though one would reasonably refrain in others. If one zealously accepts a proposition, one will act as if it is true in all situations which have a non-negligible chance of coming up, including those in which such use counts as using the proposition as evidence. But we in fact do not zealously accept most of the propositions with which we are self-consciously concerned in our deliberations. For these, we act, as practical people and as cogitators, on the assumption that such are true in some situations; and we do not so act in others. For example, if we have a drug with well- but not overwhelmingly-confirmed effectiveness and safety, we will act as if the drug is safe when we monkey around with monkeys but not when we prescribe to people.

I find Levi's account less satisfactory on two counts. First, his acceptance-rules are entirely framed in terms of epistemic utilities. But when one considers use of a proposition as evidence in practical affairs, including situations in which a scientist must worry whether the cost of running an experiment is worth the expected return in information, practical utilities must enter also. While I have no reason to think that Levi cannot explain this meshing between practical and cognitive thirsting after truth, he has not done so; and in this respect he could usefully clarify his position. I have built such meshing into the present account from the start by talking about acting as if a proposition is true whether the values are practical, moral, cognitive, or any combination of these. Second, I see a problem of near uselessness in Levi's notion of acceptance (as opposed to use) as evidence. Recall that, for Levi, an agent accepts a proposition as evidence when he accepts it with such confidence that he will use it as a premiss in any deliberations, in complete disregard of the risk that the proposition might be false. Levi argues that there are such propositions by pointing to logical truths and to empirical propositions such as that the Earth will not explode.[24] He then goes on to assume that we likewise accept serious scientific propositions as evidence – indeed he must assume something like this if the notion promises to be of much interest. I submit that this rarely happens. Consider something as fundamental to physics as the conservation of energy and momentum. As recently as the 1920s physicists ran experiments to test these principles and tried to develop theories in which they held only on the average. During the last ten years, hundreds of thousands of dollars have been spent running experiments designed to test quantum mechanics. Yet quantum mechanics and the conservation of energy and momentum are assumed without question in most physicists' deliberations. Such facts fit more naturally with the present account than they do with Levi's.

I have tried here to present the only really sound sort of criticism one can level at a scheme such as Professor Levi's: an alternative with pretentions to do better what he seeks to do. I want to be clear about my debt. Indeed, I happily describe my positive suggestions as redevelopment of ideas exclusively invented or at least mentioned by Levi. Starting with his accomplishments, I have tried to reach farther by using what I see as more natural idealizations in a more uniform application to his concerns. If nothing else, my proposal should serve to goad Levi toward further useful developments.

[24] 'Acceptance Revisited', p. 4.

§3. Comments and Replies
The Levi–Teller Session

LEVI: Teller is mistaken in alleging that I seek a system capturing 'our presystematic and qualitative use of "believes"'. I do, indeed, introduce several distinct notions of what one might call 'belief' and 'degree of belief' which I attempt to characterize in terms of their functioning in an account of enquiry and deliberation.

Thus, in *Gambling with Truth*, I introduced a distinction between 'acceptance as evidence' and 'mere acceptance'. I did not claim that either of these notions explicated our presystematic and qualitative use of 'believes'. I did assume that the growth of knowledge is manifested in the revision of a body of propositions accepted as evidence by an agent at a time. I took for granted that this corpus could be revised by adding new information obtained via observation and that it could also be revised by throwing items out – although I said very little about either of these modes of revision. I focused attention on conditions under which new information should be added to the corpus of evidence via inductive inference. In later work, I modified and improved the account of inductive inference and expansion and have commented further on expansion via observation and on contraction.

Thus, my aim has been to provide a systematic account of the improvement of knowledge construed as resources for enquiry and deliberation (borrowing and slightly modifying a phrase of Dewey's). In so far as I have attempted to explicate any notion of belief or acceptance, I have sought to do so by identifying the significance of these notions within an account of enquiry and deliberation along the lines I have been proposing without seriously exploring how well my proposals 'fit' presystematic linguistic practice.

To be sure, I have often appealed to presystematic practice in order to facilitate understanding of my proposals and to win a hearing for ideas which are, in some respects, heterodox. Thus, I do believe Shackle-like conceptions of degree of belief capture a dominant use of degrees of belief and disbelief in presystematic practice. If we were to rely on 'ordinary language', probabilistic notions would, perhaps, look like non-starters were it not for the mighty efforts of the ideologies inculcated in institutions of higher learning. But I have never relied on such a view. Indeed, I maintain that both measures of credal probability and of potential surprise have important roles to play in an account of deliberation and enquiry which are not rival to one another but are complementary. I took this view when I began commenting on these matters and continue to do so today. What does matter to me is to understand how these notions help clarify aspects of enquiry and deliberation in a systematic account of the revision of knowledge.

Teller offers his account of 'zealous acceptance' in an effort to capture salient aspects of presystematic precedents he seems to think my scheme captures. With all due respect, his proposal is neither relevant nor positive criticism of my ideas.

In any event, since Teller thinks that a Bayesian account of decision-theory and probability-judgement tells the precise version of a story told only partially and approximately in terms of zealous acceptance, it is not clear to me why Teller thinks zealous acceptance worth bothering about. We should, at least, agree that it is not worth further comment.

At the same time, I think Teller should take the notion of acceptance as evidence more seriously than he does. According to Bayesian doctrine, If X accepts h as evidence, X should assign h a positive degree of credal probability. Bayesians may not always use my jargon; but at least personalist Bayesians are committed to such a view as are any Bayesians who see their theories as being concerned with the policing of systems of probability judgements at least under idealized conditions.

My point can be put in a somewhat different form. Bayesians see judgements of credal probability as appraisals of hypotheses belonging to a space of possibilities. One of the functions of a corpus of knowledge or evidence in enquiry and deliberation is to define that space of possibilities – which I call serious possibilities. And, to my knowledge, all Bayesians who traffic in idealization contend that an ideally rational agent should accept as evidence all logical truths.

Bayesians differ among themselves concerning how a corpus of evidence or knowledge should be revised. If there is an important difference between Teller and myself it concerns this matter and not presystematic usage of 'believes'. Unfortunately Teller's view in this paper and in his other writings on the subject are too obscure for me to be sure that I can formulate his view with any clarity. He sometimes seems to claim that ideally rational agents should never accept propositions as evidence altogether – a view which ought to be anathema to every Bayesian.

But Teller is clear about one thing. If one accepts e as evidence at time t, he contends that there can be no legitimate way of removing it subsequently. He contends that my efforts to provide an account fail. He offers two reasons for claiming this.

The first is that one cannot revise a corpus of knowledge K by contraction at all but can only engage in replacement. His reason is that if a hypothesis not-H is in the initial corpus K_1, the truth of H is not a serious possibility according to the agent X at that time. Hence, at that time, so Teller seems to reason, X should accept as evidence in his corpus 'It is not possible that H is true'. But when X contracts by removing not-H so as to suspend judgement between H and not-H, he should add to his corpus 'It is possible that H is true'. But in so doing, he is replacing one proposition by another inconsistent with it.

Teller assumes in advancing this argument that if X accepts not-H as evidence and, hence, appraises H as not being a serious possibility, X should accept 'It is not possible that H' as evidence at that time. I have gone on record as rejecting that view elsewhere. Teller acknowledges the point but then claims that I have deprived my view of informative value by making this claim.

Suppose X assigns G degree of credal probability of 0.6 at time t. Does Teller think that in so doing, X is committed to accepting as evidence 'the degree of probability that G is 0.6'? Does he think that in changing from that credal judgement to one assigning G degree of credence equal to 0.5, X is committed to replacing one proposition in his corpus by another inconsistent with it? Does he think that if one refuses to embrace these consequences, the notion of credal probablity is deprived of informative value? I hope he does not endorse these absurdities. In any event, I reject them and do not see that I have to embrace kindred absurdities pertaining to possibility.

Teller also complains that prior to contraction, all items in a corpus are equally certain and infallibly true. There can be no distinction between them with respect to how well they are supported by the evidence – which consists of all items in the corpus. That there are no such distinctions on my view is correct; but that this constitutes sufficient grounds to dismiss my account of contraction is question-begging. I contend that other factors in the corpus serve as a basis for discriminating between propositions accepted as evidence with respect to vulnerability to removal.

Teller's failure to recognize that he has begged the question may be attributable, perhaps, to his commitment to a widely held dogma so well entrenched in contemporary philosophical debate that my questioning it may appear to Teller to be some sort of conceptual mistake. The dogma is this: If the falsity of h is not a serious possibility according to X at t, so that h is infallibly true according to X at t, then from X's point of view no circumstance could arise under which he would be justified in ceasing to accept h as evidence. That is to say, infallibility implies incorrigibility.

In *Gambling with Truth*, I too was seduced by this dogma to the extent that I was prepared to say that X could legitimately accept h as evidence and be fully certain that h is true even though X allowed the possibility that h is false. I did so because I continued to conflate infallibility with incorrigibility and wished to endorse the view that knowledge is corrigible. I have long since recognized the confusion ingredient in this view and have explicitly challenged the dogma. Teller seems to be caught in its toils. As a consequence, it seems inconceivable to him that grades of certainty, evidential support, or probability could be distinct from grades of vulnerability to revision. But I do question the dogma and with it the notion that vulnerability to revision (i.e., corrigibility) correlates with probability or evidential support. Once the dogma is rejected Teller's objection disappears.

To be sure, it still remains an important task to give a systematic account of contraction of a corpus of evidence. I have taken some steps in that direction but much more needs to be done. In any event, Teller should not block the path of enquiry by refusing to countenance the problem in the first place.

KYBURG: My acceptance rule is merely piecemeal cogent, but not deductively cogent: the set of statements accepted as a body of knowledge need not, on my view, be deductively closed. Levi says that it is 'entertainable' that he and I do not disagree. Much as it would delight me, and assuage any doubts I might have about the soundness of my formulations, were I to find that at long last Levi and I had arrived at the same point, it isn't obvious to me that this is so.

What is at issue are notions of belief and acceptance needed for decision-making. There are some differences in formulation of the problem that are relevant. Levi takes the corpus K of statements accepted as evidence to be deductively closed. The question he raises concerns the deductive closure of the set of statements that are *merely* accepted, MK_k. I am willing to suppose that there is a set of statements that is deductively closed; but this corresponds to Levi's urcorpus, a relatively artificial, but none the less useful, notion. In doing science, for example, I would put meter readings and the like into the urcorpus: these are statements that are *artifically* constructed to be incorrigible. So, of course, are Chisholmian statements of being appeared to, provided they turn out to serve a useful epistemological function. But I do not merely define probability relative to the urcorpus; in most situations we are willing to accept statements as evidence that are not of this extreme and artificial sort. I thus define probability relative to bodies of knowledge that are only piecemeal cogent, since their contents may be supposed to be statements that are accepted relative to some higher or more demanding corpus. The significant epistemological difference is that I want the statements accepted as evidence in a given context themselves to be justifiable – to be accepted on the basis of the same rule as warrants the acceptance of the statements MK_k. I have defined probability relative to a K that need not be deductively closed; Levi has required that it be deductively closed. That cuts no ice when it comes to making decisions relative to a set of statements acceptable relative to MK_k, so let us leave the structure of K to one side.

I want to make the same distinction that Levi does between K – the set of statements accepted as evidence in a certain context – and MK_k – the set of statements merely accepted. The set of accepted statements, MK_k, on my view is piecemeal deductively closed. Nevertheless, we may define a maximal consistent subset of MK_k. Let us call such a maximal consistent subset of MK_k a *strand* of K. Most strands of MK_k will have a lot of statements in common. Statements that occur in all strands of MK_k constitute the set of statements that ought to be accepted in the context at hand. This holds for Levi as for me. But there may be statements relevant to the decision context that appear in one strand but not in another. If there are no such statements, then for me, as for Levi, the accepted statements can be construed as truncating the alternatives open to the decision-maker. If there are such statements that appear in one strand and not in another in a given decision-context, then I would say that we should retreat to a context in which none of those statements are accepted. An illustration is at hand in the lottery situation. Suppose what is at issue is whether or not to buy a lottery ticket. At a certain level of acceptance, relative to K, for every i, I should accept the statement that ticket i will not win. But if I consider the strands of the set of statements accepted at that level, I will find that in one of them 'ticket i will not win' does *not* occur. I will therefore move to a higher level of rational corpus for that decision: I will move to the level at which none of the statements 'ticket i will not win' is acceptable, but where, relative to every strand of the corpus, the probability that ticket i will not win is $1/n$. Relative to that corpus my decision concerning whether or not to buy a ticket is dependent, in just the way Levi would have it, on the price of the ticket.

In a decision-context, what is 'solemnly' acceptable for me is a statement that appears in every strand of a rational corpus. The deductive closure of what is solemnly acceptable is consistent, and can serve to truncate the space of serious possibilities. In that sense, it may be 'entertainable' that Levi and I do not disagree over issues of deductive closure. Nevertheless, from a general epistemological point of view, it is clear that we are starting from different places and ending at different places, simply because I suppose the statements that one accepts – that is, that one is *committed* to – must all be *justifiable*, while Levi supposes that the set of statements that provide a framework of agreement in a given context are those about which we agree, and may be regarded as deductively closed and not in question in that context. The result is that Levi is free to impose deductive closure on MK_k as well as on K, (since what is at issue is the decision-context) while I am not. But in the case of a specific decision-context, I would retreat to a corpus in which all strands agree with respect to the acceptance of statements relevant to that decision; so that in that context we would agree on what is ruled out. In the case of a complex decision – for example, one that concerned complex conditional bets – we would again disagree on the assignment of probabilities, but that is a matter of the distinction (as I see it) between stochastic and conditional probability, and that is a wholly different matter.

LEVI: A corpus of knowledge or evidence in my sense is a standard for serious possibility. It partitions sentences in language L into those which are possibly true and those which are not. It is representable by the set of all sentences in L which are not possibly false according to that partition. That set should be deductively consistent and closed. I represent a corpus by that deductively closed set K.

If X contemplates expanding his initial corpus K, any potential expansion strategy should lead to a new corpus $PK \supset K$ where PK is also deductively closed; for PK should be capable of serving as a standard for serious possibility. Prior to such expansion, X might regard PK as the best potential expansion of K. In that sense, the members of PK are merely accepted.

A further terminological remark. An urcorpus UK is the weakest potential corpus or standard for serious possibility. I assume *UK* contains truths of logic, set theory, and mathematics but not, as Kyburg supposes, observation reports, phenomenological reports, or the like.

I assume that agent *X at t* should be committed to a single standard for serious possibility, so that his corpus of evidence or knowledge at *t* is unique. Of course, *X* might be schizophrenic or inconsistent; but barring such aberration, he should endorse a single standard.

Kyburg disagrees. He has contended elsewhere (and some of his remarks in his intervention echo this contention) that *X*'s corpus *K* at time *t* is vulnerable to contraction because of disagreement with others. In such contraction, *X* will be obliged to contract to shared agreements. If the disagreement with others is sufficiently drastic, *X* will be obliged to contract to a corpus *BK* consisting of the urcorpus *UK* and basic sentences such as observation and phenomenological reports together with conceptual truths. Kyburg contends that *X* should be in a position to justify membership in *K* relative to *BK*. In that way, creeping scepticism can be foiled.

I have never endorsed the idea that disagreement with others is sufficient warrant for contraction to shared agreements. A corpus is not modified in order to reach agreement with others. If *X* differs with *Y*, *X* may wish to contract to shared agreements with *Y* provided *X* regards *Y*'s views as worthy of a hearing. If *Y* is acknowledged by *X* to be an expert on the subject under dispute or if *Y*'s view has substantial value as an explanatory hypothesis, *X* might be justified in contracting to explore the merits of *Y*'s view from a non-question-begging point of view; but the mere fact of disagreement is never sufficient warrant for contraction. Who feels the need to give a hearing to the views of flat earthers?

Thus, I do not fear creeping scepticism. For me all items in *K* are, as far as *X* is concerned, certainly and infallibly true. From *X*'s point of view, none of them stand in need of justification. Justification is needed to alter *K* whether by expansion or by contraction. There is no need for a further sort of justification relative to some basic corpus *BK*.

This, in a nutshell, is the fundamental difference in epistemological outlook to which Kyburg alludes. Granting this difference, however, I do not think that the differences between our views of deductive cogency are as great as I once thought they were. I say this not in order to be pleasant but in order to emphasize that we should not be misled as to where genuine controversy does arise.

As I understand Kyburg, in so far as *BK* is a basic corpus to be used as a basic standard for possibility, it should be deductively cogent.

Suppose we identify a threshold of acceptance $k > 0.5$ such that all items in *L* with lower credal probability greater than *k* are accepted into the rational corpus RK_k. This corpus need not be deductively closed or consistent. However, from RK_k we may form the set SK_k of solemnly-accepted sentences. It is the union of all strands or maximally consistent subsets of RK_k.

According to Kyburg, the corpus *K* should be identical with the deductive closure of SK_k for some suitably specified value of *k*.

K is a standard for serious possibility to be used in computing probabilities employed in estimating risks in 'decision-contexts' of some kinds when *BK* is the basic standard for serious possibility. $K \supseteq BK$. Yet *K* is not an expansion of *BK* in the sense that *X* changes his standard for serious possibility from *BK* to *K*. According to Kyburg, both *BK* and *K* are standards for serious possibility to which the agent is committed at a given time. One is a standard to be used for practical purposes. The other is pertinent to more fundamental theoretical questions. If the propriety of using *K* in practical deliberation is challenged, the agent *X* can appeal to the basic standard *BK* for justification.

Observe, however, that even though Kyburg uses two standards where I use one, both standards are required to be deductively cogent. To be sure the rational corpus RK_k need not be deductively cogent; but RK_k is not used as a standard for serious possibility. Although it is used to 'define' probabilities as Kyburg says, it defines probabilities for use in practical deliberation only indirectly by being used to determine SK_k and, hence, *K*.

As far as I can see, Kyburg agrees with my contention that potential standards for serious possibility should be deductively closed.

In my paper, I wished to avoid drawing a distinction between inductive acceptance rules like mine which determined a set *PK* of hypotheses to be the best expansion-strategy available in an effort to add new information to the initial standard for serious possibility *K*, and rules like Kyburg's which are not rules for revision but for establishing a relation of support or justification between a basic corpus *BK* and the corpus *K* by specifying the set of sentences in the rational corpus RK_k relative to *BK*. I let MK_k represent my corpus *PK* (or, perhaps, PK_k) of merely accepted hypotheses relative to *K* when dealing with my theory and let it represent RK_k

when referring to Kyburg's theory. b-functions and d-functions can be defined relative to both interpretations. Of course, they have different meanings in Kyburg's theory and my own. However, I was concerned to draw attention to certain generic features of diverse acceptance-based measures of degrees of belief and disbelief without emphasizing differences.

Incidentally, had MK_k been equated with the deductive closure of Kyburg's SK_k, b-functions and d-functions obeying Shackle's requirements could have been generated, just as they can from rules I have proposed. So Kyburg's theory has the wherewithal to generate b-measures of several different kinds.

If we attend to the formal properties of acceptance rules without regard to their intended application, Kyburg's intervention suggests that his rules are closer to mine than I myself had thought.

Given that the selection of a corpus K relative to BK is, for Kyburg, relative to a 'decision context,' we might envisage relativizing his acceptance criterion to a partition U and the algebra $D(U)$, generated by it, of hypotheses equivalent (given BK) to disjunctions of subsets of elements of U.

If all elements of U bear upper probability relative to BK less than $1-k$, the intersection of all strands of MK_k will be empty and, as a consequence, the intersection of all strands of MK_k will consist of the elements of BK. K will be identical with BK.

If some elements of U bear upper probability relative to BK greater than $1-k$, the deductive closure of SK_k will be larger than BK. K will be distinct from BK.

Indeed, K will be the deductive consequences of BK and the negations of those elements of U whose upper probabilities are less than $1-k$.

The only difference between this criterion and my proposal in *Gambling with Truth*, modified to accommodate interval-valued probability, is that I required $1-k$ to be less than or equal to $1/n$ where n is the number of elements of U. If we attend to the formal structure of the rules and not to their intended applications, the difference between Kyburg's approach and mine approaches the subtlety of fine tuning.

Kyburg does not explicitly relativize to a partition U and, perhaps, he does not intend to. If not, however, Kyburg's criterion for determining K from BK threatens to result in $BK = K$ for virtually all situations. Kyburg's theory would lead to a single standard after all – in spite of his intention to generate two. Furthermore, the single standard would be extremely impoverished, consisting of items in the urcorpus *UK*, observational and phenomenological reports, and conceptual truths.

I do not see the need for a double standard. A corpus *K* containing strong assumptions from theories, generalizations, and statistical claims can serve as a single standard for serious possibility both for practical purposes and for scientific enquiry.

During such enquiry, the standard is subject to revision; but we should not become anxious that legitimate revisions will breed creeping scepticism.

Those haunted by the fear of such scepticism should consider the wreckage of past programmes which have sought to realize a programme for 'global' justification. I do not think we will do better with Kyburg's programme – although I think his heroic effort has much to teach us.

SWINBURNE: It is important to realize that whatever Teller means by 'accept' it is not 'believe'. He is not putting forward a theory of rational belief. For he proposes an account of the grounds which we ought to follow in choosing whether to 'accept' theories; but beliefs are not things which we can choose whether or not to have. The same point can be made with respect to many other theories of 'acceptance'; it is often very unclear what the authors mean by 'accept', of what they are giving us a theory. Pascal recommended us to believe that there is a God, but in answer to those who said 'But I can't believe', he recommended acting-as-if (we believed that) there was a God (something which we would do) as a step which might eventually have the desired effect (belief). (See B. Pascal, *Pensées*, No. 418.)

LEVI: I have explained what I mean by acceptance as evidence and mere acceptance in many places. I think my notions are as clear as Swinburne's notion of belief – indeed, they are much clearer. I also think that agents, whether they are human agents or institutions, can modify their bodies of evidence deliberately so that it makes sense to speak of choosing to accept something into evidence or choosing to remove it. In so far as believing that *h* is accepting *h* as evidence, I conclude that beliefs are subject to control.

Of course, if believing that *h* is a question of having the right intensity of conviction, belief may not be a question of choice. Those, like Hume, who sought to absolve us from responsibility for our beliefs understood belief in a manner which put it beyond our control. I maintain that our standards for serious possibility relative to which we make decisions and conduct investigations are subject to critical control. Whether such standards will be called bodies of belief depends, I suppose, on one's epistemological ideology.

COHEN: Despite Levi's interesting comparison of his own measure of belief with what I have called Baconian probability, there is an important difference between the two. Levi's function in effect identifies the degree to which given premises justify a belief with the lowest level at which an acceptance-rule operates if the belief is to be accepted as knowledge. The function is thus defined in terms of acceptance. Baconian probability, on the other hand, when it concerns matters of fact (and not legal rights, verbal meanings, or some other non-standard domain) is defined in terms of the strength with which the appropriate covering uniformity resists interference by relevant factors in the causal order of nature. I did indeed point out[1] that one can prescribe thresholds of acceptance in terms of Baconian probabilities. But the latter are defined and determined independently of the former. Thus, though Baconian probability-functions and Levi–Shackle belief-functions do share a common formal structure, they differ from one another in a way roughly analogous to that in which a propensity interpretation of the Pascalian probability-calculus differs from a personalist one. Baconian probability-functions are about reality: Levi–Shackle belief-functions are about our thoughts about reality.

A further, consequential difference emerges in relation to the criteria for assigning values to these functions. Baconian probabilities have to be assessed by applying what I call the method of relevant variables to the appropriate covering generalizations. Levi–Shackle belief-functions, however, are not thus tied to a single pattern of evaluation. They can certainly be evaluated in accordance with the corresponding Baconian probability: the justifiability of believing S, given R, can be put equal to the Baconian probability of S, given R. But any set of 'caution-dependent and deductively cogent acceptance-rules', in Levi's terminology, suffices and Levi mentions two other such sets of rules. In this respect Levi–Shackle belief-functions certainly have 'a life of their own,' as Levi puts it, independently of the method of relevant variables. But it still has to be shown that this is a useful life. *The Probable and the Provable* contains a fairly detailed and documented attempt to show that the method of relevant variables lies behind certain actual patterns of

[1] *The Probable and the Provable*, pp. 318 ff.

reasoning in the experimental sciences and in forensic proof.[2] Only when Levi has shown a comparable role for his own preferred set of acceptance-rules, will he have established the usefulness of the life that Levi–Shackle functions can have when they are evaluated independently of Baconian probabilities. Meanwhile it is in his interest to welcome the evidence and arguments that exist, via the theory of Baconian probability, for evaluating his belief-functions in conformity with the method of relevant variables.

One important point here is the nature of the formalism shared by Levi–Shackle functions with Baconian probability. Levi has not developed his own version of this system very extensively. But the system is equivalent, as I have shown, to a generalization of the C. I. Lewis modal logic $S4$. An interpretation of the formalism in terms of Baconian probabilities has the virtue of making sense of this fact. The Baconian probability of S on R gets higher and higher as the principle licensing an inference from R to S gets nearer and nearer to being a law of nature: Baconian probability is a gradation of natural necessity. That is how a modal logic comes to be apposite. Correspondingly a possible-worlds model[3] for the formalism may be seen as representing the structure of controlled experiment in accordance with the method of relevant variables.

It follows that Levi's willingness to accept the theory of Baconian *probability* while repudiating that of Baconian *support* must be based on some kind of misunderstanding. These two theories are as closely interconnected and interdependent branches of inductive logic as are systems of natural deduction and logical truth in deductive logic. Instead of speaking about the (Baconian) probability with which S may be inferred from R, we can instead speak about the (Baconian) reliability of the general principle which licenses this particular inference or (saying much the same thing in other words) about the support we suppose that principle to enjoy from observable reality. Inevitably, however, a dyadic support-function here will have certain differences from a dyadic probability-function. If there is only some degree of probability, and not certainty, that things which are R will also be S, then a statement of this fact is quite consistent with

---

[2] An assessment of Baconian probability also underlies any evaluation of a medical diagnosis that has been made in accordence with the flow-chart or decision-tree method, as I shall show in a forthcoming paper 'Bayesianism versus Baconianism in the Evaluation of Medical Diagnoses', *Brit. J. Phil. Sci.* (1980).

[3] As sketched in *The Probable and the Provable*, pp. 240–2. However several possible interpretations of the formalism concern reasoning about other topics than natural necessity: cf *The Implications of Induction* (1970), p. 142 ff. See also p. 261 ff. below.

acknowledging the existence of at least some R things which are not S. Hence a dyadic (Baconian) support-function may assign some intermediate degree of reliability to a general principle on the basis of evidence that includes mention of one or more anomalies: we can have $s[H, E] > 0$ even though E is inconsistent with H. But the (Baconian) probability with which a particular thing is S given that it is R, can obviously not be greater than zero if R contradicts S.

LEVI: Cohen acknowledges that his measures of inductive probability share a common formal structure with Shackle-like measures of degrees of confidence of acceptance or degrees of belief. He claims, however, that the two measures represent distinct interpretations of the same formalism.

But Cohen does discuss examples like the following:

(7)   There's a good (inductive) probability of rain.

On p. 214 of *The Probable and the Provable*, Cohen writes that someone who asserted (7) would 'raise the presumption that he had taken into account all of the facts that he knew'.

Now (7) is a good example of a judgement of degrees of confidence or acceptance. Cohen is plausibly to be understood as recommending that in making such Shackle-like judgements one should take into account the total relevant evidence. Moreover, as I reported in my discussion of his views, for Cohen such evidence includes knowledge of inductive support.

In his intervention, Cohen points out that he often defines inductive probability so that knowledge of inductive support is equivalent to knowledge of inductive probability objectivistically construed. He claims that such a notion of inductive probability is not a measure of degrees of confidence of acceptance. That is true; but, by the same token, (7) is not a judgement of inductive probability objectivistically construed not even when it is taken to be elliptical for

(8) On the available evidence there's a good probability of rain.

The point is, of course, that 'the available evidence' is itself elliptical for 'the evidence available to the agent or to the scientific community'. (8) is quite as subjective as (7).

Cohen's substantive thesis is that judgements of degrees of belief or confidence of acceptance in the Shackle sense ought to be made only when grounded on knowledge of inductive probability objectivistically construed which is tantamount to knowledge of inductive support objectivistically construed.

I deleted the reference to inductive probability objectivistically construed, restricting attention to the link alleged by Cohen between knowledge of inductive support and Shackle-like judgements of degrees of confidence of acceptance. In so doing, I simplified the exposition of Cohen's view without, so it seems to me, any loss in accuracy.

Thus, in admiring Cohen's endorsement of the Shackle theory while rejecting his contention that judgements of degrees of confidence of acceptance should be grounded on knowledge of inductive support, I do not think I was misunderstanding Cohen's view. I merely used his term 'inductive probability' in one of the ways he used it.

My decision to adopt that usage was based on my judgement (which I continue to think correct) that it is inductive probability construed as a degree of confidence of acceptance which is of interest and value. I do not see any clear meaning in his objectivistic notion of inductive probability nor any value to using it in enquiry any more than I see any meaning or value in his conception of inductive support. If Cohen means to disavow the subjectivistic interpretation of his measure, I think one should render a harsher verdict on his theory than I actually think it deserves.

Cohen claims that in contrast to me, he has appealed to scientific practice in attempting to establish that 'the method of relevant variables lies behind actual patterns of reasoning in the experimental sciences . . . ' But none of his examples establish the need to rank relevant variables with respect to relevance of falsificatory potential. Since Cohen has to establish that need to make his case (the need for controlled experimentation being widely conceded already), his efforts to document his theory by reference to scientific practice cannot be judged successful.

At the same time, I showed how some of his own examples of making judgements of inductive probability could be grounded on ordering combinations of relevant circumstances with respect to potential surprise even if that ordering fails to coincide with an ordering with respect to falsificatory potential. Even if one ignores the examples I have offered in my own work (as Cohen seems to have done) I think that in my paper I have shown how Cohen's illustrations of applications of his theory of inductive probability can be better understood as illustrations of applications of Shackle's theory.

Prejudiced as I am, I am inclined to the view that I have done rather better than Cohen in identifying examples conforming to my theory; but since our readings of presystematic practice scientific or otherwise are heavily laden with our philosophical commitments, I refuse to offer this as an argument for my view.

2

Induction as Information Acquisition

§4. R. D. ROSENKRANTZ
Rational Information Acquisition

Three main contexts in which information is sought are distinguished: partition problems, where one seeks the true member of a partition of hypotheses, theory construction, where, typically, no exhaustive partition of possibilities is at hand, and decision problems, where practical utilities enter. Efficient information acquistion is shown to assume quite different forms in all three contexts. In ('noiseless') partition problems, one asks questions about whose answer one is most uncertain, while in theorizing, one asks most specific questions. In decision-making, only the utility of information matters, and 'useful information' must be distinguished from 'welcome information.'

1. Introduction

With a substantial body of technical results at our disposal, the time seems ripe for an overview of the problems posed by efficient information acquisition. The contexts in which such problems arise can be grouped under three broad headings: theorizing, partition problems, and decision problems. My central thesis is that quite different strategies are called for in all three contexts.

Partition problems are characterized by a well-defined set of mutually exclusive and jointly exhaustive possible answers to the question posed. That is, one and only one member of the set is true, and the problem is to determine which member it is. Our uncertainty on this score can be precisely measured, and the optimum questioning procedure or experiment defined as that which effects the greatest expected reduction of uncertainty.

In theorizing, on the other hand, no well-defined partition of possible models is at hand. The models that occur to us, or which seem worth closer study, do not exhaust the possibilities. Of course, in a trivial, formal sense, we can always 'complete a partition' by adjoining a suitable lumpen hypothesis, but little is gained thereby, for we cannot compute the probabilities of experimental outcomes conditional on a lumpen hypothesis. The alternatives encountered in theorizing needn't even be exclusive. We often wish to compare a model with a parametric extension thereof, one which preserves the original model as a special case. A complication of this sort – adding an adjustable parameter – always improves accuracy at the cost of some simplicity. It is important to know when the trade-off is a good one, that is, when the accuracy gained is sufficient to offset the simplicity lost. This problem assumes far greater methodological importance in practice than the problem of comparing two exclusive models of roughly equal simplicity.

Given the 'open-endedness' characteristic of theorizing, it becomes more difficult to say what constitutes information acquisition or 'the growth of knowledge'. Ruling out false pretenders may bring us no closer to the truth when we lack an exhaustive list of the candidates. Nor, for that matter, is it easy to say which of two false theories is 'closer to the truth', as Miller[1] and other critics of Popper's notion of verisimilitude have stressed. The view that scientific knowledge grows by mere accumulation of facts has also been severely challenged, and, again, my sympathies lie with the challengers.

My own approach begins with the mundane observation that scientific progress comes about when additional evidence for a 'good' theory is obtained, or when a theory is replaced by a 'better' one. Now a 'better' theory might be (a) *more comprehensive*, fitting whatever data the old theory fitted and *then some*, (b) *more accurate*, fitting the same data, *only better*, or (c) *more economical*, requiring fewer concepts or independent assumptions to fit the same data. As we are interested in comparing rival theories over the entire expanding range of their intended applications, comprehensiveness can be subsumed under accuracy. Economy is achieved when free parameters are determined, and even more so, when previously disparate fields, like electricity and magnetism, genetics and cytology, or terrestrial and celestial physics, are brought together under the aegis of a single unifying theory. In all such cases, a *simplification* is achieved.

The question whether a parametric extension of a theory is a 'better' theory is clearly a special case of the general problem of balancing accuracy against simplicity and arriving at an overall appraisal of competing theories. The Bayesian index of support described in the next section accomplishes this end, and in rather compelling fashion. Using this very sensitive and powerful index, we can say that a 'better' theory is a better supported theory. And as accuracy and simplicity are alike reflected in support, the optimal strategy in theorizing is evidently to find the simplest model that fits the available data. This is a standard recommendation, but it takes on new precision. The simplest model of an experiment consonant

[1] D. Miller, 'The Accuracy of Predictions', *Synthèse* 30 (1975), 159–91.

with the data fits *only* the outcomes actually observed. For example, the heliostatic model of the planets fits only the observed frequencies with which the planets retrogress, while the Ptolemaic model, by suitably adjusting the periods of epicycle and deferent, can be made to fit any frequencies of retrogression. Intuitively, the accuracy of a simpler model is more difficult to ascribe to chance, and that intuition is beautifully captured by our Bayesian analysis which shows that, in the cases of real interest, the simpler of two equally accurate models of the same experiment is the better supported.

Simpler theories are more specific, more determinate. We can easily see how utterly inefficient the strategy of asking maximally specific questions would be if applied to a partition problem, e.g., the problem of locating a given square on a checkerboard by asking yes-no questions. The hypothesis that it is, say, the lower left-hand square is certainly as 'simple' as any, but with sufficiently bad luck, it could require as many as 64 maximally specific questions to locate the square. The optimal strategy is, rather, to divide the remaining possibilities in half with each question, and this always yields the solution in $\log_2 64 = 6$ steps. In a sense to be made precise in section 3, you cannot do better than apply that strategy.

In dealing with partition problems, one cannot even assume that simpler hypotheses are more 'falsifiable', at least not in the pragmatic sense of requiring a smaller average number of questions or experimental trials to refute them when they are in fact false. One is still tempted to think that this will tend to be true in theorizing, for a simpler theory fits fewer possible outcomes. But one cannot infer that a 'false' theory that is simpler will have a higher probability of being refuted – not, at least, without making additional assumptions of a sort non-Bayesians are usually loath to make! Nor is it clear, as I remarked earlier, that 'progress' is achieved merely by excluding false pretenders.

It is for reasons of this sort that I do not subscribe to Sir Karl Popper's attempt to justify our preference for simpler theories by appeal to their allegedly greater 'falsifiability'. Popper wants to say that simpler theories which pass through the crucible of experimentation unscathed are better 'corroborated' thereby, but he really lacks a fully independent concept of corroboration. He can only appeal to our intuition that a theory which risks more 'proves its mettle' more than a less falsifiable theory. Bayesian analysis both explains and sharpens this intuition.

Critics of Popper's views have trained their heavy artillery on his predilection for accentuating the negative, on his insistence that scientists should ever be striving to overthrow theories, to test readily falsifiable conjectures, and to state beforehand the results they will take as conclusive refutations of their conjectures. It is hard to know how seriously to take much of Popper's rhetoric, but my own position certainly *sounds* very different.

Scientists normally work within a *theoretical framework* or *scheme*, like classical mechanics or the particulate scheme of inheritance. Sneed[2] and Stegmüller[3] speak in terms of applying a set-theoretic predicate, or 'theory core', to various empirical algebras which make up the intended applications. For example, one applies the set-theoretic predicate 'is a classical particle mechanics' to an algebra comprising mass-points and their position functions by specifying the relevant theoretical functions, mass and force. Similarly, a geneticist attempts to analyse hereditary phenomena – mating experiments, changes in the gene pool of specified populations, and so forth – along particulate lines. He seeks, for example, the simplest particulate model that will fit the frequencies of the A–B–O blood types in human populations or the inheritance of coat colour in horses. This quest is less misleadingly described as 'seeking confirmation' than as 'seeking refutation'. The important point, however, is that one does not achieve high confirmation or support merely by fitting the data, no more than by weaving simple fantasies. To 'save' a theory by complicating it doesn't really save it unless a sharp improvement in accuracy results. Well-supported models are not so much accurate as *improbably accurate*, but improbable accuracy is attained neither by loose-fitting tight theories nor by tight-fitting loose theories.

Popper would perhaps lay greater stress on the importance of generating alternative theoretical frameworks, even prior to failed attempts to fit experiments that clearly fall within the theory's purview. The issues here are somewhat nebulous, but my position at least leaves open the possibility that one can increase support more rapidly by 'switching frameworks'. The problem of the planets illustrates this possibility rather well. A version of heliocentrism based on coplanar, uniform sun-centered circles – a first approximation, really – is not very accurate, and yet, it is such a simple theory that, conceivably, it is better supported than the much more accurate but far more complicated Ptolemaic theory. Moreover, it is immediately clear how to improve the accuracy of this model by exploiting the familiar devices of Ptolemaic astronomy – eccentric

[2] J. Sneed, *The Logical Structure of Mathematical Physics* (1971).
[3] W. Stegmüller, *The Structure and Dynamics of Theories* (1976).

circles, uniform motions about an equant, and so on – without sacrificing its essential simplicity, which is based, not on its paucity of parameters or epicycles, but primarily on its overdetermination. For any version of the heliostatic theory determines the relative distances of the planets from the sun and the major irregularities of planetary motion (e.g., the frequencies of retrogression, variations in brightness, the order of the inner planets, etc.) These are no mere aesthetically pleasing 'harmonies'[4] but, as I show below, the very features which render the heliostatic theory better supported.

I am maintaining that support is a sufficient basis for theory appraisal, and that recourse to acceptance-rules or extra-evidential 'epistemic utilities' is neither necessary nor desirable. Those who hanker after a stronger sense of acceptance, one that connotes a quasi-permanent commitment to premiss hypotheses or empirical findings, face the problem of explaining how such commitments can be rationally withdrawn. This formidable problem doesn't arise on my account, and, in fact, I would assume that a scientist's propensity to premiss a proposition varies continuously over time and is largely a function of the evidence. Just as variations in the prices of goods and services guide economic choices and function to ensure efficient production and distribution, variations in the support indices of different theories and effects guide scientific research and function to ensure its effective prosecution. He who violates a well-supported proposition incurs an 'evidential debit', but such debits are often willingly incurred in the expectation of arriving, in the end, at a better supported theory. It was in this spirit that Copernicus ventured to set the earth in motion.

If acceptance-rules are unduly confining, epistemic utilities raise problems of a very different kind. Lakatos and Zahar[5] invoke two desiderata in an attempt to explain why the Copernican theory superseded the Ptolemaic. The first is that a theory issue in 'novel predictions', where these turn out to be, not new predictions, but findings which the theory fits without having been expressly designed to fit. Their second desideratum is that successive modifications of the theory be 'in the spirit of its heuristic'. They claim that the use of equants was not in keeping with Plato's heuristic, to resolve the planetary motions into circles or compounds of circles. Both of their proposed desiderata strike me as very dubious merits. But what is to determine whether a proposed epistemic utility is genuine or counterfeit?

[4] T. Kuhn, *The Copernican Revolution* (1957), p. 181.
[5] I. Lakatos and E. Zahar, 'Why did Copernicus's Research Program supersede Ptolemy's?', in R. Westman (ed.), *The Copernican Achievement* (1975).

Again, the problem does not arise on my approach, nor does the equally serious problem of weighting the various desiderata. Genuine desiderata, like overdetermination, are reflected in support, and while it is helpful to know what properties of a theory render it more confirmable by conforming data, one need only concern oneself directly with support. Kuhn[6] speaks of the difficulty of weighting simplicity and accuracy, and notes that different practitioners do not even measure them in the same way. But, again, our immediate concern is with a theory's support, and ways of measuring accuracy or simplicity are illuminating or not according as they are reflected in support or not. Moreover, use of the Bayesian index has the effect of automatically weighting the appropriately defined measures of simplicity and accuracy. The judgemental element is eliminated, or, rather, the incredibly delicate and complex judgements whether a complication of theory represents 'progress' are reduced to simple and transparent discernments via Bayes's Theorem.

Without an index of support to effect the required weighting, methodological anarchy would beckon: each scientist would adopt whatever weighting suited him and become, as it were, his own methodologist. This appears to be Kuhn's position, and it is shared by many other historians of science. Yet, it is not an intrinsically attractive position; we should not rush to embrace it. Recalcitrant disagreement in science may be as well explained by conflicting evidence as by fundamental methodological disagreement, 'incommensurability', or the like. It is the task of historians of science to record the factors that actually influenced the appraisals and judgements of scientists. But philosophers of science face the rather different task of systematizing these factors and either accounting for their force by relating them to powerful principles of rationality or exposing them as spurious. Given the explanatory and not merely descriptive task confronting us, extra-evidential 'epistemic utilities' are to be viewed as onerous concepts to which we should resort only as a last resort. Simpler explanations of rational belief-changes in terms of support should be abandoned only when utterly compelling considerations force us to do so.

2. Theorizing

For a Bayesian, the comparative support which an observation E accords hypotheses $H_1, \ldots, H_n$ of a partition is given by the *likelihoods*, $P(E \mid H_i), \ldots, P(E \mid H_n)$. Thus, the 'likeliest' hypothesis is that which renders E most probable. This very natural index of

[6] T. Kuhn, 'Reflections on my Critics', in I. Lakatos and A. Musgrave (eds.), *Criticism and the Growth of Knowledge* (1970), p. 262.

support can be extended to models with adjustable parameters by thinking of such a model as the union of its special cases.

Consider, for example, the multinomial model H with category probabilities $\theta/2$, $(1-\theta)/2$, $(1-\theta)/2$, $\theta/2$. θ is a free parameter which ranges from 0 to 1. An important special case of this model, H_0, assigns θ the value $1/2$, and in that case, all four category probabilities equal $1/4$. H_0 is Mendel's original model of independent assortment, applied to the so-called double backcross, $ABab \times abab$, where A and B are 'single-factor' traits. H is the parametric extension of this model that allows the separate traits to be associated in inheritance, and the 'linkage parameter', θ, measures their degree of association.

Given a criterion of fit, each special case of H will fit a subset of the outcome space, and the union of these subsets comprises the outcomes fitted by H. Hence, H fits any outcome fitted by any of its special cases, and, in that sense, accuracy is always improved (or never reduced) when we complicate a model by adjoining another parameter. In the example before us, H_0 requires that the expected numbers in all four categories be equal, while H imposes the milder constraint that the expected numbers in categories 1 and 4 be equal and that the expected numbers in categories 2 and 3 be equal.

Whenever we add a free parameter, we increase *sample coverage*, the proportion of possible experimental outcomes which the theory fits, a criterion of fit being presupposed. In light of this, it is quite natural to measure the simplicity of a model, relative to an experiment, by its sample coverage at the assigned criterion of fit: the smaller the sample coverage, the simpler the model. The proposed measure sharpens and extends the familiar paucity-of-parameters criterion. It eliminates problems about counting parameters analogous to the problems about counting axioms. It allows us to compare the simplicity of two models with the same number of free parameters. It avoids the misleading implication that we can compare two theories as to their simplicity merely by comparing their numbers of free parameters. (All that can be said, in general, is that we complicate a theory when we add to its stock of free parameters.) It also avoids the so-called 'tacking paradox', for conjoining an 'extraneous' hypothesis need not decrease sample coverage with respect to a given experiment. Finally, the proposed measure can be extended to classes of experiments by defining 'composite' experiments and extending the definition of sample coverage, but I omit the details and content myself with the observation that the sample coverage of a theory will be reduced when it renders formerly independent experiments dependent. Such a theory may be termed a *unifying* theory. For example, the chromosomal theory, by interpreting the linkage parameter, 'linked' the previously unrelated fields of genetics and cytology, imposing the new constraint that the haploid number of chromosomes characteristic of a species coincide with its number of linkage groups (i.e., the groups of traits associated in inheritance). For 'linked' traits are those whose genes lie on the same chromosome.

The proposed measure of simplicity would be of little interest, however, if it were not reflected in support. Happily it is, as the following considerations already suggest.

Given a criterion of fit, let E assert that the outcome of the experiment falls within a $100(1-\alpha)$ per cent *direct confidence region* (or *DCR*) of K, where the $100(1-\alpha)$ per cent *DCR* contains the outcome of the experiment with probability $1-\alpha$, and has the property that the probability of any included outcome exceeds that of any excluded outcome. *DCR*'s provide convenient criteria of fit. Now if α is close to zero, the probability of E on H will be close to one, and E will be, effectively, a consequence of H. Then $P(H \mid E) = P(H)/P(E) > P(H)$, whence E confirms (raises the probability of) H, the degree of confirmation being inverse to $P(E)$. At the same time, the smaller the sample coverage of H, the smaller its *DCR*, hence, the smaller $P(E)$. Consequently, a simpler model will be better supported (and confirmed) by the bare assertion that the observed outcome falls within its (nearly) 100 per cent *DCR*. For example, we are about 99.7 per cent sure that an observation of a normally distributed random variable with known variance will fall within three standard deviations of its mean. Our proposition E would state only that the actual observation falls in that range, but, in practice, we know exactly where it does fall, and it would be foolish not to use that more precise information for the purpose of assessing competing hypotheses. To carry the analysis farther, we need the concept of average likelihood.

Recurring to the earlier example of the linkage model H with category probabilities $\theta/2$, $(1-\theta)/2$, $(1-\theta)/2$, $\theta/2$, we note that the probability of such a 'composite model' is the 'sum' (i.e., the integral) of the probabilities of its special cases. To compute the posterior probability of H, we merely 'sum' the posterior probabilities of its special cases. But this amounts to averaging their likelihoods, $p(x \mid \theta)$, against the prior distribution of θ, giving:

$$(2.1) \qquad P(H \mid x) = \int p(x \mid \theta) \, dP(\theta)/P(x)$$

where $\int dP(\theta) = P(H)$. Where the distribution of θ is uniform, this reduces to

(2.2) $$P(H \mid x) = P(H) \int p(x \mid \theta) \, d\theta / P(x)$$

which expresses the posterior probability of H as the product of its prior probability by its *average likelihood*, divided by $P(x)$. For expository convenience, I will confine attention to the special case (2.2) of (2.1).

Now the likelihood function is in no way tied to a partition of hypotheses. It is an index of comparative support, and can be used to compare the support of any number of exclusive hypotheses, whether or not they are jointly exhaustive. The same is true of the average likelihood function, which associates with each 'composite' model its average likelihood at the observed outcome. Thus, we can use average likelihood as an index of support in theorizing, where no partition of models is at hand.

In particular, average likelihood may be used to compare the support of a model with a parametric extension thereof (e.g., H_0 with H). To be sure, the model and its parametric extension are not exclusive alternatives, but that needn't trouble us. For we can take logical differences, comparing $H_0: \theta = 0.5$ with $H: \theta \neq 0.5$. Even when H is so construed, H_0 remains *effectively* a special case of H, since the latter includes values of the parameter arbitrarily close to 0.5. To appreciate the workings of the method, it will be helpful to look at some numerical data.

Of 100 offspring of a double backcross, the observed and expected numbers in the four categories are as in Table 1, where I write $\hat{H}$ for the best-fitting (i.e., maximally likely) special case of H. Is the accuracy gained enough to offset the simplicity lost? (Imagine trying to answer this question judgementally!)

Table 1

Category	AB	Ab	aB	ab
Observed	19	29	31	21
Expected: H_0	25	25	25	25
Expected: $\hat{H}$	20	30	30	20

To answer the question, we compute the ratio of the average likelihoods, neglecting the multinomial coefficient, which cancels out. The likelihood of H_0 is then $(1/4)^{100}$, while that of H, assuming a uniform prior distribution of θ, is

$$\int_0^1 [\theta/2]^{19+21}[(1-\theta)/2]^{29+31} \, d\theta = (1/2)^{100} 40! 60! / 101!$$

which is close to 5.68×10^{-61}, using the familiar beta integral,

$$\int_0^1 x^a (1-x)^b \, dx = a!b!/(a+b+1)!,$$

and the tables of $\log N!$. Since $(1/4)^{100} = 6.22 \times 10^{-61}$, support is not increased by complicating the model; the accuracy gained in replacing H_0 by H is not quite sufficient to offset the simplicity lost. In this case, the maximum likelihood estimate of θ is 0.4, which is not all that far removed from 0.5. Hence, H_0 doesn't fit the data that badly, and moreover, the sample size is not very large. At larger samples, the difference in the sample coverages of H_0 and H becomes less pronounced, the support will be increased when the ML estimate is much less farther removed from 0.5. When both conditions obtain, that is, when the ML estimate is far removed from 0.5 and the sample is a large one, we should expect H to be much better supported than H_0. The data in Table 2 for a double backcross in *Drosophila melanogaster* (from T. H. Morgan) is representative of that which, historically, prompted introduction of the linkage parameter and abandonment of Mendel's assumption. The ML estimate of θ for Morgan's data is 0.182, which is far removed from 0.5, and the sample size, 3,499, is large. The likelihood of H_0 is found to be 2.84×10^{-346}, while the average likelihood of H is 1.62×10^{-12}, which is about 6×10^{333} times as great! The evidence of linkage is entirely decisive, then, even though, as it happens, the data do not fit H at all well, the numbers in the Ab and aB categories being far from equal. (A little checking suggests that the single traits, A and B, are not assorting in their expected $3:1$ Mendelian ratios.)

Table 2

Category	AB	Ab	aB	
Observed	338	1315	1552	294
Expected: H_0	874.75	874.75	874.75	874.75
Expected: $\hat{H}$	314.9	1434.6	1434.6	314.9

The prior odds against linkage are swamped by the data in this example, but in human linkage studies, where good data are scarce, the prior odds play an important role. Bayesian methods are especially attractive in linkage studies, for they enable experimenters to keep track of the odds in favour of a posited linkage and to combine data from entirely disparate experiments. Moreover, the odds are reasonably objective. Given 22 pairs of autosomal chromosomes in human sex cells, the prior odds against linkage are $22:1$. Hence, we affix a prior probability of $21/22$ to $\theta = 0.5$, and the pattern in which chiasmata distribute themselves along the chromosomes indicates that, to good approximation, the values of the linkage parameter less than 0.5 are uniformly distributed. Values greater than 0.5 can occur, as in cases of 'affinity', but occur so rarely that they are usually ignored at the outset.

The double backcross is formally identical to a binomial experiment, where the recombinant types, AB and ab in our illustration, are 'successes', and the non-recombinant types, Ab and aB, are 'failures', θ being the probability of success. In effect, we are testing the 'simple' (or point) hypothesis $\theta = 1/2$ against the 'composite' (or interval) hypothesis $\theta \neq 1/2$, using n Bernoulli trials. The ratio of average likelihoods is

$$(1/2)^n : \int_0^1 \theta^x (1-\theta)^{n-x} \, d\theta$$

where x is the observed number of successes. Consequently, the composite hypothesis is favoured iff $(1/2)^n < x!(n-x)!/(n+1)!$, or

$$(2.3) \qquad \binom{n}{x} < 2^n/(n+1),$$

in other words, iff the observed binomial coefficient, $\binom{n}{x}$, is smaller than the average of the $n+1$ binomial coefficients $\binom{n}{i}$, $i = 0, 1, \ldots, n$. A similar result is obtained in testing a simple multinomial (or normal, or multinormal) hypothesis against a two-sided composite alternative.

To appreciate the significance of this result, imagine a very concrete embodiment of the problem. We are given a large population of urns containing various numbers of balls, each of the balls coloured black or white. Let θ be the unknown proportion of black balls in any given urn. By randomly sampling n balls in the urn with replacement, we must determine whether $\theta = 1/2$ or not. We must classify each of the urns in this way, and I will assume that our only concern is to minimize the percentage of misclassifications. (This seems a reasonable facsimile of some 'pure research problems', e.g., genetic linkage studies.) Assume, finally, that half of the urns contain equal numbers of black and white balls, and that this is known to our experimenter. Then, assuming that values of θ distinct from $1/2$ are uniformly distributed, the method of classification based on (2.4) is easily seen to minimize the probability of misclassification, and this will remain true, to good approximation, when the distribution of those values is reasonably symmetric about $1/2$.[7] In general, the Bayes rule for this problem is to multiply the prior odds by the ratio of average likelihoods and classify the urn according to the posterior odds so obtained.

Multinomial models enter here as a kind of microcosm of theorizing; they arise whenever we have categorized data. Their associated direct confidence regions are the envelopes of families of multidimensional ellipsoids. Roughly speaking, addition of a free parameter amounts to addition of a degree of freedom, another dimension along which the ellipsoids are allowed to vary. In terms of support, another parameter amounts to another variable of integration (or dimension) when we compute average likelihoods. Given the greater number of special cases over which we must average likelihoods, the tendency will be for support to decrease. But that tendency, of course, may be outweighed by the tendency of the average likelihood to increase with the accuracy of the best-fitting special case of the model. By exploiting the asymptotic normality of the likelihood function, 'one can approximate the average likelihood by a simple function of the maximum likelihood, and, using the approximation, determine the improvement in accuracy required to increase the average likelihood when a new parameter is added.[8] For multinomial models without free parameters, the *DCR*'s are ellipsoids whose volume increases with the product of their category probabilities.[9] Hence, the sample coverage of such a model is a maximum when all category probabilities are equal, and the more unequal they are, the smaller the sample coverage. At the same time, using the multinormal approximation to the multinomial, the likelihood ratio of two equally accurate multinomial models (without parameters) reduces to the square root of the ratio of their respective products of category probabilities.[10] Sample coverage (or simplicity) and average likelihood (or support) could not be more intimately related than they are in this context.

But the relationship appears in other important contexts as well. In chapter 11 of my book,[11] I apply the method of average likelihood to the problem of determining the degree of a polynomial

---

[7] G. Meeden, 'Choosing a Prior', *J. Amer. Stat. Ass.* 69 (1974), 740–3.
[8] R. Rosenkrantz, *Inference, Method and Decision* (1977), pp. 97–9.
[9] Ibid., p. 108.
[10] Ibid., p. 110.
[11] Op. cit.

regression (i.e., curve-fitting) and the order of a Markov chain (i.e., the number of previous trials on which the current trial depends), and compare its performance, empirically, with that of several orthodox (non-Bayesian) methods. It is also applied to problems from genetics (ch. 5) and to inductive generalization (ch. 4). The simplest 'strong generalization' compatible with a sample designates all and only those kinds present in the sample, and Hintikka has shown[12] that the likelihood of this hypothesis becomes infinite relative to that of all others as the sample size increases. Unfortunately, lack of space prevents my describing these interesting results in greater detail.

There is, however, one application that I can hardly omit, since it bears so directly on the issues that divide my position from others'. An influential body of opinion holds that there were no evidential reasons for preferring heliostatic theories of the planets to geostatic theories, and that, consequently, the reasons for the triumph of Copernicanism, long before physical 'proofs' of the earth's motion were found, must be sought in extra-evidential considerations. Certainly this case poses a strong challenge for the view I am maintaining: that support is a fully adequate basis for theory appraisal.

The Bayesian analysis of this case exploits a mathematical triviality, viz., that the average value of a function can never exceed its maximum value. Applied to the likelihood function, this implies that a theory with parameters can never be better supported than its best-fitting (i.e., maximally likely) special case. Now, with respect to various aspects of the planetary data, the heliostatic theory is the best-fitting special case of the geostatic theory. For instance, the heliostatic theory determines the (actually observed) order of the inferior planets and the sun, but the geostatic does not (it could accommodate the phases of Venus or the absence of such phases). In particular, the heliostatic (or equivalent Tychonic) theory is the special case of the geostatic that places the centres of the epicycles of Mercury and Venus at the point S on the line ES joining the earth to the sun, while the geostatic theory only constrains these centres to lie on ES (at all times). Again, the frequency with which a planet retrogresses is heliostatically determined (as equal to its sidereal period), but, geostatically, the periods of epicycle and deferent are independently adjustable, and so the theory can accommodate any frequencies of retrogression. In computing the average likelihood of the geostatic theory for these facets of the data, the special

---

[12] E.g. in Jaakko Hintikka, 'A Two-Dimensional Continuum of Inductive Methods', in Jaakko Hintikka and P. Suppes (eds.), *Aspects of Inductive Logic* (1966).

case (2.2) with equally weighted special cases seems entirely appropriate. For, so far as Ptolemaic theory informs us, *the universe is random in the relevant respects*. And, certainly, we want that indeterminacy of the theory to be taken into account in our evaluation of it.

Kuhn[13] labels the cited facets 'harmonies' of the Copernican system with the clear implication that, while exercising a powerful *aesthetic appeal*, they are devoid of scientific force. Bayesian analysis shows, on the contrary, that they represent *strong evidence* for heliocentrism. Owing to its greater simplicity or overdetermination, the heliostatic theory is *improbably* accurate. And that difference is registered by average likelihood, which reflects, not merely the accuracy of a theory's best-fitting special case, but the number of its ill-fitting special cases as well.

After the telescopic observation of the phases of Venus in 1610, one could oppose Copernicanism (as Tycho did) only on physical grounds, and it is not surprising that geostatic theories declined after 1632, the year Galileo published his *Dialogue*. For while, assuredly, he did not demonstrate the earth's motion therein, he did effectively undermine physical objections to a moving earth. More generally, I see little reason to suppose that the opinions of astronomers were ever greatly at odds with the evidence.[14] Finally, while I have little grip on truth in this context, much less on whether Copernicus was closer to it than Ptolemy, a Bayesian analysis does give one a grip on the evidence and shows why the very considerations Copernicus and his immediate followers found most convincing render the heliocentric theory better supported.

3. Partition Problems

Partition problems, as I remarked earlier, call for entirely different strategies of information acquisition. Let $\Theta = \{\theta_1, \theta_2, \ldots, \theta_n\}$ be a discrete partition. We want to find the true element of the partition, and to this end we seek experiments or questioning procedures whose outcomes can be expected to effect a maximal reduction of our uncertainty. Write $H(\Theta)$ for the uncertainty about Θ. Let X be an experiment with outcomes $x_1, \ldots, x_m$. When x_i occurs, our

---

[13] *The Copernican Revolution*, p. 181.
[14] Cf. R. Westman, 'Three Responses to the Copernican Theory: Johannes Praetorius, Tycho Brahe, and Michael Maestlin', in R. Westman (ed.), *The Copernican Achievement*.

uncertainty is altered to $H_i(\theta)$, and, consequently, X can be expected to reduce uncertainty to the outcome-probability weighted average of the $H_i(\Theta)$, or $H_X(\Theta) = \sum_i P(x_i)H_i(\Theta)$. Hence

$$(3.1) \qquad T(X; \Theta) = H(\Theta) - H_X(\Theta)$$

measures the expected uncertainty reduction and is called the *expected sample information* (or *ESI*) of X. (In the context of communications theory, it is called 'transmitted information'.) To complete its definition, we must, of course, define H.

One way of getting at this is to equate our uncertainty about which element of the partition obtains with the average information conveyed in finding out which element obtains, viz.:

$$(3.2) \qquad H(\Theta) = \sum_i I(\theta_i)P(\theta_i)$$

The more surprised we would be to learn that θ_i holds, the more information is conveyed by that message. Surprise is clearly at a minimum when $P(\theta_i) = 1$, and at a maximum when $P(\theta_i) = 0$, while, in between these extremes it is reasonable to require that $I(\theta_i)$ be a continuously decreasing function, $f(P(\theta_i))$, of the probability. Given a second partition, $\Phi = \{\phi_1, \ldots, \phi_r\}$, it is further reasonable to require that the information in learning that ϕ_j obtains given that θ_i obtains should equal $f(P(\phi_j \mid \theta_i)) + f(P(\theta_i))$. Alternatively, we can view ourselves as having learned which element of the Cartesian product of the partitions obtains, and that should equal $f(P(\theta_i, \phi_j))$, where $P(\theta_i, \phi_j)$ is the probability that both θ_i and ϕ_j hold. Since $P(\theta_i, \phi_j) = P(\phi_j \mid \theta_i)P(\theta_i)$, f must satisfy the functional equation

$$f(xy) = f(x) + f(y)$$

$x = P(\theta_i)$, $y = P(\phi_j \mid \theta_i)$, whose general solution is $f(x) = k \log(x)$. Because f is assumed decreasing, k must be negative, and it is most convenient to set $k = -1$, which gives

$$(3.3) \qquad I(\theta_i) = -\log P(\theta_i)$$

where the logarithm may be taken to any fixed base.

The quantity (3.2), with I given by (3.3), is known as *entropy*. It is a continuous function of the $P(\theta_i)$, and increases with any averaging of these probabilities, as well as with the number of elements in the partition. In particular, entropy is a maximum, $\log n$, when all n elements of the partition are equiprobable, and a minimum, 0, when some element of the partition is certain, with the understanding that $0 \log 0 = 0$.

$T(X; \Theta)$ measures the average entropy reduction and can be written $T(X; \Theta) = \sum_i P(x_i)[H(\Theta) - H_i(\Theta)]$. *Shannon's inequality* states that $T(X; \Theta)$ is always non-negative, so that, on the average, experimentation reduces uncertainty. Equivocal outcomes, which flatten the prior distribution, are counterbalanced by others which sharpen the prior. The *ESI*, however, measures average sharpening of one's beliefs or probabilities without regard to whether they are *true* beliefs. It is also insensitive to the direction of information flow in the sense that:

$$(3.4) \qquad T(X; \Theta) = T(\Theta; X).$$

This symmetry property follows from $H(\Theta) + H_\Theta(X) = H(X, \Theta) = H(X) + H_X(\Theta)$, where $H(X, \Theta)$ is the entropy of the joint distribution, $P(x_j, \theta_i)$. Finally, the *ESI* is additive in independent experiments or trials:

$$(3.5) \quad T(X, Y; \Theta) = T(X; \Theta) + T(Y; \Theta), \quad X, Y \text{ independent.}$$

Noiseless experiments are characterised by $H_\Theta(X) = 0$; i.e., knowledge of the true state removes all uncertainty regarding the outcome of X. For noiseless experiments, the *ESI* reduces to $H(X)$, using (3.4). That is, *we expect to learn most from an experiment about whose outcome we are most uncertain.*

We can speak, derivatively, of *noiseless partition problems*, noiseless, that is, relative to an experiment. For example, we are given twelve steel balls and must find that one of the twelve which is heavier or lighter than the others (we are not told which) by using an ordinary pan balance. If we are only allowed to weigh equal numbers of balls, we have a noiseless problem. Other examples include the problem of locating a square on a checkerboard by asking yes-no questions, which is a simplified version of 'twenty questions', concept identification problems, and code-cracking games like 'Jotto' and 'Mastermind'.

To maximize $H(X)$, we must make the outcome probabilities equal (or as nearly equal as we can). In the 'odd ball' problem, for example, the best first weighing, four against four, makes all three outcome probabilities equal to 8/24, and, by the same token, all three possible outcomes reduce the number of remaining possibilities to eight – assuming a uniform prior distribution of the twenty-four initial possibilities. In practice, of course, we cannot always make experimental outcomes equiprobable. If each question admits m possible answers (a so-called *m-ary question*), then, obviously, we cannot make the answers equiprobable if the number of possibilities remaining is not a multiple of m. (This happens on the second weighing in the 'odd ball' problem, since $m = 3$ and $N = 8$ possibilities remain after an optimal first weighing.) Idiosyncracies of the experimental apparatus or information channel can also preclude equalizing outcome probabilities. Given a version of the odd ball problem with 13 balls, you cannot partition the twenty-six possibilities into three subsets of 9, 9, and 8, using an equal-arm balance. Given these and other restrictions on the feasible partitions, the results I state below are only approximate in practice.

I address now the problem of efficiency. *Minimax procedures*, where each question minimizes the maximum number of possibilities that could remain, are appropriate where one's task is to find the true element of the partition in a prescribed number of steps, as in the odd ball problem. More typically, however, the aim is to find the solution in the fewest number of steps, on the average, as in Mastermind or Jotto. A questioning procedure with this property is called *efficient*.

For a given question, let f_i possibilities remain when the ith answer is given, $i = 1, \ldots, m$. Then if the N remaining possibilities are equiprobable, the ith answer is given with probability f_i/N, and in that case, the expected number of remaining possibilities is equal to

$$(3.6) \qquad \sum_i f_i(f_i/N) = \sum_i f_i^2/N.$$

Consequently, the efficient strategy minimizes (3.6) subject to $\sum_i f_i = N$. The solution of this constrained extremum problem is easily found to be $f_i = N/m$, $i = 1, \ldots, m$, and so the efficient strategy is also the minimax strategy (assuming, of course, that all partitions are feasible). Moreover, under our equiprobability assumption, the *ESI* of the question which effects the partition $(f_1, \ldots, f_m)$ is

$$(3.7) \qquad \log N + \sum_i (f_i/N) \log (f_i/N) = \frac{1}{N} \sum_i f_i \log f_i$$

and this quantity, subject to $\sum_i f_i = N$, is a maximum when $f_i = N/m$, as well, so that the strategy of maximizing the *ESI* is also efficient. This result is a special case of a more general theorem which asserts that minimax strategies are Bayes against a least favourable prior distribution. Simply equate 'losses' with 'number of remaining possibilities', and note that the 'least favourable' prior distribution for a noiseless partition problem is uniform.

Estimation problems are, perhaps, the most frequently encountered partition problems, and they are not 'noiseless': knowing a population proportion does not allow one to predict a sample proportion with certainty. Yet, knowledge of a population proportion does enable one to confine a sample proportion narrowly with a high degree of confidence, which suggests that estimation problems are 'nearly noiseless' in the sense that the first term of $T(X; \Theta) = H(X) - H_\Theta(X)$ dominates the second. And so the strategy of drawing samples about whose composition we are most uncertain should be highly efficient, if not optimally efficient. Thus, in stratified random sampling, drawing larger samples from strata about which we are more uncertain will increase our uncertainty about the composition of the entire sample, and that should tend to reduce uncertainty maximally, on the average. Although the technical difficulties are considerable, it would be worth analyzing this conjecture in detail.

4. Practical Decision-Making

In practical decision-making contexts, we are concerned only with the utility of information. Additional evidence of guilt is of no utility to a judge who has already found a defendant guilty as charged; only information that alters the agent's most preferred course of action has utility. 'Useful' information must also be distinguished from 'welcome' information. If you hold a hand worth twelve in a game of Blackjack and are inclined to be dealt another card, the information that the next card in the deck is a ten is anything but welcome, for it leaves you with diminished prospects. Yet, it is decidedly useful information, for it averts a sure loss. It is clearly irrational to ignore useful information, in ostrich fashion, merely because it is unwelcome, and, by the same token, irrational not to avail oneself of a cost-free observation merely because some of its possible outcomes might be unwelcome, as in the Blackjack example.

Of course, not all outcomes of an experiment can leave the agent with diminished prospects. For he would then be certain (now) that his prospects are not as bright as he now takes them to be, which is strictly impossible. To be sure, there is a sense in which an oft-disappointed 'eternal optimist' might feel sure that he is overestimating his prospects, but that really just amounts to a second-order lack of confidence in his first-order degrees of confidence. One is tempted to go farther here and assert that, just as no experiment can be expected to increase uncertainty, so too, no experiment can leave us with an expectation of diminished prospects. Surprisingly, this stronger claim is not unconditionally true. Certainly, the most direct and compelling reason for availing oneself of cost-free information is the expectation of improved prospects which it affords.[15] But since this expectation is not always met, the distinction between 'useful' and 'welcome' information becomes vital. The expectation of obtaining useful information is never disappointed, and so, at the most fundamental level, that is the reason for availing oneself of cost-free information.

It is never rational, then, not to avail oneself of cost-free information. Apparent exceptions invariably involve 'hidden costs', as in the classic cases of 'letting a sleeping dog lie'. For example, a man who suspects his wife of infidelity wonders whether he should hire a private detective to spy on her. If he realizes that he will persist in his present course whatever he finds out, then the information the investigation provides will be 'useless' to him. On the other hand, if he prefers to dissolve the marriage given that she is unfaithful, the news that she is having an affair is quite 'useful' to him, however unwelcome, and the mental suffering it occasions should not be accounted part of the cost of finding out the truth. At the same time, there are 'hidden costs' aplenty that must be included under this head: the probability that his wife will discover she is being spied upon, for one, and the probability that others will learn that the agent has been confronted with unimpeachable evidence of her infidelity, for another, which could make his social position intolerable. These possible 'side-effects' must be included in the description of the experimental outcomes. Writing $U(a, s, x)$ for the utility of performing action a when state s obtains and outcome x (of an experiment X) is observed, we see, in the case before us, that this utility depends on x. Thus, the utility of remaining married to an unfaithful spouse when others have learned that the agent knows of her infidelity may not be the same as the utility of remaining married to her when no one else knows that the agent knows. When $U(a, s, x)$ is independent of x, for each outcome x of X and each act–state pair of the relevant decision-problem, I shall speak of a *pure* observation or experiment. The idea, roughly, is that 'pure' experiments have no effect on the agent's original utility function; he assigns all act–state pairs the same utility conditional on any outcome of the experiment that he assigns them unconditionally.

(N.B., the utilities in question are to be considered utilities which the agent entertains at a single time, the specious present.)

Limitations of space preclude more than a bare sketch of the formal analysis that leads to these results. A *Bayes act* a^* of a decision-problem is an act which maximizes expected utility:

$$(4.1) \qquad U(a^*) = \max_a \sum_j U(a, s_j)P(s_j)$$

and the expected utility of any Bayes act is called the (prior) *value* of the decision-problem and equated with the agent's initial prospects. Each outcome x of an experiment X induces a posterior probability distribution, $P(\cdot \mid x)$, of states, and an action, a_x, which maximizes expected utility when utilities are expected against $P(\cdot \mid x)$, is a *posterior Bayes act,* and its expected utility,

$$(4.2) \qquad U(a_x \mid x) = \sum_j U(a_x, s_j)P(s_j \mid x)$$

is the *posterior value* of the decision-problem associated with x. If $U(a_x \mid x)$ is smaller than $U(a^*)$, I say that x *diminishes the agent's prospects,* and is, therefore, *unwelcome.*

Let X be a pure experiment, and assume, further, that the states are *act-independent* (i.e., the state probabilities are independent of the action the agent chooses). Then the utility of an outcome x, called the *conditional value of sample information* (or *CVSI*), is defined by

$$(4.3) \qquad CVSI(x) = \sum_j U(a_x, s_j)P(s_j \mid x) - \sum_j U(a^*, s_j)P(s_j \mid x)$$

where a^* is a prior Bayes act. By definition of a_x, the *CVSI* is necessarily non-negative, and hence, the same is true of the outcome-probability weighted average of the *CVSI*'s or

$$(4.4) \qquad EVSI(X) = \sum_{x \in X} CVSI(x)P(x)$$

called the *expected value of sample information* (or *EVSI*) of X. From this single-minded point of view, actions which do not alter the agent's prior Bayes act are 'useless'. And, in fact, it can happen that $ESI(X) < ESI(Y)$, even though $EVSI(X) > EVSI(Y)$.[16] Generally speaking, it behoves the agent to perform a pure experiment X

---

[16] For an example see J. Marschak and M. Radner, *Economic Theory of Teams* (1972), pp. 104–6.

just in case the *EVSI* of *X* exceeds its expected sampling costs, *C(X)*, when both are measured on a common utility scale. The difference of these quantities,

(4.5) $$ENGS(X) = EVSI(X) - C(X)$$

is called the *expected net gain of sampling* (or *ENGS*), and the optimum pure experiment maximises *ENGS*. Notice, finally, that

$$0 \leqslant EVSI(X) = \sum_{x \in X} \left\{ \sum_j U(a_x, s_j)P(s_j \mid x) \right.$$

$$\left. - \sum_j U(a^*, s_j)P(s_j \mid x) \right\} P(x)$$

$$= \sum_{x \in X} \sum_j U(a_x, s_j)P(s_j \mid x)P(x)$$

$$- \sum_j U(a^*, s_j)P(s_j)$$

using $P(s_j) = \sum_{x \in X} P(s_j \mid x)P(x)$, and reversing the order of summation. Consequently,

(4.6) $$U(a^*) \leqslant \sum_{x \in X} U(a_x \mid x)P(x)$$

and the term on the right I call the agent's *expected* (post-experimental) *prospects*, though calculated using his current probabilities (some of them conditional) and current utilities.

Given our assumptions, therefore, experimentation carries an expectation of improved prospects: on the average, the posterior value of a decision-problem will exceed its prior value. But this expectation vanishes when we admit act-dependent states and pass to Richard Jeffrey's decision model.[17] An act, a_x, which is Bayes against *x* in the special decision-model of act-independent states may cease to be Bayes against *x* in the Jeffrey model, where the posterior state probabilities, $P(s \mid x, a)$, may depend on *a*, the action chosen. We must consider, therefore, the entire family of posterior distributions, $P(\cdot \mid x, a)$, indexed by the action space, and, upon observing *x*, choose an action *a* which maximizes the difference

(4.7) $$\sum_j U(a, s_j)P(s_j \mid x, a) - \sum_j U(a^*, s_j)P(s_j \mid x, a^*)$$

[17] R. Jeffrey, *The Logic of Decision* (1965).

and take (4.7) to measure the utility of x, now written $U(x)$. I continue to write a_x for an act which maximizes (4.7), and to define the expected utility of the experiment X by

$$(4.8) \qquad U(X) = \sum_{x \in X} U(x)P(x)$$

which, as before, is necessarily non-negative. However, the above proof of the Jeffrey-analogue of (4.6) breaks down. It requires the additional assumption

$$(4.9) \qquad P(s_j \mid a^*) = \sum_{x \in X} P(s_j \mid x, a^*)P(x)$$

which is satisfied when

$$(4.10) \qquad P(x) = P(x \mid a)$$

holds for all outcomes x and actions a. I then speak of *act-dependent observations*. When (4.10) fails, both the probability and the import of experimental outcomes are influenced by the action chosen. And, though it may seem bizarre, we must allow for this possibility. Act-dependent observations may occur, for example, when the outcomes are auguries told to the agent by an augur who hopes to provide favourable omens for actions he supposes the agent disposed to perform. We encounter something very like this dependence whenever we sense that an adviser is telling us 'what we want to hear'. The notion of an act-dependent observation, like that of an act-dependent state, presupposes that we can meaningfully assign probabilities to actions, but, of course, actions and states alike have a propositional status in Jeffrey's theory, and enter as arguments of both the agent's probability and utility functions. And, indeed, in so far as we are willing to countenance present dispositions to perform future actions, this feature seems not unnatural. To summarize, then, pure experimentation carries an expectation of improved prospects when states are act-independent, or, given act-dependent states, when observations are act-independent. Pure experimentation always carries, on the other hand, an expectation of non-negative utility.

§5. HENRY E. KYBURG
Inductive Logic and Experimental Design

Many writers, including Professor Rosenkrantz, take the only logic involved in scientific inference to be deductive logic. I include in deductive logic, of course, the mathematical manipulations made within the probability calculus. Many suppose that the acceptance of statements (at least of some privileged class) is unproblematic; others suppose that no statements need be accepted. I take inductive logic to be concerned precisely with the warrant for accepting statements on the basis of inconclusive premises. Illustrations of implied inductive principles may be found in the exhortations of statisticians. These exhortations are influential in empirical research. But they are not satisfied by the classical picture of the deductive test of a fully articulated scientific theory (due to the existence of errors of measurement); it is difficult to see how they can be satisfied in the attempt to supplement and develop a partially articulate scientific theory; and the very data in terms of which a rational choice between two competing scientific theories can be made depends on a notion of inductive acceptance that conflicts with the exhortations of both classical and Bayesian statisticians.

1.

For upwards of fifty years talk about both experimental design, and scientific inference in general, has been dominated by considerations of straight-forward deductive logic. It is clearly still so dominated.

Since the phrase 'hypothetico-deductive method' was coined, many philosophers, from Dewey to Popper, and many scientists as well, have thought of the path of science as consisting of the generation of hypotheses and theories (bold, informative, probable, according to taste), and the subjection of these hypotheses and theories to tests, confirmations, potential falsifications, and so on. The picture, at least in simplified form, appears to involve no more than *modus tollens* by way of 'logic'.

It is really a little more complicated than this. We have (or generate) a hypothesis *H*. We deduce from *H* that if circumstances *C* obtain, then state or event *E* will obtain. We note that we have arranged or encountered circumstances *C*. We note that state or event *E* does not obtain. We deduce that *H* is false. The logic is perfectly deductive. What is left out is trivially unimportant in many illustrations of this procedure; it is central and crucial in any attempt to relate this picture to the actual conduct of science. It is that we must *accept* the statement that *C* obtains, and we must *accept* the statement that *E* does not obtain. In the trivial illustrations, we accept the statements (call them $S(C)$ and $S(\sim E)$) on the basis of the testimony of our senses. In ordinary life, we know perfectly well that our senses can sometimes mislead us; this does not mean that we do not or should not accept certain statements on the evidence of our senses, but merely that this acceptance is not altogether unproblematic. In science the acceptance of these statements is even more problematic. They may often be statements concerning masses or forces which are simply not the sort of statements that the direct testimony of the senses can warrant.

There are all sorts of things that may be said about this view of science; I shall say some of them later. But two things are already clear: First, that the logic involved in this description of scientific method is deductive, not inductive; and second, that the acceptance of statements, including statements whose acceptance is not unproblematic, is crucial to the operation of this method.

The hypothetico-deductive method represents a method of theorizing; let us look also at what Professor Rozenkrantz calls partition problems – problems like that of finding out which shell the pea is under. Here again the *logic* involved is purely deductive. How do you go about finding out which of nine balls is the light one in a minimum number of trials on a beam balance? The very problem is a common one in logic texts. There is more than deductive logic involved in dealing with a partition problem, of course. We must accept (on some grounds or other) the statement that the problem *is* a partition problem – that is, that the pea *is* under one of the shells, and that there is only *one* pea. We must accept statements representing the answers to our enquiries or trials: to the effect that the chosen square is in the upper half of the board, to the effect that balls 1, 3, and 5 balance balls 2, 4, and 8, and so on. In real life the acceptance of such statements is not altogether unproblematic: people do lie and make mistakes; beam balances are not arbitrarily sensitive. In scientific partition problems the acceptance of these statements may be very problematic indeed.

At least in noiseless partition problems, we note again, first, that the only logic involved is deductive, second, that the acceptance of statements is crucial to the application of this logic, and third, that this acceptance is not entirely unproblematic.

Let us look at decision-problems. Suppose we have a probability distribution over the states of the world, we obtain some evidence concerning which state of the world is actual, and we must choose one of a number of acts, each of which has consequences of known value depending on the state of the world. The classical procedure is straightforward: we take the conditional probability distribution, on the evidence, compute the mathematical expectation of each act, and choose that act which maximizes the mathematical expectation. Here again, the logic involved is strictly deductive – indeed, mathematical. Here again, also, we must accept a number of statements whose acceptance is not unproblematic. We must accept a statement describing the initial probability distribution. Such a statement, for a personalistic Bayesian, may simply characterize his state of mind, though even in this case it seems to me that its accuracy may be questioned. For a logical-type Bayesian, Jeffreys or 1950-vintage Carnap, such a statement would be logically true, and hence not problematic, if we could decide what language to talk. But for most of us statements about prior probability distributions are very problematic indeed. Furthermore, we must accept statements 'describing the evidence', in order to conditionalize on those statements. Depending on what one is going to count as 'evidence', it may not be obvious what one should accept or why.

If one accepts Rosenkrantz's partition of the process of rational information acquisition into theorizing, partition problems, and decision-problems, one is thus led to a startling conclusion and a monumental problem. The starting conclusion is that inductive logic has no role to play at all in information acquisition (or even in decision-making); and the monumental problem is that of accounting for the acceptance of statements of a wide variety of sorts.

Now of course there may be no such thing as inductive logic, or perhaps what ought to be called 'inductive logic' is really the deductive calculus of probability. And there are people who don't think we need to accept statements at all – though such people cannot employ conventional conditionalization, and there are a host of problems generated by that approach. (For example, how do you tell where a probability 'shift' originates?)

My own conviction is that there is an inductive logic; that it involves the acceptance of statements and the justification for accepting statements; and that it has a very direct bearing on the design of experiments. But since my story contradicts that of Rosenkrantz almost every step of the way, I shall have to tell it in my own way, and without much reference to him. Perhaps the contrast will be stimulating.

2.

It would be out of place for me to expatiate on what I take to be the content of inductive logic, but I do need to say something about its character and role in order to illustrate what is or should be its influence on experimental design.

I take inductive logic, like deductive logic, to be concerned with the warrant that accrues to one statement in the light of a set of other statements. The value of this warrant, in the case of deductive logic, is that if I accept the conjunction of some premises, then I am justified in accepting a conclusion; and furthermore, the value of formalized deductive logic is that if you, too, accept those premises I can *show* you that you ought to accept the conclusion. In the case of inductive logic, the value of the warrant is that if I accept a certain set of statements (at a certain level of acceptance), then I am justified in accepting another statement (at perhaps a lower level of acceptance). More precisely: if K is a set of statements representing my body of moral certainties, and S is highly probable (to degree p, say) relative to K, then I am justified in accepting S at a level of practical certainty p.

One may give both logics a stronger interpretation by saying 'obligated to accept', rather than 'justified in accepting'; and a slightly more realistic, but still very strong interpretation by saying 'committed to accept' rather than 'justified in accepting'. Suppose that I accept the conjunction of premises $P_1, \ldots, P_n$, and that the conditional whose antecedent is that conjunction and whose consequent is C is a theorem of the predicate calculus. Relative to my acceptance of the conjunction of premises, I am justified in accepting C. According to this way of talking, I may be *justified* in accepting C even if I don't know it (being ignorant of logic); even if I am not justified in accepting the conjunction; and I may be justified in accepting C and yet decline to accept it for reasons of perversity or ignorance or because (on other grounds) I am justified in accepting its denial. If you, too, accept the conjunction of premises $P_1, \ldots, P_n$, and you want me to acknowledge C, you will be quite reasonably irritated with me if I insist that while I would be 'justified' in accepting C, I'd really rather not, thank you.

One might propose a stronger principle: that if I accept the conjunction of premises $P_1, \ldots, P_n$, and if the conditional whose antecedent is that conjunction and whose conclusion is C is a theorem of the predicate calculus, then I am *obligated* to accept C. But this is surely too strong: if neither I nor anyone else knows that the theorem in question *is* a theorem, the obligation is one that I cannot reasonably be expected to fulfil. Or I may simply never have thought of C one way or the other; I should not be convicted of irrationality or of failing to meet my obligations just in virtue of my not having thought of an infinity of statements.

The more neutral notion of commitment seems about right: If I accept the conjunction of premisses $P_1, \ldots, P_n$, and if the conditional whose antecedent is that conjunction and whose consequent is C is a theorem of the predicate calculus, then I am *committed* to the acceptance of C. I may not know that I am so committed; you can show me that I am by producing a proof of the theorem. I may even, through the acceptance of the axioms of set theory, be committed to the acceptance of all statements whatever, in virtue of the inconsistency of those axioms. I don't know it; but if someone shows me that is the case, I will then reject that set of axioms.

The same considerations apply to inductive logic. If I have a corpus of knowledge K, and our inductive logic says that relative to K, conclusion C is 'acceptable', this may be interpreted permissively: I am *justified* in accepting C; but this gives you no leverage in convincing me that I *should* accept C. I don't have to do everything that is permitted me. It may also be interpreted as a duty: I *ought* to accept C. This gives you leverage, but it is an obligation that I cannot live up to; under most interpretations of inductive acceptance, I am then 'obligated' to accept all logical truths – and I just don't have the stamina to do so. Finally, it may be interpreted as a commitment: With the corpus K, I am committed to accepting C. The commitment may be unknown to me; your leverage consists in your ability (if inductive logic can be formalized) to *show* me that, given my corpus K, C is something that I am (implicitly) committed to.

No one, surely, can deny that there is such a thing as inductive *argument:* that is just what goes on when a person offers arguments for a conclusion, but does not claim that those arguments are conclusive. For example, he might claim on the basis of a sample survey whose data are accepted by the other party, that at least 30 per cent of a certain population is of Polish extraction; or he might claim, on the basis of three careful measurements, that the melting point of a new compound is 45.68 plus or minus 0.13 degrees Centigrade; or he might claim, on the basis of a number of quite different experimental results, that one general physical theory should be accepted in place of another.

That people indulge in inductive *argument* does not entail that there is an inductive *logic* – much less one having the systematic character I have suggested. Of course we can codify and organize actual instances of inductive argument, and perhaps find general principles that they seem to conform to. But that would be a mere characterization of inductive argument, and would be no logic. Just as deductive logic provides principles to which not all alleged deductive arguments conform, but to which they all *ought* to conform, so an inductive logic would provide normative standards for inductive argument.

One form of inductive argument is statistical inference. It is a commonplace, at least since the appearance of R. A. Fisher's influential book *The Design of Experiments*, that statistical considerations have an important bearing on the design of experiments. Here is one region in which inductive logic has a bearing on the conduct of scientific enquiry. Furthermore, since I regard statistical inference as not merely one form, but as an extremely pervasive form, of inductive argument, it will be useful to look at the influence that implicit principles of inductive logic, embedded in the exhortations of statisticians, have had on the design of experiments.

3.

One type of philosophical advice offered to the designers of experiments is provided by the now classical approach to statistical inference referred to as 'hypothesis testing'. This view is interestingly and intimately related to the philosophical view I mentioned at the beginning of my remarks (the hypothetico-deductive view) which denies the possibility of an inductive logic, and thus, presumably, the legitimacy of the advice offered. But we may leave that anomaly to one side.

According to this approach, we can have no inductive grounds for accepting a statistical hypothesis; nor does it make sense to assign probabilities to statistical hypotheses. We can provide grounds for *rejecting* statistical hypotheses, because often the hypothesis will provide a basis for the claim that a certain general rule will lead to a false rejection of the hypotheses no more than a certain fraction of the time. Thus we *can* have grounds for saying that *if* the hypothesis is true, the probability is only α that it will be falsely rejected. The pure advocates of this point of view are at some pains to point out that to fail to reject a hypothesis is not to have grounds for accepting it. Neyman is as staunch in his refusal to countenance the acceptance of statistical hypotheses as Popper is steadfast in his rejection of the claim that evidence can ever warrant acceptance of a theory.

This statistical point of view has had a profound influence on the design of experiments – even on the design of whole research programmes – in psychology, sociology, biology, medicine, and indeed in most fields where the hypotheses tend to be statistical and the data tend to be expensive. If the point of view were sound, we would have a demonstration not only of how inductive logic *should* influence experimental design, but how it *does* influence experimental design. I have argued elsewhere that the view is generally unsound. Here I am concerned rather to show that the view leads to general recommendations concerning scientific experimentation that come within the domain of inductive logic.

Some of these recommendations can be expressed in these three exhortations:

(1) Set up the experiment so as to test and possibly refute a null hypothesis.

(2) Ensure that the sample selection is properly randomized.

(3) Employ randomized tests to increase the power of the test to discriminate between hypotheses.

No one will deny, I think, that such exhortations as these have had a significant impact on the design of experiments in a large number of fields. The question is whether they have anything to do with inductive logic, particularly in view of the fact that those who make them often vociferously deny that there is any such thing as inductive logic. But let us look at the rationale behind these exhortations. The first depends on the assumption that evidence cannot make a statistical hypothesis probable, much less acceptable. By proper design, however, we can ensure that in the long run a null hypothesis will be falsely rejected no more than a fraction α of the time; we can do this because the null hypothesis is explicit enough that we can derive certain long-run frequencies from it (together with a random sampling assumption) that have that consequence. Thus, for example, we formulate the null hypothesis that a certain drug is without effect; we test the hypothesis against a sample by means of a rule which says that if the sample has such and such a character, reject the null hypothesis. Now to reject the hypothesis is not, on this view, quite the same as accepting its negation, namely, that the drug does have an effect. But obviously this is the way people treat the results of these tests in some degree or other. Given a persuasive enough body of evidence, we start acting as if we accepted the denial of the null hypothesis – we start prescribing the drug, taking it ourselves, and so on. In general, parameters in statistical hypotheses, or in statements derivable from them, start appearing together with numbers representing utilities in much the same role as probabilities. As far as I am concerned, this is close enough to acceptance; the exhortation concerns constraints, in terms of long-run error frequencies, to be imposed on tests which may lead to the *de facto* acceptance of statistical hypotheses.

The second exhortation, about proper randomization, is required to satisfy the conditions for the application of the first exhortation: the rationale for the first exhortation depended on its reference to long-run frequencies. The derivation of error frequencies depends on a random sampling assumption. The requirement is that the sample by means of which the null hypothesis is to be tested be drawn (selected) from the population to which the hypothesis applies by a method which will lead, in the long run, to the selection of each possible sample with equal frequency. Note that this assumption is absolutely crucial to the rationale underlying the first exhortation, and is thus a constraint to be imposed on the structure of experiments in general. It is a principle of inductive logic: if the random sampling assumption is not satisfied, we cannot use the test to justify rejection of the null hypothesis.

Here again the influence of this exhortation on the design of experiments is familiar. Any medical researcher worth his salt will assign patients to treatment and control groups in a random manner – for example, by assigning them numbers and then using a table of random numbers to determine who goes into which group. I have argued elsewhere that satisfaction of the random sampling assumption is neither necessary nor sufficient for the cogency of a statistical test. In short, the idea is that the basis for our inference is the data we have *after* we have drawn and examined the sample. The stochastically random assignment of individuals to control and experimental groups will lead, in a certain proportion of cases, to putting all the women in the control group and all the men in the test group. If there are 'bad' samples, we'll get them (rarely); and if these are 'good' ones they can have been obtained by 'arbitrary' selection as well as by 'random' selection. However much you stratify your samples, this will remain true. The point here is not who is right, but that what is at issue is (a) a matter of inductive logic, and (b) a matter that has a profound effect on the actual design of scientific experiments.

The third exhortation (to increase the power of a statistical test by using a randomized rejection rule) is less often obeyed in actual scientific practice. From my point of view, there are good reasons for this; but from the point of view of classical hypothesis testing, the rationale, concerned with long-run frequencies of error, is just as powerful as that underlying the first two exhortations. Again, whether or not the rejection of a null hypothesis is construed as the acceptance of its negation, the control of long-run frequencies of error is seen as relevant to the justification of the 'results' obtained from the experiment.

I have not taken this to be the place to criticize these exhortations. I have tried merely to indicate that they are influential in the design of experiments, that they can be construed as embodying or reflecting certain principles of inductive logic, and that they are not uncontroversial.

4.

By way of contrast, let us look briefly at Bayesian statistical theory. There we encounter quite different exhortations:
   (1) Be explicit about your prior probabilities.
   (2) Conditionalize on the results of a test.
   (3) The new set of probabilities should determine your beliefs.
   (4) Randomization is always inessential.
These, too, may be construed as reflecting principles of inductive logic. What is warranted by experimental evidence is not, in this case, the acceptance or rejection of a hypothesis, but rather the new set of probabilities resulting from conditionalizing the old ones on the evidence. Most often the prior probabilities are construed as simply subjective, and the exhortations may do relatively little to resolve interpersonal disagreement. Nevertheless, obedience to the Bayesian exhortations is intended to contribute to making explicit the warrant for new probability distributions provided by experimental evidence. Bayesianism has not had as much effect on experimental design as the classical hypothesis-testing theory; this may be due to the fact that Bayesians are a minority, and it may be due to inherent limitations in Bayesian theory. I leave that question to one side for the sake of spending some time on the question of theorizing, to which I promised to return.

5.

Early on I claimed that although the logic involved in testing scientific hypotheses usually seemed to be straightforwardly deductive, to construe tests of hypotheses this way was relatively unilluminating, and that inductive logic had much to contribute to our understanding of the relation between scientific hypotheses and theories and the evidence relative to which they are evaluated. Let me explain what I had in mind.

I shall consider first the testing and refutation of a fully articulated theory, second, the development of a partially indeterminate theory, and third, the choice between two competing theories.

Let us consider a test of a fully articulated theory. This corresponds to the classical example of the hypothetico-deductive method.

By calling the theory fully articulated, I mean that its parameters are all specified, and it is in a form which yields definite experimental predictions. If it is like a physical theory, this means it yields a prediction of the form: if the experimental set-up E is characterized by the quantities $Q_1, \ldots, Q_n$, then the outcome will be characterized by the quantity R. To test the theory, we set up the experiment, measure the Q-values and the R-value, and determine whether or not the prediction of the theory is satisfied.

But we cannot simply 'observe' the Q-values and the R-value. They must be measured, and measurement automatically involves error. Error introduces statistics. In fact, in most cases, to make an assertion about the 'true value' of a quantity, on the basis of a measurement of it, is regarded as making an assertion about a statistical parameter of a population of potential measurements. Bayesian methods allow us to make no assertions of this sort; the Bayesian approach begins with a prior distribution of the parameter Q_1, conditionalizes on the result of a measurement (which we are allowed to 'accept'), and yields a distribution (quite possibly unbounded) for the parameter Q. It is common in many disciplines to suppose that errors follow a Gaussian law – i.e., that they are normally distributed with mean 0 and variance that we can estimate from past measurements. If this is so, the error may be anywhere from $-\infty$ to $+\infty$. Conditionalize on observations as we will, therefore, the possible error may still be anywhere from $-\infty$ to $+\infty$, and the quantity Q may have any value whatever. Clearly it is hard to come by an experimental refutation of a quantitative theory this way. Of course Bayesianism could be supplemented by a principle to the effect that if a set of values satisfying the theory is rendered improbable enough by the measurements, then the theory can be rejected. But this is precisely the sort of principle of inductive logic, as opposed to deductive logic, that theory testing seems to require, and which is not allowed for on the classical view.

Confidence methods can yield, at a certain level of confidence, assertions of the form: Q_1 lies in the interval ΔQ_1. If we were to *accept* a set of such assertions, we could be in a position to apply the deductive principle of *modus tollens* and thereby to reject the theory. But we require more principles than classical statistical theory gives us to know when it is appropriate to accept such a set of assertions. The principles we require are precisely those that form part of what I call inductive logic.

Note that in any case what is involved in applying the hypothetico-deductive method to the test of a scientific theory involves the acceptance of statements that are rendered (loosely speaking) no more than probable by the evidence. We need more than deductive logic either in the simple sense of *modus tollens* or in the more complicated sense of the calculus of probability. Note further that to understand clearly what is involved is to have something useful to say about the design of experiments for the testing of fully articulated theories.

It is unclear that it very often happens that a scientific theory is developed in fully articulated form and then tested as I have described. It is fairly common that a scientific theory will be developed in a partial form, and then filled out: parameters will be evaluated, the forces called for by the theory will be sought for and related to other quantities, stochastic parameters will be filled in, and so on. Let's consider, in particular, the evaluation of a parameter.

Why should we want to do that? For a number of reasons: to have more knowledge and understanding of the way the world is; to be able to use the theory for making predictions, for designing better mousetraps, for making decisions with high expected utility, and so on. For all these purposes, what we want is not a probability distribution for the parameter, but, as close as we can get, knowledge of its value. We have here again a measurement problem – perhaps a very complicated one, since we may be able to 'measure' the parameter only very indirectly – and the same sorts of considerations as previously mentioned indicate the need for principles of inductive logic which will throw light on the warrant that observations can give to assertions of a relatively theoretical sort.

Finally, consider the choice between two alternative theories. It seems to be quite rare that a theory of any generality is subjected to test, and then rejected. Scientific progress often concerns the evaluation of parameters and the investigation of special cases, but this is most properly construed as a matter of measurement or of the articulation of a given theory. The most interesting sort of progress concerns the replacement of one theory by another, or the choice between two alternative theories.

Suppose we have two quantitative theories, T_1 and T_2, together with a large body of evidence D. The evidence D, together with theory T_1, leads to a certain quantitative statistical theory of errors of measurement, say E_1. E_1 will tell us not only that errors in the measurement of length are distributed in such and such a way *ordinarily*, but that in certain special cases (the 'anomalies') measurements of length must be construed as wildly in error if T_1 is to be preserved. Theory T_2, together with D, leads to a different quantitative statistical theory of errors of measurement, say E_2. In either case, the theory, combined with the data, determines a theory of errors of the various sorts which infect our observations. Obtaining the error theories E_1 and E_2 is a matter of statistical inference, and thus, of course, of inductive logic.

If we adopt such an approach, what can we say about the choice between one theory, together with its associated theory of error, and another with *its* associated theory of error? Inductive logic gives us grounds, (of justification or commitment or obligation) for accepting certain statements as practically certain, given a body of evidence. Given a theory T_1, together with a body of observations D, and a theory of observational error E_1, our corpus of practical certainties will contain a certain set of statements S_1. Given a different theory T_2, together with a body of observations D based on the same experiences – but quite possibly phrased in different terms – together with the corresponding theory of observational error E_2, our corpus of practical certainties will contain a different set of statements S_2. I believe we can give fairly plausible criteria of content in terms of which to make a choice between S_1 and S_2. But to prefer S_1 to S_2 is just to choose between the two theories and their associated theories of error, on the basis of a given body of observational experience.

In this way of looking at the matter the theories may be regarded as functioning in an *a priori* way. At the same time, however, inductive logic and a body of experience can give us a way of choosing rationally between them. Thus even in choosing between theories, it seems to me that inductive logic has a role to play. Much of this, at this point, is pure conjecture. But if a fully articulated system of inductive logic can be developed, it seems to me that it may very well play a role in the design of experiments to test one theory against another, just as the fragments of inductive logic we already have play – or could play – a role in the design of experiments which are intended to yield statistical knowledge.

§6. Comments and Replies
The Rosenkrantz–Kyburg Session

ROSENKRANTZ: As Kyburg observes, sufficiently strong evidence against a null hypothesis (e.g., that a new drug has no affect) will lead us to act as though the alternative hypothesis is true (e.g., to prescribe the drug to patients). If acting on a hypothesis is tantamount to 'accepting' it, then, indeed, Bayesians do it all the time (using standard decision theory). However, Kyburg appears to regard acceptance as a function of probability alone (he mentions no utilities, practical or otherwise), and so a less straightforward construal of acceptance must be intended.

Certainly we premiss all sorts of propositions in science, and, on my account, such choices are guided by support indices or (relative) probabilities, just as economic choices are guided by prices. Little of substance separates Kyburg's account from mine at this level. But he wishes to go farther and subject such choices to formal rules of acceptance, and the body of these rules constitutes what he understands by 'inductive logic'. In rough outline, the programme he sketches looks like this: given propositions are accepted *ab initio* as 'moral certainties', and these include, I take it, the truths of logic and mathematics and certain observation-statements whose probabilities (however come by) are as close to one as makes no odds. From this bedrock of certainty, one attempts to reach levels of 'practical certainty' by tacking on those propositions whose probabilities are sufficiently high relative to those accepted at the next lower rung of the hierarchy. One is led to an approach like Kyburg's by taking logical positivism and orthodox statistics (with its heavy dependence on acceptance or rejection rules) very seriously.

Without wishing to bar the way to enquiry in this area, I must admit to a certain scepticism: can the complex structure of our empirical knowledge be accounted for in such simple terms? Be that as it may, the more important point here is that Kyburg's programme fits perfectly well with the sort of Bayesian account outlined in my paper. His acceptance-rules, so far as I can judge, are purely probabilistic. The extra-evidential epistemic utilities against which I inveigh are not invoked, nor are the probabilities of hypotheses altered by their acceptance or rejection. Indeed, 'accepted' appears to mean little more than 'sufficiently probable for the practical or theoretical purposes at hand'. And, consequently, all of the propositions we premiss in science have for Kyburg the same epistemological status they have for me. If we differ, it is at the methodological level; where he sees a need for imposing formal acceptance-rules, I do not.

DORLING: The historical debate in the first half of the seventeenth century was between the Copernican and the Tychonic systems. Relative to these the Ptolemaic system is easy to dispose of by Bayesian or non-Bayesian considerations. But it was already dead by the time of the debate whose rationality we must try to reconstruct. In work I am preparing for publication, I have reinvestigated the 49 arguments for Copernicanism and 77 arguments against, which G. B. Riccioli analyzed (from an anti-Copernican point of view) in his 1651 *Almagestum Novum*. I find that some fifteen or so of the arguments Riccioli discusses, some on each side, do seem to be reconstructable as valid informal probabilistic arguments, and I have managed to translate all of these into claims about the relative likelihoods of evidential statements on the basis of the Copernican and anti-Copernican hypotheses. But it proves impossible to assess the *overall* weight of these probabilistic arguments without making them *quantitative* in a rough and ready way, without, for example, trying to evaluate at least plausible upper and lower bounds for the various likelihood ratios at issue. I have tried to do this as fairly as possible, but still cannot avoid ending with a ratio at least four hundred to one (give or take a factor of twenty or so) in favour of Copernicanism. At first one might think this was simply a factor by which one must multiply the arbitrary ratio of the prior probabilities for the two positions in order to get the ratio of the posterior probabilities. However, in converting all the probabilistic arguments into claims about likelihood ratios of evidential statements, I found that I had incorporated all the *specific* differences, between, for example, the earth and the sun, into the evidential statements. So both the Copernican and the anti-Copernican hypotheses turn out, in my ultimate shorn-down version, to assert the existence of a stationary central body, around which more than one satellite revolves, some of which satellites have one or more secondary satellites. The two hypotheses now differ merely in the *labels* attached to the bodies, and hence presumably must be assigned, in this form, the same priors. Hence my argument apparently ends up with a genuine ratio of posteriors in favour of Copernicus. (However this analysis, like Riccioli's, explicitly neglects all purely theological considerations.)

ROSENKRANTZ: In chapter 7 of my book, I deal primarily with the evidence for the Copernican theory against the Ptolemaic from planetary data. Naturally, I welcome, and eagerly await the publication of, Jon Dorling's attempt to tackle the much more difficult comparison of the Copernican and Tychonic alternatives. Frankly, I had not expected to find others treading this thorny path. But tread it we must if we are ever to assess the rationality of the reactions scientists have evinced historically to new theories in an objective way or effectively test the hypothesis that the beliefs of the members of a scientific research speciality are almost never at great variance with the evidence.

SWINBURNE: Rosenkrantz's[1] understanding of 'simplicity' is very much the same as Popper's. 'Simplicity' is a matter of content. The more precise a theory and the larger its scope, the 'simpler' it is. Maybe scientists do often seek theories of large content and therefore 'simple' in Rosenkrantz's sense. But the 'simpler' a theory in this sense, the less probable it is. This sort of 'simplicity' is no evidence of truth. There is however another sort of simplicity in science, and one more naturally so called, which is evidence of truth. Compatible with any finite number of data there will always be an infinite number of theories of similar content. Compatible with the evidence of a finite number of locations of Mars, there are an infinite number of theories about the motion of Mars. While agreeing that it passed through the observed points, they disagree about its future motion. One or two of these curves will be smooth and have relatively simple equations – e.g., the ellipse. This sort of simplicity is evidence of truth; we believe the simpler theory and its predictions to be more probable than the complicated theory and its predictions. If we did not, we would have no grounds for judging any prediction to be more probable than any other. Simplicity of this kind is a matter of mathematical simplicity of equations, naturalness of descriptive predicates, parts of a theory cohering well, fewness of new postulated entities, and fewness of new kinds of postulated entities.

This conclusion cannot be avoided by claiming that we can choose between competing theories compatible with the data by their fit with some background theory (e.g. Newton's theory). For the same point can be made with regard to the background theory. There will be an infinite number of background theories of similar content compatible with data. The choice will have to be on grounds of simplicity.

[1] For more detailed criticism of Rosenkrantz's theory of scientific inference, see my review of his *Inference, Method and Decision* in *Brit. J. Phil. Sci.* 29 (1978).

ROSENKRANTZ: My understanding of simplicity is indeed close to Popper's though of course we differ radically in our reasons for thinking simplicity important. In my view, simpler theories are preferable just because their probabilities have higher 'growth potential', while, for Popper, as for Swinburne, simpler theories (in my sense) are doomed to remain forever *less* probable. Popper's arguments are, however, not very convincing, and it has recently come to my attention that John Harsanyi answered them, much as I do in chapter 6 of my book, nearly twenty years ago (cf. ch. XIII of his *Essays on Ethics, Social Behavior, and Scientific Explanation*, 1976). Specifically, Harsanyi points out that if our interest lies in comparing, say, the hypothesis that a planetary orbit is circular with the hypothesis that it is elliptical, then we have implicitly adopted what he calls the 'exclusive' interpretation of the latter, viz., that the ellipse is one of positive eccentricity. Once we adopt that interpretation, the probability calculus no longer forces us to assign the 'elliptical' hypothesis a higher probability, even though the 'circular' hypothesis remains effectively a special case of it (since the eccentricity can be made arbitrarily small) and is certainly simpler in my sense. In his review of my book, Swinburne writes that 'theories of less content which are entailed by theories of minimal sample coverage will always have even greater posterior probabilities than the latter, whatever the evidence'. But posterior probabilities are relative to a considered partition of hypotheses, and a partition cannot include theories which are entailed by other members of the same partition. To include two such theories in the same partition, we must take them in their exclusive sense, and then conclusions about their relative probabilities can no longer be drawn from the probability calculus alone.

Brief as they are, Swinburne's own remarks about simplicity nicely illustrate the sort of approach against which I inveigh. He asserts that simplicity is 'evidence of truth' (without saying why) and presents us with a whole grab bag of properties under this head (without saying how they are to be weighted). Some of the items he mentions, like paucity of entities or kinds (and, he might have added, of parameters or assumptions) are clearly constitutive of simplicity in my sense. But the others, the naturalness of a theory's predicates and the mathematical simplicity of its equations, are harder to pin down (Is a sinusoidal curve 'mathematically simpler' than a polynomial?), and even if they could be characterized with precision, there is not the slightest reason for thinking them 'evidence of truth'. Are we to infer, for example, that theory's probability suffers a decline when it is equivalently recast using less 'natural' predicates or more complicated mathematics (as in Hamilton's reformulation of classical mechanics)? To see further into this issue, let us look at some concrete cases where the two accounts apparently conflict.

In industrial regions of Britain, where soot covers the tree-trunks, black moths are less visible to predators and so enjoy a selective advantage over white moths, while in the less polluted rural areas, where lichen grows on trees, the reverse is true. In view of this, the hypothesis H_1 that all varieties of British moth are blite [black and inhabit industrial regions or white and inhabit rural regions] is *a priori* more probable than the hypothesis H_2 that all varieties are white. Yet, 'blite' would seem to be a paradigm of unnaturalness, and so, on Swinburne's account, at a time before hardy strains of black moths had established themselves in industrial regions or before such regions were sampled, H_1 should have been accorded a lower probability than H_2. To avert this implausible implication, he must allow relevant background knowledge to override considerations of simplicity (in his sense). But, as he views matters, the question whether simplicity is overriding would arise again at the level of competing background theories, and so he must face the question: at what level does simplicity become overriding?

For a second example, consider Einstein's modification of Newton's second law, a modification to which he was led on the basis of a compelling theoretical analysis. The modified law has the same form – that the force acting on a particle is equal to the rate of change of its momentum – but relativistic momentum is mathematically more complicated, as the *relativistic mass* is defined by $m = m_0/\sqrt{1 - v^2/c^2}$, where m_0 is rest mass and c the speed of light. Although mathematically more complicated, the relativistic version is every bit as determinate, for c is an independently measurable universal constant. (True, there is some error in the measurement of c, and that makes the relativistic law a teeny bit more complicated in my sense.) Moreover, because the relativistic equations are invariant under the Lorentz group and c is a universal speed limit, Special Relativity looks to be the simpler theory of the two in my sense. Yet, given Einstein's analysis, a reasonable man would (circa 1905) have assigned Relativity Theory a higher prior probability than Newtonian Theory, and the same is true, *a fortiori*, of its predictions about the behaviour of particles travelling at speeds close to the speed of light.

In both examples we may speak (picturesquely) of a 'straight' law that is corrected by a 'bent' law at extreme ranges of the relevant variables. The discrepancy between them will often be experimentally undetectable (or, at least, undetected) at the time the bent hypothesis is put forward. And under such conditions, where data outside the domain where the straight law is well-attested are lacking, Nelson Goodman's entrenchment theory would exclude the rival bent hypothesis as an 'unprojectible' non-starter (instanced but unsupported) solely on the basis of its conflict with the (thus far supported and unviolated) straight hypothesis in question. Thus, the 'blite' hypothesis succumbs to the 'white' hypothesis, while Einstein's law is overridden (in Goodman's sense) by Newton's. Given the right background knowledge, however, a bent hypothesis can be more probable and more confirmable than its straight counterpart, as my examples attest. And, consequently, attempts to drive an epistemological wedge between the bent and the straight should strike us as fundamentally misguided. (I would even go so far as to suggest that most of the major breakthroughs in the history of science occurred when a suitable bent hypothesis was discovered.)

Swinburne argues, however, that if we lack such intrinsic reasons for preferring the straight to the bent, then we are committed to a thoroughgoing inductive scepticism: 'we would have no grounds', he writes, 'for judging any prediction to be more probable than any other'. And the conclusion cannot be evaded, he adds, by appeal to background theory, 'for the same point can be made with regard to the background theory'. In other words, we can Goodmanize our 'overhypotheses' and reverse judgements of lawlikeness or probability based on such appeals.

One could reply that the task of inductive logic is merely to state what the probabilities of competing hypotheses ought to be, *given* a body of data and background theory. Thus, the background knowledge we really do have about emeralds should enable us to locate the desired asymmetry between the bent 'grue' hypothesis and the straight 'green' hypothesis (as in ch. 2 of my book).

But one can hope to do better here. Is it really the case that the relevant background theory can always be suitably Goodmanized? How would this be done in the Relativity example? How would it be done in comparing van der Waals's first-order correction of the ideal gas law with the ideal gas law itself? Although the two-parameter van der Waals equation of state is mathematically more complicated, its predictions governing dense gases would most reasonably have been accorded higher prior probabilities than those of the ideal gas law, since, at high densities, the intermolecular forces and portion of the total volume occupied by the molecules, both of which are ignored by the ideal gas law, become appreciable. How would we Goodmanize this bit of background knowledge? Or, again, our knowledge that phylogenetically related species tend to be genetically related lends a certain presumption to the hypothesis that a given trait is sex-linked when it is known to be sex-linked in a closely related species. To be sure, we could Goodmanize this 'overhypothesis' by asserting that pairs of phylogenetically related species, other than the given pair, are genetically related. But it isn't as though the pertinent overhypothesis is believed because several phylogenetically related species have been tested and found to be genetically related! The reasons for believing it, like the reasons for believing that metals are good conductors, are at once more theoretical and more specific. It is because metallic crystals have a characteristic lattice structure that they make good conductors, and this consideration applies indifferently to all metals. Hence, to make an exception of, say, copper, without sufficient reason, would be to make an arbitrary exception, and any Goodmanized overhypothesis that did so would be justifiably accorded a very low prior probability.

Let me conclude with an example that is more recognizably a paradigm of inductive inference. In sampling balls at random with replacement from an urn containing an unknown proportion of black balls, the probability of drawing a black ball following an initial run of black balls should be higher than its initial value. This conclusion follows if we make, for example, the very mild assumption that the trials are 'exchangeable' in De Finetti's sense. That assumption is surely a realistic one, as far as it goes, and I think that, as inductive logicians, we are entitled to assume the ability to recognize which of our assumptions are realistic and which of them are gross and unworkable oversimplifications of the situation under study. Thus, a model of our urn experiment which posited a change in the proportion of black balls following each trial would flatly contradict the fact that the balls are drawn with replacement. To make his case, Swinburne must convince us that additional postulates of simplicity, analogy, or the like, are needed in the example before us to conclude that the probability of drawing a black ball is indeed higher following an initial run of black balls. I am yet to be persuaded of the need to import such global assumptions into our inductive logic to avert Humean scepticism.

3

Falsification versus Inductivism

§7. DAVID MILLER
Can Science do without Induction?

The paper seeks to defend the falsificationist approach to scientific method and scientific knowledge that was presented by Sir Karl Popper in *Logik der Forschung*. The first one-third of the paper consists of an outline of this position. There follow reports on a number of recent criticisms of Popper's views, all of them to the effect that, despite its intentions, falsificationism is as committed to a principle of induction as are the various theories of knowledge that it seeks to replace. The final one-third of the paper consists of rebuttals of these accusations, and a reaffirmation of the opinion that science does, can, and will do without induction.

1.

In 1934, in the first section of *Logik der Forschung*, Popper wrote:

Some who believe in inductive logic are anxious to point out, with Reichenbach, that 'the principle of induction is unreservedly accepted by the whole of science and that no man can seriously doubt this principle in everyday life either'. [Here there is a footnote referring to a contribution of Reichenbach's in *Erkenntnis* 1.] ... Yet even supposing this were the case – for after all, 'the whole of science' might err – I should still contend that a principle of induction is superfluous, and that it must lead to logical inconsistencies.[1]

After briefly referring to these inconsistencies, and attributing their discovery to Hume, Popper goes on:

My own view is that the various difficulties of inductive logic here sketched are insurmountable. So also, I fear, are those inherent in the doctrine, so widely current today, that inductive inference, although not 'strictly valid', *can attain some degree of* '*reliability*' *or of* '*probability*'. ...
    The theory to be developed in the following pages stands directly opposed to all attempts to operate with the ideas of inductive logic. It might be described as the theory of *the deductive method of testing*, or as the view that a hypothesis can only be empirically *tested* – and only *after* it has been advanced.[2]

There is not much more in *Logik der Forschung* about the impossibility of constructing an inductive logic. The book is very largely a detailed elaboration of Popper's theory that science grows by an

---

[1] K. R. Popper, *The Logic of Scientific Discovery* (1959), p. 29.
[2] Ibid., pp. 29 f.

involved interplay of dicey conjectures and dusty refutations.[3] With this theory Popper claims to have solved the problem of induction, though, as he concedes, 'few philosophers would support the thesis' that he has done any such thing.[4] As it happens, I do support this thesis; I do think that Popper has succeeded in developing a convincing theory of the growth of science that is quite free from any principle of induction.[5] It is the purpose of this paper to defend this position against a number of recent attacks.

2.

Like Popper in *Logik der Forschung* I shall say little here about the actual problems and difficulties that have to date beset all attempts to construct adequate systems of inductive logic. It is well known that Popper has made several sorties into this area,[6] and I have on occasion ventured there myself.[7] Most of Popper's attacks have been vigorously, though not in my opinion rigorously, rebuffed. My reason for not once more entering on to this bloodstained field is simply the fact that almost everyone acknowledges the existence of a problem with induction.[8] I take it, that is, that if Popper's theory can be shown to be both satisfactory and free from inductive taint then it is to be preferred to theories incorporating some principle of induction, even if (what I very much deny) these in their turn could effectively resist the criticisms that Popper and others have levelled against them. Salmon writes that 'Professor Popper . . . undertakes, quite appropriately I think, to reconstruct the logic of science

[3] It is strange that both B. Magee, *Popper* (1973), p. 14 and, following him, R. C. Jeffrey, 'Probability and Falsification: Critique of the Popper Program', *Synthese* 30 (1975), p. 96 find it necessary to chide Popper for being inclined 'to put forward most of his important ideas in the course of criticizing other people's [ideas]'.

[4] K. R. Popper, *Objective Knowledge* (1972), p. 1.

[5] Falsificationism does not of course on its own solve all methodological problems. Problems of statistical testing are just the most obvious ones where detailed supplementation is needed. I have no doubt, however, that such problems can (indeed must) be solved in agreement with falsificationist principles.

[6] e.g., K. R. Popper, 'Probability Magic or Knowledge out of Ignorance', *Dialectica* 11 (1957), pp. 354–72; *L. Sc. Disc.*, appendices *vii–*ix; 'On Carnap's Version of Laplace's Rule of Succession', *Mind* 71 (1962), pp. 69–73; 'The Mysteries of Udolpho: A Reply to Professors Jeffrey and Bar-Hillel', *Mind* 76 (1967), pp. 103–10.

[7] D. W. Miller, 'A Paradox of Information', *Brit. J. Phil. Sci.* 17 (1966), pp. 59–61; 'The Measure of All Things', in G. Maxwell and R. M. Anderson (eds.), *Induction, Probability and Confirmation* (1975), pp. 350–66; 'Making Sense of Method: Comments on Richard Jeffrey', *Synthèse* 30 (1975), pp. 139–47.

[8] There are one or two exceptions, such as R. Harré, *The Principles of Scientific Thinking* (1970), pp. 248 f. But Harré is mistaken in supposing that the problem of induction does not arise in his theory, as I argue in my 'Back to Aristotle?', *Brit. J. Phil. Sci.* 23 (1972), pp. 69–78.

without recourse to inductive logic';[9] and though of course he then, like so many others, casts doubt on the success of Popper's endeavour, he implicitly concedes how significant it would be if it were successful. As I shall want to argue that it is indeed successful, I shall take it for granted that the corresponding failure of inductivist theories of the growth of knowledge is itself of significantly less significance.

Another topic on which I shall not enlarge unduly here is the psychology of learning, or the psychology of discovery. In the judgement of Lakatos, Popper's 'campaign against the *inductivist logic of discovery*[,] . . . according to which a theory is scientific only if it is *guided* by facts and not *misguided* by theory[,] . . . achieved a decisive success, not only intellectually but sociopsychologically; at least among philosophers of science Baconian method is now only taken seriously by the most provincial and illiterate'.[10] In the light of this fairly characteristic piece of exaggeration it is interesting, and indeed amusing, to read in Feuer's generally favourable review of the volume in which the above cited paper by Lakatos appeared, the following remarks:

How well do Popper's central propositions fare under the test of a sociological scrutiny? . . . 'Every observation,' says Popper, 'is preceded by a problem, a hypothesis'; science is held to begin with problems, not with the collection of facts. It seems false, however, that all observation is problem-directed. . . . The collector's impulse, moreover, can evolve into important discovery. To tell one such story: an apothecary, Heinrich Schwabe, decided in 1826 to devote himself to astronomy. Every clear day for forty-three years he pointed his telescope at the sun, and counted the number of its visible spots. After his first seventeen years of collecting observations, it suddenly struck him that there was a periodicity in the occurrence of the sunspots, which he later confirmed as that of a ten-year cycle. [In fact the cycle is an eleven-year one.] The collection of facts *can* precede the formulation of a hypothesis.[11]

So there we have it. Altogether passing over the fact that in the telling of this story Popper's point is systematically missed (Schwabe was by no means collecting facts at random, but was already guided by a hypothesis, however ill-formulated), we have a beautiful example of a typical episode of scientific discovery: the conjecturing of a

[9] W. C. Salmon, 'The Justification of Inductive Rules of Inference', in I. Lakatos (ed.), *The Problem of Inducitive Logic* (1968), p. 24.

[10] I. Lakatos, 'Popper on Demarcation and Induction', in P. A. Schilpp (ed.), *The Philosophy of Karl Popper* (1974), p. 258 f.

[11] L. S. Feuer, 'Karl Popper: Humanist Philosopher', *The Humanist* (Nov./Dec. 1974), p. 38.

hypothesis unsupported by any evidence whatever. For without having observed one single instance of a particular regularity Schwabe was visited by, and obviously impressed by, the hypothesis that this regularity was universal. Not even once had the sunspot cycle repeated itself before Schwabe was conjecturing that it would always repeat itself. Truly a belief in the hypothesis that we learn directly from experience – that is, that we make inductive inferences from instances to generalizations – can persuade one to see inductive inferences being made where no inductive inference could conceivably exist.[12]

3.

Having said in the last section what I shall not say in the rest of the paper, let me say in this section what I shall say, and in the rest of the paper say it.

In section 4 I shall briefly sketch Popper's theory as I currently understand it. I assume, of course, that everyone has some familiarity with Popper's ideas, so I shall try to present them in as unfamiliar a way as is compatible with fidelity. In section 5 I shall enumerate some of the respects in which Popper's theory has been held to be as committed to a principle of induction as are the theories it sets out to challenge. Having enumerated the objections I shall at once proceed to eliminate them, and this will be the business of section 6. Section 7 will conclude.

4.

Fallibilism might be characterized as the doctrine that no factual assertion, let alone scientific theory, can be established with absolute certainty. It disputes, in other words, the reality of certainty – of certain knowledge. Popper is of course a fallibilist. But his central achievement, in my view, has been to recognize that the ideal of certain knowledge is quite as pernicious as the reality. Science, according to Popper, is not, need not be, and should not be, dominated by this ideal. In rejecting what Dewey called 'the quest for certainty' Popper is not just acknowledging the truth of fallibilism. It is the quest that Popper is opposed to quite as much as the

---

[12] It might be objected that the particular phenomena that Schwabe conjectured to comprise the sunspot cycle had indeed been observed once, and that some of them had actually been observed twice. This objection would hold a little water only if Schwabe's hypothesis indeed was that a particular sequence of phenomena would occur repeatedly, rather than that there was some largely unspecified cycle of sunspot activity. In any case, Schwabe's conjecture was preceded by not more than a single instance, so hardly amounts to evidence for the view that we learn by repetition.

certainty. That is to say, the crucial disagreement between Popper and other fallibilists is methodological rather than epistemological. We all agree that certain truth cannot be achieved. As far as I know, Popper was the first to say that it ought not to be attempted, that it should not even be approached. Probable truth, reliable truth, and so on are therefore not suitable or even worthwhile goals. Nor is there any point in aiming to make our knowledge more certain, or more probable, or more reliable. For the aim of science is simply truth; not some epistemically distinguished variety of truth, but truth alone. Or, more enterprisingly, more truth, as much truth as can be achieved. According to the simplest version of the falsificationist doctrine, a doctrine that is almost entirely due to Popper, that is all that we should try to achieve in science; it is on truth alone that the methods of science should be concentrated. This does not mean, of course, that the methods we adopt need guarantee in any degree the attainment of this goal; only that they should not demonstrably frustrate it. It is in this sense that methodology should be minimal. As the appropriate method for the search for truth Popper proposes the method of conjectures and refutations.

The main difference between this method and all justificationist methods – that is, all methods that seek to justify, if only in part, the theories that scientists propose – is that it relies on expulsion procedures, rather than entrance examinations, as the chief way of maintaining academic standards. For justificationists a hypothesis has to pass tests, or be confirmed, or something of the sort, if it is to be admitted to the realm of scientific knowledge; if it fails these tests, or is disconfirmed, or even if it fails to be confirmed, it is excluded. Popper, in contrast, subjects a hypothesis to test only after it has been admitted. If it fails any of the tests to which it is put then it is expelled, removed from science; if it passes them all then nothing happens – that is to say, it is retained. The passing of tests therefore makes not a jot of difference to the status of any hypothesis, though the failing of just one test may make a great deal of difference. For justificationists, in contrast, the passing of tests is just as important as the failing of tests, for it is just this that determines whether a hypothesis is admitted or not to the body of science. Of course, justificationists need expulsion procedures as well as entrance examinations; for even the most rigorous entrance examination fails to guarantee the quality of a successful candidate. But the expulsion procedures are the sole means that Popper allows for the control of scientific knowledge. He adopts a policy of open admission, subject naturally to the condition that no hypothesis may be admitted unless it is clearly understood that there are conditions under which that hypothesis will be expelled. This natural qualification is Popper's criterion of demarcation between science and pseudoscience: a hypothesis may be admitted provisionally to the realm of scientific knowledge only if it is falsifiable by experience.

Popper's methodology insists that, if we are seriously searching for the truth, we should submit any hypothesis proposed to the most searching barrage of criticism, in the hope that if the hypothesis is false we shall be able to show that it is false. To the extent that we conform to the principle of empiricism ('the principle that only "experience" can decide about the truth or falsity of a factual statement')[13] our criticism will take the form of empirical tests, of confrontation between the hypothesis under fire and the kinds of phenomena – photographs, movements of pointers, etc. – generally regarded as making up the empirical basis of science. If our hypothesis clearly and unambiguously fails one of the tests to which it is submitted we shall at once eliminate it as a candidate for the truth. And if the aim of science is just the truth we shall want to retain anything that might be true, but nothing that cannot be true. In this simple situation falsification will lead to rejection, and lack of falsification will mean no change: the hypothesis will be retained.[14] But as Popper clearly saw, science often operates as though it aimed not at the truth but at close approximations to the truth. In such an enterprise a hypothesis will not be rejected as soon as it is falsified, but only as soon as it is shown to be a worse approximation to the truth than some other available hypothesis. As I suppose is generally known, this attempt of Popper's to broaden the base of falsificationism has led to some intransigent logical problems, namely the extreme difficulty of explaining what there can be about a couple of hypotheses that makes one of them a better approximation to the truth than is the other. I shall not elaborate further on these difficulties here, since they do not, in my opinion, have much bearing on the non-inductivist character of Popper's theory of the growth of knowledge.

'Science advances *conjectures*, not *certain* information', writes a recent commentator,[15] summing up one aspect of Popper's theory.

---

[13] *L. Sci. Disc.*, p. 312.

[14] I should briefly note here the popular contention, stemming apparently from T. S. Kuhn, *The Structure of Scientific Revolutions* (1962), that '[no] process yet disclosed by the historical study of scientific development at all resembles the methodological stereotype of falsification by direct comparison with nature' (p. 77). The logical situation is not affected by this historical generalization, even if it is true.

[15] R. J. Ackermann, *The Philosophy of Karl Popper* (1976), p. 3.

The statement is of course correct, but it highlights a false contrast. The conjectural character of scientific hypotheses lies not so much in the fact that they cannot be shown to be right as in the fact that they may be shown to be wrong. The falsifiability (whether by strict empirical means, which have the advantage of being easy to agree on, or by some more comprehensive scheme of criticism) of scientific hypotheses is quite crucial to any methodology that practises a policy of open admission to the domain of science. For unfalsifiable hypotheses, if appointed, would effectively have security of tenure; and such security is, to say the least, undesirable if what we are seeking is the truth. How could we, even in principle, end up with a science full of truths if there are false but unfalsifiable hypotheses permantly dug into the woodwork?[16] Thus the falsifiability, even the high falsifiability, of scientific hypotheses, is a crucial factor, and is very far from being a property that can be casually dispensed with. Of course all falsifiable hypotheses have amongst their consequences a host of unfalsifiable sentences, which enter science as it were on the coat-tails of their parents (this seems to have been overlooked by Good).[17] But these unfalsifiable consequences – to the extent that that is all that they are – cannot be regarded as scientific in their own right, but only by courtesy. If their parents have to be rejected from the realm of scientific knowledge, they will be rejected too.

---

[16] It might be thought that there do exist means by which some unfalsifiable hypotheses, for example unrestricted existential statements like 'Seaserpents exist', can be expelled from science: such a hypothesis is to be expelled if it contradicts an unfalsified hypothesis that is also scientific. The trouble with this suggestion is that it makes the fate of a theory depend less on what the world is like than on which hypotheses about it happen to be put forward. There need be no harm, to be sure, in using unfalsified hypotheses in order to eliminate conjectures with which they conflict. We do this whenever we make a singular prediction (though in such a case we eventually have a check on whether we have properly eliminated alternative predictions; that is, the eliminated conjectures are themselves falsifiable). More importantly, we may have to do it when we make use of auxiliary hypotheses in the evaluation of some sophisticated empirical test. But in these cases we have a pretty good idea in advance of what sort of unfalsified (auxiliary) hypotheses we intend to summon to our aid – we do not (anyway we should not) propose conjectures whose claim to falsifiability depends on entirely unspecified auxiliary theories. Indeed, the rule that we should never propose a conjecture whose disposal we cannot contemplate is not one that can be lightly discarded; not, anyway, as long as we continue to be interested in what is true. A conjecture is a way of going into debt; and it is unwise, to say the least, to take out a loan that one has no prospect at all of ever being able to repay.

For some comments on the role of existential statements in science the reader may care to consult Popper's 'Replies to My Critics', in P. A. Schilpp (ed.), *The Philosophy of Karl Popper*, pp. 1038 f.

[17] I. J. Good, 'Explicativity, Corroboration, and the Relative Odds of Hypotheses', *Synthese* 30 (1975), p. 66.

So much for theoretical concerns. We turn now to the matter of practice. It has often been maintained that, however defensible Popper's deductive theory of testing may be in the realm of theories, in matters of practice and of practical action a principle of induction becomes essential. Popper's advice on this matter has been given as follows.

From a rational point of view we should not 'rely' on any theory, for no theory has been shown to be true, or can be shown to be true. ... But we should *prefer* as a basis for action the best-tested theory ... [,] the one which, in the light of our *critical discussion*, appears to be the best so far .... [I]n spite of the 'rationality' of choosing the best-tested theory as a basis for action, the choice is *not* 'rational' in the sense that it is based upon *good reasons* for expecting that it will in practice be a successful choice: *there can be no good reasons* in this sense, and this is precisely Hume's result.[18]

In other words, in the lucky event that we have an unrefuted hypothesis relevant to our practical problem we shall normally plan our actions on the assumption that this hypothesis is true. Nothing, of course, justifies our choice of action, let alone our choice of theory. But we may be able to justify our preference for one action over another. As I say, this proposal of Popper's has been widely condemned as involving some covert principle of induction. In section 6 below I shall argue that it involves nothing of the kind.

In sum, Popper offers us the following picture of science. Science is a system of hypotheses, usually universal hypotheses, proposed and incorporated into science before there is any evidence in their favour. The main critical activity of the scientific community consists of attempts to expel these hypotheses, by showing that they conflict with relatively uncontroversial test statements, or, if you like, data. If a hypothesis passes all the tests to which it is subjected then it stays where it is; unless, that is, there is proposed some more informative, more falsifiable, hypothesis that performs at least as well with respect to the experimental tests. In this event the earlier hypothesis may no longer be retained within science, despite its being well supported by the empirical evidence; though it may of course reappear as a consequence of the hypothesis that supersedes it. In other words, good empirical support (in the sense of inductivist theories of the growth of knowledge) is neither necessary nor sufficient for retention within the body of science. Inductive support has very little to do with what we conjecture to be true.

[18] *Objective Knowledge*, pp. 21 f.

5.

The objections to falsificationism that are to be considered can be loosely collected into six categories.[19]

(i) First are those objections that assume that all our knowledge of the world must either be direct (observational) or inferred; more particularly, if we know anything of the unobserved, then what we know must have been obtained by means of some process of inference. Salmon, for example, writes:

> If science is to amount to more than a mere collection of statements describing our observations and various reformulations thereof, it must embody some other methods besides observation and deduction. Popper has supplied the additional factor: *corroboration*. . . .
>
> Corroboration is, I think, a nondemonstrative kind of inference. It is a way for providing for the acceptance of hypotheses even though the content of these hypotheses goes far beyond that of basic statements. *Modus tollens* without corroboration is empty; *modus tollens* with corroboration is induction.[20]

---

[19] By no means all criticisms of falsificationism can be mentioned, even obliquely, here. Amongst those that I cannot really discuss are those that are not really discussable – criticisms that do little more than deny categorically things that Popper has asserted. One such is Giere's remark (R. N. Giere, 'Popper and the Non-Bayesian Tradition: Comments on Richard Jeffrey', *Synthese* 30 (1975), p. 127) about 'the Popperian idea that only refutation is possible – positive support does not exist' that 'strict adherence to this Popperian dogma is simply perverse'. Giere makes no mention of the fact that the passing of a test always leaves a hypothesis where it was, though the failing of a test may well cause it to be removed. His dogmatic accusation of dogmatism, on an issue where many arguments have been given, is the more serious in that, a few pages earlier, he had disdainfully remarked that (p. 119) 'I found that many of Popper's views harmonized well with my previous scientific experience. . . . I soon found, however, that the *arguments* Popper offered for those intuitively appealing views did not measure up to my newly acquired philosophical standards.' It is one of the cornerstones of Popper's philosophy that arguments are offered against hypotheses, not for them. It looks as though Giere regards this critical attitude as a form of dogmatism.

There are indeed many other comments in Giere's paper with which I might take issue. One in particular is his endorsement of 'Jeffrey's comments on Popper's broad-brushed style and minimal success in employing Carnap's formal apparatus' (p. 122). I think that it should be pointed out that Popper's own achievements in the formal theory of probability are far from negligible. It is good to see that his beautiful axiomatizations of the calculus of probability (see for example his *L. Sci. Disc.*, appendices *iv, *v) have recently begun to attract serious attention (e.g., R. Stalnaker, 'Probability and Conditionals', *Phil. of Sci.* 37 (1970), pp. 64–80; W. L. Harper, 'Rational Belief Change, Popper Functions and Counterfactuals', *Synthese* 30 (1975), pp. 221–62; and H. H. Field, 'Logic, Meaning and Conceptual Role', *J. Phil.* 74 (1977), pp. 379–409). The depicting of Popper as a philosopher unable to cope with technicalities is one that must be firmly resisted. And in as much need of resistance is the widespread untruth that Popper's technical criticisms of Carnap were ineffective.

[20] Op. cit., pp. 26–8.

Salmon repeats this criticism in a recent paper.[21] Similar objections have been made by Good[22] and O'Hear.[23]

(ii) The second species of objection is concerned with the repetition and the repeatability of tests. A classic objection in this genre is that of Warnock.[24] Here, however, I quote Hesse:

> Objections can be made to Popper's view on the grounds that it is impossible even to state it without making some inductive assumptions. For example, it is not clear that the notion of a 'severe test' is free of such assumptions. Does this mean 'tests of the same kind that have toppled many generalizations in the past', which are therefore likely to find out the weak spots of this generalization in the future? Or does it mean 'tests which we should expect on the basis of past experience to refute this particular generalization'? In either case there is certainly an appeal to induction. Again, one past falsification of a generalization does not imply that the generalization is false in *future* instances. To assume that it will be falsified in similar circumstances is to make an inductive assumption, and without this assumption there is no reason why we should not continue to rely upon all falsified generalizations.[25]

Very much the same point is also made by Levison.[26]

(iii) The third variety of objection is also concerned with the repeatability of tests, but it focuses specifically on their severity. As stressed above, Popper requires that our proposed hypotheses be subjected to the most strenuous tests that we can devise, in the hope that any hypothesis that is false will be falsified. Suppose that H is the hypothesis that we are testing. Then any test can be regarded as an adjudication among the elements of a class of possible results. Let B be our background knowledge. Then a test is severe if for one of its possible results E the probability $p(E, HB)$ is high while the probability $p(E, B)$ is low. More precisely, a test is the more severe the higher is $p(E, HB)$ and the lower is $p(E, B)$ for some possible result E. The most severe sort of test is therefore one for which $p(E, HB) = 1$ and $p(E, B) = 0$, which will be obtained in particular if the hypothesis H contradicts background knowledge B and the

---

[21] W. C. Salmon, 'Unfinished Business: The Problem of Induction', *Philosophical Studies* 33 (1978), pp. 11 f.

[22] Op. cit., p. 61.

[23] A. O'Hear, 'Rationality of Action and Theory-Testing in Popper', *Mind* 84 (1975), p. 273.

[24] G. J. Warnock, Review of K. R. Popper, *L. Sci. Disc.*, *Mind* 69 (1960), pp. 99–101.

[25] M. B. Hesse, *The Structure of Scientific Inference* (1974), p. 95.

[26] A. Levison, 'Popper, Hume, and the Traditional Problem of Induction', in P. A. Schilpp (ed.), *The Philosophy of Karl Popper*, pp. 328–30.

prediction *E* is a consequence of *H*. Popper has written:

A serious empirical test always consists in the attempt to find a refutation, a counter example. In the search for a counter example, we have to use our background knowledge; for we always try to refute first the *most risky* predictions . . . . Now if a theory stands up to many such tests, then, owing to the incorporation of the results of our tests into background knowledge, there may be, after a time, no places left where (in the light of our new background knowledge) counter examples can . . . be expected to occur. But this means that the degree of severity of our test declines. This is also the reason why an often repeated test will no longer be considered as significant or severe: there is something like a law of diminishing returns from repeated tests . . . [27]

Contesting this claim, O'Hear writes:

both the use made here of background knowledge and the consequent explanation of the law of diminishing returns from repeated tests seem to be in conflict with Popper's characteristic rejection in *L.Sc.D.* (pp. 367–369) of any schema of the form

$$p(a_n, a_1 a_2 \ldots a_{n-1}) > p(a_n)$$

where *p* is the measure of probability, a_1 is a singular statement referring to an event and $p(a_j, a_i)$ is the probability of a_j given a_i . . . . Without assuming some version of the principle of induction, every test of a given type should be considered as severe as every other test of that type.[28]

Pretty well the same objection has been voiced by Musgrave.[29] Musgrave's criticism is endorsed by Grünbaum,[30] who does not accept, however, Musgrave's solution. I shall return to this in the next section, when I respond to this third variety of objection.

(iv) The fourth sort of objection that I have in mind is that which claims that Popper's theory, no less than any inductivist theory, is troubled by problems raised by Goodman's paradoxes. Vincent, for example, summarizing a discussion of Popper's theory of how one sentence can corroborate (or confirm) another in the presence of a third, writes:

From the foregoing we may conclude that according to Popper's [theory] . . . '*a* is green' confirms 'All emeralds are grue' relative to '*a* is an emerald and *a* is examined before time *t*'. . . . Indeed, we may conclude that '*a* is green' confirms the conjunction of 'All emeralds examined before time *t* are

---

[27] *Conjectures and Refutations* (1963), p. 240; cf. pp. 390f.

[28] Op. cit., p. 275.

[29] A. Musgrave, 'Popper and "Diminishing Returns from Repeated Tests"', *Austr. J. Phil.* 53 (1975), pp. 250 f.

[30] A. Grünbaum, 'Is Falsifiability the Touchstone of Scientific Rationality? Karl Popper versus Inductivism', in R. S. Cohen, P. K. Feyerabend, and M. W. Wartofsky (eds.), *Essays in Memory of Imre Lakatos* (1976), pp. 236 f.

green' and any other logically contingent hypothesis relative to '*a* is an emerald and *a* is examined bofore time *t*'. I take it as obvious that these results are unsatisfactory.[31]

In other words, according to Popper's theory many conflicting hypotheses may be equally well confirmed by exactly the same evidence. Kyburg delivers the judgement that 'R. H. Vincent has shown that Popper's criteria, like everyone else's, founder on Goodman's reef'[32]. No doubt others (perhaps including Levison)[33] would agree.

This criticism, of course, contains no direct accusation that Popper's theory of testing and corroboration is inductivist despite its intentions. But the accusation is there in the form: there can be no solution to Goodman's paradox that does not distinguish between soundly and unsoundly made predictions – that is, sound and unsound inductive inferences.

(v) The fifth context in which critics have been prone to see the need for a principle of induction has already been mentioned: the context of practice. We read, for instance, in Niiniluoto and Tuomela's book:

Popper's answer to Salmon and Lakatos can thus be taken to show that his theory of corroboration has nothing to do with induction. At the same time it shows how implausible a full-blown deductivist₂ theory of scientific inquiry is. Even if cognitivism were rejected, reliance on science in technological applications is still an every-day fact. Of course, this reliance is not 'absolute' in any sense; still, it may have good reasons. ... Popper's discussion of practical action is considerably oversimplified. At the same time, it makes a complete mystery of the trust and deliberate reliance on science.

The fundamental problem which Popper fails to answer is this: why is it *rational* to base one's practical decision upon the best-tested theory, if there are *no good reasons* for expecting that it will be a successful choice?[34]

This criticism is as old as falsificationism itself, and has been voiced recently by Lakatos,[35] Howson and Worrall,[36] Jeffrey,[37] Salmon,[38]

[31] R. H. Vincent, 'Popper on Qualitative Confirmation and Disconfirmation', *Austr. J. Phil.*, 40 (1962), pp. 162 f.

[32] H. E. Kyburg, *Probability and Inductive Logic* (1970), p. 158.

[33] Op. cit., pp. 330 f.

[34] I. Niiniluoto and R. Tuomela, *Theoretical Concepts and Hypothetico-Inductive Inference* (1973), p. 203.

[35] I. Lakatos, 'Changes in the Problem of Inductive Logic', in I. Lakatos (ed.), *The Problem of Inductive Logic*, pp. 390–405.

[36] C. Howson and J. Worrall, 'The Contemporary State of Philosophy of Science in Britain', *Zeitschrift für allgemeine Wissenschaftstheorie* 5 (1974), p. 368.

[37] R. C. Jeffrey, 'Probability and Falsification: Critique of the Popper Program', *Synthese* 30 (1975), pp. 111 f.

[38] Op. cit., pp. 12 f.

and Cohen.[39] I have argued elsewhere[40] that the question that Niiniluoto and Tuomela pose is one that remains without an answer in most modern theories of induction – for example, in the variety of Bayesianism espoused by Jeffrey. In the next section I shall show how naturally and easily it is answered by Popper's theory.

(vi) The final type of criticism that I wish to consider is one that was resorted to by Lakatos[41] in an attempt to bolster his doctrine that in practical affairs Popper's theory was irremediably ridden with inductivism. The criticism was that, even in purely theoretical concerns, Popper's methodology was in need of some principle of induction. He wrote that Popper's theory of verisimilitude makes it

possible, for the first time, to define *progress* even for a sequence of false theories. . . . But this is not enough: we have to *recognise* progress. This can be done easily by an inductive principle . . . which reinterprets the rules of the 'scientific game' as a – conjectural – theory about the *signs* of the *growth of knowledge*, that is, about the signs of *growing verisimilitude of our scientific theories* . . . Popper's methodological appraisals are interesting primarily because of the hidden *inductive assumption* that, if one lives up to them, one has a better chance to get nearer to the Truth than otherwise . . . [But] he still will not say unequivocally that the positive appraisals in his scientific game may be seen as a – conjectural – sign of the growth of conjectural knowledge; that corroboration is a *synthetic* – albeit conjectural – measure of verisimilitude.[42]

In an accompanying footnote Lakatos wrote of this 'inductive principle' that he prefers it

in the form that – roughly speaking – the methodology of scientific research programmes is better suited for approximating the truth in our actual universe than any other methodology.[43]

He concedes that such an 'inductive principle' is 'sadly irrefutable'. It is comforting, therefore, that neither it, nor anything resembling it, is needed in the methodology of science.

This concludes my exposition of six ways in which Popper's methodological proposals have been thought to be tinged with inductivism. I now proceed to show that none of these accusations holds any water at all.

---

[39] L. J. Cohen, 'Is Popper more Relevant than Bacon for Scientists?' *The Times Higher Education Supplement*, 348 (14 July 1978), p. 11.

[40] D. W. Miller, 'Making Sense of Method: Comments on Richard Jeffrey', *Synthese* 30 (1975), p. 146.

[41] I. Lakatos, 'Popper on Demarcation and Induction', in P. A. Schilpp (ed.), *The Philosophy of Karl Popper*, pp. 241–73.

[42] Op. cit., pp. 254, 256.

[43] Op. cit., p. 269.

6.

(i) The first objection, to which Salmon, Good, and O'Hear were instanced as parties, was that without some process of inductive inference we can have no knowledge of the world beyond the content of our own observations. To this the falsificationist reply is extremely simple: most of our knowledge, particularly our theoretical knowledge, is obtained neither by observation nor by inference, but by guesswork. One may of course call guesswork a process of inference, if one likes, but one must remember that such inferences are not performed according to any rules, nor are they in need of any sort of justification. One may even refer to guesses of universal form as inductive inferences, despite their not being at all based on evidence – and indeed in most cases actually preceding any evidence that would normally be thought to support them. But it is hard to see any point in adopting this way of speaking. Whatever one calls them, Hume's problem simply does not arise for guesses. Nor is there anywhere else that it could arise in the lifetime of a scientific theory, since once guessed a theory remains in the body of science until it is expelled. And the logic of expulsion, of falsification, and of supersession, is entirely deductive. No inductive inference is needed to put a hypothesis into science; no inductive inference is needed to keep it there; and no inductive inference is needed to prise it out.

When Salmon says that 'Popper's deductivism remains pure; science has no predictive import',[44] his premiss is true but his conclusion false. As Popper has repeatedly stressed,[45] science does have predictive import: the conjectures of which science is composed are universal, and are highly informative with regard to both past and future. But this does not mean that they are inferred inductively (or in any other way). The fact is that the rule of inference that Salmon uses here, 'if [science] has predictive import, it must incorporate some form of ampliative inference',[46] is an ampliative one, and so invalid. Of course, the predictions that science makes are not justified, or warranted, or reliable predictions. But as Hume clearly showed, this they cannot be. I cannot understand what is supposed to be rational about pretending that some ampliative rule of inference or another leads to reliable predictions, when there is an incontestable (and largely uncontested) argument to show that it does nothing of the kind.

(ii) The second objection concerned the repeatability of tests. It

[44] Op. cit., p. 12.
[45] In particular in 'Replies to My Critics', in P. A. Schilpp (ed.), *The Philosophy of Karl Popper*, section 15.
[46] Op. cit., p. 13.

should be said at once that, on its own, the fact that a theory has
passed a test provides no evidence at all that it will pass a repetition
of that test. Nor does its failing a test give reasons for believing that
it will fail a repetition of that test. But it does give reasons for
believing that the theory is false.[47]

In reply to Hesse we might note that it is background knowledge,
rather than past experience, to which all assessments of the severity
of tests are relativized. But background knowledge itself is by no
means restricted to hypotheses and theories that have passed anything resembling a severe test. It is quite likely to include all variety
of unexamined prejudice and presumption; indeed, it often happens
that it is through a severe test of a theory that we discover how
inadequate parts of our background knowledge are. For example, it
was presumably part of background knowledge at the time of the
Michelson–Morley experiment that the length of a body in motion
is independent of its velocity; this assumption, previously un-
criticized, and surely never obtained by any sort of inductive inference, was eventually recognized to be false. Thus no appeal to
induction is needed to explain what a severe test amounts to. For
severity is not relative to some privileged sector of our knowledge,
the well-corroborated part say, but to all our knowledge at the time
of testing except the theory under test and some of the known
difficulties that it set out solve. I can see that for an inductivist, who
hopes to learn something positive from a severe test that the theory
fails to fail, this is an unsatisfactory state of affairs; for severity
should surely not depend on the whims of some arbitrary accumulation of background knowledge. But for a falsificationist, who puts no
absolute value on the passing of a severe test (severity concerns
methodology, not epistemology), nothing is here amiss. There is an
absolute value, of course, in the failing of a test; but if a test is
failed, it does not matter at all whether it is severe.

The passage quoted above from Hesse concludes with her remark
that without 'an inductive assumption . . . there is no reason why we
should not continue to rely upon all falsified generalizations'. The
answer to this is that there is a very good reason for not relying on
any generalization at all – namely that we have no good reason for
supposing it to be true. The additional reason that we do not rely on
a falsified generalization is that we know it not to be true. Of course,
one may if one wishes suppose that a generalization holds in just
those instances in which it has not been shown to fail. Hesse doesn't
explain what problem such a hypothesis might solve. Nor does she

---

[47] See also Popper, 'Replies to My Critics', p. 1043.

explain how such a hypothesis might be falsified. In fact, similar issues arise with regard to Goodman's paradoxes, which will be dealt with in (iv) below.

(iii) To the third objection, raised by O'Hear and Musgrave, and repeated by Grünbaum, that a non-inductivist approach to science fails to explain 'the law of diminishing returns from repeated tests', my reply is that the point of repeating a test in fact is to check that one has got hold of a repeatable effect. This is obvious when we consider tests that actually refute the hypothesis under investigation. All we need to know, once we have refuted the hypothesis, is that the effect recorded was not a freak; provided that is so, nothing is to be gained by repeating the test, for we already know that the hypothesis is false.[48] Exactly the same goes for a test that the hypothesis passes – we do not learn more from the repetition of the test result than that the test can be repeated with the same result.

Quite often, of course, we may discover that the test cannot be repeated with the same result – that the first effect discovered was indeed occult. Rather more seldom we may be led to conclude that there is no repeatable effect, even a statistical one, to be had. That this rarely happens, anyway in the natural sciences, is of course an important factor in the success of the natural sciences. That is to say, the truth of 'Most apparatus eventually behaves uniformly' (if it is true) is an important ingredient in the success of science. But nothing justifies, or could justify, our assuming this sentence to be true; like every other sentence, it is tolerated largely because no sufficiently good case has yet been made out against it.

Musgrave's own response to his objection is that a hypothesis only becomes refuted (or corroborated) when, as he puts it,[49] 'sufficiently many' repetitions of the test have been performed for 'warranted acceptance of a falsifying hypothesis … or of a corroborating hypothesis'. But as Howson remarks, 'in declaring the acceptance of some experimental generalization, as opposed to its negation, sometimes rational after "sufficiently many trials", Musgrave is proposing a thesis inductivist in everything but name.'[50] Musgrave's explanation has also been attacked by Grünbaum, who objects that it 'leaves unsolved for Popper the problem of "*how* often is sufficiently often" when repeated performances of a corroborating test are held

---

[48] K. R. Popper, *Logik der Forschung*, 1934, trans. as *L. Sci. Disc.* (1959), section 22.

[49] Op. cit., p. 251.

[50] C. Howson, 'Why Once May be Enough', *Austr. J. Phil.* 55 (1977), p. 145.

to be adequate for incorporating the *universal* hypothesis ... into the background knowledge'.[51] But the point is that the claim that we are dealing with some repeatable effect or other is normally already a component of background knowledge – otherwise the test would hardly be worth performing even once. And we repeat a few times any test that we have performed, not further to test the substantive hypothesis, but simply to check that the effect that we have recorded is indeed one that can be repeated. Thus no question arises of the acceptance of a universal hypothesis in the wake of a number of repetitions of the same test. What might happen is that we have to reject the claim that the result of the first test could be repeated. But otherwise nothing happens, and since nothing happens it cannot be important exactly when we stop testing. Anyone who objects is perfectly free to carry on with the tests. They will gradually decline in severity, one suspects, as they gradually cease to test any hypothesis of any significance. But this is hardly a reason for supposing that some inductive argument is involved.

(iv) We turn now to problems arising out of Goodman's paradoxes. My response here is an utterly trivial one: there cannot be any empirical reason for expressing a preference between two hypotheses that are empirically indistinguishable. The fact that the hypotheses may seem to be empirically well-supported is irrelevant. After all, many metaphysical hypotheses are thought by some to be empirically well-supported.

Let us take the predicate 'grue' to mean 'green if and only if first examined before the year 2001'. It is claimed that the sentence 'All emeralds are grue' will pass all tests conducted before the year 2001 that are passed by the sentence 'All emeralds are green': and so they will be equally corroborated by the evidence.[52] But how, then,

[51] Op. cit., p. 237.

[52] Actually I think that this claim is false, since a test for grueness involves not only a colour test but also a date test. The mere fact that a test for colour takes place before the year 2001 contributes nothing towards its being a test for grueness. For a similar reason I reject a similar contention of A. N. Maxwell, 'The Rationality of Scientific Discovery. Part I: The Traditional Rationality Problem', *Phil. of Sci.* 41 (1974), p. 128, that given a well-tested theory *T*, 'we can very easily invent an unlimited number of aberrant versions of *T*, each of which will differ in predictive content from *T*, and yet will be ... just as well corroborated as *T* itself is'. For the examples of tests that Maxwell sketches, though tests for *T*, are incapable of falsifying its supposed rivals. The rivals to *T* must be specified before the tests are conducted if these tests are to test these rivals. But in this case we shall not regard either *T* or its rivals as well tested if no crucial experiment has been attempted. It seems to me that, if we know that at least one of two theories is false, we are not pursuing the truth very vigorously if we neglect to perform a crucial test between them. Thus Maxwell's criticism, though no doubt effective against some inductivist theories of scientific knowledge, is irrelevant to falsificationism.

can we have any reason for preferring one of these hypotheses to the other? And if we do not have any reason for preferring one of them to the other, which prediction concerning the first emerald examined after 31 December 2000 shall we endorse: that it is green or that it is grue? For it seems that these predictions contradict each other.

After all, although 'All emeralds are green' may have been quite well tested, it certainly has not been tested well enough for us to justify a strictly empirical preference (that is, one that does not appeal to other, perhaps more comprehensive, hypotheses) for it over 'All emeralds are grue'. If we are not at present interested in justifying any such preference, then no harm is done. Science can quite well accommodate both hypotheses until the year 2001, at which time a simple crucial test will become available. But if we do wish to justify a preference like this in advance, then we must make it possible for ourselves to do so. We must not admit into science two empirically indistinguishable hypotheses if we are not prepared to countenance non-empirical ways of effecting a distinction between them; likewise, we must not admit hypotheses that are empirically indistinguishable until a certain date, unless we are prepared to put off until that date the task of distinguishing between them, or are prepared to accept methods that are not strictly empirical. These restrictions are really nothing but a refinement of the principle of demarcation: if decisions have to be empirical then we should not allow disputes on which no empirical decision is possible. We may not have any strictly empirical reason for preferring one of 'All emeralds are green' and 'All emeralds are grue'. Equally, there is no strictly empirical argument against preferring the one that actually we do prefer. But it is no part of falsification-ism to deny that there are questions that cannot be settled by strictly empirical methods. Indeed, there are questions that cannot be settled by any empirical method at all.

Goodman's paradox is seen to be a difficulty, I believe, because it is mistakenly thought that it is empirical support that makes a hypothesis eligible for admission into the body of science. But as I said above, empirical support is neither necessary nor sufficient for this. Indeed, the sentence 'All emeralds are first examined before the year 2001', or even the sentence 'All emeralds are examined', might be thought to be well supported.[53] In accordance with the empirical facts, maybe; but a genuine component of empirical

---

[53] Cf. K. R. Popper, *Conjectures and Refutations*, p. 284.

science, no. No prediction based on 'All emeralds are first examined before the year 2001' can claim to have any serious empirical backing.

(v) This brings us immediately to the problem of the practical application of our scientific theories, and the extent to which this can be sustained without recourse to a principle of induction. My discussion here does not deviate very significantly from that of Popper,[54] except that I tend to emphasize our practical proposals where Popper emphasizes the theories on which they are based.

Briefly the point is this. We make our practical decisions in the light of our best-tested theories not because we have some positive reasons for supposing these theories to be true – and therefore some positive reasons for supposing predictions made from them to be true – but simply because these decisions (and the proposals from which they emanate) stand up best to criticism and rational comparison with other proposals.[55] It is the rational criticism of proposals, not their rational justification (or even the rational justification of the preference for one proposal over another) that is at issue. Usually there are many proposals, and accordingly many possible decisions, and several of them are equally rational. To act rationally, therefore, all we need to do is to 'avoid the irrational courses of action. Of the others, any one will do, from the rational point of view.

Why do proposals made in accordance with our best-tested theories stand up best to criticism? And anyway, what sort of criticism are we going to allow? It is obvious, I think, that the fewer lines of criticism we are prepared to tolerate, the more proposals will survive the ordeal, and the more therefore will count as rational. If, for example, we are squeamish about applying our theoretical knowledge critically, then very many pretty clearly dotty proposals will get through. (If we are sufficiently finicky, and insist on the eternal possibility that nature will entirely change its course just before our action is performed, then no proposal whatever will get rejected.) But what is important is the survival of those proposals that we would normally count as sensible ones. What is more, these proposals will still count as rational when we wield our theoretical knowledge in a highly critical way. But the same would not be true if we were to try to use falsified and superseded theories as ammunition; for these falsified and superseded theories are

[54] In 'Replies to My Critics', section 14.
[55] For the criticizability of proposals, if not of decisions, see paragraph (3) of note 5 to chapter 5 of K. R. Popper, *The Open Society and its Enemies*, 5th ed., (1966).

themselves incapable of standing up to any sort of counter-criticism. And after all the criticism is over, after all the returns are in, it will be found that many proposals, including those that everyone agrees to be rational, those that appear to be based on the assumption that our best-tested theories are true, will still be there. Our decisions are not instructed by science, but selected. But it must be admitted that in some cases the simulation of instruction is extremely good.

Two points are crucial to this explanation of the rationality of our scientifically informed decisions. One is that a rational decision is one based on a proposal that survives criticism, not one that we have reason to suppose to be successful. The other is that the best we can do in the way of criticism is to deploy all the theoretical knowledge that we have at our disposal. For criticism has to make use of what we know now, not of what we shall know when our decision is implemented. Of course, we could do worse than this, and criticize more mildly. But that cannot undermine the rationality of our best decisions.

It seems to me that this provides a complete answer to the criticisms, cited on p. 120 f. above, of Lakatos, Jeffrey, Niiniluoto and Tuomela, Salmon, and Cohen.

(vi) To the last line of criticism I shall be extremely brief, as I have said it before:

> In fact, of course, the epistemological significance of falsificationism, in its simplest form, depends not on an 'inductive principle' but on logic. Systematic elimination of false theories prevents us from becoming entrenched in acknowledged falsity, and to that extent assists us in the search for what is true. Whether Popper's methodology (or any other) can do more, and allow us to discriminate among the false theories, is a different matter ... But even if such discrimination is possible, no 'inductive principle', will ever have any role to play.
>
> The advice not to go down obvious *culs-de-sac* cannot be expected to guide us successfully (or even moderately successfully) through a maze of infinite complexity. But it is nevertheless significant and valuable advice. I am at a loss to see how it can be thought otherwise.[56]

I am still at a loss to see how it can be thought otherwise.

7.

Rather little of what I have said in this paper has been novel. Much, indeed, was already said in Popper's *Logik der Forschung* (1934), and almost all the paper was foreshadowed there. Why, then, do

[56] D. W. Miller, 'The Accuracy of Predictions: A Reply', *Synthese* 30 (1975), p. 211.

these criticisms that falsificationism is ridden with inductive elements recur, time and time again? The answer, I think, has to be in the new theory of scientific knowledge that is an essential concomitant of falsificationist methodology. I mean the theory that, in the normal run of things, scientific knowledge is everything that a classical epistemologist says it ought not to be: it is unjustified, untrue, unbelief. From this point of view a logic of induction would not be wanted, even if it were available – for no effort is made, or should be made, to justify even the tiniest fragment of our knowledge. This new epistemology is, obviously, one that philosophers find so hard to digest that most would rather commit themselves to the absurdities of inductive logic and the search for justification. But, indeed, it need never be asked again whether science can do without induction. It does.

§8. KEITH LEHRER

Truth, Evidence, and Error: Comments on Miller

David Miller offers a clear and bold defence of the anti-inductivism espoused by Popper. According to Miller, the simplest version of Popperian doctrine is that the aim of science is simply truth – it is on truth alone that the methods of science should be concentrated. My criticism of Miller is that the theory he articulates contains internal conflict and is an inadequate account of science. The conflict is between three principles. The first, which I will call *anti-refusalism*, is that we should not refuse to admit or retain any true hypothesis as a candidate for testing. The second, *falsificationism*, is that we should eliminate any candidate that has been falsified by empirical test. The third, *fallibilism*, is that reports of empirical tests are not certain. The external inadequacy results from the fact that hypotheses that are pairwise inconsistent, especially all hypotheses about the future, should, on his theory, be admitted and retained in science until falsified. Such inconsistent hypotheses cannot be employed for scientific prediction and decision-making. Moreover, it will prove impossible to decide between such hypotheses on the basis of how well-tested they are because of the Goodman paradox. Hence the theory Miller offers requires supplementation, and the supplement required appears to be induction.

Science and Truth

It will be most effective to begin with a quotation from Miller concerning science and the quest for truth.

For the aim of science is simply truth; not some epistemically distinguished variety of truth, but truth alone. Or, more enterprisingly, more truth, as much truth as can be achieved. According to the simplest version of the falsificationist doctrine, a doctrine that is almost entirely due to Popper, that is all that we should try to achieve in science; it is on truth alone that the methods of science should be concentrated.

This quotation commits Miller to the doctrine of anti-refusalism, a doctrine which he may not gladly embrace. Suppose that truth and only truth, the more truth the better, is our aim in science, as Miller affirms. According to Miller, *empirically testable* statements are the concern of science, and I shall use the term 'hypothesis' to refer to such statements and only such. What hypotheses should we then admit and retain in science as candidates for testing? From the supposition about truth being the only aim of science, Miller is committed to answer that we should never refuse to admit or retain any *true* hypothesis as a candidate for testing. The interest in truth and only truth would not be well served by refusing to admit or retain a hypothesis that is true. Thus, Miller is committed to anti-refusalism, to wit, to the doctrine that one should never refuse to admit or retain any true hypothesis as a candidate for testing in science.

The doctrine of anti-refusalism leads to conflict when combined with other doctrines within Miller's theory. The most famous of such doctrines is falsificationism, the doctrine that we should eliminate from science any hypothesis as a candidate for testing that has been falsified by empirical test. The doctrine of falsificationism does not by itself conflict with anti-refusalism. The elimination of false hypotheses does not conflict with the admission or retention of true ones. However, there is a third doctrine, fallibilism, which creates discord within the system. This doctrine says that reports of empirical tests, like other empirical statements, are not certain.

The Basic Conflict

The conflict between anti-refusalism, falsificationism, and fallibilism results as follows. If our aim is truth and only truth, we must not refuse to admit or retain any hypothesis as a candidate for testing that is, in fact, true. If we could be certain that all hypotheses that are falsified by empirical test are, in fact, false, we would lose nothing in the quest for truth by refusing to retain falsified hypotheses in science. But, since it is not certain that the results of empirical tests are true, it is also not certain that the hypotheses they falsify are, in fact, false. Indeed, the term 'falsify' is somewhat misleading. Suppose that we have some reports of empirical tests R and that these results are logically inconsistent with a hypothesis H, that is, the denial of R is deducible from H. Then Popper and Miller say that H has been *falsified* by R. Since R is not certain, however, it by no means follows from the fact that H is inconsistent with R that, therefore, H is false. For R might be false and, consequently, H might be true. So, given the assumption of fallibilism, falsificationism directs us to eliminate hypotheses that might be true. This directive then conflicts with aiming at truth and only at truth, the commitment of anti-refusalism.

The crux of the preceding argument is that when we eliminate hypotheses that have been falsified by empirical test we run the risk of eliminating true hypotheses from science by so doing. Given fallibilism, it is by no means certain that hypotheses that have been falsified by empirical tests are, in fact, false. If our only aim in science is truth, the more truth the better, how can we eliminate hypotheses as candidates for testing which might be true? The answer is that we cannot. When we eliminate a hypothesis that is inconsistent with the reports of empirical test we risk eliminating a truth. For the reports might be false and the hypothesis true. How are we to defend taking this risk? If our aim is truth, only truth, and the more truth the better, there is no defence. Miller says that the reports of tests may be noncontroversial. But that does not resolve the conflict within his account. For the aim of science is, according to him, truth, not agreement. So he cannot defend the policy of risking the elimination of a true hypothesis from science by appeal to agreement concerning the results of empirical test unless he equates truth with agreement. Miller is not, I believe, inclined to do so.

Evidence and the Risk of Error

Often it is worth the risk of eliminating hypotheses from science when they are inconsistent with the reports of empirical tests. The reason for this, however, is that we are often interested in something other than admitting and retaining what is true in science. We are also interested in avoiding the retention of error. When we eliminate a hypothesis on the basis of test reports, we take some risk that the reports might be false and the hypothesis true, but we think the risk sufficiently small, and our interest in eliminating an erroneous hypothesis from science makes the risk worth taking. If, however, our only aim is truth, the more truth the better, then this policy would be indefensible. It is indefensible to risk losing a truth if your only aim is truth.

Thus, to avoid conflict, Miller would need to modify his account of the aim of science to include the objective of avoiding the retention of error as well as the objective of admitting and retaining truth. The elimination of hypotheses that are inconsistent with test reports could then be defended on the grounds that the risk of eliminating a true hypothesis is small and counterbalanced by avoiding the high risk of retaining a false hypothesis. We eliminate hypotheses that contradict the reports of tests in the interest of avoiding error in the hypotheses we retain as candidates for testing in science. This position may not be one that Miller would accept, but I do not discern any plausible alternative in his paper.

This objection becomes more telling once it is noticed that Miller's account allows for the admission and retention of hypotheses that are logically inconsistent with one another. If two hypotheses are inconsistent with each other and neither has been falsified by empirical test, then neither may be eliminated as candidates for empirical test. So there is no reasonable objection, on his account, to retaining two hypotheses, H and K, such that H is logically inconsistent with K. In that case, what objection is there to retaining a hypothesis H and a report O that is logically inconsistent with H? The mere logical inconsistency of one statement with another does not, on his theory, require that either be eliminated. Thus, it might be some feature of the reports of empirical tests other than contradicting a hypothesis that sustains the policy of eliminating the hypothesis from science. What sustains it is the conviction that the elimination is worth the risk.

The Problem of Evidence

The objection I am raising against Miller could be raised against a considerable variety of theories of inductive logic as well. It is customary to treat empirical reports as unproblematic and then proceed to construct and defend some theory of the admission or elimination of hypotheses in science on the basis of such reports. But such an approach is, I contend, epistemologically unsatisfactory. It reflects a completely artificial division of labour within philosophy between epistemology and philosophy of science. To take some empirical report as evidence in science is a critical decision, no matter how routine and non-controversial it may be. It is a decision made under risk of error. In this way, it does not differ from the decision to retain or eliminate a hypothesis in science for the purpose of testing. This too is a decision made under risk.

Our intellectual decisions may be divorced from practical concern. But once one understands that when one takes statements as evidence in science one confronts an intellectual decision, the Popperian argument against induction is undermined. For, as Isaac Levi argued convincingly, the decision to accept statements as evidence is a form of induction.[1] On this account of induction, a scientist is engaged in induction, though he may be quite unaware of it, when he accepts the reports of empirical test as evidence. Therefore, the elimination of hypotheses inconsistent with accepted test reports is indirectly based on induction. One might dispute about whether to call the decision to take some statement as evidence *induction*, but that would be a verbal dispute. The best account of such decision-making is one that directs us to maximize expected utility, perhaps of a rather intellectual variety. Miller may tell us that in making such decisions scientists ignore their expectations. I do not believe

[1] Isaac Levi, *Gambling with Truth* (1967).

that. Nor do I believe that they should. I find it extremely difficult to believe that he believes that they do or should.

Prediction and Decision

The foregoing remarks concern an internal conflict in the theory Miller advocates. One criticism of a theory is that there is conflict between principles of the theory. A second kind of criticism is that a theory is inadequate to the appropriate subject-matter. Miller's theory provides an inadequate account of scientific prediction and decision-making. I shall argue that this inadequacy could be readily rectified. The rectification leads, however, to a theory antithetical to the one Miller defends.

The problem of prediction and decision arises from the fact that they both concern the future and no hypotheses about the future have been empirically tested.[2] Scientific knowledge enables us to predict the future in some instances and to base our practical decisions on that knowledge. According to Miller, however, scientific knowledge includes all those hypotheses that have been admitted as candidates for testing and have not been falsified by empirical testing. Consider any two hypotheses about the outcome of some future event, for example, that E will occur and that E will not occur. Neither of these hypotheses has been falsified by empirical test. If both have been seriously proposed, then neither can be eliminated from science. This is a consequence of the passage quoted at the beginning of my remarks. If truth and only truth is the aim of science, then no statement about the future can be eliminated because any such statement might be true. The commitment to anti-refusalism disallows the elimination of any prediction about the future.

This illustrates that what Miller calls 'scientific knowledge' is nothing of the sort. The set of statements that are admitted and retained in science as candidates for empirical testing are not all part of scientific knowledge. This is no verbal quibble over the use of the word 'scientific knowledge'. What Miller calls 'scientific knowledge' is inadequate for any prediction of the future. We can, of course, deduce statements about the future from what Miller includes in scientific knowledge, but we can deduce the contradictory of every prediction from it as well.

Moreover, this problem is exacerbated when we consider using what he calls 'scientific knowledge' for the purposes of practical

[2] Cf. Wesley C. Salmon, *Foundations of Scientific Inference* (1966), pp. 21–7, 114–15, 117–20, 129, 131.

action. When we consider whether to adopt some course of action, we must consider the possible outcomes. Suppose we are deliberating about whether to do *A*. We wonder whether *C* will be the outcome. The statement that if we do *A*, then *C* will obtain has not been falsified by empirical test. Neither has the statement that if we do *A*, then *C* will not obtain. If it is *C* we desire to bring about, 'scientific knowledge' will offer us no guidance. For each course of action we contemplate, it will tell us that if we adopt that course of action, we will obtain *C*, but, unfortunately, it will also tell us that if we adopt it, we will not obtain *C*. Moreover, the same results would be obtained with respect to some alternative course of action, *B*. That is, we will be told that if we do *B*, then we will obtain *C*, and also that if we do *B*, then we will not obtain *C*. Neither of these conditionals can be eliminated. Thus, under Miller's account, science is of no use whatever when we are deciding whether or not to perform an action or whether to perform some alternative action instead. If all unfalsified hypotheses are retained in science so that we may aim at truth and only at truth, no hypotheses about the future can be eliminated, and the resulting body of science will be useless for prediction and practical action. Science is not useless for these purposes. So there is more to science than Miller allows.

Testable Hypotheses and Goodman Predicates

Miller has a reply to this line of criticism. He claims that we may *select* from among unfalsified hypotheses for some purposes, for example, to guide practical enquiry. His suggestion is that some among the unfalsified hypotheses are better-tested than others, and the better-tested hypotheses may be used to guide action. But the problem here is that Goodman's problem concerning odd predicates like 'grue' and 'bleen' may be used to show that for any hypothesis that could be used to make predictions about the future to guide our actions, we can construct an equally well-tested hypothesis, or at least a hypothesis that would be equally well-tested if we reflected upon the relation between the hypothesis and the results of testing other hypotheses.[3]

Suppose, for example, that the hypothesis 'for any *x* and any *t*, if *x* is *A* at *t*, then *x* is *B* at *t*' is a very well-tested hypothesis. It might appear that we could conclude that if at some future time *T* we were to perform an action yielding *A*, then *B* would obtain. If so, the selection of such a hypothesis to guide practical action would be

---

[3] Nelson Goodman, *Fact, Fiction, and Forecast* (1955).

useful. Notice, however, that we can define a predicate yielding an equally well-tested hypothesis which would make the prediction if we perform the action yielding A at T, then non-B would obtain. Let us say that x is B^* at time t if and only if, either t is prior to T and x is B at t, or t is not prior to T and x is non-B at t. Assuming that T is the future time in question, the hypothesis 'for any x and for any t, if x is A at t, then x is B^* at t' would be equally well-tested. From it we should infer that if we perform an action yielding A at T, then non-B would obtain. Now it might be tempting to reply that the B^* hypothesis has not been as well-tested at the original B hypothesis, but that is not so. The original B hypothesis will be tested as severely as possible before T by trying to produce a case of an A that is non-B, and the B^* hypothesis will be tested as severely as possible before T in exactly the same way. Moreover, as Goodman has noted, there is a definitional symmetry between the original predicates and such a defined predicate as 'B^*' with respect to temporal reference. Let us say that x is non-B^* at t if and only if, either t is prior to T and x is non-B at t, or t is not prior to T and x is B at t. Then we may define 'B' in terms of 'B^*' by saying that x is B at t if and only if, either t is prior to T and x is B^* at t, or t is not prior to T and x is non-B^* at t. Given this definition of 'B', it contains a reference to T. So, if we take B^* and non-B^* as primitive, then 'B' will be defined with respect to T. Hence, the reference to T in the definition of 'B^*' cannot be exploited to show that the B hypothesis is better tested than the B^* hypothesis. Therefore, any attempt to select a hypothesis for prediction or practical action on the grounds that it is better-tested than hypotheses that make contradictory predictions must fail. There is always an equally well-tested hypothesis that makes a contradictory prediction.

Miller has a reply to the Goodman problem, and if that reply is successful, then the preceding argument could be circumvented. His reply is that we must not admit empirically indistinguishable hypotheses into science unless we are either willing to distinguish between them by non-empirical means or wait until we can distinguish between them by such means. But this reply is useless if the foregoing argument is correct. Given any hypothesis from which we draw conclusions about the future, there will always be an empirically indistinguishable hypothesis, indistinguishable in terms of tests that have already been performed, that makes contradictory predictions about the future. So either we admit both the B and B^* hypotheses, in which case they will be useless for predicting whether

B will obtain at *T* if *A* does, or we admit neither, in which case they will be equally useless. And the same argument applies to any other hypothesis.

It remains open to Miller to allow that the admission of one hypothesis in science and the refusal to admit another is an arbitrary matter, the luck of the draw so to speak. If one hypothesis is selected for prediction or to guide our practical actions, perhaps there are other hypotheses that could be constructed which would be equally well-tested by the tests we have performed and which would make contrary predictions, but those just happen not to have been advanced for scientific consideration. Others that conflict with them concerning future predictions do not get admitted, not because they are eliminated by falsification, but because they have not been seriously advanced for consideration. I do not know whether Miller subscribes to this line of thought, but when he appeals to background knowledge, his remarks suggest that he might. For on his view, what is in background knowledge is just a matter of what has been advanced and has got admitted into science one way or another. If we allow for the arbitrary admission of hypotheses into background knowledge, then we might also allow for the arbitrary selection of one hypothesis rather than another as a guide to action.

However, the appeal to background knowledge is ineffective for the purpose of refusing to admit hypotheses into science given that the aim of science is truth and only truth. As we noted above, such a policy commits one to anti-refusalism in science. That is, if one is interested in truth and only truth, the more truth the better, then one could not defend refusing to admit a hypothesis as a candidate for testing in science that is unfalsified on the grounds that background knowledge contains a contrary hypothesis. For the refused hypothesis might be true. Moreover, since we have no reason to think that hypotheses arbitrarily admitted into science as background knowledge are true, we have no reason for refusing to admit hypotheses that conflict with background knowledge. Again, the use of the term 'knowledge' is misleading here. What Miller calls 'background knowledge' is nothing but a set of hypotheses admitted into science as candidates for testing. When the aim is truth and only truth, the inclusion of hypotheses in 'background knowledge' cannot offer us a reason for refusing to admit contrary hypotheses.

The preceding observation as well as a number of my other remarks amounts to the contention that the set of hypotheses included in 'scientific knowledge' on Miller's account is incoherent in a way that makes it useless for prediction or practical action. If, for example, we wonder whether to repeat some test that has been performed but once, our 'background knowledge' might tell us that people have often made errors in carrying out scientific tests, and, therefore, it is worth repeating. When we consider what such 'background knowledge' tells us about the future, however, we confront incoherence. For the hypothesis that no repetition of tests in the future will expose any error, as well as the hypothesis that the repeating of tests in the future will expose errors, are both unfalsified. Neither can be refused admittance into science when one is only interested in truth. Either might be true. Everyone, however, Miller included, will opt for the policy of repeating tests that have been performed but a single time. The hypothesis that errors will be exposed by repeating tests is one that guides our action. For Miller, the selection of that hypothesis as a guide to action would be arbitrary.

Expected Utility and Falsification

I should now like to advance a positive proposal. Incoherence may, of course, be avoided, and one may do so without abandoning the Popperian emphasis on the importance of empirical testing and the falsification of hypotheses. One may simply supplement the account Popper and Miller offer with what is almost the standard theory of rational decision-making without asking Miller to retract a single contention. The standard account to which I refer is that one that tells us that a rational action is one that maximizes expected utility. To determine whether an action maximizes expected utility one must ascertain both a probability assignment and a utility assignment, and the former might be thought to carry inductive presuppositions to which Miller would object. However, the standard subjective or personalist theory of expected utility is constructed so that both a utility assignment and a probability assignment of a person may be extracted from a sufficiently complete articulation of the preferences of that person. Now Popper, Miller, and the sort of scientist they envisage in their account of science, have preferences just like the rest of us. They will prefer some states of affairs to others, and they will be indifferent between some states of affairs. With a sufficiently complete and coherent articulation of preferences, a person can ascertain his probability and utility assignment and then proceed to maximize expected utility.

In short, I propose Miller reply to his critics that the set of hypotheses admitted and retained as candidates for testing is not the only consideration germane to practical action. Preferences of the individual are also relevant. Once that is admitted, then it may be argued that our practical decisions should not be based on the assumption that any specific outcome will result from a course of action. It should be based on the probability and value we assign to outcomes of that action and alternative actions, that is, on the expected utility.

By adopting this strategy, Miller would escape from the incoherent guidance of hypotheses that make contrary predictions about the outcomes of actions. Once one adopts the probability of hypotheses rather than the hypotheses *simpliciter* as the guide to action, the incoherence vanishes. One should consider the probability of getting each of the contrary outcomes to compute the expectation of an action, and there is nothing incoherent about doing so. Moreover, Miller is not, I believe, entitled to resist this suggestion on the grounds that the probability assignments extracted from preferences are subjective. For Miller notes that background knowledge 'is quite likely to include all variety of unexamined prejudice and presumption'. The subjective or personalist theory of expected utility provides us with a method for using such a background in a coherent way for practical decision.

Of course, a subjective or personalist account of decision-making is open to one line of criticism that has been directed against Popper and Miller, to wit, that the basis for such decision may be nothing more than the unexamined prejudice and presumption to which Miller refers. At any rate, Miller may agree that the rational action is one that maximizes expected utility without sacrificing any thesis or line in the general Popperian theory. The resultant theory is subject to the objection based on the arbitrariness of individual preference and judgement. Since Miller must confront the objection, he might as well obtain the advantage of coherence.

Beyond Miller and Popper

I shall now propose a natural development of the present line of thought that leads us to a theory of evidence and induction. Suppose we obtain a probability assignment by subjective or personalist methods. We must render such an assignment coherent. That yields internal consistency. However, one might also wish to render the personal probability assignment consistent with whatever objective probabilities we have, say those obtained from observed samples and frequencies. It is natural to think of these objective probabilities as intervals. We may then require that our subjective probability assignments be internally coherent and also fall within the intervals of the objective probability statements. The mapping from objective to subjective probability statements is, of course, non-trivial. Suppose we are to assign a probability to the statement '*a* is *F*'. The object that '*a*' denotes will belong to a variety of different classes that might have different probability relations to the class that '*F*' denotes. So we have the problem of deciding which of those objective probability relations should restrict the probability assigned to '*a* is *F*'. This is only one problem that will arise in the attempt to limit the way in which objective probabilities should limit subjective ones. Fortunately, a good deal of the problem is solved by the work of Kyburg.[4]

Assume we obtain subjective probabilities that are consistent with whatever objective probabilities are available. I have argued elsewhere that subjective probability assignments together with logical relations suffice to enable us to decide what statements it is reasonable to select as evidence.[5] My treatment of the matter shares some assumptions with Miller. I too am a fallibilist and, therefore, believe that there is some chance that any statement we select as evidence in science has some chance of being in error. I interpret this to mean that the statements that we select as evidence should be assigned some probability less than unity.

I follow Levi in applying epistemic utilities but specify those utilities in a different manner.[6] On my proposal those utilities may be defined in terms of probabilities and logical relations. The disutility or loss that is incurred when you select a false statement as evidence is measured in terms of the probability of the most probable competitor. Competition is a logical relation, and the utility of selecting what is true is the maximum, or unity, minus the probability of the strongest competitor. The basic philosophical difference from Levi is that I think of evidence in terms of *function* and aver that statements can fulfil the function of evidence without being assigned a probability of unity. Given the specifications of utilities in terms of most probable competitors, we can decide what to select as evidence in terms of expected epistemic utility on the basis of just logic and the probabilities. Since Miller is a fallibilist concerning evidence, it is consistent with his falsification theory to decide in this way. Moreover, I have argued elsewhere that it is

---

[4] Henry Kyburg, Jr., *The Logical Foundations of Statistical Inference* (1974).

[5] Keith Lehrer, 'Truth, Evidence, and Inference', *American Philosophical Quarterly* 11 (1974), 79–92, and *Knowledge* (1974).

[6] Levi, loc. cit.

possible to obtain a *consensual* probability assignment from the weights we assign to the expertise of others.[7] Thus, when Miller says that we adopt statements as evidence because they are non-controversial, I believe he is partly correct. Given a probability assignment constrained first by coherence and objective probability relations that is in accord with an intersubjective consensus as well, the selection of evidence based on such a probability assignment will be as non-controversial as the problem allows.

There is a reason for Miller to resist this line of thought, however. Firstly, the decision to select statements as evidence on the basis of epistemic expected utility is very similar to induction. It is probability-based selection under risk. Secondly, when we have selected some statements as evidence, it is natural then to ask whether by using the same probability assignment, this time considering the probability of statements on the evidence, it is reasonable for us to select statements for other scientific purposes, say as the best explanation of the data, as the best scientific description at the present time, and so forth. There are a variety of scientific purposes for which we wish to single out individual statements and sets of statements. To decide what to select, we may maximize expected utility, epistemic or practical, depending on whether our interests are purely intellectual or coloured with practical concerns. Different utility assignments will be appropriate to different purposes, and no monolithic theory will capture that variety of purposes that are germane to science.

Perhaps the attainment of truth is paramount among them. However, concern with explanation, simplicity, and computability are legitimate scientific interests as well, and the connection between these interests and those of truth and the avoidance of error are tenuous. I may hesitate to predict on the basis of the hypothesis that provides the best explanation of data. Truth and explanatory power are not so happily wedded as we may assume, nor are simplicity and truth perfectly mated. Thus, I suggest, that given our intellectual as well as practical interests, and the utilities that correspond to each, we confront a variety of decisions which are, in their own way, part of scientific enquiry. Decisions made in terms of probabilities that are as objective and consensual as any can be, and that maximize utilities which express those interests, are rational. It is, however, perfectly consistent with our selection of statements as I suggest that we retain other statements as candidates for testing. Since the

[7] Keith Lehrer, 'When Rational Agreement is Impossible', *Nous* 10 (1976), 327–32, and 'Social Information', *The Monist* 40 (1977), 471–87.

statements we select are not assigned a probability of unity, we may admit and retain contradictory statements as candidates for testing. After all, there is some chance that such statements might be true.

In summary, I have sketched a programme for the selection of statements as evidence and for other scientific purposes on the basis of probabilities and preferences. Such acceptance may properly be called induction. I have no proof that the statements thus selected will all be true, or even true in some fixed percentage. That implies that this programme does not solve the problem Hume raised. The rationality of the sort of decision-making I envisage is not a guarantee that one will succeed in hitting upon the truth, but consists instead in making the most consistent use of individual and collective judgement. If such judgement falls wide of the mark of truth, there is no way the hazard can be avoided by method. For the acceptance of any method will ultimately depend on such judgement as well. That is not an argument against method or discipline. It is an exposure of the spring from which method flows.

§9. Comments and Replies
The Miller–Lehrer Session

MILLER: Lehrer makes two substantial criticisms of the position outlined in my paper. The first alleges a conflict between fallibilism and falsificationism, doctrines that I endorse, and the unprepossessingly named doctrine of anti-refusalism, to which Lehrer thinks I am committed. The second criticism is a more familiar one, and it is that I give no satisfactory explanation (even in section 6 (v) of my paper) of how theoretical science is applied in practical action and decision making. Both these criticisms emerge from Lehrer's attribution to me of this doctrine of anti-refusalism, and I shall contest them by showing that I reject the doctrine. Anti-refusalism, to my mind, far from promoting the search for truth, would seriously obstruct it. It is a doctrine indeed not unlike socialism. Its heart is in the right place; it is well-intentioned; but unless severely restricted it simply does not work.

The aim of science, I have said, is truth and only truth. Falsificationism proposes that, in order to achieve as much truth as we can, we should invent imaginative theories and submit them to varied and stringent tests, in the hope that if they are false they will been seen to be false.[1] Perhaps because of infelicitous wording on my part, perhaps because he characterizes falsificationism as the weak principle that 'we should eliminate any candidate that has been falsified by empirical test',[2] Lehrer fails to appreciate that in advocating falsificationism I was indeed urging that 'the aim of science · · include the objective of avoiding the retention of error as well as the objective of admitting and retaining truth'.[3] If mere aggregation of truths, without concern for what falsehoods might be present, were the aim of science, there would be no rationale for subjecting scientific hypotheses to tests, and therefore no rationale for restricting them to those that are testable – a restriction that Lehrer accepts without demur.[4] I do not feel at all committed by my interest in truth to the principle of antirefusalism that we 'should never refuse to admit or retain any true hypothesis as a candidate for testing in science'[5] (despite the fact that we would thereby enrich our hoard of truths); especially as this policy of antirefusalism is not

[1] David Miller, 'Can Science do without Induction?', p. 114 above.
[2] Keith Lehrer, 'Truth, Evidence, and Error: Comments on Miller', p. 131 above.
[3] Lehrer, p. 132 above.
[4] Lehrer, p. 130 above.
[5] Loc. cit.

an effective one (because we never quite know what is true). Still less am I committed to the stronger, methodologically significant, version that we should not refuse to admit or retain as a candidate for testing any hypothesis not known to be false; in particular, that we should never risk eliminating a hypothesis that might be true. It is this form of anti-refusalism that Lehrer actually exploits to provoke the clash with fallibilism and falsificationism; and I can only say that the clash is reason enough to reject such anti-refusalism out of hand. As Lehrer notes, in combination with fallibilism it would prevent us from ever eliminating any hypothesis at all, and would thus condemn the testing process to futility. Popper's demarcation principle advised us to admit to science only those hypotheses that we would be able to expel; it follows that if nothing may be expelled then nothing may be admitted. Anti-refusalism leads unwittingly to pro-refusalism, which it contradicts. Thus anti-refusalism must be rejected.

My repudiation of anti-refusalism also draws the fangs, I trust, from Lehrer's second criticism: the criticism that if all unfalsified hypotheses are admitted into science then science is unable to offer any guidance about the future. In my paper I discuss this issue at some length, and suggest (banally enough) that we must not admit empirically indistinguishable hypotheses into science if we have any concern to distinguish empirically between them. Thus we must not admit both 'All emeralds are green' and 'All emeralds are grue'[6] unless we are prepared to delay a decision between these two hypotheses until the year 2001. Lehrer understands this suggestion to imply that we must either deny admission to all hypotheses about the future (in which case science offers no guidance) or accept that 'the admission of one hypothesis and the refusal to admit another is an arbitrary matter, the luck of the draw so to speak. . . . [But] then we might also allow for the arbitrary selection of one hypothesis rather than another as a guide to action.'[7] He notes in support of the second alternative (which I am obviously driven to) that no appeal to background knowledge does more than shift the difficulty; for background knowledge too, on this construal, has been accumulated in a quite arbitrary fashion. Although in fact we may very well have excluded 'All emeralds are grue', even before testing, on the grounds that it contradicted background knowledge, it is an historical accident that what we knew was not instead incompatible with

[6] Miller, p. 126 above and Lehrer, pp. 135–7 above.
[7] Lehrer, p. 137 above.

'All emeralds are green'. Indeed, it seems not impossible (and I can concede the possibility, despite its being really a very silly one, making no biological sense) that human knowledge might have developed so differently that gruelike hypotheses were pervasive; so that, to our way of thinking, a vast panoply of changes in the world was predicted for the onset of the year 2001, or for some other time in the future. This must pose a vexatious problem for inductivists, and for others who think that our knowledge can be justified; but it has no force against falsificationism, which acknowledges without embarrassment an element of arbitrariness in all our knowledge. Even at the practical level this arbitrariness has no serious effects.

Although the admission of one hypothesis rather than another may initially be a pretty arbitrary affair, its retention when it passes all the tests to which it is exposed and, even more, its expulsion if it fails any test are far from arbitrary. Our background knowledge may be in part a random collection of barely scrutinized anticipations, but a considerable part of it is the product of a long process of conjectures and refutations (albeit at a biological level). It could have been quite different, to be sure; though not in any old way. But I cannot see that there is anything epistemologically objectionable about this. There are many routes to the truth, and we shall tread but one of them. This may be arbitrary, but it is not wrong. As has been said before, if we are going in the right direction it does not matter very much where we are.

Yet when we consider practical propsals it does at first sight seem to matter where we are. Surely we need to choose between a proposal in accordance with our present knowledge, and one in accordance with a system currently indistinguishable from it empirically and composed entirely of gruelike hypotheses? My answer is that there is no need to choose. Despite the conflict between the predictions of two such systems for the third millennium there will be no conflict in the guidance they give about what we should do now. For each will advise that we prepare for an event after 2001 just as though it were to happen before 2001. Since they agree about everything before that date, they will agree on what ought to be done (even though they may phrase their advice differently). In other words, provided each of the systems is a system of temporally universal hypotheses (as is implied by the use of general terms 'green' and 'grue') they will coincide in any advice that they can give. Of course, they will differ in their advice about what we should do from 2001 on, but by then we shall know which of the systems is false. I also grant that there could be a conflict of advice if 'All emeralds are grue' and similar hypotheses were taken to mean that there will be some causally relevant change at the end of the year 2000. But as I said in my paper, if we 'insist on the eternal possibility that nature will entirely change its course just before our action is performed, then no proposal whatever will get rejected'.[8]

AGAZZI: An important question raised in Miller's paper is whether the goal of science is that of reaching truth. His Popperian orientation makes it difficult to him to answer this question satisfactorily. On the one hand, he has to answer this question in a positive sense, at least in order to safeguard, even in some corrected and more or less sophisticated way, the core and the purpose of the falsificationist methodology. On the other hand, Popper's fallibilistic doctrine claims that we never reach truth, but must be satisfied with an indefinite approximation to it, and this makes the first claim quite platonic and seriously challenges his falsificationism.

I think that the positive answer is correct and that the anti-instrumentalist view of science it implies is sound (I also think that the central idea of the falsificationist methodology is tenable, provided it is equipped with suitable explications about how it concretely applies). What is responsible for many undesirable complications and inconsistencies is, in my opinion, the misleading notion of truth which lies behind the discourse of Popper and of the Popperians. I shall call it the 'substantival notion' of truth, which I shall contrast with an 'adjectival notion' of the same. Popper conceives of truth as something existing in itself, as a kind of hypostatized entity, which we must therefore denote by a substantive, like 'the truth' (or 'the truths') and which science continuously tries to know in a perpetual labour of Sisyphus. This conception is mirrored in the seemingly innocent statement 'science's goal is to know truth'. But, unfortunately, truth is not a *substance*, which may be denoted by a substantive, but a *property* which must be denoted by an adjective, i.e. by 'true' (sentence or proposition). If one is clear about that, one immediately sees that the object of scientific *knowledge* is not *truth*, but *reality*, and this eliminates much of the difficulties. For it is not at all difficult to maintain that we progressively increase our knowledge of reality, by establishing more and more 'true propositions' about it, even if the task of a total knowledge of reality may remain a perpetually unfulfilled enterprise. This, in particular, allows to say that a single 'true proposition' may falsify, under suitable circumstances, a particular conjecture. On the other hand, it avoids all

[8] Miller, p. 127 above.

the intriguing questions connected with the very controversial notion of the Popperian 'verisimilitude'.

On the contrary, it seems to me that, if one gets rid of the substantival notion of truth, one can find a rather effective tool for expressing the idea of verisimilitude by adopting something of the kind of L. J. Cohen's methodology for grading inductive support. It has been argued against this methodology that it makes not much sense to give more credit to a hypothesis which has survived n subsequent tests before being disproved, than to a hypothesis that has survived only $n - p$ of the same series of tests. Such an objection conceives truth in a substantival way, which makes of it an 'all-or-nothing' question. An adjectival conception of truth, instead, allows us to say that the first hypothesis was 'true about reality' to a greater extent than the second and the tests which eventually 'disprove' a hypothesis can be seen rather as sound information about reality or, better, as information about which restricted or actual domain of reality it holds true of. For example, if the statement 'Drug D has no dangerous side-effects on humans' has resisted several tests of increasing complexity in the sense of Cohen's theory, until bad side-effects appear when D is administered to pregnant women, we should not say that it has proved false, but rather that it has proved true under the restricted form 'Drug D has no dangerous side-effects on non-pregnant humans'.

MELTZER: David Miller in his presentation unequivocally supported the view, apparently an important part of the Popperian account of scientific method, that induction cannot be done by rules – in contrast to deduction, which has well-studied and well-understood rules of inference. There are many statements to this effect both in *The Logic of Scientific Discovery* and also elsewhere than in the Popperian literature. A typical one is from Hempel: 'There are, then, no generally applicable "rules of induction", by which hypotheses or theories can be mechanically derived or inferred from empirical data. The transition from data to theory requires creative imagination.'[9] It is possible to show constructively that this view is false.

Let us suppose the knowledge of some particular domain of science expressed in a formal language, for example that of predicate calculus, with explicit and effective rules of *deductive* inference. Let S be the conjunction of sentences which state the existing body of knowledge of the subject, including so far unrefuted general laws as well as particular facts (though the distinction between these two

[9] C. G. Hempel, *Philosophy of Natural Science* (1966).

categories is not as clear-cut as one might think).[10] Now what does it mean to find a hypothesis or theory to explain some so far unexplained, and within the terms of *S*, unexplainable 'fact' *A*, whatever its degree of particularity or generality may be? It means generating a sentence *B*, such that the conjunction of *B* and *S* deductively imply *A*. Each step in the deduction of *A* from *B* and *S* will be the application of some explicit rule, e.g. instantiation or *modus ponens*. Since the direct inverse of each such rule is also an effective operation, it would be possible to make the exact inverse sequence of steps from *A* to *B* and *S*, by the application of the exact inverses of the deductive rules (for example the inverse of a rule of instantiation would be a rule of generalization). If this were done the hypothesis *B* would have been generated by the successive applications of rules of inference which are just as explicit as the deductive rules of which they are the inverse. (Some of the technical issues arising when the inverse rule has more than one consequent as in reverse *modus ponens* are discussed by Morgan.)[11] Furthermore, it can be easily shown that in cases where the deductive system of rules is complete in the sense that all semantically valid inferences from given premises can be generated by their application, the same is true of the inverted system of rules, namely, *all* the hypotheses expressible in the language which imply *A* can be generated.

Of course there is a restriction that must be imposed if such a system of inductive rules were actually to be used, namely, at each application of a rule the resulting sentence or conjunction of sentences must be checked for compatibility with *S* and rejected if found to contradict it (or, alternatively, as sometimes happens in the history of science, *S* itself altered to remove the contradiction). Two things need to be said about this test of compatibility. First, it is purely a deductive matter and can be done by a rule-governed automatic theorem-prover, for example. Secondly, although not of much practical significance, I believe, the test of incompatibility – in, for example, the first-order predicate calculus – is undecidable in the technical sense, so that a theorem-prover may not succeed in carrying out the test. Therefore we have got to be content here with a notion of relative completeness. If we take into account the actual context in which induction is or would be done, whether by people

---

[10] B. Meltzer, 'Power amplification for theorem-provers', *Machine Intelligence* 5 (1970).

[11] C. G. Morgan, 'Hypothesis Generation by Machine', *Artificial Intelligence* 2 (1971), 179–87.

or machines, we observe that any proof of logical compatibility must be done with an apparatus of limited deductive power. For certain deductive systems, e.g., what are known as 'resolution-type' automatic theorem-provers, it is possible to specify the maximum deductive power precisely, usually by means of an integer parameter l.[12] The test for compatibility in such a system is entirely finite and decidable. This measure is usually related to the length or complexity of proof allowed. This may prove to be possible for other deductive programs – it may even be possible to specify numerically upper bounds to the deductive power employed by people.

So it seems appropriate to introduce a notion of relative completeness of systems of inductive inference of the type considered, namely, such a system may be complete *relative* to a body of knowledge S and level of deductive power l. The hypothesis generated is not absolutely reliable – its reliability depends on the reliability of S and on the magnitude of l (a parameter usually readily adjustable in automatic theorem-provers).

So far only the logical adequacy of such systems has been considered. Obviously in making a choice from the theoretically infinite number of logically adequate hypotheses such a system could generate to explain a given fact, heuristic criteria of various kinds, such as simplicity, explanatory power, etc. may be employed. Some of these issues have been discussed and analyzed very interestingly by Plotkin.[13] But the fact that such issues have to be faced is no support for the view that rule-governed generation of hypotheses to explain facts is not possible. For this kind of pruning of the space of possible inferences is also entirely characteristic of deductive inferences, and nobody would suggest that rule-governed deductive inference is impossible in principle.

Finally, if one may have the temerity to suggest it, the falseness of the Popperian claim is immediately established by the existence of many computer programs which have carried out successful theory formation, e.g., Buchanan's[14] and Meltzer's.[15] The latter, using the inverse of only one deductive rule, generated a fair approximation to the axioms of group theory from 10 facts about two simple groups.

[12] B. Meltzer, op. cit.

[13] G. Plotkin, 'Automatic Methods of Inductive Inference', Ph. D. thesis, Department of Machine Intelligence and Perception, University of Edinburgh, 1971.

[14] B. G. Buchanan, 'Scientific Theory Formation by Computer', Proceedings of the NATO Advanced Study Institute on Computer Oriented Learning Processes, Bonas, France, 1974.

[15] Op. cit.

In a certain sense the reconstruction of the process of inductive inference offered above is not so very interesting, since it tacitly assumes a given formal language and hence a given set of concepts in terms of which the body of knowledge is formulated. As such however it formalizes a great deal of the reasoning involved in what is usually known as 'normal science'. But, of course, some of the most interesting work of science involves the creation of new concepts. Ways of bringing this into the formal reconstruction given above are briefly referred to in a paper of mine,[16] but the most impressive computational modelling of this that has yet appeared is to be found in the recent work of Lenat.[17]

KYBURG: All of our knowledge is fallible; even test statements are only 'relatively uncontroversial' (Miller, p. 116). What is required to give 'all *A*'s are *B*'s' scientific content is an understanding of what circumstances would yield a relatively uncontroversial judgement that some thing was an *A* but not a *B*. Miller may be correct in asserting that no induction is involved here, and no contradiction between fallibilism and falsificationism.

2. But 'All *A*'s are *B*'s' is not very interesting science. Consider instead a quantitative theory *T*. Suppose it (together with boundary conditions, which we leave out of account) yields the result that a certain distance is *d*. What is required is an understanding of the circumstances which would render relatively uncontroversial the judgement that the distance is not *d*.

3. The result of our measurement of the distance will not be *d*; according to usual theories of error, the probability of its being *d* is zero. Indeed, under conventional Gaussian theories, any amount of error in the measurement is possible. But we may refer to convention or practice: e.g., we may regard an error of three standard deviations as 'practically impossible'. And this may characterize circumstances under which we may regard the prediction as falsified.

4. But if the appeal to convention or practice is taken to solve the problem of falsification, it raises its own problems. Cannot convention and practice themselves be subject to criticism? Are not some conventions better than others? In this case, and in statistical cases in general, conventions of rejection can be and are subjected to criticism.

5. To reject the hypothesis that the true value of *d*, i.e., the mean

[16] B. Meltzer, 'Generation of hypotheses and theories', *Nature* 225 (1970), 972.

[17] D. Lenat, 'AM: An Artificial Intelligence Approach to Discovery in Mathematics as Heuristic Research', Ph. D. thesis, Computer Science Department, Stanford University, 1976.

of the set of hypothetical unbiassed measurements of d, falls outside the acceptable interval i, is to accept the hypothesis that it falls inside the interval i. We are thus concerned with conventions concerning both acceptance and rejection of statistical hypotheses.

6. The exploration, consideration, criticism, evaluation, development, formalization, and study of such conventions, I take to be the main business of inductive logic. If this is so, the falsificationist has as much need of induction as the straw inductivist whom Miller characterizes as looking for ways of 'inferring' theories from raw data.

7. I believe, though I cannot prove it to be so, that an adequate understanding of inductive logic will eventually lead to rational criteria for preferring one theory to another (say for the purposes of building bridges), in a given state of knowledge. I suspect Miller would deny this; but it is a matter of conjecture that has yet to be put to the test. What he should not deny is that the part of inductive logic which is concerned with the critical assessment of statistical inference is of value to the realistic falsificationist.

KUIPERS: That there is something like a law of diminishing returns from repeated tests is one of those few intuitions shared by inductivists and Popperians. However, unlike the former, the latter appear to have much trouble in giving an account of it. I would like to present an objective and deductivistic explanation which seems to me conclusive.

Let us agree that a repeated test is a test which is, according to our background knowledge and as far as the experimental set-up is concerned, a copy or replication of a foregoing test. In other words, we are considering test-tokens of a test-type. Now, either the background knowledge implies that from one positive test-token result it may be inferred that all others will be positive, or not.

In the first case repetitions are check-replications, i.e. they are performed to guarantee that the test-conditions and the result have at least once been established unambiguously. If I have understood Miller correctly, this comes close to his view on the role of repeated tests.

In the second case the background knowledge leaves room for the possibility that there is some constant objective probability p that a test-token leads to a counterexample of the universal hypothesis under test. Our further concern is an n-test, the performance of n test-tokens; and for our present purposes it suffices to identify the severity S_n of an n-test simply with the probability of getting a counterexample.[18] Now, even if p is zero, we get of course: $S_n = 1 - q^n$, where $q = 1 - p$. The additional severity $A_{n+1} = S_{n+1} - S_n$ of an extra test-token is easily shown to be pq^n. Hence it follows that, although an extra test-token increases the severity of the compound test, the additional severity diminishes from p, for $n = 0$, to 0 for n is infinite, i.e. extra test-tokens have diminishing returns.[19]

It is worthwhile to note that this analysis is formally equivalent to the non-controversial explication of intuitions concerning random sampling for the occurrence of a failure: although a large sample is better than a small one, enlargement of the sample with 1 increases the quality of the failure-test more in case of a small sample than in case of a large one.

Besides simplicity, the key to the proposed analysis is of course the *a priori* point of view. But attempts at a non-inductive *a posteriori* account necessarily confuse objective and inductive probabilities in the same way as the child who guessed that he would get a sister because he knew that he was to become a brother. On the other hand, if my analysis is sound, I consider it as inductive support for the claim that science can do without induction, because and although it might be (merely) a handsome way of talking, even in meta-empirical matters, provided it is carefully done.

NEWTON-SMITH: Miller follows his bold conjecture that 'Popper has succeeded in developing a convincing theory of the growth of science that is quite free from any principle of induction, (p. 110) with a spirited defence on Popper's behalf against a number of standard objections. My concern in this comment is not with Miller's sins of commission but with two sins of omission. The first concerns the ultimate grounds on which hypotheses are shown to be false within the Popperian model of science. What counts against a hypothesis is its incompatibility with an accepted basic statement. Clearly the grounds for rejecting a hypothesis can be no stronger than the grounds for accepting one of its falsifying basic statements. What then should ground the acceptance of a basic statement? In the case of observationally simple basic statements the naive non-Popperian's natural inclination is to talk of the evidence of his

---

[18] A more sophisticated measure might include a measure for the severity of the test-type as a whole, although one may also argue that this is essentially given by S_1, i.e., p.

[19] Note that if p turns out, in the end, to be 0, the (additional) severity was in fact uniformly equal to 0. If one finds this counter-intuitive, take p then as estimate of the objective probability on the basis of the background knowledge. If this estimated value is 0, the foregoing feature is not surprising because we are in fact back to the first case.

senses. But, if we understand as we should that the hall-mark of inductive reason is that an inference to a proposition p is inductive if and only if the grounds cited as warranting the assertion of p support the claim that p is true but do not entail that p is true, the naive non-Popperian is guilty of 'pernicious inductivism'. What then is to be the move of the sophisticated Popperian? Apparently the acceptance of basic statements is purely a matter of convention. As Popper is a realist this cannot be construed as the untenable thesis that such statements are made true by fiat. It seems that the thesis is to be interpreted as some form of 'epistemological conventionalism' whereby an ungroundable (ungroundable because the only grounding could be inductive) decision is made by the scientist to hold the statement to be true. But in that case we have no grounds for counting this decision against the claim that the hypothesis in question is true. Consequently there can be no grounded falsification without induction. If Popper's model of science is completely free of the taint of induction it is an account of science in which not only are there no 'entrance examinations' there are no justifiable 'expulsion procedures' (p.113).

The second sin of omission concerns the vexed question of the relation between verisimilitude and falsification. Admittedly Miller notes this problem (p.114) but fails to appreciate its full force. Setting aside the apparently intractable problem of the analysis of the notion of verisimilitude one wants to know what possible grounds a deductivist can advance for thinking that one false theory, say, relativistic mechanics, has greater verisimilitude than another false theory, say, Newtonian mechanics. Clearly Popper wishes to be able to ground such claims, for otherwise his view of science as progressive is unjustified. Miller departs from Popper in boldly claiming that 'no "inductive principle" will ever have any role to play' in choosing between false theories. For Popper in his infamous 'whiff of induction' footnote[20] argues that it would be surprising that relativistic mechanics provides better predictions than Newtonian mechanics if it were not a better approximation to the truth. To defend a thesis of convergence to the truth in this way is to use inductive argumentation (whether or not we decide to *say* an 'inductive principle' is involved). But once Popper admits inductive argumentation here there is no reason not to admit it from the start. Thus what is constitutive and unique in Popper's account of science seems to have been abandoned *ex cathedra*. One hopes for Popper's

[20] P. A. Schilpp (ed.), *The Philosophy of Karl Popper* (1974), pp. 1192–3, note 165b.

sake that Miller's promissory note offering non-inductivist grounds for discriminating between false theories will, unlike the British government's perpetual War Bonds, be cashed in finite time.

MILLER; In response to the five interventions to my paper I can, I think, be extremely brief. I have no quarrel with Agazzi's suggestion that we view science as a pursuit of true propositions, rather than of truth; but I do not at all see how what seems only a verbal reformulation can avoid any of the problems concerning verisimilitude. Nor do I have any real objection to what Meltzer says, except that it has little to do with most of my paper (which was non-inductivist, rather than anti-inductivist). No doubt we can in a well-defined language generate all the consistent hypotheses from which a particular sentence follows (Hempel explicitly says so in the work cited, though Meltzer suggests the contrary). The problem, however, is why we should prefer any of these hypotheses to any of the others. They surely cannot all be the results of valid inductive inferences, in the way that all the consequences of the sentence are the results of valid deductive inferences. If Kyburg's message is simply that in the testing and evaluation of scientific hypotheses we make heavy use of a variety of statistical methods, then of course I agree. I tried to hint as much in footnote 5 on p. 110. Where I don't agree is that these methods involve any appeal to any principle or rule of induction. Kyburg says that to reject the hypothesis that the value of some parameter d falls outside some interval i 'is to accept the hypothesis that it falls inside the interval i'.[21] But it is obvious from the way such measurements are performed that both these hypotheses are admitted to science prior to test; and to reject the one is not to accept, but merely to retain, the other. No inductive inference is involved even in the adoption of basic statements. For these need not be justified as Newton-Smith supposes; it is enough if they are accessible to further test if required. To Newton-Smith's second point I would say that according to any adequate theory of verisimilitude the claim that we have progressed towards the truth would be conjectural and open to falsification, but neither in need of, nor open to, verification.[22] Science may progress, but I would hardly expect a demonstration that it does. Thus no inductive inference is involved here either. Finally I must thank Dr Kuipers for his interesting explanation of the diminishing returns we

---

[21] Henry E. Kyburg, Jr, 'Intervention Ad Miller', p. 151 above.

[22] See David Miller, 'The Accuracy of Predictions', *Synthese* 30 (February/March 1975), section VII, and also Karl R. Popper, *Objective Knowledge* (1972), the first complete paragraph on p. 265.

obtain from the repetition of tests. But, alas, it seems to me not quite adequate. For if Kuipers is right then there will be diminishing returns from any sequence of tests, repeated or otherwise (provided only that the probability of a counterexample remains constant from test to test). Kuipers's suggestion can distinguish one test of a kind from a later test of the same kind; but being formal it cannot distinguish a test of a new kind from a mere repetition of a test of an old kind. I am therefore inclined to stick with my own explanation of why the severity of repeated tests decreases.

4

Application Conditions for Eliminative Induction

§10. L. JONATHAN COHEN
What has Inductive Logic to do with Causality?

1. *A Statement of the Problem*

According to J. S. Mill,[1] 'the notion of Cause' is 'the root of the whole theory of Induction', and Mill's view has been echoed in recent times by A. W. Burks. However it turns out that this view cannot be sustained even if one grants (as I should certainly be willing to do) that the inductive logic of experimentation in natural science is eliminative, and not enumerative. The proposition that, so far as induction is concerned with causes in controlled experiments, it is eliminative cannot be validly converted into the proposition that all eliminative reasoning is induction about causes. The fact is that when one develops and systematizes Bacon's tables of presence and absence, or Mill's methods of agreement and difference, as criteria of evidential support, one comes up against a method of relevant variables that is realized not only in reasoning about causes and effects but also in reasoning about quite different kinds of subject-matter – for example, about legal or linguistic problems. At the same time all assignments in accordance with this method of relevant variables have a certain underlying logical structure: their interrelations conform to principles that are representable within a certain kind of generalized modal logic. I have given a detailed argument for both propositions elsewhere[2] and shall give only the briefest appropriate summary here. My object in the present paper is rather to enquire into the general conditions for the presence of the underlying logical structure. Why is it open to other employable interpretations than as a calculus of causes? What is there in common to all the types of subject-matter that admit inductive reasoning of this kind? What makes them admit it? What are the application-conditions for the generalized modal logic that is the logic of Baconian eliminative induction?

---

[1] *System of Logic*, Bk. III, ch. iv, sect. 2 (1896 ed., p. 213).

[2] In *The Implications of Induction* (1970), and *The Probable and the Provable* (1977). Levi's theory of potential surprise establishes yet another possible interpretation of this underlying logic: cf. p. 1 ff above.

The nature of the problem may be seen most clearly at the outset if it is regarded as the analogue of a question that can be raised about the classical calculus of probability. If we define a probability-function in terms of a formal axiomatization for the calculus, like Popper's, several different interpretations of the formalism are available, as is well-known, that may reasonably be regarded as reconstructions of pre-analytic concepts of probability. For example, the two-place functor may be construed as an empirically evaluatable function from pairs of sets into real numbers $(0 \leqslant n \leqslant 1)$ and thus as graduating a relative frequency; or it may be construed as an *a priori* evaluatable function from pairs of propositions into real numbers and thus as graduating a logical relation. The question then arises whether some unitary explanation can be found for the availability of these alternative interpretations of the classical function as determining relative frequencies, logical relations, belief-intensities, natural propensities, or whatever. Are there any general semantical conditions, common to all these interpretations, that enforce a mathematical structure of the classical kind? J. L. Mackie[3] has given a negative answer to this question, on the ground that the interrelationships between the various concepts involved are merely those of a Wittgensteinian family-resemblance. But, as I have argued elsewhere,[4] the family-resemblance thesis is not defensible and an affirmative answer can instead be given. The various familiar concepts of probability all measure gradations of provability by criteria analogous to rules of inference in a complete deductive system for the elements of a Boolean algebra (where a complete system is understood as being one in which a proposition is provable if and only if its negation is not provable). The main differences between these different concepts of probability can then be accounted for, as I have shown, by the fact that the analogous statements of provability may also be of different kinds. They may be either general or singular, either necessary or contingent, and either extensional or non-extensional. For we must not think here of proof just in some single, metamathematical sense. There are many other kinds of proof besides mathematical ones.

Now I want to raise here a similar question about another mathematical structure. The structure that I have in mind is not the classical calculus of probability (which I shall henceforth call the Pascalian calculus) but the generalized modal logic that seems to

---

[3] *Truth, Probability and Paradox* (1973), pp. 155 and 188 f.
[4] *The Probable and the Provable*, pp. 11 f.

control the implications of statements about evidential support when this support is graded in accordance with the Baconian tradition. Suppose, that is, you rank generalizations in a particular area of natural-scientific enquiry by their capacity to pass cumulatively tougher and tougher tests, i.e., to resist falsification by cumulatively richer and richer combinations of relevant factors. This is a form of what I call the method of relevant variables, and is a generalization of Mill's methods of agreement and difference. It was succinctly described long ago by J. F. W. Herschel's remark[5] that experiments 'become more valuable, and their results clearer, in proportion as they possess this quality (of agreeing exactly in all their circumstances but one), since the question put to nature becomes thereby more pointed, and its answer more decisive'. The kind of reliability that is discernible by this method mounts grade by grade towards the necessity that is normally attributed to laws of nature. For example, the wider the range of relevant causal factors that fail to interfere with the operation of a generalization about, say, the colour-sensitivity of bees, the nearer we may suppose that generalization is to stating either a law of nature or at least a logical consequence of one or more such laws. Correspondingly, to formulate the logic of such reliability-rankings, we need to have not just one primitive square-operator, as in an ordinary modal logic, but a series of them $\Box^1, \Box^2, \ldots, \Box^d$, where $\Box^d$ represents logical necessity, $\Box^{d-1}$ represents natural law, and $\Box^1, \Box^2, \ldots, \Box^{d-2}$ represent thresholds of increasing reliability that fall short of natural law. $\Box^i H \rightarrow H$ is provable only where $i \geq d-1$. Any wff (or part of a wff) $\Box^i H$ may be rewritten, in functional notation, as $s[H] \geq i$, to represent rankings by a monadic support-function[6] that maps propositions of the appropriate category on to positive integers $(0 < i < d)$. Similarly a dyadic support-ranking $s[H, E] \geq i$ may be analysed out as $\Box^{d-1}(E \rightarrow \Box^i H)$. We shall then have axiom-schemas like $\Box^j A \rightarrow \Box^i A$, where $j > i$, $\Box^{d-1} A \rightarrow A$, $\Box^i (A \rightarrow B) \rightarrow (\Box^i A \rightarrow \Box^i B)$, $\Box^i A \rightarrow \Box^i (x) A$, and so on – in short a generalization of the Lewis–Barcan calculus S4.

It is, however, not only the reliability of natural-scientific generalizations, as inferable from reports of experimental test-results, that may be graded by functions that have this underlying logical structure, which I shall henceforth call Baconian functions. One may also grade thus the reliability of a legal rule that is inferred

[5] *A Preliminary Discourse on the Study of Natural Philosophy* (1833 ed.), p. 155.
[6] Cf. *The Implications of Induction*, pp. 219 ff.

from judicial precedents, as in the Anglo-American system of common law, or the reliability of a hypothesis about the meaning of a word that is inferred from known contexts of its use. Both types of hypothesis may be graded by the cumulative variety of situations to which they apply. But the relevant factors for testing hypotheses of these legal or lexicographical types are not ones that characteristically operate in the causal order of nature: they are instead nexuses of legally recognized relations, or features designated by semantical markers, respectively. For example, the generalization that an innkeeper always has a duty to safeguard the property of his guests may be falsified by cases that have arisen in conditions of war or civil riot, but these conditions have operated juridically, not causally, on the duties of the individual landlords involved. And the assumption that similar causes have similar effects is matched by the principle of natural justice that like litigants should be treated alike: *similia similibus*. Compare the golden rule of universalizability in ethics. Moreover in addition to their interpretation as rankings for the reliability of generalizations, whether these be natural-scientific, legal, semantical, or of any other appropriate kind, Baconian functions also have – consequentially – a rather different, though closely connected, type of interpretation. They can also be used to grade how small is the extent of the qualification that such a generalization needs in order to resist falsification by any relevant factor and thus attain full reliability. For example, it is possible in this way to rank the degree of precision with which a rule of law has been formulated in a particular branch of a precedent-based legal system, or the degree of adequacy with which a lexical entry has been formulated in a particular field of a vocabulary within the compositional semantics for a natural language.

What then is there in common to these various modes of inductive reasoning – in such diverse fields as experimental science, common-law jurisprudence, or compositional semantics – so as to require Baconian functions for their proper evaluation? Or, if we look at the problem in the other direction, why is it that such diverse interpretations are available for the underlying modal logic? I see this as an analogous problem to the question I mentioned earlier about the classical, Pascalian calculus of probability. But it is only an analogous problem. It is not the same problem, or part of the same one, as an objector might be inclined to suppose who thought that all evaluations of inductive reasoning were representable in terms of Pascalian probability-functions. Nor is this just because the latter are countably additive while the former (for reasons that will emerge later) are not even finitely additive. There is also quite a different reason. A generalization may pass a test that has a certain degree of severity, but fail a tougher one. That is to say, it may be fully reliable over a certain range of combinations of circumstances, but not over a more extensive range. It may have a certain grade of reliability and yet still be false. Hence statements reporting counter-instances for a particular generalization are often compatible with statements ascribing a non-zero grade of reliability for that generalization. And it turns out that because of this the logic of Baconian functions cannot be mapped on to any form of the calculus of probability in which $p[B, A] = 0$ wherever A is incompatible with B (with $p[A] > 0$). The argument is quite simple.

We first show[7] that if the two-place Baconian support-function $s[H, E]$ is a function of the probabilities involved it is a function of $p[E, H]$, $p[H]$, and $p[E]$, where $1 > p[E] > 0$. Now consider two logically independent generalizations, H and H', such that $p[H] = p[H']$. Let E report an unfavourable result of a certain kind of test on H, plus a favourable result of this test on H' and an unfavourable result of a more severe test on H'. Then we shall have $s[H', E] > s[H, E]$. But at the same time we shall have $p[E, H] = p[E, H'] = 0$ and $p[H] = p[H']$. So here is a by no means abnormal type of case in which the grades of Baconian support for two generalizations are different while each pair of mathematical probabilities concerned is identical (since presumably $1 > p[E] > 0$). It is thus quite impossible to represent Baconian support-functions in terms of Pascalian probability; and the problem that I am raising in this paper about Baconian functions is therefore quite a different one from the corresponding problem about Pascalian probability-functions, even though the two problems may be regarded as analogues of one another in important respects.

2. *Two False Starts*

Perhaps the most obvious suggestion to consider is that eliminative induction is appropriate only in areas of enquiry where there are non-logical uniformities to be discovered and that accordingly Baconian functions apply to the appraisal of evidential support only in those areas. These uniformities may be the familiar regularities of nature, or the man-made principles that are determined by judicial precedent or linguistic convention. Indeed it is arguable that the conception of nature as a system of uniformities derives

[7] Cf. *The Probable and the Provable*, pp. 189 f.

originally from the monotheistic conception of God as a divine legislator and of nature as powerless to disobey Him; and presumably this conception derives in turn, by an analogical extension, from human experience of human legislators. So on this view it is man's capacity to legislate for himself and his fellows that one way or another gives rise to domains of study for which eliminative induction is the appropriate mode of reasoning. In each case the object is – broadly speaking – to find those generalizations that conflict as little as possible with other well-evidenced generalizations. Correspondingly, it is to be presumed, in domains where there is no reason at all to expect the existence of uniformities we have a field for some kind of Pascalian reasoning, not for eliminative induction and Baconian functions.

This is an attractively simple gloss on the situation, but it doesn't really do the trick, or does only a small part of it. It certainly doesn't account for the specific type of modal logic that controls assessments of eliminative induction, because it says nothing to preclude us from applying classical probability-functions in the appraisal of evidential support for universally quantified propositions, as in, say, Hintikka's version of the theory that measures E's confirmation of H by the ratio of $H \& E$'s range-measure to that of E. All it does achieve is to account for the axiom-schema $\Box^i A \rightarrow \Box^i (x)A$, which tells us that if a singular proposition enjoys a particular level of inductive support so too does the first-order generalization of which it is a substitution-instance – a principle that is in effect shared by Baconian logic with the Hintikka–Hilpinen theory of acceptability.[8]

So we might as well start instead from what we can establish about the underlying semantical features that suffice to ensure a function's being an evaluation of probability that conforms to the axioms of the classical, Pascalian calculus. And I have already remarked (on the basis of work published elsewhere) that the various familiar concepts of probability all measure gradations of provability by criteria analogous to rules of inference in a complete deductive system for the elements of a Boolean algebra (where a complete system is one in which a proposition is provable if and only if its negation is not provable). In what respects, then, do the conditions of application for Baconian functions differ from these? In both cases the fillers of functional argument-places are elements of a Boolean algebra. But there must also be substantial differences,

---

[8] J. Hintikka and R. Hilpinen, 'Knowledge, Acceptance and Inductive Logic', in J. Hintikka and P. Suppes (eds.), *Aspects of Inductive Logic* (1966), p. 18.

in order to account for the resistance of Baconian logic to any form of representation in Pascalian terms.

What are these differences? It might perhaps be thought that eliminative induction, of the kind so far discussed, had nothing to do with gradations of provability. When we appraise the grade of support that a report of experimental evidence, E, gives to a hypothesis H, we in effect infer from E to a certain level of reliability for H. The inference is validated by whatever background knowledge we have about the sorts of variations in experimental circumstances that are relevant to hypotheses of H's type. If H has been tested successfully but only over relatively few variations, we can infer only a rather low floor for H's reliability: if it has survived a more thorough test, its minimum level of reliability must be higher. From the report of the test-result, we may infer – as experimental scientists often do – a statement about the hypothesis's level of reliability. So even if we think of the report as proving the truth of the latter statement, even if we think of $s[H] \geqslant i$ as being provable from E, it is not *that* provability which is being graded. Equally, if $s[H, E]$ graded the provability of H from E, we should no more be entitled by the truth of E to detach $s[H] \geqslant i$ from $s[H, E] \geqslant i$ than we are so entitled to detach the monadic Pascalian probability $p[H] = n$ from $p[H, E] = n$. So $s[H, E]$ does not grade the provability of H from E. At first sight therefore it looks as though no grading of provability is at issue in Baconian evaluations of evidential support, but only the proof of a grade of reliability. What varies, and is subject to graded evaluation, is the reliability of H that may be inferred from E, not the reliability of inferring H from E.

However this is not to be thought a serious point of difference between Pascalian and Baconian functions. It depends too much on just how we line up these two structures against one another in order to compare them. The fact is that we do get a gradation of provability in Baconian terms if we consider not the dyadic support-function $s[H, E]$ but the monadic grading of reliability $s[H]$. Suppose H is a conditional, then a grading for H's reliability is also a grading for the provability of H's consequent from H's antecedent. For example, if we establish by eliminative induction from experimental evidence a suitable ranking for the reliability of the generalization that all bees are colour-sensitive and thence for the proposition that if this insect is a bee it is colour-sensitive, then we have also established a suitable ranking for the provability of the conclusion that this insect is colour-sensitive from the premiss that this insect is a bee.

Unfortunately, in discussing Baconian reasoning, the title of 'inductive inference' has sometimes been given to such a move from the antecedent to the consequent of H, where $s[H] > 0$, and sometimes to the move from a report of experimental evidence, E, to $s[H] = i$, where $i > 0$. But this is unnecessarily confusing and I shall differentiate between a (dyadic) Baconian probability-function $p_I[H, E]$ and a (dyadic) Baconian support-function $s[H, E]$. We need to put $p_I[H, E]$ equal to $s[E \rightarrow H]$, and we can then define a monadic Baconian probability-function $p_I[H]$ as equal to $p_I[H, Hv \sim H]$. The logical liaisons of Baconian probability-functions are thus derivable within the same modal logic as those of Baconian support-functions. But, though $p_I[H]$ turns out to be demonstrably equal to $s[H]$, the dyadic functions $p_I[H, E]$ and $s[H, E]$ do not have the same logical structure. Most notably, if E contradicts H and $p_I[E] > 0$, then $p_I[H, E]$ must be zero, analogously to the Pascalian probability $p_M[H, E]$, but $s[H, E]$, as we have already seen, need not be zero in these circumstances.

Now a Baconian probability-function is not just a spin-off from the formalism. It has an important role to play in the analysis of human reasoning, especially in any matters, like human conduct, where rather simple uniformities are not at all common. That is because we can upgrade the inductive reliability of a conditional by introducing qualifications into its antecedent that will exclude falsifying circumstances. So $(x)((Ax \& Bx) \rightarrow Cx)$ may be more reliable than $(x)(Ax \rightarrow Cx)$ and correspondingly $p_I[Cy, Ay \& By]$ may be higher than $p_I[Cy, Ay]$. In this way Baconian probability-functions can reflect a build-up in the weight of evidence, and can in fact provide, as I have shown elsewhere,[9] a foundation for criteria of acceptance, or rational belief, that is free from the paradoxes which notoriously beset us when we try to employ Pascalian probability-functions in that role.

It is clear, therefore, that Baconian reasoning has a form of provability-gradation that may legitimately stand comparison with the Pascalian gradation of provability. So, if it is not in being concerned with statements about provability (for the elements of a Boolean algebra) that a Pascalian logic differs from a Baconian one, it must be in the type of provability and in the mode of graduating it.

3. *The Completeness–Incompleteness Issue*

Gradations of provability that have a Pascalian structure are analogous to criteria of proof in a complete deductive system. At the limiting case we have $p_M[B, A] = 1$ if and only if $p_M[\text{not-}B, A] = 0$,

[9] *The Probable and the Provable*, pp. 265 ff. and 310 ff.

and in general $p_M[B, A] = 1 - p_M[\text{not-}B, A]$. One is naturally in-clined to enquire, therefore, what kind of logical structure is re-quired for gradations of provability that are analogous to criteria of proof in an *in*complete deductive system.

Clearly the negation-principle in such a logic cannot be com-plementational, for it must be possible to have neither B nor not-B provable from A. That is to say, $p[B, A] = 0$ must not imply the falsehood of $p[\text{not-}B, A] = 0$. And certainly this implication does not hold in the logic of Baconian functions: we obviously cannot[10] derive $\sim\Box^1(A \rightarrow B) \rightarrow \Box^1(A \rightarrow \sim B)$ as a theorem-schema for that logic.

But, if a zero-value for the provability/probability of B on A does not imply a positive value for the provability/probability of not-B on A, then $p[B, A] = 0$ must be taken to signify the non-provability of B on A without implying its disprovability. Hence the kind of probability-function that grades provability in an incomplete system must be ascribed values that run from conclusive provability at one extreme to non-provability at the other, not from provability to disprovability. Such a function must be taken to grade the build-up of evidence in favour of a stated conclusion – the build-up from 'not in favour of (though not necessarily against)' to 'no room left for excluding the truth of'. That is to say, if we are given that $p[B, A] > 0$, we know that on balance the evidence stated in A favours the truth of B and that the specific value of $p[B, A]$ will grade how large a part of the totality of relevant facts is actually stated by A. Only if the evidence is, on balance, in favour of not-B would we instead, by grading the amount of relevant facts constituted by the evidence, obtain a positive, non-zero value for $p[\text{not-}B, A]$. So, when this kind of probability-function gives the provability of B on A a positive value it must give the probability of not-B on A a zero value. Or at least it must do this in any normal case, i.e., where A is not self-contradictory or otherwise anomalous as evidence. In short, we cannot have, in normal cases, both $p[B, A] > 0$ and $p[\text{not-}B, A] > 0$, which we can have in the Pascalian system, but have instead two non-complementational negation-principles ($p[B, A] > 0$ & $p[\text{not-}A] = 0) \rightarrow p[\text{not-}B, A] = 0$ and $p[A] > 0 \rightarrow p[\text{not-}A] = 0$.

Now it really does not matter very much whether or not you are willing to call such gradations of provability in an incomplete system a scale of 'probability'. Those who are unwilling to do so are presumably motivated by the desire to retain a formal, mathematical

[10] Cf. the interpretation into second-order quantification-theory that is given in *The Implications of Induction*, p. 236.

definition for the concept of probability. For them the axioms of the Pascalian calculus determine what is to count as a probability. They must then, of course, accept any non-standard interpretations of those axioms as also being probabilities, but they could – appropriately enough–take over Keynes's term 'weight' for the gradation of provability in an incomplete system. On the other hand if a philosopher is interested in the semantics of our concepts as well as in their logico-mathematical syntax, and accepts the analysis of probability in terms of provability, he can have no reason to reject the relevant distinction between provability in a complete system and provability in an incomplete one and must therefore recognize the latter as generating what can properly be called non-Pascalian probability-functions.

It turns out that Baconian probability-functions are of just this kind. Not only is $\sim\Box^1(A \to B) \to \Box^1(A \to \sim B)$ not derivable as a theorem-schema in their logic, but we *can* derive as theorem-schemas $(p_I[B, A] > 0 \ \& \ p_I[\sim A] = 0) \to p_I[\sim B, A] = 0$ and $p_I[A] > 0 \to p_I[\sim A] = 0$. But even when these facts have been established we are still rather far from having solved the problem with which the present paper is concerned. We have discovered features that admit of representation within a logic of Baconian reasoning, not features that require such representation. Our object was to discover general conditions for the application of such a logic, conditions that will govern eliminative inductions about both causal and non-causal domains. But what has been established so far is by no means sufficient to generate the axioms of this logic. In particular we cannot get from the negation-principles $(p[B, A] > 0 \ \& \ p[\sim A] = 0) \to p[\sim B, A] = 0$ and $p[A] > 0 \to p[\sim A] = 0$ to either of the logic's crucial modal principles $\Box^i(A \to B) \to (\Box^i A \to \Box^i B)$ and $\Box^i(A \to B) \to \Box^i(\Box^i A \to \Box^i B)$.

4. The Additivity Issue

We obviously, therefore, need to explore further the dissimilarities between the kind of provability graded by Baconian eliminative induction and the kind of provability graded by Pascalian functions. Now, one essential feature of the latter, in its classical form, is that it should be countably additive. Indeed, given this requirement, plus the restriction to elements of a Boolean algebra, we need little else to derive[11] the multiplicative law for the probability of conjunctions, which is one of the most important principles of the Pascalian

---

[11] Cf. R. T. Cox, *The Algebra of Probable Inference* (1961), pp. 4 ff.

calculus. But there is a good reason for supposing that the gradation of provability which is evaluated by eliminative induction is at best a rank-ordering. The reason is that the property fundamental to such gradations is not an additive one. If a property is additive, there must be an operation with it that corresponds in the ideal case to arithmetical addition, like the prolongation of a line when length is added to length. In this operation the sums of equal amounts of the property must also be equal, since if $a = b$ and $c = d$ then $a + c = b + d$. Hence the magnitude of the system that results from adding one amount of the property to another must depend only on the separate magnitudes of what are added and not on anything else, such as the order of addition or an interaction between the elements added. And though this is a necessary condition for additivity it is a condition that is not satisfied by the properties that standardly underlie eliminative induction.

In the paradigm case of eliminative induction about nature, for example, the fundamental property that underlies gradation of evidential support is the power of appropriate variations of circumstance to cause interruptions in the operation of a certain kind of natural uniformity. The reliability of a hypothesis is graded by its ability to survive tests under more and more powerful variations of circumstance, where power is increased by introducing more and more types of relevant circumstances into the variations. But, though the combination of one circumstance with another, or of one type of circumstance with another, is the only fundamental operation that could conceivably correspond to arithmetical addition in these inductive variations, it does not in fact do so. Nature is such that the combination of two factors often has a causal potency far greater than knowledge of their potencies in isolation would entitle us to expect. The match and the gas that combine to cause an explosion, or the barbiturates and whisky that may be lethal if taken together, are relatively harmless in isolation. In short it is no accident that experimental scientists have never themselves introduced a measure for the strength of evidential support by eliminative induction, despite their awareness of the advantages gained in so many fields of scientific enquiry by the introduction of quantitative terminology. They could not have introduced such a measure even if they had wanted to, because causal efficacy is not an additive property.

The only way to achieve an additive measure for evidential support would be to grade the latter in some other way than by the method of relevant variables. For example, one can build up a measure on the basis of an *a priori* selected language as in the range-theoretical tradition. But then, if there is no empirical constraint on the importance attached to particular primitive predicates or families of primitive predicates in the language, there is no reason whatever why H's being highly confirmed by E should in fact make H's truth worthy of being expected by observers of nature if E states all the evidence they know. Now Baconian evaluations of evidential support avoid this kind of objection because they are empirical judgements, falsifiable by appropriate increases in our background knowledge about relevant variables. Perhaps, therefore, a range-theorist may think that he can avoid the objection by somehow contriving that his choice of language should be sensitive to adverse experience. But if he tries to introduce empirical constraints on the importance attached to different basic units in the language he may well go astray if he does not relate their importance to the causal efficacy of the factors that these units designate, since that causal efficacy determines what an intelligent and knowledgeable observer of nature should expect to happen. And he is then involved in much the same difficulties about additivity as those confronting the method of relevant variables.

Analogous considerations affect the two other modes of eliminative induction that I mentioned earlier. For example, in most common-law jurisdictions the right of two people to co-habit is not restricted merely because they intend to have sexual relations. Nor is it restricted merely because one is an adult and the other a child. But the co-occurrence of these two circumstances is a rather potent factor in restricting people's legal rights. Again, the semantic feature +ARTIFICIAL is too widespread in our lexicon for it to be regarded as of particularly high significance, and even +CELESTIAL is used just to mark off the rest of reality from our sublunary world. But a combination of the two might once have been felt as an offence against lexical restrictions, and its occurrence today must be attributed a correspondingly high significance.

It looks therefore as though evidential support by eliminative induction must be regarded as a non-additive property. Or at the very least we can say that reasons exist for thinking it rash to assume that it is an additive one. It follows that additive measure-functions for eliminative induction are bound to lack credibility, and that we should be content with rank-orderings if we can devise them. So here is another respect in which a logic of Baconian reasoning must differ from the Pascalian calculus. It must not only be applicable to the generalization of provability in an incomplete system and so have a non-complementational negation principle. It must also control a kind of ranking-function, rather than a mode of quantitative measurement.

But now we have enough, in substance, to resolve the rest of our problem (bearing in mind that we have already accounted for the axiom-schema $\Box^i A \rightarrow \Box^i (x) A$). If the semantic requirement is a function that ranks propositions on a scale that runs from provability to non-provability, then on certain reasonable assumptions we can derive the crucial modal principle $\Box^i (A \rightarrow B) \rightarrow (\Box^i A \rightarrow \Box^i B)$: whether we use the method of relevant variables or any other method for assessing these probability-rankings, our assessments are forced into the same modal framework.

The argument begins by establishing a conjunction principle for monadic (unconditional) probablities, viz, if $p[H] \geqslant p[H']$, then $p[H \& H'] = p[H']$. Its premisses are:

  (i) The values of any function of the required kind are any sequence of integers $0, 1, 2, \ldots$ (This represents the restriction to ranking.)

 (ii) If $p[H] > 0$, then $p[\sim H] = 0$. (This is the negation principle generated by taking non-provability as the lower end of the scale of probabilities.)

Two assumptions are made:

(iii) What is a logical consequence of A must be at least as probable as A itself. (This is a corollary of taking probability to be a gradation of provability).

(iv) For any H and H' that are mutually consistent, and for any value of $p[H]$ such that $p[H] \geqslant p[H']$, and for any $n \geqslant 0$, $p[H \& H']$ must have different values for $p[H'] = n$ and $p[H'] = n + 1$, respectively: it must be strictly monotonic increasing with $p[H']$. (Otherwise the probability of a conjunction would be independent of the probability of one of its conjuncts in an undesirable respect: note that where $p[H] \geqslant p[H']$ it follows from (iii) that if H entails H', $p[H] = p[H']$.)

The argument then proceeds:

 (v) According to (iii), $p[H] \geqslant p[H \& H']$.

 (vi) It follows from (i) and (iv) that, if H and H' are mutually consistent and $p[H] \geqslant p[H']$, then $p[H'] \leqslant p[H \& H']$.

(vii) If H and H' are mutually inconsistent, then according to (iii) $p[\sim H] \geqslant p[H \& \sim H] \geqslant p[H \& H']$.

(viii) According to (i) and (ii) either $p[H]=0$ or $p[\sim H]=0$.

(ix) It follows from (iii), (vii), and (viii) that, if H and H' are mutually inconsistent, then $p[H \& H']=0$.

(x) It follows from (v), (vi), (viii), and (ix), that if $p[H] \geqslant p[H']$ then $p[H \& H']=p[H']$.

We can now establish the crucial modal principle: if $p[H$ only if $H'] \geqslant n$, then $p[H] \geqslant n$ only if $p[H'] \geqslant n$, corresponding to $\Box^i(A \to B) \to (\Box^i A \to \Box^i B)$ in logical notation:

(xi) By (x), if $p[H$ only if $H'] \geqslant n \leqslant p[H]$, then $p[(H$ only if $H') \& H] \geqslant n$.

(xii) By (iii) and (xi), if $p[H$ only if $H'] \geqslant n \leqslant p[H]$, then $p[H'] \geqslant n$.

(xiii) By exportation from (xii), if $p[H$ only if $H'] \geqslant n$, then $p[H] \geqslant n$ only if $p[H'] \geqslant n$.

And, on the further assumption that on the null set of premisses there is no difference between proving H and proving that one has proved H (i.e., on the assumption that, if $p[H] \geqslant n$, then $p[p[H] \geqslant n] \geqslant n$), we easily obtain from (iii) and (xiii) that if $p[H$ only if $H'] \geqslant n$, then $p[p[H] \geqslant n$ only if $p[H'] \geqslant n] \geqslant n$.

5. *Some Final Comments*

Perhaps I should just make three further clarificatory comments.

First, some philosophers may be tempted to suppose that the problem which I have been discussing could have been solved by describing a possible-worlds model for the modal logic in question. Such a model is easily sketched.[12] Physically possible worlds are defined as those logically possible worlds that are subject to the same appropriately testable uniformities as the actual one, and are then ranked by their possession of cumulatively more and more relevant circumstances, with the actual world having a plenitude of them. The Baconian reliability of an appropriately testable hypothesis H is then evaluated by the highest grade of relevantly eventful world in which H is true (or in which some proposition H' is true such that H is true in all logically possible worlds in which H' is true). Though this kind of model-building, if realistically intended,

[12] Cf. *The Probable and the Provable*, pp. 240 ff. This model follows the scheme for the method of relevant variables that is sketched ibid., pp. 143 f. That is, it is assumed that each test incorporates every previous test. It thus becomes possible to discard the requirement mentioned ibid., p. 139, that a more important relevant variable can never have its falsificatory power nullified by a less important one; and the account of probability-grading that is given ibid., pp. 202 ff., needs to be modified in the light of the assumption that each test incorporates every previous test.

is subject to the kind of anti-metaphysical criticism that Kant levelled against its Leibnizian antecedents, it does provide a useful basis for comparison between monadic Baconian functions and monadic Carnapian ones. Carnap may be construed as having measured the logical range of a proposition by the sum of the values severally assigned to each logically possible world in which the proposition holds good, while a monadic Baconian function ranks its inductive reliability by the fullness of the fullest possible world in which it holds good. But this model is at best just one amongst many intelligible interpretations for the modal logic in question. As such it cannot explain why certain other interpretations are possible in which, for example, reference may be made to the isolation of certain combinations of circumstances in laboratory experiments rather than to their lonely existence in a jejune world that is conceivable but not actual.

Secondly, the problem that I have been talking about is a philosophical, not a psychological or sociological one. It is not the problem of how to explain the fact that in such-and-such areas of our culture we employ evaluations of evidential support which – at least in their idealized form – obey Baconian principles. Presumably a capacity for inductive reasoning of this kind would have immense survival value in a physical universe that is governed – or at least largely governed – by causal laws, and brains that were innately equipped with such a capacity would economically conceive socio-political laws, semantic conventions, or other uniformities, in terms of the same underlying logical structure. In some such way we might hope one day to explain the fact that human beings use Baconian reasoning in cognitive enquiry, judical procedure, semantic learning, etc. But we could still wonder whether there is any non-disjunctive description that would cover all such forms of Baconian reasoning and would non-trivially entail the kind of modal logic which the method of relevant variables requires. By having such a description we have a deep philosophical elucidation why the logic of hypothesis-gradings in experimental science is as it is, instead of needing to fall back on the claim that this logic somehow matches the causal order about which the reasonings that it regulates are concerned.

Thirdly, even when we have the desired description, we still have on our hands the problem of explaining how different forms of Baconian reasoning are possible. The analogous problem in the case of Pascalian reasoning can be dealt with, as I said, mainly by drawing certain familiar distinctions between different kinds of provability in order to generate niches into which the various recognized types of Pascalian probability – relative frequencies, logical relations, etc.,–may be seen to fit. But the distinctions appropriate for this purpose in the case of Pascalian reasoning do not all seem fruitful in relation to the present problem. For example, the provabilities established by eliminative induction are all non-extensional. However the contingent/non-contingent distinction is obviously relevant here. There is an obvious difference between the contingent provabilities that are graded by inductive reasoning about nature, and the non-contingent ones graded by inductive reasoning about numbers.[13] And there is another kind of obvious difference between the gradation of proofs about what is the case, as in mathematics or natural science, and the gradation of proofs about what ought to be the case, as in ethics or jurisprudence. Moreover, as I pointed out in my comment[14] on Levi's paper, Levi–Shackle belief-functions stand to Baconian probability-functions in a relationship analogous to that in which a personalist interpretation of the Pascalian calculus stands to a propensity interpretation of it. They share a common underlying structure, but whereas Baconian functions are about reality, Levi–Shackle ones are about our thoughts about reality. Some philosophers will no doubt wish to insist, as Levi does, that one such interpretation of this underlying structure is the correct one, and that other interpretations are incorrect, just as it has often been argued that, say, the personalist interpretation of the Pascalian calculus is the correct one, and the propensity interpretation is incorrect, or vice versa. But it is more fruitful here, just as in the case of Pascalian probability, to investigate the conditions under which the various possible interpretations or theories are severally applicable than to seek reasons for holding one such theory universally true and the others universally false. For example, Levi–Shackle functions can concern themselves, in a rather heavily idealized way,[15] with beliefs about any topic whatever and not just about those justifiable by the method of relevant variables. But, just so far as they are indeed concerned with beliefs, the substitutivity of their argument-places must always be very heavily restricted, whereas the substitutivity of the argument-places in Baconian functions is restricted only in accordance with the nature of their subject-matter.

[13] Cf. ibid., p. 127, and *The Implications of Induction*, p. 181.

[14] Cf. p. 64 above.

[15] Cf. Teller's remarks on pp. 31–7 above. Also Levi's system does not include a rule of universalizability analogous to my $\Box^i A \to \Box^i(x)A$.

§11. Arthur W. Burks
Enumerative Induction versus Eliminative Induction

1. *The Problem*

Jonathan Cohen has formulated a rule of inductive proof which he calls the 'method of relevant variables'. Suppose a scientist wishes to show that there is a lawlike connection from antecedent property A to consequent property C. He considers those properties P_1, $P_2, \ldots, P_n$ which are *prima facie* relevant to the occurrence of C, and tests A in the context of various compounds of $P_1, P_2, \ldots, P_n$. He finds that C does indeed follow A in all these contexts, and concludes that A is sufficient to produce C.

The method of relevant variables clearly encompasses Bacon's tables of instances and Mill's methods of experimental enquiry. The relevant variables may be quantitative, in which case Cohen's method becomes the controlled experiment, and the conclusion is some quantitative relation between A and C rather than a simple 'if A then C'.

In classical terminology, the method of relevant variables is a rule of eliminative induction. As such it is to be contrasted with the traditional rule of induction by simple enumeration, a rule of enumerative induction. This is a rule in which instances count probabilistically towards the verification of a generalization of the form 'for all x, if x is A, x is C'. Assuming no counterinstances, the probability that 'if A then C' holds, increases with the number of instances in which C follows A. The universal generalization may state a quantitative functional relation from A to C, in which case the instances must exemplify that relation. The concept of probability employed here is that of inductive probability.

Both the method of relevant variables and the rule of induction by simple enumeration can be stated to cover statistical generalizations also. Since argument forms that conclude to universal generalizations are more applicable to legal statements, Cohen concentrates on these. I will do likewise.

In his earlier books[1] and the present paper, Cohen makes several claims about the superiority of his method of relevant variables over induction by simple enumeration: that it is a more accurate description of the inductive inferences actually made in science; that it is more widely applicable outside of science, particularly in the sphere

---

[1] *The Implications of Induction* (1970) and *The Probable and the Provable* (1977).

of law; and that it is philosophically more basic. I will focus on the last of these claims.

2. Complexity, Hierarchy

However, before doing that I shall make some remarks on two topics that will be useful as background, namely (1) the complexity of rules, and (2) hierarchies in natural and artificial systems. The experiences of computer scientists with these topics are relevant to our present discussion of induction.

(1) Consider a set of formal objects (e.g., statements, computer programs, automata) which are built from primitives. One can assign weights to the primitives and define the complexity of a compound (or system) as the sum of the weights of its primitive parts. For example, the complexity of a computer may be defined as a weighted sum of its switching (logic) and storage elements. Having that definition, one can then define the complexity of a particular computer function (rule, algorithm) as the complexity of the simplest computer that performs that function.

One can also move up a level and define the complexity of an object in terms of the complexity of a meta-object which produces it. For example, given a computer and a suitable program language that the computer understands, we can define the complexity of a particular computer function as the length of the shortest program in that language which will direct the machine to perform that function.

This idea has been used by Kolmogorov and Chaitin to give an excellent definition of randomness.[2] A suitable computer and programming language are chosen. A finite binary sequence is random if it is of approximately the same length as the shortest program that produces it. Intuitively, a random sequence is patternless – it has no pattern which repeats. An infinite binary sequence is random if an infinite number of its finite initial segments are random.

The guiding idea of this method of defining complexity is that a reference basis is established for a formal system, and the complexity of a formal object is then taken to be the weighted sum of the parts of that object, or the weighted sum of the parts of a meta-object which describes or produces that object. For appropriate

[2] A. N. Kolmogorov, 'Tri Podhoda k Opredeleniju Ponjatija "Kolicestvo Informacii"', *Problemy Peredaci Informacii* 1 (1965), 3–11. Gregory Chaitin, 'On the Length of Programs for Computing Finite Binary Sequences: Statistical Considerations', *Journal of the Association for Computing Machinery* 16 (1969), 145–59.

A discussion of this and other senses of 'random' is given in my *Chance, Cause, Reason* (1977), pp. 592–603.

choices of formal systems, weighting schemes, and levels, one may obtain intuitively reasonable measures of complexity. In many applications one does not need a very good measure, for rough or comparative measures will suffice. This will be the case when we talk about the complexity of rules of induction. I will illustrate this point now by sketching my explanation of the phenomenon of vagueness in terms of complexity.

A concept is vague in relation to a domain of application, which is a set of objects to be classified by the concept. The concept is a kind of pattern-recognition rule, classifying some pattern-instances of the domain as falling under the concept, some pattern-instances as excluded, and failing to classify some pattern-instances. Being a rule, the pattern-recognition rule has a certain complexity by some plausible definition of complexity.

Consider next those properties of the objects of the domain that are relevant to the classification process. These are related in various ways, and hence constitute a structure. This structure also has a complexity.

I think vagueness can be understood in terms of the comparative complexity of the pattern-recognition rule associated with the concept, and the complexity of the structure of properties involved in the instances of the domain of application. When the latter complexity is greater than the former, some instances of the domain will be too complex for the rule to analyse successfully.[3]

This completes my background discussion of the complexity of rules, which I will apply later to rules of induction. I take up next the topic of hierarchies.

(2) The notion of hierarchy is applicable to both natural and artificial systems. In nature, atoms combine to make molecules, small molecules join to make large molecules, large molecules are components of cells, cells make up organs, and organs are parts of organisms. In computers, components are connected into circuits, circuits make up subsystems, and so on. Similar remarks can be made about computer software.

Man is the highest known product of evolution. It has been argued that there has not been time for evolution to produce this result by chance.[4] The argument is worth analysing because of the light it throws on the notion of hierarchy.

---

[3] This theory of vagueness is explained more fully in my 'Computer Science and Philosophy', *Current Research in Philosophy of Science*, ed. by Peter Asquith and Henry Kyburg (1979), pp. 408–9.

[4] P. S. Moorhead and M. M. Kaplan (eds.), *Mathematical Challenges to the Neo-Darwinian Interpretation of Evolution* (1967). See the papers by Murray Eden and M. Schutzenberger.

The argument goes like this. Man is composed of certain primitive components which existed at the beginning of the evolutionary process. Evolution mixes these components randomly at certain rates. The complexity of man in terms of his components can be estimated to an order of magnitude. From these assumptions one can calculate the probability that such a complex object will be formed by random mixing over the given time span. On this calculation, it is unlikely that man would have been produced by evolution.

The flaw in the argument concerns the mode of construction of the final product. The argument assumes that the original parts are combined directly to make the final product. In fact, evolution proceeds in stages, moving up a hierarchy of levels.[5] Small compounds are made from the initial parts, medium compounds from the small compounds, and on up to organs, and finally organisms. Enzyme operators, genetic programmes, and the heart are all examples of such compounds.

It is critical to evolution, and to its rate of progress, that the structures produced at each level are both stable and capable of change. Their stability allows them to serve as parts of larger structures, on up through higher levels of the hierarchy. Their adaptability allows them to perform the same function in many different contexts, that is, in many different kinds of structures at higher levels. This combination of stability and adaptability enables evolution to build small compounds, test these, combine the successful small compounds into larger compounds, then test these, and so on up the hierarchy. The final product is definitely *not* constructed directly from its most elementary parts, as the argument that evolution has not had time to produce man assumes.

There is a significant analogy between natural and artificial systems here. A complex computing system is built in a similar manner. Components are made into circuits and the circuits tested. The circuits are made into subsystems, perhaps with modifications for different contexts. Et cetera. There is a difference in that biological subsystems are generally more dependent on the rest of the system for their existence and operation. Thus enzymes operate only in a certain chemical environment, and it is hard to maintain a heart outside a body. But this is only a difference in degree. The ordinary computer fails to operate at extreme temperatures, and at one time computers were air-conditioned even though humans weren't.

Incidentally, I think that functional statements in biology, such as

[5] Herbert Simon, *The Sciences of the Artificial* (1969), pp. 90–5.

'the function of the heart is to pump blood', should be analysed in these hierarchical design terms.

3. *Enumerative Induction is Basic*

This completes my discussion of hierarchies, which I will apply later to rules of induction. I turn now to Cohen's claim that the method of relevant variables is more fundamental than induction by simple enumeration.

The opposing view was stated very nicely by David Hume.

Nothing so like as eggs: yet no one, on account of this appearing similarity, expects the same taste and relish in all of them. It is only after a long course of uniform experiments in any kind, that we attain a firm reliance and security with regard to a particular event. Now where is that process of reasoning which, from one instance, draws a conclusion, so different from that which it infers from a hundred instances that are no-wise different from that single one? This question I propose as much for the sake of information, as with an intention of raising difficulties. I cannot find, I cannot imagine any such reasoning.[6]

I think Hume's fundamental point is correct, though his formulation of it is misleading.

It is misleading for Hume to say that induction by simple enumeration is not reasoning. It is not *deductive* reasoning, to be sure. But it is *inductive* reasoning. Hume recognizes this fact in other places, where he calls this type of reasoning 'reasoning from causation', 'reasoning concerning matters of fact', and 'probable reasoning'.[7]

Language aside, Hume is stating a profound thesis about induction. He sees that induction has an essential feature which distinguishes it from deduction: each instance affects the probability of the conclusion.

Since inductive reasoning involves repetition, it presupposes both a repeatable factor and a matrix or framework in which repetition can occur. On my view, non-indexical properties are the repeatable factor of induction, and space-time is the framework in which repetition occurs. For example, 'green', 'being in a magnetic field', and 'dissolving in aqua regia' refer to non-indexical properties; 'occurring today', 'being in my house now', 'living in the Himalayas' contain implicit references to space or time and denote indexical

---

[6] *An Enquiry Concerning Human Understanding*, sec. 4, part 2 (in *Enquiries*, ed. by L. A. Selby-Bigge, 2nd ed., 1902, p. 36).

[7] Hume's misuse of ordinary language here is related to his scepticism concerning induction. See sec. 3.3.2 of my *Chance, Cause, Reason.*

properties.[8] The basic rule of induction by simple enumeration states that the more often non-indexical properties are associated in space-time the more likely it is that they are always so associated.

If Hume is right, and repetition does play an essential role in inductive reasoning, what is the status of the method of relevant variables? I suggest that it is compatible with, and depends on, induction by simple enumeration. For one thing, after an hypothesis has been eliminated by the method of relevant variables, several alternative hypotheses usually remain. Enumerative induction generally gives information about the relative probabilities of those alternatives.

More basically, I suggest that our inductive rules are arranged in a hierarchy, with induction by simple enumeration at the lowest level and the method of relevant variables at a fairly high level. I will elaborate this speculation by means of Charles Peirce's notion of a 'habit'.[9]

I follow Peirce in holding that there is a strong analogy between the evolution of species, the evolution of individual belief, and the evolution of science. Peirce used the term 'habit' in this connection, employing it in a sense sufficiently general to cover the hereditary action patterns of the individuals of a species as well as learned habits. The concepts, rules, methods, procedures, etc., of social institutions, such as science and the law, are also included. In science the 'habits' are the procedures and methods of enquiry which are used, as well as the accepted theories as they are employed in scientific enquiry.

Peirce intended his notion of habit to cover any operative set of rules embodied in a system or subsystem in the most general sense. He talked about 'habits' rather than 'systems' because he was focusing on function, law, behaviour, input-output relation, etc., rather than on the physical or biological embodiments of these. Any entity, organ, or subsystem (e.g., an enzyme, the heart, a computer memory) performing a function would be executing a habit. It follows that Peirce's concept of a habit covers algorithms, strategies, and computer programs when they are used to recognize input patterns, to produce transformations, to act, or to respond to stimuli.

Peircean habits are both stable and adaptive, and thus have the

---

[8] The distinction is explained in sec. 9.2 of my *Chance, Cause, Reason*.
[9] *Collected Papers of Charles Sanders Peirce*: vols. 1–6 ed. by Charles Hartshorne and Paul Weiss (1931–5); vols. 7–8 ed. by Arthur Burks (1958).

two characteristics essential to the construction of complex compounds by an evolutionary process. Thus Peircean habits are appropriate building blocks in a natural hierarchy as I described this concept early on.[10]

Let us now look at the complex of human habits concerned with reasoning in the broadest sense, including learning, problem-solving, discovery, and enquiry, as well as the logic of argument, justification, and proof. A person applying an inductive rule employs many habits that he has acquired during his life and these have a hierarchical structure. I'll illustrate this in a moment with the pattern-recognition rules whereby one classifies groups of qualities together as more general properties.

Now, individual habits are acquired and modified by a statistical process similar to the rule of induction by simple enumeration. Successful exercise of a habit strengthens it, so instances do count in the way Hume said they did. Indeed. when analysing causal inferences, Hume was doing psychology as well as inductive logic.

As with the individual, so with science, for science is an institution of the 'community of investigators'. Scientific knowledge arises from common-sense knowledge, and the intellectual habits of individuals are constituents of the higher-level 'habits' of science. Within science, advances are based on various experimental procedures and established theories. These procedures and theories are generally stable. But they are also subject to revision and incorporation in improved procedures and theories.

My thesis is that learning and induction involve a hierarchy of concepts and properties, statements and laws, rules and methods. The materials of one level incorporate those of lower levels and are incorporated in those of higher levels. The method of relevant variables is high in the hierarchy, and hence fits scientific practice more directly than enumerative induction. Enumerative induction is basic, operating from the lowest level on up.

4. Causal Hierarchies in Induction

Let us look further at the structure of this hierarchy and the role enumerative induction plays in it.

The hierarchy has an epistemological part, containing concepts,

---

[10] Peirce expresses some of his assertions about hierarchies when treating successive stages of evolutionary, common-sense, and scientific learning. He expresses others as iterations of his three categories: First, Second, Third. Thus a particular kind of Thirdness may have three subsidiary forms (First, Second, Third) with respect to some subordinate principle of classification. For examples, see my paper with Paul Weiss, 'Peirce's Sixty-Six Signs', *J. Phil.* 42 (1945), 383–8.

statements, rules, and methods. It also has an objective part, containing laws of nature and the properties and variables interconnected by these laws. The concepts, properties, statements, laws, rules, and methods of one level are interrelated among themselves and to their counterparts on other levels in various ways. For example, a method of enquiry presupposes certain laws and is employed to discover and confirm other laws. The search for new laws is guided by probability estimates as to what properties are likely to be connected by law.

As Peirce emphasized, science grew out of a body of commonsense generalizations. These were used as a basis for establishing elementary theories, and on up the hierarchy. This process continues. Generalizations, laws, and theories established at one level become the background assumptions for those tested at the next level. For example, in conducting an experiment, scientists rely on the laws governing the apparatus. At each level various generalizations and procedures are established by repeated success, while other generalizations and procedures are eliminated because they are not confirmed or perform poorly.

Another hierarchical way in which eliminative induction depends on enumerative induction concerns our knowledge of what properties are likely to enter into laws. Cohen calls his rule of induction the method of *relevant* variables. To apply it an investigator must know which variables are relevant in the given context.

Cohen's method is very similar to what I call 'the method of varying causally *relevant* qualities'.[11] Both methods were designed to encompass Bacon's tables of instances, Mill's method of experimental enquiry, and the controlled experiment. All these inductive procedures involve varying certain properties by experiment or observation, and observing the effects.

It has long been recognized as a weakness of these rules of eliminative induction that some properties are plausible candidates for variation and others are not. This point is sometimes made to an elementary class by means of the simplistic argument: sufficient amounts of bourbon and soda result in drunkenness, and so do sufficient amounts of scotch and soda; therefore, soda causes drunkenness!

Inductive relevance may also be viewed in Bayesian terms. Suppose A is followed by C in the presence of B. Is the correct generalization 'if A then C' or is it 'if AB then C'? This last hypothesis has initial plausibility only if variable B is relevant to variables A and C.

---

[11] *Chance, Cause, Reason*, pp. 101–2.

Now relevance is a relation, questions of relevance being of the form: Is property Q relevant to the properties $P_1, P_2, \ldots, P_n$? Such questions are clearly inductive questions, for 'relevance' means 'inductively relevant', not 'deductively relevant'. Information about relevance is gained by prior use of the rule of induction by simple enumeration. To show this we need to examine how man's hierarchically organized conceptual apparatus has been produced by evolution, learning, and scientific enquiry.[12]

A conceptual structure represents a corresponding hierarchical structure of properties. Properties on one level may be combinations of properties of lower levels. For example, many distinguishable shades of red are lumped together under the generic term 'redness'. In turn, red, blue, green, etc. are classified together as colours. These combinations of properties become more and more inclusive and complicated at higher levels in the hierarchy of properties. Quantitative measures are often involved, as they are in the states of a physical system, the utilities of acts, and the strengths of chess positions.

Suppose a person has formed a concept of some property of his environment. According to Peirce's theory that a concept is a habit, this concept is a pattern-recognition rule or program whereby the person identifies and can respond to instances of the property. Concept rules are also employed for other purposes, such as imagining the property or thinking about it. Concept rules may be combined logically to form single unified rules that are concepts of compound properties. Such unified rules are very analogous to computer programs compounded of other computer programs.

We are now in a position to see how our conceptual structures contain information about property relevance that has been obtained by enumerative induction throughout the processes of evolution, learning, and scientific enquiry. Concepts are rules or programs which men employ in adjusting to their environment. The development of these programs has been governed by the same basic laws that apply to the development of man as a whole.

The conceptual structure we have at birth is the product of the evolution of our species.[13] This structure grows as we learn from

---

[12] This theory of causal relevance is derived from Peirce's idea that general properties are Thirds and from general evolutionary considerations.

[13] It is part of what I have called our *innate* structure-program complex, which under the influence of experience develops into our *acquired* structure-program complex. *Chance, Cause, Reason*, sec. 10.2.1.

See also my treatment of these ideas in relation to Kant's categories and evolutionary theory. 'Computer Science and Philosophy', op. cit., pp. 404–7, 416–17.

experience, including scientific experience. I suggest that our concepts have developed during the evolutionary, common-sense learning, and scientific stages in a manner similar to the way that our genetic programmes have evolved. Concept rules have been modified, compounded with other concept rules, tested for their utility in helping us adjust to the environment, with the most useful ones being retained at each stage. As noted earlier, this genetic-like learning procedure is a statistical process, similar to induction by simple enumeration. The more often a concept has proved useful the more likely it is to be retained in our conceptual structure. There are many ways in which concepts are useful. For example, it is convenient to have simple concepts for those objects, situations, and properties which we experience often, or which are very important for us.

We are especially interested here in those features of concepts which facilitate inductive reasoning. It is better to have simple rather than complex concepts for those properties which are likely to enter into causal laws. This explains why 'red' and 'swan' are simple and natural notions for us in comparison to 'red square or blue circle' and 'is a swan near this brick house'. It is also of adaptive value for us to group properties together according to their likely causal interrelations. How do we acquire this second-order information about which properties and which groups of properties are likely to enter into causal laws?

We learn it by enumerative induction from our experiences, both successful and unsuccessful, in searching for and finding causal laws. The more often a property occurs (or two properties are connected) in a successful hypothesis, the more likely we take it to be that property will occur (or those two properties will be connected) in other successful hypotheses. Thus the relevant information on which the method of relevant variables depends is derived from experience by enumerative induction.

I think it will clarify this account of how we learn about the causal relevance of properties to explain an analogous situation in computer learning. This is the way Arthur Samuel's checkers-playing-and learning program selected good general measures of the strength of a board position in checkers (draughts).[14] Such specific measures as the number of men, the number of kings, mobility, and centre

[14] A. L. Samuel, 'Some Studies in Machine Learning Using the Game of Checkers', *IBM Journal of Research and Development* 3 (1959), 211–32; 'Some Studies in Machine Learning Using the Game of Checkers II–Recent Progress', ibid., 11 (1967), 601–17.

control are relevant to the relative strengths of the board positions of the two players. To assess the strengths of its possible moves, the checker-playing part of the program used a general measure consisting of a weighted sum of certain chosen specific measures.

I'll first explain how the program used this general measure to play checkers, and then how it improved the general measure by an inductive learning process.

When it was its turn to move, the program needed to decide which of its possible moves was best. It could apply the general measure directly to each possible move and choose the one with the highest value. But the program did better by choosing its moves on the basis of their consequences, in the following manner. It explored the game tree representing its possible moves and the possible countermoves of its opponent, for as long a span of play as could be calculated in the time available. It used the general measure to calculate the strength of each board position reached at the end of this span of play. Making the assumption that its opponent would choose optimum countermoves, the program chose the move that would leave it with the best board position.

Starting with a poor general measure given to it by Samuel, the learning part of the program made an inductive search for a better general measure of the strength of board positions. It did this on two levels, within a game and over successive games. Within a game it modified the weights assigned to specific measures according to a uniformity requirement, and over successive games it tried general measures composed of different specific measures to see which won the most games.

The fact that the value of a board position calculated directly was inferior to the value of that position calculated in terms of its consequences after a short span of play reflected an imperfection in the general measure. A good general measure would give approximately the same value for these two calculations, though the general measure with which the program started did not. This requirement of uniformity was used by the program to improve its general measure during the course of a game. To search for a more uniform measure, the program modified the weights it assigned to the specific measures of which the general measure was composed. It then used this new measure to select its moves. If the new measure gave more uniform results, it was adopted. This procedure was iterated during the course of each game to find a good set of weights for a given set of specific measures.

The specific measures employed were sometimes changed between games. The program replaced one specific measure by another, and modified the weighting system of this new general measure over several games. If the new general measure won more games than the old, it was adopted provisionally. For our purposes, it is important to note that replacing one specific measure by another is closely analogous to trying one relevant variable in place of another in a scientific experiment.

This two-level evolutionary procedure of modifying, testing, and selecting general measures was iterated repeatedly. In this way the checkers program found general measure of the strength of board positions, and thus learned to play tournament-calibre checkers.

We are now able to see the analogy between the operation of Samuel's checkers-playing-and-learning program and the way we learn which properties enter into natural laws. The program's general measure of position strength was a compound concept. This compound concept was constructed out of simple concepts, namely, a set of specific measures of position strength. The program began with a general concept that measured actual strength poorly, and hence the program played poorly. The program then modified this general concept on the basis of repeated experiences until it had constructed a concept which was a good measure of the actual strength of board positions, so that the program played successfully.

Similarly, to learn what properties enter into natural laws, we construct compound concepts from simple ones. We modify these constructions in an inductive fashion according to their success in enquiry, until we find compound concepts that correspond to the properties and variables that are interconnected by laws of nature. This is done at successive levels of the hierarchy, beginning with common-sense concepts and generalizations, moving to scientific concepts and causal laws, and on up to the concepts and theories of highly advanced science.

This concludes my account of how we learn about the likely causal relevance of a property or group of properties. Before leaving this topic, I should like to point out that it has implications for the formulation of the rule of induction by simple enumeration.

Positive instances do not always raise the probability of a generalization. The more often a metal wire is bent without breaking, the more likely that it will break the next time it is bent. A run of heads on a fair coin does not make a head on the next toss more likely; or less likely, as gamblers sometimes think.

These apparent counterinstances to enumerative induction can be understood in terms of our idea of an inductive hierarchy. The primitive form of the rule of induction by simple enumeration occurs at the ground level of the hierarchy and applies to the non-indexical properties of this level. The relatively complex concepts of fatigue and randomness occur several levels up. At this level we have learned by enumerative induction that metal wire is subject to fatigue and that certain elaborate procedures generate random sequences.[15]

Let us now summarize the results of this section. Eliminative induction depends on enumerative induction in several ways: for probabilistic information as to what properties are likely to be involved in causal laws, and which groups of these are likely to be casually interconnected and hence are worthy of experimental test; for laws and procedures assumed in an experimental test; and, when an hypothesis is eliminated, for information about the respective likelihoods of the remaining hypotheses. Thus a use of the method of eliminative induction presupposes that a good deal of inductive work has already been done by means of enumerative induction. The converse is not the case, so enumerative induction is more basic than eliminative induction.

5. *Formalization of Induction*

It is natural to ask: Could my claims about induction be demonstrated constructively and in detail, by developing a hierarchical system of inductive logic in which higher-order inductive inferences could be modelled formally? Such a formal system would put the whole idea of a hierarchy of inductive rules on a firm basis, and show that induction by simple enumeration does provide a solid foundation for induction, as Hume thought.

In my opinion, if the traditional philosophical notion of formalization is extended to include computer modelling, then all human behaviour is in principle formalizable.[16] A *fortiori*, inductive and learning behaviour is formalizable, in principle. In fact, however, we are a long way from being able to show by formal methods and computer models how a hierarchy of inductive rules operates. For the remainder of my time I'll review briefly the state of formalization of inductive logic, both in philosophy and in computer science, from the perspective of this paper.

Rudolf Carnap's quantitative systems of confirmation were the

---

[15] This issue is discussed in sec. 3.3.3 of my *Chance, Cause, Reason.*
[16] I argue for this general thesis on pp. 308–11 of 'Logic, Biology, and Automata – Some Historical Reflections', *International Journal of Man–Machine Studies* 7 (1975), 297–312, and in 'Computer Science and Philosophy', op. cit., near the end of sec. 2.

first formal models of inductive argument that contained both the probability calculus and the rule of induction by simple enumeration.[17] In these systems, repeated instances of 'if A then C' raise the probability that the next instance of A will be C.

However, repeated instances of 'if A then C' do not raise the probability of 'for all instances x, if Ax then Cx'. For when there are infinitely many individuals in the model, all universal generalizations have a zero prior probability and are unconfirmable. This weakness in Carnap's formalization of induction was overcome by Jaakko Hintikka, who extended Carnap's system so that universal generalizations have non-zero prior probabilities and may be confirmed by enumerative induction.[18]

These inductive logics are based on first-order quantification theory, and so the universal generalizations confirmed in them are extensional rather than modal. This is a serious defect for anyone who holds that basic scientific generalizations are modal, involving a kind of necessity. Both Jonathan Cohen and I hold this non-extensionalist position on scientific laws. I'll say a few words about our views, and then review what has been done to incorporate modality into formal inductive models.

The necessity in question is not logical necessity, but a different kind, called variously 'natural necessity', 'physical necessity', and 'causal necessity'. Cohen calls it 'natural necessity'. I call it 'causal necessity', partly out of respect for Hume and Kant, the former not finding this kind of necessity after a careful search and the latter making it one of his basic categories. I do not, however, restrict causal necessity to statements of cause and effect, as Hume and Kant did, but apply it to laws of nature and true scientific theories generally.

In my logic of causal statements I employ the usual $\Box$ for logical necessity, and $\Box^c$ for causal necessity.[19] Cohen has a finite sequence of necessity operators $\Box^d$, $\Box^{d-1}$, $\Box^{d-2}$, ..., $\Box^1$, the number of operators d depending on the complexity of each application of his method of relevant variables. For him, $\Box^d$ symbolizes logical necessity and $\Box^{d-1}$ symbolizes natural necessity. The remaining $d-2$ modal operators correspond to certain stages in the process of

---

[17] *Logical Foundations of Probability* (1950), and *The Continuum of Inductive Methods* (1952).

[18] 'A Two-Dimensional Continuum of Inductive Methods', pp. 113–32 of *Aspects of Inductive Logic*, ed. by J. Hintikka and P. Suppes (1966).

'Induction by Enumeration and Induction by Elimination', pp. 191–216 of *The Problem of Inductive Logic*, ed. by I. Lakatos (1968).

[19] *Chance, Cause, Reason*, chs. 6 and 7.

eliminating variables or properties which the investigator thought might be relevant but which turn out not to be.

Consider again the investigator who wishes to ascertain whether A by itself is sufficient by itself to produce C, or whether some of the variables $P_1, P_2, \ldots, P_n$ enter into the production of C. He tests A in the context of various compounds of the properties $P_1, P_2, \ldots, P_n$ and finds that A does bring about C in all these contexts. Now imagine these tests ordered in a sequence numbered $1, 2, \ldots, d-2, d-1$. Abbreviate the generalization '(x) (if Ax then Cx)' by G. As G passes the i'th test, the investigator is warranted in making the corresponding assertion $\square^i G$. Thus over the complete series of tests, the investigator is warranted in asserting $\square^1 G$, $\square^2 G, \ldots, \square^{d-2} G$, and $\square^{d-1} G$ in turn. Note that $\square^{d-1} G$ asserts that G is necessary or lawlike, and is warranted after G passes all the tests of this application of the rule of eliminative induction.

Without objecting to Cohen's analysis, I would describe the sequence of tests in a different way, replacing each of Cohen's assertions $\square^i G$ by

$$\mathbf{P}(\square^c G, e_i) = x_i,$$

where $\mathbf{P}$ is inductive probability or degree of confirmation, $\square^c$ is causal necessity, e_i is the total evidence after test i, and x_i expresses the strength (qualitative or quantitative) of the confirmation after test i. Each test, if correctly carried out and interpreted, eliminates some hypothesis alternative to C and raises the probability of G. For example, if A results in C even in the absence of P_1 the hypothesis 'A causes C only in the presence of P_1' is eliminated, and the probability of G increases. Thus the confirmation of G increases as successive tests are performed.

Even at the end there are grounds for uncertainty. Some of the tests may have been performed incorrectly. This possibility might be reduced by repeating the tests. But there will always be uncertainty over the set of 'relevant' variables $P_1, P_2, \ldots, P_n$. This set may not be complete. Perhaps all cases of A being followed by C really depend on the presence of a property Q which has not yet been observed.

The preceding analysis of eliminative induction combines causal necessity and inductive probability. In my book *Chance, Cause, Reason* I have suggested some formal models which combine my logic of causal statements with Carnap's inductive logics. I call them 'causal models of standard inductive logic'.[20] The term 'standard

---

[20] *Chance, Cause, Reason*, sec. 10.3.

inductive logic' connotes adherence to the standard rules of induction employed by common sense and science.

A causal model of standard inductive logic has a two-level hierarchy of possible universes. A *causal model* contains a set of *possible causal systems*, each of which contains a set of *causally possible universes*. One possible causal system is designated as actual, and one of its causally possible universes is designated as the actual universe. The designated actual causal system corresponds to nature, its laws corresponding to the laws of nature. The designated actual universe corresponds to our world, its facts corresponding to actual fact. The other possible causal systems are the alternatives to nature considered in enquiry. These alternatives are restricted by various assumptions, which I call presuppositions.

Inductive probabilities are assigned *a priori* to possible causal systems and to the universes in them. This is done in such a way that actual instances of a causal universal raise the probability of that causal universal, in accordance with induction by simple enumeration.[21] Thus causal necessity and inductive probability can be combined in a single formal system of enumerative induction.

This completes my brief sketch of formal inductive models. It is important for our present discussion that these models incorporate enumerative induction and yet allow eliminative induction to work as well. These formal models constitute philosophical evidence for Hume's claim that the enumeration of instances is an essential feature of inductive reasoning, and distinguishes it from deductive reasoning.

On the other hand, these formal systems of induction are much, much simpler than the system of inductive rules actually employed by humans, and hence are highly idealized models of human inductive reasoning. These formalizations do not incorporate a hierarchy of rules, and hence cannot show how enumerative induction functions in such a hierarchy to establish generalizations at successive levels, and to give probabilistic information as to what properties and groups of properties are likely to enter into causal laws. In particular, these formal models of induction cannot explain the relevance that one property or variable has for another.

6. *Computer Modelling of Inductive Activities*
To convey a sense of how idealized these formal systems are when taken as models of actual inductive inference, I'll comment briefly

[21] See sec. 10.3.2 ('Verification of causal laws') of my *Chance, Cause, Reason*; and Soshichi Uchii, 'Induction and Causality in a Cellular Space', pp. 448–61 of *PSA 1976*, vol. 2, ed. by P. Asquith and F. Suppe (1977).

on the experiences of computer scientists, psychologists, and linguists in programming computers to perform intelligent human functions.[22] Their efforts have covered such topics as game playing, language translation, problem solving, proof discovery, language use, grammatical analysis, and learning. The scope of these studies is much broader than inductive argument *per se*, but the connections are close enough (especially the connections to learning and problem solving) for these efforts to be relevant to the task of formalizing induction.

To program a computer to perform an intelligent task one formulates an appropriate rule or algorithm and then expresses this as a program for the machine. People generally approached these problems optimistically. They saw in a general way how to formulate the rules involved with sufficient precision for intelligent and educated humans to communicate with one another. It therefore seemed that the creation of successful programs for computers was a straightforward development task, to be achieved by careful analyses, ingenious schemes, and extensive programming.

There were important successes, and notable failures. Overall, progress was considerably slower than anticipated and often required that a large amount of information specific to the particular topic be incorporated in the computer program.[23]

I think these experiences show a lot about the complexity of the rules needed to perform intelligent tasks, both the actual rules used by humans in performing these tasks, and the algorithms needed for programming computers to perform the same tasks. These rules and algorithms are very complex. They are much more complex than the formulations and descriptions of them employed in the relevant sciences, such as psychology, linguistics, and inductive logic. They are much more complex than was realized by most of those who have attempted to write them as programs for computers.

Two final comments are needed on my application of the concept of complexity to induction. First, I have assumed that the human is a relatively efficient computer. Man is not actually an optimum reasoner, but he is a product of evolution and hence is somewhat of an optimizer. Second, learning, reasoning, and intelligent activities

---

[22] For a comprehensive review of this subject see Margaret Boden, *Artificial Intelligence and Natural Man* (1977).

For an approach to this problem that is very different from the usual one, see John Holland, *Adaptation in Natural and Artificial Systems – An Introductory Analysis with Applications to Biology, Control, and Artificial Intelligence* (1975).

[23] See Sir James Lighthill, 'Artificial Intelligence: A General Survey', and responses to it, in *Artificial Intelligence: A Paper Symposium* (1973).

generally involve much more than inductive reasoning, and inductive reasoning includes inductive discovery as well as inductive proof. But even when all these distinctions are taken into account, the conclusion remains that a fully detailed and operational formalization of a complete system of inductive logic will be very complex. For example, it will take a very long program to specify for a computer the conditions for a variable to be worthy of consideration in eliminative induction.

7. Conclusion

Let me conclude with a maxim of discovery that applies to Hume's idea that induction by simple enumeration is the basic rule of induction.

A *new idea* may be likened to a new-born babe: it is to be carefully nurtured and given every consideration rather than attacked with the choking diet of a *multitude* of so-called *facts* because it cannot prove at once that it will one day grow into a Samson.[24]

There is a multitude of facts about actual inductive inference that the rule of enumerative induction does not directly and simply account for. Among these are the hierarchy of natural laws and inductive rules, our knowledge of what properties and groups of properties are likely to be involved in causal laws, and the verification of causally necessary laws of nature. A full demonstration that enumerative induction can account for these facts will require a Samson-size formal and computer model of inductive reasoning.[25]

[24] R. A. Lyttleton, 'The Nature of Knowledge', p. 11, in *The Encyclopedia of Ignorance*, ed. by R. Duncan and M. Weston-Smith (1977). Italics added.
[25] This paper was written under NSF Grant No. MC 576-04297.

§12. Comments and Replies
The Cohen–Burks Session

COHEN: In reply to Burks I should like to emphasize that in explicating what I call the Baconian conception of inductive reliability I certainly do not suppose, or wish to imply, that this is the only way of gauging evidential support. Indeed in *The Implications of Induction* (secs. 12–13) I discussed enumerative induction at some length and tried to explore its various interconnections with eliminative (Baconian) induction. One certainly cannot gauge support properly by the method of relevant variables without appreciating the significance of an experimental result's replicability. Since failure to replicate invalidates the result, successful replication must correspondingly go at least some way towards establishing its validity. Looked at this way enumerative induction seems more fundamental than eliminative induction. But it is possible to look at it also from the point of view of someone faced with a given situation from which he seeks to predict what will happen next. He may think up any number of generalizations 'All A_1 are B_1', 'All A_2 are B_2', etc., that might be testable by enumerative induction. But his title to apply any one of these generalizations for predictive purposes will depend on the extent to which his given situation resembles the observed A_i in relevant aspects, as Hume saw,[1] and this must determine which generalizations he should test. So here eliminative induction is the more fundamental of the two procedures.

In sum one can indeed envisage a hierarchy of inductive rules, as Burks suggests. But the relative positions in it of enumerative and eliminative induction will depend on the point of view from which the overall program is constructed.

BLACKBURN: I am perplexed about the interpretation we are meant to give to monadic Baconian probabilities. For instance, if they are supposed to correlate with such things as confidence or the acceptance of a legal case, then the monotonicity property seems very strange. According to it if we have independent H and H', and $p(H) > p(H')$, then $p(H \& H')$ is an increasing function only of $p(H')$. This then entails that a case which has several components one of which is not strong but the rest of which are extremely strong, is no better than if the rest were on the weak side too, provided that they remain a bit better than the weakest. That seems wrong to me.

[1] *A Treatise of Human Nature*, Bk. I, pt. III, sec. XII.

Of course I see that in a legal case where someone is shouldering the onus of proof his case can be no stronger than its weakest link: Pascal gives us that too. But if we take an example where there is symmetry (say, each of a husband and wife is contending for care of the children by showing that they have means, are not feared by the children, never struck them, care for their welfare) I don't at all see that a judge should treat them equally if one has but one weak part of their contention, but the other has one equally weak and all the others nearly as bad.

COHEN: The answer to Blackburn's interesting puzzle lies, I suspect, in the rather special nature of the example that he has chosen. Each of the facts to be established in his imaginary case concerns what is normally a matter of degree: *how much* means does the husband or wife have, *how much* loved is he or she by the children, *how* gentle, *how* attentive, and so on. Clearly a judge has to sum the merits of both parties under these heads, and he ought not to treat both parties equally in the kind of case that Blackburn describes. But the point to be established by this summation seems to be a single one, viz. which spouse is better fitted to be given custody? The gradations that press on our intuition about the case are not gradations of evidential probability, but gradations of personal conduct or character. (If there were gradations of evidential probability too, the situation might get rather complex, but a case for superior overall fitness could no doubt be made out on the basis of a sufficiently large number of weakly established superiorities in particular features.)

HILPINEN: According to Jonathan Cohen, the concept of inductive support is formally analogous to the concept of necessity, and the ('Baconian') logic of support can thus be regarded as a variety of modal logic. In his publications Cohen has presented excellent arguments for the latter thesis, but the former claim (regarding support and necessity) seems dubious.

In the present paper Cohen assumes that the degree of support of a generalization depends on its 'capacity to pass cumulatively tougher and tougher tests, i.e., to resist falsification by cumulatively richer and richer combinations of factors'.[2] A hypothesis is refuted by an experiment or a test if and only if it is inconsistent with the results of the test, and it is able to 'resist falsification' by the test if it is consistent or *compossible* with the test-results. This suggests that

[2] p. 158 above.

the 'Baconian' logic of support is indeed a species of modal logic, but that the concept of support resembles the concept of possibility, not the concept of necessity, and satisfies neither the conjunction principle nor the negation principle (or consistency principle) defended by Cohen. It is conceivable that these principles hold for certain special cases, e.g., when the tests concern a simple universal generalization $(x)(Rx \rightarrow Sx)$ and its 'modifications' of the form $(x)(Rx \ \& \ C_ix \rightarrow Sx)$, where C_i is some combination of the values of various 'relevant variables'. However, if the conjunction principle and the negation (or consistency) principle are regarded as general principles of the logic of support, it is difficult to understand e.g., the logic of crucial experiments, as Hesse points out in her paper.[3]

According to Cohen's logic of support, a test statement E may give a positive degree of support to a hypothesis inconsistent with E. This result reflects the fact that even if E shows (is conclusive evidence) that a hypothesis H is false, it may also show that H possesses some degree of reliability, that is, holds good in some combinations of circumstances. In this respect Cohen's concept of inductive support resembles Popper's concept of verisimilitude, and this also suggests that the logic of support should be analogous to the logic of possibility, not the logic of necessity. But the concept of verisimilitude does not satisfy Cohen's conjunction principle or his negation principle: two mutually incompatible hypotheses or theories may both possess a high degree of verisimilitude.

I am inclined to agree with the view that 'the kind of reliability that is discernible by this method [the method of relevant variables] mounts grade by grade towards the necessity that is normally attributed to laws of nature',[4] but I would like to suggest that this approach towards (natural) necessity takes place through various degrees of possibility, not through lower degrees of necessity.

COHEN: Hilpinen suggests (in regard to scientific theories, as distinct from more elementary hypotheses) that in a modal-logical representation of inductive support it is degrees of possibility rather than degrees of necessity that should be taken to represent grades of inductive support, because this permits a high grade of inductive support, on appropriate occasions, to each of two mutually incompatible theories. Inductive support would thus resemble Popperian verisimilitude.

However the Popperian concept of verisimilitude, as is well

---
[3] pp. 202 ff. below.
[4] Cohen's paper.

known, has run into deep trouble, which the Baconian concept of inductive support avoids. The Baconian concept is based squarely on the idea that the relevant kind of experimental reasoning is out to establish natural *laws*. Hence to arrive at an intermediate stage – a partially supported hypothesis – is to mount some way towards natural *necessity*. Consequently, any acceptable support-function must ensure that two positively supported theories have a positively supported conjunction; and since there cannot be positive support for a contradiction no two mutually incompatible theories can both be positively supported according to an acceptable support-function. Baconian methods of assessing support are empirically corrigible, however, and the evidence that *seems* to establish positive support for the conjunction of two mutually inconsistent theories must instead be taken to show that the support-function which produces this result is unacceptable and needs revision. In any comparative assessment of the two theories a crucial experiment must be introduced in order to arbitrate between them; and then, according to the new support-function, support for one of the two theories will fall to zero.

At any rate this[5] is what happens when you think of experimental science as being out to discover laws of nature by the method of relevant variables. An assessment of scientific theories in terms of graduated possibility would represent a substantially different conception of scientific enquiry. The main objection to it springs from the old modal principle *ab esse ad posse valet consequentia*. What this principle entails, for a possibilistic analysis of inductive support, is that every true proposition has next-to-maximum positive support. Hence the moment we discover an anomaly for a particular theory, we know that the negation of the theory has next-to-maximum positive support, even though the theory itself may have an immense range of valid applications. And it seems very paradoxical to conclude, just on the basis of some minor anomaly, that the negation of the theory is importantly superior to the theory itself. Of course, there is a clear sense in which the negation is superior: it is true and the theory is false. But this kind of superiority may seem rather trivial in comparison with the other merits – explanatory and predictive applications – that the theory has, and it is the value of these other merits that the Baconian analysis seeks to capture.

It will be open to Hilpinen to try to meet this objection by restricting the formalism in such a way that the principle $A \rightarrow \Diamond^i A$

---

[5] Cf. *The Probable and the Provable*, pp. 179–81.

is demonstrable only where i is minimal in the hierarchy of support-grades, just as in the Baconian hierarchy $\Box^i A \rightarrow A$ is demonstrable only where i is maximal. But the plausibility of the interpretation is now at stake. To say that A is not quite a law of nature seems obviously consistent with the risk of A's being false. But what kind of possibility, or compossibility with the actual, can $\Diamond^i A$ signify for A, if A could be true without having it? Whereas Baconian gradings mount towards necessity, possibilistic gradings mount towards actuality. Hence, just as a law of nature is conceived to surmount every inferior Baconian threshold, so a true proposition must be conceived to surmount every inferior possibilistic threshold.

MARGALIT: The ecumenical atmosphere of 'Let a hundred notions of probability blossom in the garden of Philosophy' hides an important fact. The many interpretations of probability (necessitarian, personal, frequency, propensity, and what not) do have a common property. They are all interpretations of the same calculus, the one axiomatized by Kolmogorov. However, while there exists a family of probability notions that share a common calculus, there are also bastards. The concept of probability advanced by Jonathan Cohen was born out of Kolmogorov's wedlock. The question is: does this render it illegitimate? Cohen, I take it, says no; we should not be dogmatic. After all, the history of non-Euclidean geometries ought to teach us a lesson. But I believe that there are good reasons to adopt Kolmogoroff's axioms if one wants to be rational – unless being rational is a way of being dogmatic.

One such reason seems to be De Finetti's theorem according to which the credence function is coherent ('No Dutch Book') if and only if it satisfies the classical (Kolmogoroff) axioms of probability.

Nevertheless, let us take up Cohen's challenge and give his non-classical calculus a fair hearing. His notion should be tested where it matters most and where he believes that the accepted mathematical notion of probability is feeblest. I take it that Cohen's home ground is legal reasoning, an area which has in fact not been covered in Cohen's paper but to which he devoted his most interesting and provocative new book. Cohen's argument for the comparative advantage of his notion of probability over the classical one runs roughly as follows. The Anglo-Saxon legal system is more or less a paradigm of rationality. The reasoning in this system is inductive reasoning but it deviates from the inductive prescribed by the mathematical probability theory. Hence a different calculus is required which, in Cohen's view, has to be Baconian in spirit.

To substantiate his claim that mathematical probability is no good, or at best limited, in the context of legal reasoning, Cohen brings forward some hard cases, one of which he dubs the gate-crasher paradox of legal reasoning. In a rodeo show entrance fees are charged but no tickets are given. It is known that on a certain occasion 51 per cent of those inside the stadium managed to get in without paying, while only 49 per cent paid. Someone was picked there at random and was brought to civil court, accused of not having paid his entrance fees. The only evidence against him was the fact just cited, namely that 51 persons out of every hundred in the stadium cheated their way in. In other words, there is a prior probability of 0.51 against him. The paradox is that while according to the received mathematical calculus the balance of evidence is sufficient for him to be found guilty, no (Anglo-Saxon) court will indict on such a 'proof'. Incidentally, even if we sharpen the paradox and assume that 80 per cent of the audience did not pay, still the court will indict no one on the basis of this evidence alone.

One may react to this problem in the three following ways:

(a) regard the recommendation of the mathematical calculus as irrational;

(b) regard the judical system as irrational for rejecting a proof which is based on prior probability – even in cases where it is high;

(c) take both the received mathematical calculus and the judical system to be all right as they are, but to consider the possibility that there is more to proof in court than mere inductive reasoning.

Cohen has opted for (a), whereas I would opt for (c). My own conjecture is that the reasons why prior probability, on its own, is not accepted as a proof and specific evidence – even weak – about the accused is required have to do with such considerations as the existence of certain presumptions of the law (like the presumption of innocence), the prevalence of the 'moral' intuition that one cannot be accused on the basis of evidence that might equally have applied to others, and possibly more. I am not claiming that *this* is the explanation for the deviation from the received mathematical calculus of probability in legal procedures. What I do claim is that this is the spirit of the explanation called for.

Finally, if attempts at explanation along the lines of (c) fail, then I believe that option (b) should be taken up. The reason is that ultimately I do not share Cohen's respect for the rationality of traditional institutions.

COHEN: The most that the Ramsey–De Finetti–Savage argument

about coherence can show is that *when* you measure credence by a betting quotient you are rational to use a credence function that conforms to Kolmogorov's axioms. But when is it fully rational to measure credence by a betting quotient? Only when two conditions are satisfied: all available evidence must be taken into account and it must be at least in principle possible for a bet to be settled. Obviously these two conditions can both be satisfied in very many kinds of cases, and in particular when credence is concerned with future events, such as the winning of a horse-race. Here one can get to know the facts on which the betting-quotient is based quite separately from getting to know the fact that determines the outcome of the bet. But the two conditions cannot be jointly satisfied in the case of credence about past events, which is the characteristic pre-occupation of forensic proof. If the choice of betting quotient is based on *all* available evidence, then no further facts are available to determine the outcome of the bet. Of course, the evidence available to the bettor (or at an earlier date) may not include all the relevant facts available to others (or at a later date) and then the bet might be settlable by reference to these other facts. But in that case (if we abstract from questions of utility) the rationality of measuring credence by a betting quotient will vary inversely with the extent and importance – the weight, as Keynes called it – of the relevant facts that are unknown to the bettor. The coherence of your credence function will not save you from bankruptcy if you persistently bet with people who are better informed than yourself. So, after all, we do need another function, to assess evidential weight, and this turns out to have a Baconian structure. There is no way that the Ramsey–De Finetti–Savage argument can be used to undermine the case for Baconian evaluations in appropriate contexts.

The appeal to Anglo-American norms of legal proof, in order to establish a context of legitimacy for Baconian reasoning, does not rest, *pace* Margalit, on a superstitious reverence for the rationality of traditional institutions. The underlying assumption is rather that very large numbers of highly intelligent judges, whose profession requires great analytical acumen, are hardly likely to have been content with a system of proof at the heart of which has lain a major element of irrationality. Perhaps in the end here we have to fall back on a choice between the intuitions of a few philosophers, who have a vested interest in finding support for their own theories, and the intuitions of very many judges, who have no philosophical interest at stake in the matter and have always been able to re-interpret the norms of legal proof if they had wished to do so (as so many other common law rules or principles have been re-interpreted). It is not easy to defend a preference for the philosophers' intuitions as against the judges' on this issue.

Accordingly we should try to resolve the paradox of the gate-crasher in a way that does not rely on supposing some deep irrationality in the norms of forensic proof. Margalit suggests that this can be done by assuming that those norms must be taken to include some appropriate additional principle or principles, such as that a person cannot be accused on the basis of evidence that might equally have applied to others. Now it is certainly possible, as is pointed out in *The Probable and the Provable*, that each of the half-dozen or so paradoxes in a Pascalian, mathematical analysis of the standards of forensic proof can be accounted for in some such way. But each paradox requires a different kind of extra principle to be posited, some of these extra principles are rather implausible, and none are needed for any other purpose than to buttress up the Pascalian analysis against the paradoxes that otherwise assault it. The Baconian analysis, on the other hand, needs no *ad hoc* auxiliary hypotheses of this type, and also makes sense of a number of other puzzling facts, such as some of the results of psychologists' experiments about probability-judgements. My claim is therefore that, by familiar criteria for theory-choice, the Baconian analysis is preferable to the Pascalian one.

MACKIE: Cohen's criticism[6] of a view of mine seems to rest on a misunderstanding. I would not speak of 'Wittgensteinian family-resemblance', since I am eager not to give Wittgenstein the credit for recognizing a process which is clearly described by Mill and other earlier writers. My substantial thesis was that the term 'probability', whose core meaning concerns imperfectly supported statements, has been transferred to such very different things as class ratios, limiting frequencies, propensities, and items in an uninterpreted calculus. Such transfers are comprehensible because, for example, a frequency may be the evidence that gives partial support, a propensity may generate a frequency, or a known or postulated propensity may give partial support. Admittedly if all these are Pascalian there will be a formal resemblance between them all, but if Cohen is right and some partial support is non-Pascalian, there will not be even a formal resemblance, but only an indirect connection, between, say, a Cohen-type support and a Pascalian frequency. Cohen is himself committed to the view of mine which he criticizes.

[6] p. 157 above.

On something more central in Cohen's paper, I would point out that his use of Baconian induction is at least non-standard. He uses the method of relevant variables to yield measures of partial support, whereas the standard use (for example by Mill, in methods whose logic I have made more explicit in an Appendix to my *The Cement of the Universe* and in the article 'Mill's Methods of Induction' in *The Encyclopedia of Philosophy*, edited by Paul Edwards) is to establish generalizations conclusively, given the assumptions used. The generalizations are typically, but not necessarily, causal, and they are typically incomplete – as Mill says, the method of difference shows that one item is 'the cause, or an indispensable part of the cause' of another; in my terms, the conclusion is that the differential factor between the experimental case and the control case is at least an inus condition of the differential result.

This contrast is, no doubt, linked with the fact that Cohen's gradations of support are related to a (hypothetical?) series of imperfect tests, in which fewer or more of the possibly relevant variables are controlled, whereas the standard use requires that *all* possibly relevant variables except the differential one (or, as I have pointed out, the differential cluster) are matched between the experimental and control cases. However, even after reading chapter 13 in *The Probable and the Provable*, I am not clear exactly how Cohen is modifying the standard procedure or just how he extracts a measure of support from it. Part of my difficulty is that he seems to mix up the range of application of a generalization with the degree of support for it. But a generalization which passes an imperfect test may have *no* range of correct application at all; the imperfect test may seem to designate as a relevant factor one which is in fact totally irrelevant in all circumstances, all the work being done by some factor not controlled in the imperfect test.

Cohen's main question in this paper is, what are the general conditions for the applicability of his account of support. The corresponding question about the standard use of Baconian methods is easily answered: they reveal relations of conditionality wherever it can be assumed that *some* possibly complex combination of items (some disjunction of conjunctions of presences and absences of relevant factors) is both necessary and sufficient for a certain other item. Causation is only the leading special case of such conditionality: legal relations are another, and so on. If Cohen's re-use of the methods is sound at all, I expect that it will have the same range of application as the standard one.

COHEN: In reply to Mackie, I should like to point out, *en passant*, that it was not J. S. Mill but Dugald Stewart, as Mill himself acknowledged,[7] who deserves primary credit among British philosophers of language for explicitly recognizing the historical process by which family resemblances, as Wittgenstein later called them, are generated. Stewart's recognition of this in his *Philosophical Essays* (1810) was the outcome of the general movement towards the acceptance of semantic change which took place, especially in Germany, in the latter half of the eighteenth century.[8] If Wittgenstein is to be denied credit for originating the idea of family-resemblance meanings, it is perhaps worth while to trace this idea to its real source.

But does the family-resemblance idea have any application to the problem of probability in the way that Mackie thinks it does? Mackie has still said nothing to meet the objection I raised three years ago.[9] That objection relied on both a historical and a philosophical argument, since Wittgenstein (*pace* Mackie) does not seem to think of family-resemblance meanings, like Mill, in terms of a historical process.

On the historical side the argument against Mackie is that historical claims must be backed by historical evidence, and quite a lot of evidence would be needed to show that the concept of probability has undergone a process of successive transfers like that which Stewart and Mill describe, whereby 'names creep on from subject to subject, until all traces of a common meaning sometimes disappear'.[10] But not only has Mackie himself given no evidence at all to support this historical thesis. He has also ignored the substantial case that Hacking has been making out, since 1971,[11] for the opposite view. Hacking has now established quite a strong presumption in favour of the view that various specialized conceptions of probability (relative frequency, logical relation, propensity, etc.) all developed at about the same time in the seventeenth century. And

[7] *System of Logic*, Bk. IV, ch. IV, sec. 5.

[8] I have discussed this movement at length in *The Diversity of Meaning* (1966), pp. 1–23.

[9] In *Probability – the One and the Many* (1975), p. 7, reprinted in *Proceedings of the British Academy* 61 (1975), 83–108.

[10] Mackie quotes this passage from Mill in his *Truth, Probability and Paradox* (1973), p. 155, but the reference there to Mill's *System of Logic* is incorrect: it should be Bk. I, ch. II, sec. 5.

[11] I. Hacking, 'Jacques Bernoulli's Art of Conjecturing', *Brit. J. Phil. Sci.* 22 (1971), 209 ff.; 'Equipossibility Theories of Probability', ibid., pp. 339 ff.; *The Emergence of Probability* (1975).

on my view the Baconian conception of probability would be another such seventeenth-century development (albeit a slightly earlier one).

Mackie also passes over, without making any attempt to answer, the philosophical argument against his family-resemblance thesis. This argument, which I have developed at length elsewhere,[12] is that if one thinks of probability as the gradation of provability then the various different conceptions of probability that are familiar may all be accounted for in terms of familiar types of distinction between different kinds of provability. So there need be no creeping on from subject to subject and no disappearance of common meaning, any more than there is when we speak of a good gardener or a good car as well as of a good man. 'Probable' is an evaluative term, like 'good', and it naturally comes to be used with different criteria of evaluation in different contexts.

Mackie's next point is that my use of Baconian induction to grade partial support 'is at least non-standard', since on his view the standard use, as typified by J. S. Mill, is to establish generalizations conclusively. Now, even if this were true, it would be of no great significance, unless one supposes that philosophy just consists in picking over the bones of a standard set of theories. But in fact it is far from being true. Mill is the odd man out within the mainline tradition of inductive logic, though his somewhat degenerate conception of the subject may well have had more impact on text-books and encyclopedias than it has deserved to do. Bacon certainly thought of his own method as setting up degrees of certainty;[13] and, as I remarked in my paper, J. F. W. Herschel[14] said that experiments 'become more valuable, and their results clearer, in proportion as they possess this quality (of agreeing exactly in all their circumstances but one), since the question put to nature becomes thereby more pointed, and its answer more decisive'. The main

---

[12] In *Probability – the One and the Many*, and *The Probable and the Provable* (1977), pp. 5–39.

[13] Cf. the preface to his *Novum Organum*. A fuller account of Baconian views about probability, from the seventeenth century to the nineteenth, is given in my 'Some Historical Remarks on the Baconian Conception of Probability', forthcoming in *Journal of the History of Ideas* (1980), which supplements and in part corrects sec. 14 of my *The Implications of Induction* (1970). Some contemporary philosophers will no doubt be unhappy with my use of the term 'probability' in connection with Baconian functions: they want to reserve it for Pascalian ones. But the weight of history, along with a great deal of current forensic and other non-philosophical usage, is against them.

[14] *A Preliminary Discourse on the Study of Natural Philosophy* (1833), p. 155. Even Mill saw analogical reasoning as a matter of degree: *System of Logic*, Bk. III, ch. XX, sec. 3.

innovation in my treatment of Baconian induction is not the gradation of partial support but the exploration of the logical constraints imposed by one judgement of Baconian probability on another – the systematic articulation of the principles controlling conjunction, negation, etc.

Finally, Mackie objects that a generalization which has passed an intermediate test – a test that is not as thorough as it could be made – may have no range of correct application at all, because the results of the test were in fact produced by some hidden factor that was not controlled. But this objection is based on a misconception of such tests. Mackie has overlooked the fact that, according to the method of relevant variables,[15] the report of a test in which relevant variables $v_1, v_2, \ldots, v_i$ were manipulated must also state that no variants of any other relevant variable were present. Hence the kind of case described by Mackie cannot arise.

[15] Cf. *The Implications of Induction*, pp. 54 ff., and *The Probable and the Provable*, p. 134.

5

Inductive Appraisal of Scientific Theories

§ 13. MARY HESSE

What is the Best Way to Assess Evidential Support for Scientific Theories?

The paper discusses two theses which have led many philosophers of science to reject inductive logic as a useful explication of scientific theories:

(1) The sceptical view that no scientific generalization over an unbounded domain can be an object of knowledge.

(2) The view that inductive logic cannot show that universal generalizations are given any inductive support by evidence.

Among those who still pursue inductive logic as a probabilistic theory, Carnap accepted (2) but regarded scientific knowledge as finite in character; and Hintikka and the personalists in different ways reject both (2) and (1). L. J. Cohen also rejects both (2) and (1), but on the basis of a non-Pascalian confirmation function. In this paper I reserve judgement on (2) as a purely formal matter, but argue that its truth or falsity is not a very important feature of a confirmation theory, since there are more profound reasons why scientific knowledge should be regarded as essentially finitist in character. In support of this thesis I sketch a Carnap-type probabilistic confirmation theory using the positivist relevance criterion, and show why a sharp distinction has to be made between confirmation of generalizations and confirmation of (a finite domain of) next instances.

Next I examine Cohen's non-Pascalian support function, and show how all the conditions he stipulates for it can be interpreted into a probabilistic confirmation function by means of a redescription of his ideal model of experiments. I suggest that his implied separation between the logic of enumerative and that of eliminative induction offends against the desirable unity of an inductive logic, and show how the Carnapian enumerative theory just described can be extended in a more natural way to account for inferences to and within scientific theories. I conclude that while the sceptical spirit of (1) with regard to universalizability is correct, this does not have the sceptical and anti-realist consequences for scientific knowledge often claimed for it.

At the end of his book *The Probable and the Provable* (*PP*) Jonathan Cohen concludes that 'Sceptical philosophers · · · have fallen into error because of the backwardness of inductive logic' (p. 356). He bases this conclusion on two characteristics of the views of many recent philosophers of science, including Carnap, Popper, Kuhn, and Toulmin, which are as follows:

(1) The sceptical view that denies that 'the truth of a scientific

generalization over an unbounded domain is a possible object of proof or knowledge' (p. 347), and

(2) The view that inductive logic cannot show that universal generalizations are given any inductive support by evidence.

For reasons such as these most philosophers of science now reject inductive logic as useless for the understanding of scientific theories, and give alternative highly fallibilistic accounts, while Carnap continued to pursue inductive logic, but restricted it to showing how singular statements are given support by evidence. There is of course also a minority view that rejects (2) and to whom it is therefore open to reject the scepticism of (1). This includes the Hintikka school, about which I shall not speak here, except to say that they seem to me to follow the Carnap method too closely to be successful, and also the personalists, a version of whose theory I shall develop below.

Cohen also rejects (2) on the basis of his own logic of inductive support, which uses an 'inductive probability' function not satisfying the axioms of mathematical probability. I shall have more to say about this suggestion later, but first I want to put the whole debate in a wider context by suggesting that the equation of scepticism with regard to science with the rejection of universal generalizations as possible objects of knowledge conflates various issues that ought to be kept separate. To explain this I shall briefly outline the theory I myself put forward in *The Structure of Scientific Inference* (*SSI*), as far as it is relevant to the inductive support of theories, and then look at some difficulties that have been found in it. In this theory I differ from the other philosophers of science just mentioned in the following respects. Firstly I differ from Cohen in using Pascalian probability functions. Secondly, although I agree with Cohen and Hintikka in rejecting view (2), I do not regard the possibility of giving support to universal generalizations either as a very difficult problem or as a criterion of primary importance for a confirmation theory. Thirdly, I accept the spirit of the so-called sceptical view (1), but deny that it has the sceptical and anti-realist consequences drawn from it by, for example, Feyerabend, Kuhn, and Toulmin.

Confirmation as Positive Relevance

My argument starts with one of the paradoxes of confirmation detected by Hempel,[1] the importance of which has not been given widespread recognition. Indeed it had no name until I suggested it be called the 'transitivity paradox' (*SSI*, p. 141). It is particularly

[1] 'Studies in the Logic of Confirmation', in *Aspects of Scientific Explanation*, p. 3

important in the present context, because it not only refers to confirmation within deductive systems such as scientific theories, but it is also independent of the particular confirmation function adopted within wide limits, and in particular does not presuppose Pascalian probability. It rests on four intuitive criteria which would be accepted *prima facie* by all scientists concerned with theoretical inference:

(H1)   *The Principle of Equivalence*
　　　 If f confirms g, and $f \leftrightarrow f'$, and $g \leftrightarrow g'$, then f' confirms g'.
(Read '$\rightarrow$' as 'Entails').
(H2)   *The Principle of Entailment*
　　　 If $f \rightarrow g$, then f confirms g.
(H3)   *The Principle of Converse Entailment*
　　　 If $g \rightarrow f$, then f confirms g
(H4)   *The Principle of Special Consequence*
　　　 If f confirms g, and $g \rightarrow h$, then f confirms h.

The rationale for (H1) and (H2) is fairly obvious, although there has been some discussion about their desirability, mainly for reasons connected with Hempel's other paradoxes. But I know of no well-developed confirmation theory that rejects them, and I shall not give them further consideration here. (H3) and (H4) are a different matter however. (H3) seems very desirable in the context of the confirmation of the premisses and general theorems of a scientific theory when some of its deductive entailments are observed to be true. (H4) seems very desirable in the context of the confirmation of deductive predictions derived from a theory which has already been confirmed by other evidence. But it is unfortunately easy to show that if all four principles are adopted, then any evidence at all confirms any hypothesis at all (including both a given hypothesis and its negation), and that therefore any theory of confirmation is useless if it satisfies all four principles. If only (H3) and (H4) are taken to be at risk, which is the culprit? Probabilistic theorists with a positive relevance criterion of confirmation (Carnap's) maintain (H3) and reject (H4); probabilistic theorists with a k-criterion of confirmation maintain (H4) and reject (H3); Cohen's theory is a little difficult to characterize in these terms, but he appears to reject both (H3) and (H4) for arguments that range over all propositions.

　　The first decision to be made, therefore, is whether to adopt a probabilistic theory of confirmation or not. I do so on grounds that can be argued in a variety of ways, but I shall take it here that the justification is primarily that proof of the pudding is in the eating, especially in relation to the confirmation of theories. The next decision is whether to adopt the positive relevance criterion of confirmation (PR), or the k-criterion. These can be expressed in terms of conditional probabilities as follows:

PR Criterion: f confirms g iff $p(g/f) > p(g)$
> k-*criterion:* f confirms g iff $p(g/f) > k \geqslant \frac{1}{2}$, where k is a real number less than 1 chosen according to the stringency required in the circumstances.

There are various arguments for not adopting the k-criterion, among which are that it depends on a special decision about the value of k, and that it permits f to confirm g even if f *reduces* the probability g previously had, as long as the probability remains above k, and this seems a counter-intuitive use of the notion of 'confirming evidence'. Moreover, the k-criterion as such is an all-or-none decision, whereas the *PR* criterion has built into it the notion of comparative confirmation relative to $p(g)$. The k-criterion is in fact a more suitable explication for the all-or-none concept of *acceptance*, which is not the same as the concept of degrees of support given to a hypothesis by evidence.[2]

Let us assume, therefore, that we adopt a support function for g relative to f, to be read 'f confirms g', and that its criterion is the *PR* criterion. We then have the following conditions satisfied by the confirmation function: (H1), (H2), (H3), and also, to pick out three of the most important consequences of the probability axioms.

Falsification: If f is logically incompatible with g, then $p(g/f) = 0$,
Entailment: If $g \rightarrow f$, then $p(g) \leqslant p(f)$,
Bayes Theorem: $p(g/f) = p(g)p(f/g)/p(f)$, provided $p(f) \neq 0$.

It is now convenient to separate consideration of the confirmation of universal generalizations and predictions derived from them, from confirmation relations within theories, although, as we shall see, theories are later to be dealt with as extrapolations from the principles involved for generalizations.

(i) *Confirmation of generalizations.* We take generalizations in the form $h = (x) (Px \supset Qx)$, where the domain of quantification may be finite or infinite. A *positive instance* is an x that is both P and Q; a *negative instance* is an x that is P and not Q. We will assume for the moment that all instances are known to be P, and this is assimilated

---

[2] *The Structure of Scientific Inference* (1974), pp. 133f., 147f.

to background information b supposed given. Consider the confirmation of $h \& b$ on evidence e_n which reports that, of n instances mentioned in b and examined, all are positive and none negative. We have $h \& b \to e_n$, and hence $p(h \& b/e_n) \geqslant p(h \& b)$ according as $p(h \& b) \geqslant 0$, and assuming $p(e_n) \neq 0$. If $p(h \& b) > 0$, e_n confirms $h \& b$, and this confirmation will increase with increasing positive instances.

(ii) *Confirmation of next instances.* A problem now arises about the confirmation by e_n of the prediction that next instances of p will be Q. Call these x_{n+1}, x_{n+2}, etc. Since (H4) is not satisfied by the confirmation function we cannot argue that since e_n confirms $h \& b$, and $h \& b \to x_{n+1}$, etc., therefore e_n confirms x_{n+1}. If this is required as a consequence of our normal expectations about universal generalizations, then we must find out under what conditions it is expected and build these in specifically to the prior probabilities of this particular situation. De Finetti suggests how this process might be understood in his personalist concept of exchangeability of instances of a (statistical or universal) generalization when instances are believed to be sufficiently analogous to each other to count as instances of the same generalization. That is, when we recognize an x as being 'P and Q again', our prior probability distribution contains the entry $p(x_{n+1} \& b/e_n) > p(x_{n+1} \& b)$. This prior probability can be assigned quite independently of the probability, either prior or posterior, of the generalization h itself. Indeed the two problems described under (i) and (ii) are quite distinct from each other. Under (i), we have substitution-instances confirming the generalization, providing the prior probability of the generalization is non-zero, but not necessarily confirming next substitution-instances. This is exactly what is pointed out in Goodman's paradox, where the same evidence e at this date provides confirmation for each of two hypotheses 'All emeralds are green' (h), and 'All emeralds are grue' (h'), when 'green' and 'grue' refer now to the same extension of objects in the evidence. After doomsday, however, the substitution-instances x_{n+1} of h are green and not grue, while those, x'_{n+1}, of h' are grue and not green, so that whereas e confirms h and e confirms h', we cannot have e confirming of the same object x after doomsday that it is both x_{n+1} and x'_{n+1}. Confirmation of next instances must fail for either h or h', and hence is not entailed by confirmation of both h and h' themselves.

With regard to problem (ii), however, we have to include in the prior distribution whatever inductive expectations we have about the substitution-instances of a given generalization (or in the case of Goodman's paradox we have to reject either the set of green objects or the set of grue objects as exchangeable in this sense). And we can do this whether or not e confirms h, that is, whether or not $p(h) > 0$, or $p(h) = 0$. We need not assert any prior belief that h has any probability of being true over all possible P's, only that it has some probability of being true over the next few or many of a finite number of instances in which we are interested. So whether or not h is true universally, we can retain in our prior distribution the belief that h in a finite number of instances has an initial probability of being true. This finitude may be expressed by stating h within a limited spatio-temporal domain, or over a finite number of kinds of objects, or in many other ways which are sufficiently flexible to deal with all the universal generalizations that are in fact considered in science.

Cohen's Eliminative Induction

Now I shall compare this treatment of universal generalizations with Cohen's, since he states some requirements for support of generalizations which imply objections to the above account, and in general he adopts the standpoint of eliminative induction, whereas my account is enumerative. I hope to show that when all Cohen's implied assumptions are made explicit, the appearance of conflict is illusory, and moreover that his account also needs a foundation of enumerative induction to work at all. I shall claim that the enumerative account is more fundamental and more comprehensive, and that it provides natural suggestions for extrapolation to scientific theories that Cohen's fails to provide.

I shall first show that the desirable requirements Cohen places on support of universal generalizations are satisfied by the *PR* theory if suitably interpreted. Cohen sets up his ideal inductive situation by referring to von Frisch's investigation of the sensory discriminations of bees. I shall change Cohen's terminology in describing this model in order to ease comparison with the *PR* theory. Frisch begins with the hypothesis, h, that 'All bees make colour discriminations'. His first test t_0 varies colours and observes that these variations are correlated with variation in bees' behaviour, *where all other relevant variables are kept constant.*[3] But what is a relevant variable? Cohen

[3] Cohen says at this point (*PP*, p. 136) that other variables are to be supposed *absent* in test t_0, that is, for example, still air is reckoned as absence of the variable 'colour'. It is not clear why this very artificial assumption is required, for the account seems to go through just as well by simply assuming that during t_0 the other relevant variables have some 'normal' value which is kept constant.

refers here to the general consensus of scientists about what is relevant to particular investigations, and relates this with the concept of 'replicable evidence'. When evidence of a single test result is taken as sufficient to guarantee that repetition of that test in the same relevant circumstances will yield the same result, repetition does not contribute any more support to the hypothesis in those circumstances. Cohen is prepared to admit at this point that judgements about relevance and replicability are based on previous experience, and may be an application of something like enumerative induction. But he thinks nothing is gained by 'confusing' this question with that of the conduct of experiments like Frisch's where these judgements are taken for granted. (*PP*, p. 175).

What we have now is a hypothesis h supported by replicable evidence of bees that are colour-discriminatory under specific values of all other known relevant variables, $v_1, v_2, \ldots, v_n$, and whatever other specific circumstances C obtain that are held to be irrelevant to h. I shall call these values of the variables respectively $V1$, $V2, \ldots Vn$. The hypothesis we are now concerned with is essentially h in a domain bounded by these particular values. I shall call this hypothesis $h_{V1,\ldots,Vn,C}$, or h_{V1} for short. Now Cohen takes it that the evidence e_0 that report the result of test t_0 is sufficient to give maximal support to h_{V1}, since in the domain defined by $V1$, $V2, \ldots, Vn$, C, there is no point in doing t_0 again for more instances of h_{V1}. In a probability theory this assumption would be represented by $p(h_{V1}/e_0) = 1$.

The next step is test t_1 which varies the values of v_1 over its whole range and for every value of colour previously tested. If h survives this test, that is, if it is shown to be independent of the variable v_1, we can say that it has been shown to be maximally supported in domain $V2, \ldots, Vn$, C. We now have $p(h_{V2}/e_1) = 1$, where e_1 is the total evidence. In Cohen's terminology, the support function $s(h, e_1)$ is greater than $s(h, e_0)$, and s of h increases with every subsequent test which varies $V2, \ldots, Vn$, up to the maximum where h_C may be said to be equivalent to h, if we are prepared to accept that the particular conditions in C are known to be irrelevant to h. At this point, ideally, every possible hypothesis other than h has been eliminated by tests on all possible combinations of the relevant variables.

Let us see how far s can be expressed as a probability. I suggest that Cohen's intentions about replicability at test t_{i-1} are representable by $p(h_{Vi}/e_{i-1}) = 1$. In probabilistic terms this can be justified by the usual assumptions of eliminative induction. Evidence e_{i-1} is supposed to have eliminated all hypotheses regarded as possible rivals to h in the domain $V1, V2, \ldots, Vn, C$. Hence $p(h_{V1}/e_{i-1}) = 1$. We may now remove e_{i-1} from further calculations of conditional probabilities by noting that

$$h \rightarrow h_C \rightarrow h_{Vn} \rightarrow \cdots h_{V2} \rightarrow h_{V1}, \quad \text{and} \quad h_{Vi} \rightarrow e_{i-1}.$$

Hence $p(h/e_{i-1}) = p(h \ \& \ h_{Vi}/e_{i-1}) = p(h/h_{Vi})$.

Now I propose to put

$$s(h, e_{i-1}) = p(h/h_{Vi}).$$

This equation is merely a numerical identification of values,[4] and is to be understood to apply only to support functions where the arguments are respectively a universal generalization and a report of the results of successive tests of the kind just described. It does not, for example, imply in general that $s(h \ \& \ h'/e_i) = p(h \ \& \ h'/e_i)$, for $h \ \& \ h'$ is not generally in a form $(x)(Px \supset Qx)$ of which e_i reports substitution-instances.

The successive grades of support offered to h by the tests reported by e_i can now be expressed probabilistically as follows. After test t_{i-1} the total evidence is sufficient to eliminate all possible hypotheses in domain $Vi, \ldots, Vn, C$ except h_{Vi}. The probability of h after t_{i-1} is therefore $p(h/h_{Vi})$. We have to show that this is greater than $p(h/h_{Vi-1})$. We have

$$p(h/h_{Vi}) = p(h)/p(h_{Vi})$$
$$p(h/h_{Vi-1}) = p(h)/p(h_{Vi-1}) < p(h'/h_{Vi}),$$

since $h_{Vi} \rightarrow h_{Vi-1}$, and we assume $p(h_{Vi-1}) \neq p(h_{Vi})$

Cohen has four principal requirements for the support of universal generalizations:

1. We should *not* be able to increase the support of a generalization by evidence of more than a single replicable test. This condition is satisfied by the interpretation of eliminative induction in probabilistic terms, because *once the initial decision is made about what finite set of hypotheses is possible* (which is assumed in Cohen's concepts of relevance and replicability), a probability theory can certainly allow a single test of the kind described to make hypotheses such as h_{Vi} maximally probable.

---

[4] This is permissible because the values of s are rational numbers between 0 and 1, depending on what proportion of tests of the sequence have been carried out. The numerical identification is merely a way of assigning prior probabilities to $p(h)$, $p(h_{V1})$, etc. It does not, as we shall see, determine joint priors of conjunctions of hypotheses, so the total prior distribution remains underdetermined.

2. Cohen points out (following Duhem, Polanyi, and many other writers on scientific inference) that a few anomalies do not lead in practice to abandonment of whole theories. He proposes to represent this by a theorem satisfied by his support function to the effect that $s(h, e)$ is not necessarily zero when e contradicts h. Instead $s(h, e)$ retains the value it had at the stage of testing just before the falsifying test. This can also be represented perfectly well in probability theory. We simply modify the numerical identification of $s(h, e_{i-1})$ to read

$$s(h, e_j) = p(h/h_{Vi}), \quad \text{for} \quad j \geqslant i - 1,$$

where e_i reports that stage in the sequence of evidence e_j where the first anomaly was discovered, if one has been discovered. This seems to capture all that is meant by saying that h is retained but in restricted circumstances where it is successful, that is in the domain $Vi, \ldots, Vn, C$.

3. Cohen's support function satisfies a principle of *conjunction* that is non-probabilistic. He argues that, taking s to mean that grade of support reached by h up to date if it is unfalsified, or if it is, that grade reached before it was falsified, we should have $s(h \& h', e) = s(h, e)$, where $s(h, e) \leqslant s(h', e)$. This is because $h \& h'$ as a conjoint hypothesis cannot be said to have been supported to a *higher* grade than the least supported of the conjuncts in the same series of tests reported by e. On the other hand, it cannot be said to have been supported to a *lower* grade than h, because if $s(h, e) \leqslant s(h', e)$, h' and hence $h \& h'$ must have passed all the tests that h passed and perhaps more.

Whatever the force of this argument, it clearly implies that s is not a conditional probability function. But the intention here can be represented by stipulating a probability value for the support of conjunctions as follows:

$$s(h \& h', e_j) = p(h/h_{Vi}), \quad \text{where} \quad p(h_{Vi}/e_j) \leqslant p(h'_{Vj}/e_j),$$

and e_{i-1} reports the last test in the sequence e_j that gives support to h.

4. A similar stipulation can deal with Cohen's *negation* principle. Here his system gives rise to a theorem

$$\text{If } s(h, e) > 0, \quad \text{then} \quad s(\sim h, e) = 0.$$

Let us see what this means. The hypothesis $\sim h$ is not of the form $(x)(Px \supset Qx)$, but of the form $(\exists x)(Px \& \sim Qx)$. Cohen correctly argues that there is no hypothesis of the canonical form that entails

$\sim h$ that is not refuted by the sequence of test reports e. Therefore $\sim h$ can get no support of the kind required from e, and we may put $s(\sim h, e) = 0$. Again we can represent this in probability terms by stipulating: If $p(h/e) > 0$, then $s(\sim h, e) = 0$.

Thus examination of the assumptions of the inference model used by Cohen shows that his demonstrations that the 'inductive probability' derived from s is non-Pascalian are beside the point. What he has in fact done is to assimilate into the argument h of the s–function a number of *different* hypotheses h_{v_i} etc., each of which separately can perfectly well be given probability-values on the evidence described.

Choice of Support or Confirmation Function

How should we choose a support or confirmation function? Comprehensiveness and accuracy in explicating inductive behaviour, formal manipulability, naturalness of extra-logical assumptions, and absence of *ad hoc* restrictions having nothing clearly to do with normal inductive behaviour, are all desirable characteristics. I have suggested how the apparent advantages of Cohen's theory in explicating four features of eliminative induction are illusory advantages with respect to *PR* theory, because they are translatable into its terms. There may be other advantages not so translatable that I have missed. But now some disadvantages of his theory must be pointed out. The first concerns the relation between enumerative and eliminative induction, and offends against the need for unity of different types of inductive behaviour. Cohen is prepared to admit that some elements of enumerative induction may be present in the first or 'pre-scientific' states of an investigation when the relevant variables have not yet been identified. He does not expand on the enumerative inductions that might be required, but it is clear that he sees them as requiring a quite different logic from his eliminative model. The possibility of unification here in *PR* theory is an advantage. Moreover, to banish enumeration to early or prescientific stages of investigation is to assume that after these stages scientists are not concerned with statistical hypotheses, for his model starts with the assumption that no relevant variables are related by statistical generalizations of the kind '$p\%$ of P's are Q's'. It is true that in his earlier book *The Implications of Induction* (*TIOI*), he does show how support gradings may be extended to statistical hypotheses, but a consequence of their non-Pascalian character is that there is no 'measure of credibility that would somehow amalgamate the probability estimated *by* a hypothesis with the grade of inductive support that exists *for* the hypothesis' (*TIOI*, p. 117). Again, there is an absence of unity in the formal foundations of the theory.

There are more serious problems. In defining his sequences of tests for *h*, Cohen introduces the notion of an *order* into the sequence, depending on the 'falsificatory potential' of the relevant variable whose variation is being tested. The need for this restriction is not explained when it is first introduced (*PP*, p. 139), but it later turns out to be necessary to avoid inconsistencies in the axiom system. It is certainly not suggested by the examples of inductive reasoning given by Cohen, that is von Frisch's bee discriminations, Mill's methods, and Newton's investigations on spectral colours, for in all these cases there seems to be no assumption that the order of testing for different variables is crucial. Certainly there is no discussion in these authors or in similar scientific reports about how experiments on different variables should be ordered for importance as falsifiers. As in other places, Cohen assumes very strong and not always explicit intuitions on the part of scientists, which are only related in an *ad hoc* manner to his inductive theory. And it turns out that this assumption of ordering implies that a scientist already has to presuppose that the same evidence cannot give support to more than one of two conflicting hypotheses (*PP*, p. 179). On the face of it, this is a severe restriction of the inductive theory, because it means that no account can be given of crucial experiments, where all evidence *e* up to date is consistent with two conflicting hypotheses, and an experiment is designed to decide between them. But Cohen merely concludes that this situation shows that we have ordered two sequences of tests wrongly, for if two hypotheses are still potentially conflicting *after* evidence *e* has supported both, that means we should have done the crucial test earlier, before we had any evidence that supported a false hypothesis:

· · · emergence of such contradictions · · · enables us to elucidate how the actual progress of science in a particular field of enquiry imposes a continuing local readjustment in our criteria of evidential support. Inductive appraisal has a vitally important internal dynamic that must not be ignored. (*PP*, p. 181.)

But an inductive theory is surely unsatisfactory that not only demands of scientists that they make judgements about all possible hypotheses in the field before they can undertake a well-ordered series of tests, but also that when a series fails to be well-ordered, the process of well-ordering lies wholly outside the inductive theory whose support-gradings have at that point broken down. At best it has to be conceded that the support-gradings do not at that point represent all that a scientist has learned, although all of what he has learned is surely inductive knowledge.

A question that arises here is 'what exactly is the function s supposed to be grading?' It is certainly nothing as straightforward as scientists' confidence in a hypothesis, for this does not go back to zero when it is discovered that the series of tests must be reordered. Moreover, it seems that something more drastic is required at this breakdown point than mere reordering of experiments that have already been carried out, because those experiments later in the sequence are intrinsically more *complex* than those earlier, in the sense that they test a greater number of permutations of co-variation. When a sequence has to be reordered, experiments already performed cannot be assumed to give *any* support in the new ordering, since they are not experiments of the proper complexity for their new place in the sequence. Cohen places very strong emphasis here on the notion of an ideal *ontological* ordering of importance of relevant variables, and this ideal could only come to light when we have the true generalizations. But is not inductive logic primarily an epistemological, not an ontological matter?

A final point about Cohen's theory will take us onto the problem of the confirmation of theories. How does Cohen approach this problem? Let me quote him:

To be in keeping with the type of procedure already discussed, a testable scientific theory must take the form of a universally quantified conditional that is in principle capable of having its antecedent and consequent co-instantiated in each possible combination of the variants of the appropriate series of relevant variables. Admittedly no normal scientific textbook contains a theory in this form $\cdots$ But on the assumption that any scientific theory H is in fact axiomatizable one can construct an equivalent of H that takes the form, as required, of a universally quantified conditional. An exact statement of the form this equivalent can take will be rather complicated. (*PP*, p. 153.)

Cohen goes on to sketch a procedure for expressing a theory as a hierarchy of generalizations, each level of which can be expressed as a universal generalization of which the antecedent and consequent can ideally be co-instantiated with the aid of propositions bridging the gap between theoretical and observational concepts. However, it is difficult to see how in practice such a reduction of theoretical concepts and generalizations to observational correlates could be carried out. Theories seem to be internally too tightly connected to permit such piece-by-piece support.

Analogy in Theoretical Inference

Finally I come to the suggestion developed in my *SSI* that the confirmation of a theory involves judgements of analogy between situations of application of the theory.[5] This is an extension of enumerative induction, and it might be thought at first sight that a development of eliminative induction might be more appropriate. For suppose we take theories to be expressed in familiar deductive form, and suppose further that we are concerned only with comparing rival theories that are (to use Shimony's terminology) 'seriously proposed'. Then crucial experiments can be set up to falsify some of these theories, thus raising the posterior probability of the disjunction of the remainder, until ideally all are eliminated except one, which then has probability 1. But this is much too crude a representation. There is no reason to assume that all possible theories in a given domain have been thought of, or that they are finite in number. Moreover, we are interested not just in all-or-none falsification, but in the comparative confirmation given to theories by evidence that falls short of conclusive verification. Eliminative induction may just be a possible procedure for low-level local generalizations, where the consensus on background assumptions is high, but is too blunt an instrument to represent more complex and interesting features of theories.

Enumerative induction of *PR* type, however, immediately faces the problem of transitivity. That is to say, as with universal generalizations and their instances, we have to separate the problem of the confirmation of a theory by evidence deducible from it, from that of confirmation of further predictions of the theory by the same evidence. There have been various suggestions for evading this problem by replacing *PR* confirmation by some other function in theoretical contexts:[6] some of them depend on adopting a form of 'acceptance' theory for theories when these are highly confirmed by evidence of their consequences so that transitivity of confirmation to predictions goes through with high probability; other suggestions depend on adopting some criterion of 'explanatory goodness' for theories which does not circularly depend on the notion of confirmation, and which gives high confirmation to their consequences. In the case of the acceptance approach, it is difficult to see how any scientific theory comprehensive enough to make powerful predic-

---

[5] *SSI*, ch. 9
[6] *SSI*, p. 147

tions in domains as yet untested, could ever satisfy the normally stringent conditions on degree of confirmation required for acceptance – how could one 'accept' Newton's theory of universal gravitation as true on the basis only of the acceleration of falling bodies and the orbit of the moon? And yet even such limited evidence would be taken to be highly confirmatory of as yet untested predictions such as the orbits of other planets and the comets. In the case of the 'explanation' approach, this cannot depend simply on the deductive meaning of explanation, because this brings us back via the converse entailment condition to PR-type or k-type confirmation theory which we are trying to improve upon. But no stronger sense of explanation which satisfies our requirements has been suggested other than the one I am now going to describe. And in general it appears better to look more fundamentally at the *reason* for the transitivity paradox in this context, than merely to tinker about *ad hoc* with the related circle of concepts: confirmation, acceptance, explanation.

The suggestion I have developed in *SSI*, and to which I can do little more than allude here, is that the goodness of theories with respect to the high confirmability of their predictions is a question of how high a degree of *analogy* they represent between their entailments that constitute evidence (i.e., those already observed) and those that constitute predictions in domains that are accessible but not yet tested for. To take Newton's theory again as the most striking historical example, Newton had confidence (high personalist probability) in predicting the orbits of the comets, the motions of the tides, etc., as deductions from his theory, not because he necessarily had a very high personal probability for his theory in universal form, but because he believed material substance in all the domains concerned to be sufficiently analogous ('exchangeable') as being massive bodies, to give high probability to the consequences of an analogy argument from evidence to prediction. To put it another way, a 'good theory' (and this means 'a good explanatory theory' in a sense richer than Hempel's) is one that abstracts from a number of domains of analogous objects or events, those features which turn out to be essential features relative to a system of laws – in the case of Newton's theory, mass, motion, and central forces. It is this characteristic of exhibiting analogies in a finite number of phenomenal domains that is important about laws and theories, not their universal quantifiability or the merely formal deductive relations within their domains of application.

If such an account of confirmation in theoretical systems can be made to work it seems to score high on several of the dimensions of a good confirmation theory. It operates with a single confirmation function, positive probabilistic relevance, which is a familiar function with clearly understood axiomatic structure. The confirmation theory does not adopt different principles for scientific theories and universal generalizations, or for enumerative and eliminative induction; it rests on a single primitive concept of 'analogy' which is already overtly present in some theoretical reasoning in advanced science as well as in the presupposition of the notion of 'next instance'; it is successful in explicating most types of elementary inductive inference recognized in the textbooks and other types not so elementary; and it gives natural solutions of some of the classic paradoxes of induction.

The major difficulties of the theory lie in its dependence on the concept of analogy. Firstly, the relation of analogy between two objects or events has to be supposed to be an objective and recognizable characteristic of the world, for anything less than this will not be a strong enough basis for the objective success of a sufficient proportion of predictions based on high posterior probabilities derived from the theory. This requirement involves a theory not unlike a realist theory of universals.[7] The second major difficulty is that, while analogy relations may be acceptable in an analysis of the confirmation of simple generalizations, their application is not so obvious in the case of theories. For example (an example of Putnam's) exactly what analogy in the phenomena is being appealed to when laboratory-sized experiments in nuclear physics are taken to give sufficiently high probability to the predicted results of nuclear theory to justify the risk of the high energy test at Los Alamos? Or similarly with the Mars probes? To run through the confirmation relations in a complex theory like these would be a largeish research programme for some Ph.D student. I have attempted some such analysis in the case of Maxwell's prediction of the displacement current in his electro-magnetic theory.[8]

In conclusion, let me return briefly to the question of scepticism and realism raised by Cohen's attribution of two characteristics to recent philosophy of science. They were

(1) The denial that 'the truth of a scientific generalization over an unbounded domain is a possible object of proof or knowledge' and

(2) The view that inductive logic cannot show that universal generalizations are given any inductive support by evidence.

[7] *SSI*, ch. 2.
[8] *SSI*, ch. 11

My claim is that a *PR* confirmation theory, together with high prior probabilities given to the conclusions of analogical arguments, shows that enough inductive support can be given to generalizations over finite and practically relevant domains to make (2) a misleading conclusion. Since universal generalizations and theories are thus given probability-values in these domains, it follows that they have truth-values in these domains, which shows that (1) is too strong a demand. The truth of a scientific generalization over practically relevant domains *is* a possible object of inductive proof and knowledge, and this is sufficient to restore a modified sense of realism against some of the extreme forms of scepticism and relativism.

§14. Ilkka Niiniluoto
Analogy, Transitivity, and the Confirmation of Theories

In this comment, it is argued that the main conclusions of Mary Hesse's paper 'What is the Best Way to Assess Evidential Support for Scientific Theories' can be defended without limiting the applications of inductive logic to restricted generalizations. Everything which Hesse hopes to accomplish in her finitist approach can be done within systems of inductive logic which deal with strictly universal generalizations.

An axiomatic treatment of inductive generalization, due to J. Hintikka and I. Niiniluoto, is outlined for multinomial sampling situations with cells $Q_1, \ldots, Q_K$. In the resulting K-dimensional system of inductive probability measures, Carnap's λ-continuum is the only special case which does not attribute non-zero prior and posterior probabilities to some strictly universal generalizations. It turns out that non-Carnapian measures in this system automatically satisfy Hesse's requirement for theoretical analogical inference (*The Structures of Scientific Inference*, pp. 210–12). Moreover, two different ways of treating singular analogical inference are suggested; they are both based on the idea that the probabilities given by the K-dimensional system are systematically modified by weighting them with numbers which depend on the distances between the relevant cells.

The so-called transitivity paradox is important as a problem concerning indirect support, but in connection with prediction it does not seem to be so serious as Hesse suggests. Predictions are reliable if they are probable; thus for the evaluation of predictions it is more appropriate to know how probable they are on the evidence than to know whether they are supported in the Positive Relevance sense by the evidence. Hesse's example concerning Newton's predictions of the orbits of comets can be treated in probabilistic terms by taking into account the approximate character of such predictions.

Mary Hesse's paper 'What is the Best Way to Assess Evidential Support for Scientific Theories?' has two main conclusions:

(i) The view that inductive logic cannot show that universal generalizations are given any inductive support by evidence is 'misleading', since a positive relevance theory of confirmation, 'together with high prior probabilities given to the conclusions of analogical arguments, shows that enough inductive support can be given to generalizations over finite and practically relevant domains'.

(ii) Some of the extreme forms of scepticism and relativism are wrong, since 'the truth of a scientific generalization over practically relevant domains is a possible object of inductive proof and know-ledge'.[1]

For me it is easy to agree completely with these conclusions – and yet to disagree partly with the grounds that Hesse presents for them. The conclusions (i) and (ii) are too weak: in defending them it is unnecessary to follow Hesse's policy of considering only restricted generalizations. There are systems of inductive logic which are capable of handling strictly universal generalizations – i.e., generali-zations over unbounded or infinite domains rather than over 'finite and practically relevant' domains. Moreover, it can be argued that everything which Hesse hopes to accomplish in her finitist ap-proach can be done at least equally well within these systems. Even though it may be useful for some methodological purposes to deal with generalizations restricted to finite domains, there is nothing in our formalism of inductive logic which compels us to limit our attention to such situations. Thus, no real gains can be won by excluding strictly universal generalizations – and, hence, genuine scientific theories – from the applications of inductive logic.

In this comment I shall take up some of the main themes which Hesse discusses in her paper and in her book *The Structure of Scientific Inference*.[2] The programme for developing an inductive logic of theories has been defended in a number of my earlier works and papers.[3] As one can easily see from them, Hesse's excellent work on scientific inference has very much influenced my own views – in spite of the remaining disagreement about some of the basic issues.

One important part of Hesse's paper is the reconstruction of L. J. Cohen's account of inductive support in terms of the probabilistic theory of confirmation. To me it seems to give a satisfactory (partial) answer to Cohen's interesting challenge to Pascalian probabilities. I shall not discuss this topic here; I rather leave the reply to Cohen himself.

---

[1] M. Hesse, 'What is the Best Way to Assess Evidential Support for Scientific Theories?' p. 202 f. above.

[2] M. Hesse, *The Structure of Scientific Inference* (1974).

[3] See I. Niiniluoto and R. Tuomela, *Theoretical Concepts and Hypothetico-Inductive Inference* (1973); I. Niiniluoto, 'Inductive Logic and Theoretical Concepts', in M. Pzrelecki, K. Szaniawski, and R. Wojcicki (eds.), *Formal Methods in the Methodology of Empirical Sciences* (1977), pp. 93–112; J. Hintikka and I. Niiniluoto, 'Axiomatic Foundations for the Theory of Inductive Generalization', ibid., pp. 57–81; I. Niiniluoto, 'On a *K*-dimensional System of Inductive Logic', in F. Suppe and P. D. Asquith (eds.), *PSA 1976*, vol. 2 (1977), pp. 425–47.

1.

Hesse distinguishes sharply the problems of supporting universal generalizations and of supporting the predictions ('next instances') of generalizations. She thinks that these problems are 'quite distinct from each other'.[4] The first problem is, she claims, neither 'a very difficult problem' nor 'of primary importance for a confirmation theory'.[5] The latter problem is more serious, since it involves the 'transivity paradox'.

It seems to me that all these points are, to some extent, exaggerated. Confirmation of generalizations is more problematic, more important, and less distinct from problems of prediction than Hesse claims, and therefore the transitivity paradox is not quite so serious as she suggests. I shall start by considering some aspects of the problem of supporting generalizations.

Let h be a universal generalization or a scientific theory formulated as a universal axiomatic system. Let e be an accepted evidence statement,[6] and let b represent all the background assumptions which are accepted or taken for granted in the given situation. Here b may contain, e.g., background theories which are needed in the interpretation of the observational evidence or auxiliary assumptions needed in an attempted derivation of e from h. Then evidence e *confirms h relative to b* if and only if $P(h \mid e \ \& \ b) > P(h \mid b)$. A sufficient (but by no means necessary) condition for this inequality is

$$(1) \qquad h \ \& \ b \vdash e, \qquad b \nvdash e, \quad \text{and} \quad 1 > P(h \mid b) > 0.$$

On the basis of this observation one can give an account of the hypothetico-deductive view of scientific inference (with its variants) on the basis of probabilistic confirmation theory.[7] In a similar way, if

$$(2) \qquad h \ \& \ b \vdash e, \qquad h \nvdash e, \quad \text{and} \quad 1 > P(b \mid h) > 0,$$

then e confirms b relative to h. In other words, if we take the generalization h for granted, then e gives support to the assumption

[4] This volume, p. 206.

[5] Ibid., p. 203.

[6] Hesse makes a distinction between 'observation reports' and 'observation statements' and uses it in a model for dealing with uncertain evidence (see *The Structure of Scientific Inference*, pp. 127–30). For criticism, see R. Hilpinen's review in *J. Phil.* 62 (1975), 485–91.

[7] This includes (part of) Popper's view of scientific inference; cf. J. Hintikka, 'Induction by Enumeration and Induction by Elimination', in I. Lakatos (ed.), *The Problem of Inductive Logic* (1968), pp. 191–216; Niiniluoto and Tuomela, op. cit.; R. C. Jeffrey, 'Probability and Falsification: Critique of the Popper Program', *Synthese* 30 (1975), 95–117.

of the initial conditions b (or 'cause') of e. This corresponds to the inference which was called 'abduction' by C. S. Peirce.[8]

These simple observations suggest that the confirmation of generalizations indeed is 'not a very difficult problem': all we need is a probability function P which gives them non-zero probabilities relative to the background assumptions. But in fact this account seems to make it too easy for generalizations to gain evidential support: for example, the observation of one white thing confirms the claim that this thing is a unicorn and all unicorns are white.[9] To make the notion of confirmation more interesting, additions to the positive relevance criterion or additional requirements to the probability measure P seem to be needed.[10] In the next section, I shall show how P can be chosen so that $P(h \mid b)$ has finite values.

In the account given above, the inductive probability $P(h \mid e \& b)$ is usually interpreted as a reasonable degree of belief in the *truth* of h in the light of e and b.[11] It might be argued, however, that in the methodologically relevant situations we all have reason to believe in the *falsity* of h on the given evidence $e \& b$. As Duhem, Feyerabend, Popper, and others have pointed out, scientific theories are often inconsistent with the data they are invented to account for. Just like in curve-fitting problems, theories explain data by correcting them at the same time. Hence, $P(h \mid e \& b)$ should be expected to be zero. Similar arguments have been presented by Hesse: she claims that there is *no* chance that a strictly universal generalization is true, since it may not be reasonable to believe that it states a law accurately even in one instance. For example, a proposed law 'All P are Q' may have to be replaced by 'All PP' are Q' or by 'All P are Q or Q''. It is impossible, she argues, to know in any single instance of a proposed law that 'all relevant predicates have been taken into

---

[8] See C. S. Peirce, *Collected Papers*, ed. by C. Hartshorne and P. Weiss (1931–5), ii. 712.

[9] Note that Hesse says, in her paper, that e confirms the conjunction $h \& b$ under the condition (1). I have preferred to speak here of relative confirmation.

[10] For discussion about the Positive Relevance Criterion of confirmation, see W. Salmon, 'Confirmation and Relevance', in G. Maxwell and R. M. Anderson, Jr. (eds.), *Induction, Probability and Confirmation* (1975), pp. 3–36. For the possibilities of defining the confirmation relation by means of the notion of explanation, see Niiniluoto and Tuomela, op. cit., pp. 222–8, and R. Tuomela, 'Confirmation, Explanation, and the Paradoxes of Transitivity', in R. J. Bogdan (ed.), *Local Induction* (1976), pp. 319–28. For a proposal that only 'seriously proposed' hypotheses should be given non-zero prior probabilities, see A. Shimony, 'Scientific Inference', in R. Colodny (ed.), *The Nature and Function of Scientific Theories* (1970), pp. 79–172.

[11] For a different view, see Shimony, 'Scientific Inference'.

account'. Therefore, it is reasonable to take the probability of laws to be 'always properly zero'.[12]

Let us use the name *Falsity Thesis* for the claim that all scientific laws are strictly speaking false.[13] This thesis is a serious one: it gains some support from the history of science and we cannot claim to be certain of any counter-example to it. But, on the other hand, there are no conclusive or convincing arguments for it, either. As long as you admit that there is some chance for the Falsity Thesis to be false, you also have to admit there is some chance that some universal laws are true.

Fortunately, in developing inductive logic one need not solve such metaphysical problems as the validity of the Falsity Thesis. The reason for this is simple: the problem of confirming strictly universal generalizations would be methodologically interesting even if the Falsity Thesis were valid. We may indeed admit that all scientific laws are false in the actual world, since they always involve idealizing assumptions – counterfactual assumptions about the absence of certain disturbing factors, the irrelevance of certain variables, the values of certain parameters, etc.[14] Hence, they are at best *approximately true* in the actual world, whereas they may be *strictly true* in those counterfactual states of affairs where the idealizing assumptions hold.[15] The discrepancy between a scientific law h and evidence e – e.g., between Newton's theory and Kepler's laws – is usually based upon the fact that they involve conflicting idealizing assumptions. In those cases, the probability of h on e may be zero, but nevertheless e gives strong support to another law h' which is closely similar to h. (See Fig. 1.) Alternatively, it may be that

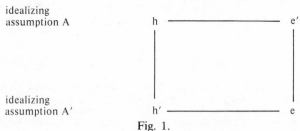

Fig. 1.

[12] See Hesse, *The Structure of Scientific Inference*, pp. 181–3.

[13] This thesis is accepted in a view which I call 'fallibilism in the strong sense' in I. Niiniluoto, 'Notes on Popper as Follower of Whewell and Peirce', *Ajatus* 37 (1978), 272–327.

[14] Cf. e.g., W. Krajewski, *Correspondence Principle and the Growth of Knowledge* (1977).

[15] Cf. F. Suppe, 'The Search for Philosophic Understanding of Scientific Theories', in F. Suppe (ed.), *The Structure of Scientific Theories* (1974), pp. 223–4.

evidence e' gives support to h, where e' tells what e would have been under the idealizing assumptions connected with h.[16] The relations between e and h', and between e' and h, are then precisely of the sort which can be studied by means of an inductive logic for universal generalizations.

2.

Let us now consider the familiar situation of multinomial sampling with K mutually exclusive and jointly exhaustive classes $Q_1, \ldots, Q_K$. Let L be a monadic first-order language with the primitive predicates 'Q_i', $i = 1, \ldots, K$, and individual constants $a_1, a_2, \ldots$. Let e be a description in L of a sample of n individuals from universe U such that $n_i \geqslant 0$ of them are found in cell Q_i $(i = 1, \ldots, K)$. Thus, $n = n_1 + \cdots + n_K$. Further, let c be the number of different kinds of individuals in sample e, i.e., c is the number of n_i's such that $n_i > 0$. The more explicit notation 'e_n^c' for 'e' will be occasionally used below.

Let us assume that a measure P for the sentences of language L satisfies the following conditions:

1^0 Probability axioms.
2^0 Regularity: for singular e and h, $P(h \mid e) = 1$ if and only if $e \vdash h$.
3^0 Symmetry with respect to individuals: $P(h \mid e)$ is invariant w.r.t. permutation of individual constants.
4^0 Symmetry of Q-predicates: $P(h \mid e)$ is invariant w.r.t. permutation of Q-predicates.
5^0 c-principle:

There exists a function f such that

$$P(Q_i(a_{n+1}) \mid e_n^c) = f(n_i, n, c).$$

Here 3^0 is essentially de Finetti's exchangeability assumption.

If 5^0 is replaced by the stronger condition that function f is independent of c and depends only on n_i and n, it can be shown that P belongs to Carnap's λ-continuum of inductive methods. On the other hand, measures P which satisfy conditions 1^0–5^0 constitute a K-dimensional system with free parameters

$$\lambda = \frac{Kf(1, K+1, K)}{1 - Kf(1, K+1, K)} - K$$

$$\gamma_i = f(0, i, i), \quad \text{for} \quad i = 1, \ldots, K-1),$$

---

[16] Ibid., pp. 225–6.

where $\lambda > -K$ and

$$(3) \qquad\qquad \gamma_i \leqslant \frac{\lambda/K}{i+\lambda}$$

When all parameters γ_i are given their maximum values, Carnap's λ-continuum is obtained as a special case of the K-dimensional system. Another important special case of this system is the 'generalized combined system' of Hintikka.[17]

Constituents of L are generalizations of the form

$$(4) \qquad\qquad C_i = \bigwedge_{j \in W_i} (\exists x) Q_j(x) \ \& \ (x)\left[\bigvee_{j \in W_i} Q_j(x) \right]$$

Here $w_i = |W_i|$ is the *width* of C_i. Constituents are mutually incompatible, and each consistent generalization in L can be expressed as a finite disjunction of constituents. Let C^K be the maximally wide constituent with width K. If C^K is true in universe U, then there are no universal laws (expressible in L) true in U. It can be proved that in the K-dimensional system $P(C^K) = 1$ if and only if all parameters γ_i have their 'Carnapian' (i.e., maximum) values (cf. (3)). Carnap's λ-continuum is thus the *only* special case of this system which does not attribute non-zero prior probabilities to some strictly universal generalizations.

This result gives a diagnosis of Carnap's failure in accounting for inductive generalization in his λ-continuum: the reason for this failure (and for a similar failure of the classical Bayesians like Laplace and Jevons) is the assumption that the representative function – that is, probabilities of singular inductive inference – is purely enumerative, i.e., independent of the variety of evidence e as expressed by the number c. Further, it refutes the view that zero probability has to be assigned to universal generalizations in 'all obvious modifications' of Carnap's confirmation theory,[18] thereby making unnecessary all *post hoc* rationalizations (by Carnap and

---

[17] The K-dimensional system was introduced in Hintikka and Niiniluoto, op. cit. Further results are given in Niiniluoto, 'On a K-dimensional System of Inductive Logic'; T. Kuipers, 'On the Generalization of the Continuum of Inductive Methods to Universal Hypotheses', *Synthese* 37 (1978), 255–84; T. Kuipers, *Studies in Inductive Probability and Rational Expectation* (1978); T. Kuipers, 'A Survey of Inductive Systems', forthcoming in R. C. Jeffrey (ed.), *Studies in Inductive Logic and Probability*, vol. 2. For Hintikka's generalized combined system, see J. Hintikka, 'A Two-Dimensional Continuum of Inductive Methods', in J. Hintikka and P. Suppes (eds.), *Aspects of Inductive Logic* (1966), pp. 113–32, and Niiniluoto and Tuomela, op. cit.

[18] Cf. Hesse, *The Structure of Scientific Inference*, p. 176.

others)[19] of why after all it is rational to give zero probabilities to laws. Finally, we see that, under conditions 1^0–5^0, bets on universal generalizations are equivalent to finite betting systems for singular sentences (choice of the K parameters), which refutes the widespread view that there is something strange in the idea of interpreting the probabilities of laws as coherent betting ratios.

3.

Some additional comments on the K-dimensional system are in order here. As we noted above, it is essentially a generalization of Hintikka's 'generalized combined system' (with more flexible prior probabilities for constituents) which in turn is essentially a generalization of Carnap's function c^*; the latter again is a generalization of Laplace's rule of succession. Kuipers has suggested that this system is *the* rational generalization of Carnap's inductive logic.[20] I find this doubtful, however, for the reason that it may sometimes be reasonable to violate some of the conditions 3^0–5^0: condition 3^0 may be replaced by an assumption of partial exchangeability;[21] condition 4^0 does not apply in cases involving Q-predicates of different width; and condition 5^0 excludes some interesting forms of analogy arguments (see section 4). Moreover, the system does not – and is not intended to – handle statistical generalizations of the form 'A proportion p of P's are Q's' in infinite domains.[22]

---

[19] See e.g., W. Stegmüller, 'Carnap's Normative Theory of Inductive Probability', in P. Suppes *et al.* (eds.), *Logic, Methodology, and Philosophy of Science IV* (1973), pp. 501–13.

[20] Kuipers, 'On the Generalization of the Continuum of Inductive Methods to Universal Hypotheses'. Note, however, that in his *Studies in Inductive Probability and Rational Expectation* Kuipers himself considers more liberally defined systems.

[21] Cf. the article by B. de Finetti in R. C. Jeffrey (ed.), *Studies in Inductive Logic and Probability* (forthcoming).

[22] Hesse has argued that Hintikka's system is unsatisfactory, since 'it is not capable without further ad hoc additions of dealing with statistical generalizations' (see M. Hesse, 'Confirmation of Laws', in S. Morgenbesser, P. Suppes, and M. White (eds.), *Philosophy, Science, and Method: Essays in Honor of Ernest Nagel* (1969), p. 76). This remark concerns infinite domains only: if we limit our attention to finite domains, as Hesse proposes elsewhere, then statistical generalizations can be handled in the Hintikkian systems by computing the probabilities of structure descriptions. Hesse has also suggested that the problem of confirming universal laws of the form 'All P are Q' should be replaced by the problem of finding an interval estimate $[\theta, 1]$ for the parameter p in 'proportion p of P's are Q' (see ibid., p. 77). More generally, in the multinomial case with K cells, one may be interested in finding a region estimate for the true value of the parameter $\langle p_1, \ldots, p_K \rangle$, where p_i is the proportion of individuals in the ith cell and $p_1 + \cdots + p_K = 1$. However, I agree with Shimony and Levi that there may sometimes be a 'special pressure' for obtaining a point estimate (see Shimony, 'Scientific Inference' and I. Levi, 'Acceptance Revisited', in R. J. Bogdan (ed.), *Local Induction*, pp. 45–6). Moreover, I assume that from the

On the other hand, it should be strongly emphasized that the results concerning the K-dimensional system are extremely general. L. J. Cohen has argued against Niiniluoto and Tuomela that 'to publish an inductive logic for scientific theory which turns out to be confined to monadic, qualitative predicates . . . is like publishing a textbook of mechanical transportation which turns out to apply only to bicycles'.[23] This remark would be more to the point if the purpose of inductive logic would be to produce manuals for working scientists for computing the numerical degrees of confirmation of their theories. But the situation is different if its aim is rather to analyse the notion of confirmation and to study the characteristic properties of this notion. For then the important question to ask about such books as *Theoretical Concepts and Hypothetico-Inductive Inference* is the following: to what extent are the monadic cases representative of the more general cases? In this respect, the results concerning the K-dimensional system are very interesting and satisfactory.

Note that we have so far not said or presupposed anything about the nature of the Q-predicates. It can be assumed that they are defined by conjunctions

(5) $$(\pm)O_1(x) \& \cdots \& (\pm)O_k(x)$$

of k primitive, qualitative monadic predicates. (Then $K = 2^k$.) Equally well they can be defined by means of families of predicates which may involve (suitably partitioned) value-spaces of quantities.[24] But for us it is perhaps even more interesting to note that

viewpoint of scientific theory formation the interest in such extreme values as $\langle 1, 0, \ldots, 0 \rangle$, $\langle 0, 1, 0, \ldots, 0 \rangle$ etc. is a legitimate one, so that there are situations where the only 'seriously proposed' hypotheses are non-statistical generalizations (cf. section 1). Because of the interplay with enumerative and eliminative aspects of induction, resulting from the falsifiability of such non-statistical hypotheses, this special case is qualitatively different from the statistical problem of interval estimation and from point estimation with respect to non-extremal points of the parameter space. In recommending the K-dimensional system and its modifications for this special problem, I am not forgetting that other techniques may be needed for other problems (cf. Levi's remarks on 'the Finnish School', op. cit., p. 61). The K-dimensional system is similar to Shimony's approach in the sense that hypotheses which from the statistician's viewpoint correspond only to a singular point of the parameter space may have non-zero prior probabilities; moreover, because of the limiting behaviour of the posterior probabilities, constituents satisfy Shimony's 'tempering condition'. But it should be noted that, as Levi points out, at least in his system 'it is unnecessary to assign positive probabilities to universal generalizations in order to accept them' (ibid.).

[23] L. J. Cohen, 'A Conspectus of the Neo-Classical Theory of Induction', in R. J. Bogdan (ed.), *Local Induction*, p. 239.

[24] Cf. R. Carnap, 'The Basic System of Inductive Logic, Part I', in R. Carnap and R. C. Jeffrey (eds.), *Studies of Inductive Logic and Probability*, vol. 1 (1971), 33–165. Part II is forthcoming in Jeffrey, op. cit.

the individuals in cells Q_i need not be simple individuals (such as individual objects or singular events) but they may as well be ordered pairs, m-tuples, or even finite trees with branches of length m. It is known that each universal generalization in a polyadic first-order language (with a finite set of primitive predicates) is equivalent to a finite disjunction of constituents of the appropriate quantificational depth $m > 0$; each of these constituents is expressible in the form (4) where Q-predicates are now finite trees consisting of sequences of individuals with the length m. The K-dimensional system tells then how the inductive probabilities of such first-order generalizations depend on a sample e which consists of a set of observed trees of the length m. This gives, in principle, a general solution to the problem of confirming generalizations in full first-order languages – and it also shows that the solution of this problem has the same general features as the confirmation relations of the K-dimensional system when applied to monadic situations.[25]

4.

Hesse's principal objection to Hintikka's system of inductive logic – and *a fortiori* to the K-dimensional system – is the fact that it is 'not capable of explicating analogy arguments of a kind fundamental for science'.[26] It is known that the K-dimensional system satisfies the principle of Positive Instantial Relevance, viz.

(6) $P(Q_j(a_{n+1})/e_n^c) < P(Q_j(a_{n+2})/e_n^c \ \& \ Q_j(a_{n+1})).$[27]

What Hesse has in mind, however, are stronger arguments by analogy, such as

(7) $P(D(b)/e) > P(\sim D(b)/e)$

   if $e = A(a) \ \& \ B(a) \ \& \ C(a) \ \& \ D(a) \ \& \ A(b) \ \& \ B(b) \ \& \ \sim C(b).$[28]

Such inferences can be handled in Carnap's η-theory, and Pietari-nen has shown how the analogy parameter η can be incorporated

[25] These observations give at least a partial answer to P. Teller, 'Comments on Niiniluoto and Uchii', in F. Suppe and P. D. Asquith (eds.), *PSA 1976*, vol. 2, p. 498. For an extension of Hintikka's system of inductive logic to cases involving relations, see R. Hilpinen, 'Relational Hypotheses and Inductive Logic', *Synthese* 23 (1971), 266–86.

[26] Hesse, *The Structure of Scientific Inference*, p. 177.

[27] See Niiniluoto, 'On a K-dimensional System of Inductive Logic', p. 433.

[28] See Hesse, op. cit., pp. 167–70. Here A, B, C, and D are primitive predicates – not Q-predicates.

into Hintikka's system.[29] But even though Hesse herself has contributed to the development of the η-theory,[30] she seems now quite sceptical over its possibilities – 'it is not profitable, at least at present, to pursue such an approach to analogical arguments', she concludes.[31] As a consequence of this attitude, it remains unclear to the readers of Hesse's book on scientific inference how precisely the analogical arguments are to be reconstructed within a probabilistic theory of confirmation.

It is interesting to note that in her argument against Hintikka's system Hesse claims that 'explication of analogy arguments requires that higher initial probability be assigned to relatively clustered universes', i.e., to constituents with a small width.[32] No wonder that she has lost her faith in Carnapian systems, since in infinite universes the λ-continuum assigns the whole probability mass 1 to the maximally wide constituent C^K! Hintikka's system – and all non-Carnapian members of the K-dimensional system, too – gives high posterior probabilities to the constituent which, among those compatible with evidence, exhibits the greatest amount of 'clustering' in the universe. In this respect it differs from the behaviour of Carnap's λ-system even on finite domains. This feature should make Hintikka's system look more promising than Carnap's for explicating analogy arguments.[33]

It is interesting to note that in Hintikka's system we have $P(e_2/e_1) > P(e_2)$ if e_1 is the generalization $(x)(F(x) \& G(x) \supset P(x) \& Q(x))$ and e_2 is $(x)(G(x) \& H(x) \supset P(x) \& R(x))$ and if the probabilities are calculated in the monadic language L with primitive predicates F, G, H, P, Q, and R. This is Hesse's paradigm example of theoretical analogical inference.[34]

I shall now outline a modification of the K-dimensional system which takes into account analogy arguments without introducing new parameters such as Carnap's η. There seems to be a very

[29] See J. Pietarinen, *Lawlikeness, Analogy, and Inductive Logic*, Acta Philosophica Fennica 26 (1972).

[30] See M. Hesse, 'Analogy and Confirmation Theory', *Philosophy of Science* 26 (1964), 319–27.

[31] Hesse, *The Structure of Scientific Inference*, p. 170.

[32] Ibid., p. 177.

[33] It is not quite clear to me why one should require high *prior* probabilities for clustering, as Hesse does, rather than high *posterior* probabilities for clustering, as in Hintikka's system. In any case, in the K-dimensional system it is possible to choose the parameters so that wider constituents have smaller prior probabilities than the less wide ones. See also T. Kuipers, 'A Two-Dimensional Continuum of a Priori Probability Distributions on Constituents', in Przelecki *et al.* (eds.), *Formal Methods in the Methodology of Empirical Sciences*, pp. 82–92.

[34] Hesse, *The Structure of Scientific Inference*, pp. 210–12.

natural way of doing this which, as far as I know, has not been tried before. A basic assumption which is needed for this account is the existence of a function d which measures the *distance between Q-predicates* and thus also the *degree of similarity* between individuals exemplifying these predicates. For two Q-predicates of the form (5) function d can be easily defined by

$$(8) \quad d(Q_i, Q_j) = \frac{1}{k} \cdot \text{the number of different conjuncts in } Q_i \text{ and } Q_j.$$

(Here of course $O_r(x)$ and $\sim O_r(x)$ are counted as different conjuncts.) For the more general case with families of predicates a definition of d has been given by Carnap,[35] and for the case with Ct-predicates of polyadic languages (i.e., trees of length $m > 0$) this has been done by myself.[36] I shall restrict my attention here to cases involving the simple definition (8).

The simplest way of modifying the K-dimensional system in order to account for analogy seems to be the following. As the posterior probability that the next individual will be found in one of the already exemplified cells is influenced, in accordance with (6), by the observed individuals, let us assume that probabilities $f(n_i, n, c)$, $n_i > 0$, remain unchanged. On the other hand, the posterior probability that an individual will be found in a so far unexemplified cell Q_j should depend upon whether we have already observed individuals which are similar to Q_j. In other words, this probability should increase when the following distance decreases:

$$(9) \qquad\qquad d(Q_j, e) = \min_{i \in I_e} d(Q_j, Q_i)$$

where I_e is the set of the indices of the c Q-predicates which have been exemplified in evidence e. In the K-dimensional system the probability $P(Q_j(a_{n+1})/e_n^c)$ would be $f(0, n, c)$; we can now propose to redistribute these probabilities by assigning $f(0, n, c)$ with a weight $a(e_n^c)/d(Q_j, e_n^c)$ where the normalizing factor $a(e_n^c)$ is defined by

$$a(e_n^c) = \frac{K - c}{\sum\limits_{i \notin I_e} \dfrac{1}{d(Q_i, e_n^c)}}$$

---

[35] Carnap, op. cit., Part II.
[36] See I. Niiniluoto, 'Truthlikeness: Comments on Recent Discussion', *Synthese* 38 (1978), 281–328.

Thus,

$$(10) \qquad P(Q_j(a_{n+1})/e_n^c) = \frac{a(e_n^c)}{d(Q_j, e_n^c)} f(0, n, c).$$

This definition violates in some cases the condition 3^0, and thereby creates a sort of partial exchangeability situation. It also violates the c-rule 5^0, since it is now essential to know, not only that c cells have been exemplified in e, but also *which* c cells have been exemplified. For example, if $n = c = 1$ and one individual of type $ABCD$ has been observed, then it is more probable on this evidence that the next individual to be observed is of type $A \& B \& {\sim}C \& D$ than of type $A \& B \& {\sim}C \& {\sim}D$, since by (8) the former predicate is closer to $A \& B \& C \& D$ than the latter. This is equivalent precisely to the analogy requirement (7) above. When applied to arguments involving two individuals, this measure seems to satisfy Hesse's basic requirements of analogy: the strength of analogy considerations depends on the amount of positive analogy between the individuals; clustering is favoured; a principle of 'negative analogy' is not assumed.[37]

A more complex account of analogical inference could be based upon the assumption that *all* observed individuals have some *similarity influence* to the probabilities of next instances. This would involve a more radical departure from the c-rule 5^0 than the simpler account. The n individuals observed in e_n^c will be distributed into c cells in an uneven way.[38] Intuitively, the claim $Q_j(a_{n+1})$ is the more probable the closer Q_j is to the most frequently occupied cells. Let us define

$$h(Q_j, e_n^c) = \sum_{i=1}^{K} \frac{n_i}{1 + d(Q_j, Q_i)}$$

Then we can propose:

$$P(Q_j(a_{n+1}) \mid e_n^c) = \frac{h(Q_j, e_n^c)}{h_1(e_n^c)} f(0, n, c), \quad \text{if } n_j = 0,$$

$$= \frac{h(Q_j, e_n^c)}{h_2(e_n^c)} g(n, c), \quad \text{if } n_j > 0,$$

where $g(n, c)$ is the probability in the K-dimensional system that the next individual will be of the same kind as the one of the earlier

----

[37] Hesse, *The Structure of Scientific Inference*, pp. 160, 173.
[38] Teller (op. cit., p. 497) seems to suggest that this sort of system would be desirable.

kinds, and

$$h_1(e_n^c) = \sum_{i \notin I_{e_n^c}} h(Q_i, e_n^c),$$

$$h_2(e_n^c) = \sum_{i \in I_{e_n^c}} h(Q_i, e_n^c).$$

These two accounts of singular analogical inference would also affect inductive generalization: while in Hintikka's generalized combined system the probability $P(C^w \mid e_n^c)$, for large n, if non-zero, covaries with the difference $w - c$ between the claimed width w and the observed width c, in the analogy account this probability would also depend on how close the claimed but yet unobserved kinds of individuals are to the already observed ones. For example, if e_n^1 contains n AB's, then the constituent which claims that there are AB's and A & $\sim B$'s is more probable on e_n^1 than the constituent which claims that there are AB's and $\sim A$ & $\sim B$'s.

5.

The Positive Relevance Criterion (PR) of confirmation does not satisfy the Special Consequence Principle

(SC)   If e confirms h and $h \vdash g$, then e confirms g.

In fact no reasonable notion of confirmation which satisfies the Converse Entailment Principle

(CE)   If $h \vdash e$, then e confirms h,

as PR does, can satisfy SC. On the other hand, the High Probability Criterion (HP) satisfies SC but not CE.[39] It therefore seems that there is no reasonable way to account for the fact that evidence e which supports a theory h (by being deducible from h) is often taken to support also h's deductive predictions. This problem is called the 'transitivity paradox' by Hesse.[40] Her solution to this problem is based on the suggestion that good theories represent a high degree of analogy between their entailments: if theory h entails e_1 and e_2, then by revealing and expressing a real or objective relation of analogy between e_1 and e_2 theory h justifies the claim

(11) $P(e_2 \mid e_1) > P(e_2)$

and thereby makes possible a *direct* inference from e_1 to e_2.[41]

---

[39] According to HP, e confirms h iff $P(h/e) \geqslant k > 1/2$, where k is a constant.
[40] Hesse, *The Structure of Scientific Inference*, pp. 141–50.
[41] Ibid., pp. 209–12.

It seems to me that as a problem concerning *prediction* the transitivity paradox is not as serious as Hesse thinks. Predictions are *reliable* if and only if they are probable on the accepted evidence – and what is interesting about predictions is not how much evidence supports them (in the PR sense) but how reliable they are on the evidence (in the HP sense). If a theory h is accepted as evidence, then a prediction e_2 is maximally reliable on h in case e_2 is deducible from h, and it is reliable on h in case $P(e_2 \mid h)$ is high. If h is not accepted, but only supported by evidence e_1, i.e., $P(h \mid e_1) > P(h)$, then the increase in the probability of h increases the lower bound of the degree of reliability of e_2, since $e_1 \ \& \ h \vdash e_2$ guarantees that

(12) $$P(e_2 \mid e_1) > P(h \mid e_1).$$

Knowledge of (12) may be important especially in those cases where $P(h \mid e_1)$ is high or the value of $P(e_2 \mid e_1)$ cannot be evaluated directly.[42]

For these reasons it seems quite misleading to say that confirmation of generalizations by means of enumerative induction is 'useless for prediction'.[43] In the same way, it is misleading to treat the PR relation (11) as a criterion for the prediction of e_2 on e_1.[44]

Formula (12) guarantees that a rational degree of belief for the truth of a deductive prediction based on a theory is always at least as high as the degree of belief in the truth of the theory itself. But Hesse is nevertheless right in pointing out that $P(e_2 \mid e_1)$ may be high even if $e_1 \ \& \ h \vdash e_2$ and $P(h \mid e_1)$ is low or even zero. She suggests that Newton was willing to attribute a high probability to predictions concerning the orbits of comets, not because he had 'a high personal probability for his theory in universal form', but because he believed comets to be sufficiently analogous, as massive bodies, to already tested applications of his theory.[45] But, as this sort of prediction is only approximate, it might be equally well suggested here that Newton was highly confident of the truth of a suitably restricted and approximate – but universal – version of his theory which was still

---

[42] On the other hand, if there are several rival theories which make conflicting predictions, then at most one of them may have a probability larger than 1/2. In such cases it may be impossible to justify any predictions with the help of inequality (12): for example, we may have $e_1 \ \& \ h_1 \vdash e_2$, $e_1 \ \& \ h_2 \vdash \sim e_2$, $1/2 > P(h_1/e_1) > P(h_1)$, and $1/2 > P(h_2/e_1) > P(h_2)$. This conclusion is just what we should expect; cf. J. Dorling, Review of *The Structure of Scientific Inference*, *Brit. J. Phil. Sci.* 26 (1975), 61–71.

[43] Hesse, op. cit., p. 152.

[44] Ibid., p. 210.

[45] This volume, p. 215.

sufficient for the derivation of the predictions concerning comets. This argument can be reconstructed by the relation (12).[46]

The transitivity paradox is important, not in the context of evaluating the reliability of predictions, but as a problem concerning *indirect support*. If evidence e_1 supports a theory h, is a deductive consequence e_2 of h also supported by e_1?[47] Can theories be indispensable for achieving such indirect confirmation? I have suggested elsewhere that indirect support *via* a theory h should be reconstructed as direct theoretical support by h itself.[48] Thus, a theory h achieves inductive systematization (in the PR sense) between e_1 and e_2 if e_1 alone is *not* positively relevant to e_2, but e_1 and h together are positively relevant to e_2 or e_1 is positively relevant to e_2 relative to h. In contrast with Hesse's analogy construal of inductive systematization, it is assumed here that (11) is *false* – while Hesse's idea is to show that the theory justifies the assumption (11). While in my construal it can be shown that universal theories employing theoretical concepts may be logically indispensable for inductive systematization among observational statements,[49] in Hesse's approach one wonders whether anything like theories are needed as a solution to the transitivity problem: a simple singular sentence asserting that the relation of real analogy holds between e_1 and e_2 seems to be enough for justifying a positive relevance relation between e_1 and e_2.[50]

What seems to underlie the two different approaches is the following: my notion of inductive systematization is a generalization of a notion of deductive systematization (viz. $e_1 \nvdash e_2$ but $e_1 \& h \vdash e_2$) in which h does not reveal an antecedently existing link between e_1 and e_2, but rather serves as an indispensable premiss for deriving e_2 from e_1. Hesse's basic idea is a generalization – for the *analogy* relation – of the 'consilience' situation, i.e., of the case where evidence for one of two independently reached laws comes to support

[46] Equally well, we might say that, since Newton believed in the approximate truth of his theory on the relevant domain, he also believed in the approximate truth of its predictions. This argument cannot be reconstructed by probabilities (e.g., by (12)), but a suitable notion of 'estimated truthlikeness' is needed. Cf. I. Niiniluoto, 'On the Truthlikeness of Generalizations', in R. E. Butts and J. Hintikka (eds.), *Basic Problems of Methodology and Linguistics* (1977), pp. 121–47.

[47] Cf. Hesse, *The Structure of Scientific Inference*, p. 207.

[48] See I. Niiniluoto, 'Inductive Systematization: Definition and a Critical Survey', *Synthèse* 25 (1972), 25–81; Niiniluoto and Tuomela, op. cit.

[49] See Niiniluoto and Tuomela, op. cit., ch. 9.

[50] We noted above that in Hesse's paradigm example of analogical inference (11) is automatically satisfied by inductive probabilities.

the other, when a theory shows that these laws are in fact *identical* with each other. While the former approach is thus related to theoretical explanation, the latter is more concerned with domain-combining reduction. That may suggest that these approaches are, after all, not rivals but rather complement each other.

§15. Comments and Replies
The Hesse–Niiniluoto Session

HESSE: Ilkka Niiniluoto has essentially three comments on my outline of the positive-relevance type confirmation theory I developed in *The Structure of Scientific Inference* (SSI). The first concerns the importance of finding a theory where generalizations in unbounded domains have greater than zero prior probability. Here I would merely remark that I certainly do not deny that such are possible and have been instantiated by Hintikka-type theories. I have only claimed that for practical scientific induction they are not required. Niiniluoto and I differ only in our interest in developing confirmation theories whose postulates 'are at best *approximately true* in the actual world, whereas they may be *strictly true* in those counterfactual states of affairs where the idealizing assumptions hold'.[1] Niiniluoto's second main point concerns the possibility of accounting for analogy arguments of various kinds in an axiomatic confirmation theory, and here I can only welcome the recent developments of Hintikka-type theories which demonstrate that this can be done in neat and natural ways.

It is over Niiniluoto's third point, about transitivity, that I find myself in disagreement. Niiniluoto wants to regard a prediction (e_2) as *reliable on h* if and only if it satisfies the condition that $p(e_2/h)$ is high, and h is either accepted as evidence, or has itself a high probability on other evidence e_1. (The case is what I discussed as 'limiting transitivity' in SSI, p. 148). It rests essentially on the assumption that it is possible to find conditions under which $p(h/e_1)$ is close to 1. I argued in my book that such conditions obtain only for inference from statistical samples which are not typical of evidence in science in general, or when there are only a finite number of conflicting hypotheses, some of which are eliminated by e_1. Thus if h is a universally quantified generalization in a real physical domain, then $p(h/e_1)$ for inevitably local evidence e_1 can never become close to 1. Niiniluoto half admits this when he suggests that 'Newton was highly confident of the truth of a suitably *restricted* and *approximate* [my italics] – but universal – version of his theory.[2] If he means by 'restricted' here, restricted in time and space to the historical solar system and all bodies sufficiently analogous to it, then I have no quarrel, and Newton's belief thus expressed is indeed equivalent to a belief that comets are 'sufficiently analogous,

[1] P. 222 above.
[2] P. 232 above.

‚as massive bodies, to already tested applications of his theory'. But why then does Niiniluoto add that this version of his theory is 'universal'? Certainly it is not universal in the sense of Newton's 'universal law of gravitation' for *all* pairs of masses in the universe. On the other hand, by 'restricted and approximate – but universal' Niinuloto *may* mean a theory restricted by idealizing assumptions, which only approximately fit the real world, but in which laws have universally quantified form. If *this* is what he means, then I still have a quarrel with him, because I am not talking about the confirmation of predictions in an ideal world, but in the real world, and the inductive grounds for our beliefs about the relation of ideal models to the real world is precisely one aspect of the question at issue.

BLOOR: One of the great virtues of Mary Hesse's work on confirmation theory is that it keeps in close contact with the history of science, and is concerned to capture and describe the actual processes of scientific inference. It has also been developed against the background of a most interesting description of knowledge called the Network model. I should like to pose a question to Hesse designed to draw her out on the connection between what she has said today and these background concerns. In particular I should appreciate a more explicit statement of the relation between her solution to the so-called transitivity paradox and the Network model. In order to sharpen my question I shall pose it in the form of a challenge: that Hesse's solution to the transitivity paradox has been presented in a way which contradicts some of the important insights of her general philosophy. This charge is an overstatement but I think that there is enough *prima facie* evidence to make it worth pressing.

The background to this issue lies in the early chapters of Hesse's *The Structure of Scientific Inference*. These define the Network model and hence the base-line from which I detect deviation. We are told that knowledge is to be looked upon as an interacting and negotiable network of classifications. This can be thought of as arising, in the first instance, from a primitive ability to group things together by selectively perceiving their similarities and differences. Nevertheless, orderly knowledge cannot be grounded on this alone. The reason is that similarity is not transitive: A can be similar to *B*, *B* to *C*, but *A* may be dissimilar to *C*. So similarity does not tell us whether *C* is to be grouped with *A* and *B*. In general, all the objects and processes we encounter will always bear to one another a complex set of similarities and differences which need to be selected, judged, and weighed. Similarity alone indicates no natural way of drawing boundaries and would only yield meandering chains of association and loose, syncretic groupings. To see why knowledge is not in fact in this state we need to appreciate its conventional component. One way to bring out the role of convention is to imagine an initial classification, based on similarity alone, being tidied-up by active reclassification. We could reclassify so as to preserve and make more exact some of the rough law-like regularities that began to emerge in the initial classification. If most Xs are Ys we can turn this into the law that all Xs are Ys by adjusting the boundaries of the classes X and Y. The degree of similarity necessary for class membership may be made more or less strict; other correlated properties might be invoked as reasons for inclusion or exclusion. A detailed illustration of these processes of adjustment and negotiation would be out of place here, but all we need imagine is the repeated application of those operations made famous by Duhem in his *La Théorie physique: Son objet et sa structure* (1906). The room for all this manoeuvring, of course, lies in the indeterminate nature of the similarities available in the initial classification.

We can now see how the order and coherence of our knowledge depends on something other than similarity and difference. It must depend crucially on something like a collective decision to hold fast to certain classifications, boundaries or law-like regularities. The parts of the Network which are held fast Hesse calls 'coherence conditions'. A law which is given this protective treatment and whose preservation leads to adjustment elsewhere is just such a coherence condition. Clearly these features of the Network would be unnecessary if there were a natural and obvious way of classifying things and if, as a consequence, the Network were not so fluid.

Just two further points about the Network model need to be born in mind. First, Hesse's carefully argued rejection of empiricism rests upon these same considerations. If there were natural classifications and boundaries that could be directly intuited there would be no problems with the empiricist idea of a data language. Second, Hesse denies that as time goes by the network settles into a fixed, natural correspondence with the world. There is no place in the model for any permanent, privileged classifications that are immune from alteration or the threat of alteration as all the other adjustments and their ramifications are carried through. There is, we are told, no 'entrenchment' of an epistemologically significant kind in the Network.

Now let us look at Hesse's account of our inductive intuitions about theoretical inference and relate them back to the model. Scientists frequently have confidence in the yet untested predictions of a theory. Reasonably enough this confidence might stem from the past successes of the theory. One way of characterizing this is to say that if we already have evidence e_1, which confirms theory T, and T entails prediction e_2, then e_1 will confirm e_2. But this principle, called the special consequence condition, leads to the result that in the Carnap-type theory Hesse adopts any proposition can confirm any other proposition whatever. It cannot therefore explain selective preferences. Rather than supplement or complicate the special consequence condition Hesse totally replaces it. In its stead we are offered the principle that evidence only confirms a prediction when there is an analogy between them. So plausibility depends on precedent. Formal deduction from a confirmed theory alone will not convince us of the reasonableness of a prediction. Our minds will only be carried along from e_1 to e_2 by the analogy of the predicted case with the evidence.

This is a powerful and elegant idea about how our minds work, but what is the precise status of the analogical resemblance involved here? Clearly it must be assumed to work in ways which conform to the Network model. This means that the analogies in question will depend on the state of the Network which provides the background to their use. They will depend upon a conventionally grounded selectivity or weighing-up of the various similarities and differences that are potentially available to their users. In short the analogies will depend on theoretical traditions or cultural backgrounds. They represent an educated grasp of the relation between evidence and prediction – and that means that coherence conditions will have been tacitly at work. The example given by Hesse of Newton's inferences is ample evidence for this: their plausibility rested on the analogy between terrestrial and celestial phenomena. Seeing this analogy is no naive response to the world. Nor could it be, for on the Network model this would have meant that thought was functioning on the level of the 'initial classification' of the environment. And this was just what the model was meant to rule out.

Given the necessary involvement of coherence conditions in this account of confirmation why, then, does Hesse deny any role for the process of 'acceptance'? If my understanding of the Network model is correct then coherence conditions are exactly those parts of the Network which are indeed 'accepted'. If coherence conditions are those parts of our knowledge which are held stable whilst negotiation and elaboration take place elsewhere, then surely they must be 'accepted'. Using Hesse's example of Newton: isn't it reasonable to say that his continuity assumption, his sense of analogy between the terrestrial and the celestial, was something that he "accepted"?

Clearly it is proper for Hesse to object to existing formulations of the notions of acceptance on the grounds that they do not capture the idea in the right form for her work. I appreciate that the k-criterion does not fit in with a positive relevance approach to confirmation and that thresholds of acceptance generate technical problems. But don't the facts of the history of science make it overwhelmingly obvious that parts of knowledge achieve a taken-for-granted status? The concept of acceptance may well have to be reinterpreted or re-explicated before it is appropriate for the Network model. But surely confirmation theory must find some place for this notion if it is to do justice to the role of coherence conditions in the underlying model?

The inconsistency between Hesse's attitude towards 'acceptance' on the one hand, and coherence conditions on the other, might be resolved by saying that we are here witnessing a move away from the Network model. A piece of evidence that favours this interpretation – or perhaps just heightens the inconsistency – lies in what Hesse says at the end of her paper about a realist theory of universals. Here we are given some guidance about the nature of these important analogies which convey our confidence from evidence to prediction. We are told that 'the relation of analogy · · · has to be supposed to be an objective and recognizable characteristic of the world'. We are told that this involves a theory 'not unlike a realist theory of universals'. Hesse introduces this idea to explain the success of predictions, but let us concentrate on the effects it has on the previous analysis of our intuitions of plausibility. To relate the analogies involved in this process to 'real' universals is to fly in the face of the Network model again. Surely the Network model denies that we have any direct access to universals or to identical properties that things share? Instead of being able to intuit universals we are said to be confronted with particulars which never partake of the same identical observable properties. Every particular has a complex relationship to other particulars and their being grouped together or separated into different classes is always open to adjustment. We never have access to identity, only to more or less similarity. This is why the Network model provides grounds for rejecting empiricism and its data language, for that language can only be a report about the directly accessible properties which things partake in or share and which are recognizable as identical from case to case. But if the primitive universals of the kind that interest the empiricist are not acknowledged to be shared identities, properties, or universals, then how much less should this be granted to the complex, sophisticated theoretical analogies being discussed here? Why deny that we can directly experience observable properties or coherently respond to simple truths about the world, only to grant that we can 'recognize' the complicated and deeply-laid real universals involved in high-level theory? Of course it might be argued that the real universals in question can only be 'recognized' by a properly trained eye. For example it might be said that over time the Network of classifications gradually assumes a correspondence with the real or true classification of things; the real universals or objective properties of things are progressively unveiled. But I do not think that this is what Hesse can mean. For what could be the point of saying this if it were not a prelude to deeming some parts of the Network different from the rest in virtue of their correspondence with reality? And this would be just a reintroduction of the idea that parts of the Network will be more stable or 'entrenched' than others – a point strongly contested in *The Structure of Scientific Inference.*

In summary, I feel that what has been said about 'acceptance' and the 'real universals' involved in theoretical analogies is at odds with the Network model. If confirmation is indeed mediated by analogies, and this seems to me wholly convincing, then surely the account needs to be squared with the Network model by doing the *opposite* of what Hesse has done. This means acknowledging the role of 'acceptance' and rejecting real universals, rather than discarding 'acceptance' and embracing real universals. I might be quite wrong in all this but I would appreciate clarification.

HESSE: David Bloor asks a very pertinent question about how I understand the relationship between an ever-revisable and culturalty conditioned network of theoretical classifications of empirical objects, and my use of the notion of *objective* analogies between those objects as the basis of inductive inference. My answer may well appear to him to be an uneasy compromise which does not yet amount to a coherent account.

Let us see what the problems are that lead to this apparent contradiction. They derive from two conflicting accounts of scientific development, which may roughly be called the progressive empirical and the revolutionary views.

(a) First there is the point that science exhibits progressive success in organizing the empirical world, at least *for certain purposes.* These are the purposes that involve rigorous testing, feedback correction of false theories, and subsequent successful prediction and potential control of nature. Now it can be admitted at once that the fact that *these* are the purposes of the classificatory knowledge we call science *is* something that comes to us with our culture, and not all cultures have exploited this particular kind of interest in the natural world. It is indeed at least a necessary feature of what we call 'objectivity' and 'realism'.

(b) The question is however, how to reconcile (a) with another insight into the development of science, namely the ever-revisable character of the concepts, categories, and 'self-evident truths' that are presupposed as the framework of every scientific theory – a thesis which is accepted and excellently summarized by Bloor. Have I gone back on this thesis in my paper?

I should first make clear that my arguments about analogical inference within a confirmation theory were mainly directed to explicating (a) and not (b). But if (b) is accepted, then a confirmation theory to deal with (a) can only be regarded as a comparatively local affair, applicable as it were to 'normal' science, where inductive methods are more or less routine. Hence my emphasis on finite domains and the rejection of metaphysical universals, causal necessities, etc. Now Bloor has rightly seen that the question of *acceptance* becomes a problem for such a local view, not so much because individual universal *theories* cannot attain high probability on the evidence in my theory, but because any applicable confirmation theory has to presuppose ('accept') some stock of predicate constants and some conditions on the prior distributions, and according to thesis (b) *these* are what are in principle always subject to revision. 'Recognition' of analogies will likewise be expressed in terms of the basic classifications made in a given society, and these recognitions, Bloor thinks, 'will depend on theoretical traditions and cultural backgrounds', and hence cannot have the objectivity required for my arguments about reasonable confidence in predictions.

My reply has to be that the basic classifications are not *wholly* dependent on cultural background. That they could be wholly dependent is surely unbelievable – it is not a *conventional* matter that Venus probes arrive near Venus – when it is predicted with the aid of some theory that they will do so, they either do or do not. The question is, how can we explain the fact that the underlying theories are so successful in this new domain of application? As in my reply to Dorling below, my suggestion is in terms of the *local* character of all our actually formulated theories and the conceptual classifications they presuppose. No such classification has any right to claim universal application, but compared to such a *logical* claim, all scientific problems are local and finite problems. Many basic classifications would reproduce the same local laws and entail the same local inductive inferences,[3] but most of these would be much too cumbersome for use in testing and prediction. Which classification is adopted at any given time may well be a matter of cultural tradition and convention, but it is the empirical resistance of the world, not cultural convention, that determines whether they are or are not convenient and successful instruments for scientific prediction.

DORLING: Hesse considers that scientific theories, at least when their domains are relativized to practically relevant ones, get finite personal probabilities, but that these are still always far too small to solve her transitivity problem. I on the other hand think that they often get large personal probabilities, for two reasons.

First, even if the personal probability of Newtonian Celestial Mechanics were only one in a million million million, say, in 1720, it would still only take half a dozen confirmations, E, of a kind which involve an average $p(E, \sim N)$ of $1/1000$, to raise the posterior probability of N to greater than $1/2$ by 1850. Examples of such confirmations would be Clairaut's solution of the problem of the moon's nodes, Laplace's explanation of the change in eccentricity of the earth's orbit and of the moon's secular acceleration, Laplace's explanation of the exact commensurability of the periods of Jupiter's satellites, the Adams–Leverrier prediction of Neptune. So once finite personal probabilities are let in, it seems that Bayesian conditionalization on subsequent evidential statements will before long raise posteriors high enough to solve Hesse's transitivity problem.

Secondly, it seems to me that the fact that scientists are prepared not only to entertain but to believe *prima facie* very improbable auxiliary hypotheses in order to save their preferred theories from refutation, only makes sense if those theories themselves (relativized to the appropriate relevant domain) have already acquired personal probabilities close to 1. (I have in mind the various explanations

[3] I have discussed the problems of 'translating' between theory languages in such domains of empirical overlap in 'Truth and the Growth of Scientific Knowledge', in F. Suppe and P. D. Asquith (eds.), *PSA 1976* (1977), p. 261.

proposed for the acceleration of Enke's comet, the acceptance of *prima facie* very improbable distributions of invisible matter to explain away the advance of Mercury's perihelion, the acceptance of an amount of tidal friction greatly in excess of estimates based on direct measurements to explain away Adam's rediscovered discrepancy concerning the moon's secular acceleration, the belief, in order to save both Newtonian Mechanics and General Relativity from refutation by the anomalous motion of Venus's nodes, that random errors in measurements and in well-tried calculations had, by a very unlikely chance, all accumulated in the same direction.) It seems to me a Bayesian personalist analysis of such examples will only lead to such beliefs when the preferred theory starts off with a very high personal probability, one very much larger than 1/2.

HESSE: To show the fallacy of supposing that any probability of the form $p(N/E)$ can obtain a value greater than a half when N is Newton's theory and E is evidence for it, consider a case in which there are at least two theories that conflict with N (call them S and G) and conflict with each other, but are both sufficiently consistent with E. Suppose for simplicity that all have the same very small prior probability, and that the values of such expressions as $p(E/\sim N)$ are also the same. Then by symmetry we must have

$$p(N/E) = p(S/E) = p(G/E)$$

and hence none can get a value greater than 1/3. That means that if there are such theories as S and G, Dorling's numerical calculation must be based on false postulates for the probabilities involving N.

Now Dorling will doubtless say that we do not have situations in which there are alternative conflicting hypotheses like S and G. Here a distinction ought to be made between theories that might historically come to mind, and theories that are logically possible. Dorling is a more whole-hearted personalist than I am, and might be content to say that personalist probabilities are based on what happens to be 'seriously considered' at any given time, whereas I would prefer to interpret personalism less subjectively as referring to measures of what is reasonable at any time, given the *logical* possibilities. It is only the second interpretation that would give *objective* grounds for confidence in predictions. It is therefore necessary either to show that there cannot be alternative theories like S and G, or to explain Dorling's examples in a way that does not assume their absence.

The first alternative is excluded by the fact that there is a pair of theories which could easily, in say 1850, have satisfied the conditions on S and G. They are the theories of special and general relativity. If N, S, and G are all taken to be strictly universal theories, the evidence then available was sufficiently consistent with all of them, and it is not unreasonable to suppose they all had very small, and more or less equal, *prior* probabilities.

What, then, about Dorling's argument from his examples? He says that the fact that scientists believe very improbable auxiliary hypotheses in order to save preferred theories 'only makes sense if those theories themselves (relativized to the appropriate relevant domains) have already acquired personal probabilities close to 1'. I have no need to disagree with this. Dorling's statement contains a slide from 'their preferred theories' to theories 'relativized to the appropriate relevant domain'. There is a difference. All a scientist need believe to account for his behaviour with respect to Mercury's perihelion is that Newton's theory is very likely to apply to *that* particular domain, and I would express that by saying that he has a very strong belief in the analogy in all mechanical respects between Mercury and the other planets, so that *apparent* deviation from Newton's laws must be explained by dissimilarity in the local mechanical situation, i.e., by invisible matter. This is a far cry from giving Newton's *universal* law of gravitation over all time and space high probability.

It may be that Dorling and scientists in general are not interested in such universalized theories – rightly so in my opinion – but some philosophers certainly claim to be, otherwise what becomes of Popper's insistence on universal laws, and the claims of more recent rationalists that scientific laws and properties are paradigm sources for causal modalities, necessity, natural kinds, rigid designators, etc.?

KUIPERS: In my *Studies in Inductive Probability and Rational Expectation* (Synthese Library 123 1978) I showed that a K-system is equivalent to a Special Hintikka (SH-) system, which is based on some prior distribution for constituents and conditional Carnapian (C-) systems related in a certain way. The following remarks on Niiniluoto's paper are based on this equivalence-theorem.

1. My second comment will make clear how I can agree with Niiniluoto's qualitative claim that the K-system approach can accomplish for the infinite case what Hesse aims at for the finite case. This might suggest the reversed claim that K-systems can be applied to essentially finite cases, such as random sampling *without* replace-

ment in a finite universe. Using the SH-formulation I have given in my book several reasons for serious doubt on this point, in particular, because our intuitions seem to call in question a key feature of K-systems, viz. positive relevance, as soon as the universe is almost exhausted. To be clear, this extrapolation-problem seems to me not a shortcoming of the K-system for I consider the case of (actually or potentially) infinite universes as far more interesting than the case of essentially finite universes.

2. Niiniluoto's attempts to introduce *analogy* are very difficult to evaluate, but they seem to lead easily to violations of the exchangeability (or order indifference) principle. In my book I have shown how *SH*-systems can be generalized (to *GSH*-systems) in such a way that they can be obtained from the exchangeability principle and a weakened version of the c-principle. Now, in a *GSH*-system the prior probabilities of constituents of the same size may differ and this gives room for the possibility of introducing *analogy* in the prior distribution in a very transparent way. For example, let there be 4 cells or Q-predicates defined by $Q_1(x) = O_1(x) \& O_2(x)$, $Q_2(x) = \sim O_1(x) \& O_2(x)$, $Q_3(x) = O_1(x) \& \sim O_2(x)$ and $Q_4 = \sim O_1(x) \& \sim O_2(x)$. A distance-meaure $D(Q_i, Q_j) = Dij$ needs to be symmetric, $Dij = Dji$, and such that $D12 = D13 = D24 = D34 < D14 = D23$. A constituent C_{ij} ($i \neq j$) of size 2 tells that Q_i and Q_j are the only non-empty cells. Now the prior distribution can be defined such that $p(C_{ij}) > p(C_{kl})$ iff $Dij < Dkl$. This procedure can be extended to constituents of size 3. We assign equal probabilities to the 4 constituents of size 1 in order to keep the system symmetric with respect to the Q-predicates. For the size 4 (and O) there is no problem. Now it is easy to show that in such a *GSH*-system, with conditional patterns as in an *SH*-system, we get, e.g., if e_n tells that all n individuals are Q_1, for the next individual x, $p(Q_1(x)/e_n) > p(Q_2(x)/e_n) = p(Q_3(x)/e_n) > p(Q_4(x)/e_n)$. From the second inequality follows a third: $p(O_1(x)/e_n \& \sim O_2(x)) > p(\sim O_1(x)/e_n \& \sim O_2(x))$. All three inequalities express essential parts of the intuitive notion of analogy; but, in contrast with Niiniluoto's approach, there is in the present approach no risk of violating the exchangeability principle.

Fortunately I see no reason why Niiniluoto's interesting suggestion for treating polyadic predicates cannot be used in the *SH*- and *GSH*-approach.

COHEN: I am grateful to Mary Hesse for her stimulating comments on the theory of what I call Baconian probability. But I don't think that any of these criticisms have the bite which she, and Ilkka Niiniluoto, attribute to them. She has three main points.

The first point is that Baconian grades of inductive support, represented by my function $s[H, E]$, can be equated, in a certain way, with Pascalian conditional probabilities. Actually the purported equation would have to be with conditioned, not conditional probabilities. It would be between $s[H, E] \geqslant i/n$ and $E' \to p[H] \geqslant i/n$ (not $p(H, E') \geqslant i/n$) in order to allow the detachment that $s[H, E]$ permits. But this is a minor issue. The real objections to Hesse's criticism are more deep-rooted.

1. The purported equation is achieved by taking the evidence, on which an evaluation of support for H is to be made, as being a generalization that is considerably more restricted than H. It is in effect the generalization that asserts the replicability of a certain test-result. But, though such a generalization is implicit in what I take to be the canonical form of a report of experimental evidence, it is by no means all that is implicit in the latter. In particular what my Baconian logic also brings out, in quite a simple theorem, is that, if the evidence is that a certain test-result has failed to be replicated (though, so far as is known, the same factors have been controlled), it follows that a hidden variable must have operated somehow in one of the reported experiments. Hesse's Pascalian function is not fine-grained enough to capture this important feature of the logic of experimental science. It cannot claim therefore to give an adequate representation of Baconian assessments of evidential support.

2. Hesse's purported equation, in order to establish its probability-space, assumes that each relevant variable is equally important, and that the combination of two relevant variables makes a test that is exactly twice as powerful as the manipulation of either variable on its own. But this double assumption is one that Hesse never defends, and which I have explicitly argued to have no general validity (*The Probable and the Provable*, pp. 226 ff.). The toughness of Baconian tests is not normally an additive property, any more than the co-presence of lighted match and petrol vapour has just twice the causal force of the lighted match.

3. Hesse's mapping of $s[H, E]$ on to Pascalian probability applies only where H is a generalization of the appropriate kind and E reports the results of a test on the generalization. It does not apply where H is, say, a conjunction of generalizations, or the negation of a generalization, or a substitution-instance of one, or where E reports irrelevant matters. About such cases special ad hoc stipulations have to be made by Hesse in each case. So, even if for the

moment we were to disregard the inability of Hesse's mapping to accommodate the problem of hidden variables or its rather questionable assumption about equipotency and additivity, she has still not shown how to capture the logic of Baconian assessments wholly within the Pascalian calculus.

Of course I don't wish to deny the enormous importance of Pascalian assessments and I've tried to explore some of the many ways in which they interlock with Baconian ones. Perhaps there may even be ways of mapping ordered pairs of Baconian and Pascalian probabilities on to some third kind of grading. But we cannot hope to achieve such unifications successfully unless we are very careful first to note all the important differences between what are to be unified.

A second main point of Hesse's is that inductive logic should be an epistemological rather than an ontological enterprise, whereas my $s[H]$ seems to grade something in nature rather than something that might be entertained in the mind of the scientist. But this is quite right. Any inductive logic that is built around testing scientific hypotheses by the manipulation of relevant variables is concerned with establishing the degree to which certain kinds of tendencies in nature resist interference by other causal factors. The investigator's object, on this view, is to discover what that degree of resistance is, by examining the evidence afforded by appropriate experimental tests. Moreover he has to be prepared at any time to revise his views about what tests are appropriate, which may well mean revising his views also about how well-established his previously tested hypotheses were. Such revisions take place constantly in any developing scientific enquiry. It therefore seems to me to be a virtue, not a vice, in my inductive logic that it has an ontological as well as an epistemological element. This is quite indispensable if assessments of inductive support are to be empirically corrigible. There must be something in nature to correct them against.

Hesse's third point is that I have no warrant in natural science to assume an ordering of relevant variables for each main field of enquiry. But I'm afraid that one just *has* to do this if one wants to make comparisons of inductive support on the basis of tests against relevant variables, as Bacon long ago implicitly recognized with his ordered list of what he called 'prerogative instances'. The reason is that, since as I've already said, one can't assume equality or additivity for the importance of such variables, it follows that the only defensible way to ensure comparability between test-results is to construct a hierarchy of cumulatively more and more complex tests, which absorb more and more from an ordered list of relevant variables. In fact experimental scientists show considerable signs of recognizing this when they regard certain variations of circumstance to be quite crucial in a particular area of research; others to be important though not crucial; others to be capable, even if they falsify, only of generating anomalies; and yet other variations to be scarcely worth making at all. Or again a distinction often has to be drawn in practice – in agricultural research, say, or in cognitive psychology – between the more important factors, which have to be controlled even in a test that is only as thorough as time or money allows, and a fuller list of factors that admit of being usefully controlled in a relatively more thorough test. Indeed, even if part of an ordering had to be purely conventional, at least it would avoid the kind of non-comparability that results when one test manipulates variables A, B, C, D and the other manipulates B, C, D, E. But in fact the theory provides for such an ordering to be empirically corrigible in various ways. And, even if no other method were available, relevant variables could be objectively ordered in importance, in a particular area of enquiry, by the number of testable generalizations that they falsify (where the number of primitive non-logical terms is finite). In short, there is a considerably better warrant in natural science for orderings of this kind (which a philosophically constructive idealization naturally has to make systematic and comprehensive) than there is for Hesse's assumption, which Niiniluoto apparently endorses, about the equipotency and additivity of relevant variables.

However, rather than conclude on a somewhat polemical note, I should like to suggest that in such a very difficult and controversial area we may do better to try to uncover the conditions and assumptions under which this or that form of inductive logic is best suited to operate, rather than to try to construe the inapplicability of an inductive logic to different conditions and assumptions as a knock-down refutation of that logic.

Now the fact is that if you want to judge the reliability of a scientific hypothesis by the thoroughness of the controls on a controlled experiment by which it fails to be falsified you are committed to Baconian inductive logic. It *is* the logic of controlled experiment. One way to see this is by reflecting on the fact that in a controlled experiment we aim ideally to control every relevant factor that is present. Or, to put it the other way round, the experimental situation is insulated from every factor that is not controlled. So if, in a kind of Leibnizian theodicy, we could examine a physically possible world in which the only initial conditions were relevant factors and their various controls and combinations, we could save ourselves the trouble of actually carrying out the experiment. But when such possible worlds are ordered by the cumulative richness of their relevant circumstances, analogously to the ordering of controlled experiments by their toughness, the logic to which we are unavoidably driven is a generalization of the modal system $S4$ that cannot be mapped on to the Pascalian calculus. Indeed it surprises me very much that those, like Niiniluoto, who are keen enough to explore systems that rely ultimately on the relative numbers of possible worlds in which a proposition holds good, are somehow reluctant to look seriously at what happens when we rely instead on the relative richness of the possible worlds in which a proposition holds good. The upshot is that, if you want to judge hypotheses by the toughness of the controlled experiments they survive, you cannot replace Baconian logic by any system based on the Pascalian calculus. That option is closed. The option that is open, if you don't like Baconian inductive logic, is to judge hypotheses in some other way. But you will then need to justify your apparent disregard for the probative value of controlled experiment.

HESSE: In his comment Jonathan Cohen has greatly clarified the relation between Pascalian (probabilistic) confirmation theory and his own non-Pascalian theory. (I would make a plea for minimizing the possibility of confusion by restricting the term 'probabilistic' to the Pascalian calculus.) In the light of the points he makes I would now like to describe my attempt to reconcile the two theories as follows. My assignments of values to his s-function in such a way as to satisfy the standard probability axioms may be seen as a proof that his support function is *consistent* with a probabilistic theory, and therefore that it is not open to the charge of representing support for incoherent betting. Cohen has sometimes spoken as if such an assignment is logically excluded in his system, but it seems to me that he ought to welcome proof that this is not so. The correspondence thus shown between part of Cohen's theory and probabilistic theory has the additional merit of exhibiting the special conditions (those of eliminative induction) under which a probabilistic theory goes into correspondence with the theory of support functions.

On the other hand, as Cohen rightly points out, his theory has advantages over probability theory in enabling certain of the assumptions of what he calls 'controlled experiment' to be derived naturally from his calculus, whereas they have to be injected as special *ad hoc* assumptions into the probabilistic theory. This is more than a mere matter of aesthetics, because the elegance and economy of a postulate system can surprise us by bringing out results that might not have been noticed if they had to be dredged up *ad hoc* from scientific practice. These remarks apply to Cohen's points 1–3. For example, under 2, it is certainly the case that a probabilistic theory *could* accommodate the requirement of non-additivity in its assignment of values to the s-function if it were known what the relative importance of each variable is, but only at the cost of more *ad hoc* conditions.

On Cohen's second main point, that his s-function is an *ontological* grading of something in nature, I do not feel so conciliatory. Surely what there is in nature to correct both theories and 'assessments of inductive support' against, is an empirical reality which we express as best we can in terms of laws and theories. There seems no case for interposing between the empirical and our best theories an intermediate level of gradings of variables measured by the s-function. What in Cohen's view is the relation between this grading and actual theories? Without an answer to this question it is difficult to regard the s-functions as more than an *epistemological* device which represents the particular kind of inductive method which Cohen calls Baconian induction. This point is related with the next one, with regard to the ordering of relevant variables. Again, it is difficult to know what corresponds in actual scientific theories to this apparently ontological requirement. Cohen's remarks about the practical need to order experimental factors show only that this is often a matter of convenience, not that it is an attempt to realize some ordering intrinsic to nature. Indeed it may of course turn out that the convenient ordering is an unsuccessful one in Cohen's terms. I remain unclear about what is represented by $s[H]$ when s becomes zero as a result of the need to reorder relevant variables.

6

Statistical Hypotheses

§16. RONALD N. GIERE
Causal Systems and Statistical Hypotheses

The immediate aim of this paper is to develop an account of *simple causal hypotheses* typified in pronouncements of public health officials, e.g., 'Smoking causes lung cancer'. The paper also has a broader aim, which is to further the development of a philosophical framework different both from the positivism inherited from the Vienna Circle and from the historically grounded studies of recent years. Two possible components of an emerging analytical empiricism are (i) a *semantic* account of scientific theories, and (ii) acceptance of *causal modalities* such as physical necessity and its weaker cousin, physical propensity. No direct arguments for the acceptability of such concepts are given. The strategy, rather, is to show how fruitful such concepts can be in the resolution of philosophical and methodological problems.

The paper begins by applying a semantic conception of scientific theories to simple *discrete state systems*. Such systems may be either *deterministic*, with transitions from input to output governed by *physical necessity*, or *stochastic*, with the inputs determining only a distribution of *propensities* over the outputs. *Simple causal hypotheses* are then analyzed as being about *finite populations* of such systems. Two similar analyses are given, one assuming the *individual* systems are deterministic, the other assuming they are stochastic. Finally, the analysis is connected with real scientific practice by showing why scientists are correct in thinking that *randomized experimental designs* are best for demonstrating causation. This latter connection is shown to hold whether one assumes that individual systems are deterministic or stochastic.

1. *Introduction*

The immediate aim of this paper is to develop an account of simple causal hypotheses typified in pronouncements of public health officials, e.g., 'Smoking causes lung cancer' or 'Saccharin causes bladder cancer'. This task has considerable intrinsic interest. Coming to a clear understanding of the meaning of such statements would resolve a long-standing philosophical debate. It might even have some desirable practical consequences as well. But the paper has a further, broader aim which it is well to make explicit at the outset.

The philosophy of science is currently in a transitional stage. The positivist framework inherited from the Vienna Circle is no longer simply assumed by large numbers of working philosophers, but no single alternative framework has yet taken its place. Historically minded philosophers of science have developed the most visible alternative, but many others still seek a different approach. This third alternative would be empiricist, though not narrowly so; analytical rather than historical in method; and carefully attuned to both the content and methods of real science. It is by no means clear what the central doctrines of a new analytical empiricism might be, but two appear quite often and will provide the underpinnings for this paper. One is a *semantic* rather than a *syntactic* approach to scientific theories. The other is an indulgent attitude toward the concept of natural *necessity* and its weak cousin, physical *propensity*.

Even those who deny there are paradigm shifts in science would have to admit that the concept applies fairly well to philosophy. Reality exercises only the weakest constraints on the development and acceptance of philosophical doctrines. If what we face, then, is something like a conflict between competing paradigms, we cannot expect direct, 'internal' arguments to be decisive. It is also important to develop the competing paradigm in ways that show it can provide solutions to recognized problems. Adopting that strategy, this paper begins by applying a semantic conception of scientific theories to simple discrete state systems. Such systems may be either *deterministic*, with transitions from input to output governed by physical necessity, or *stochastic*, with the inputs determining only a distribution of propensities over the outputs. Simple causal hypotheses, e.g., saccharin causes bladder cancer, are then analyzed as being about finite populations of systems. In fact, two similar analyses are given, one assuming the individual systems are deterministic, the other assuming they are stochastic. Finally, the analysis is connected with real scientific practice by showing why scientists are correct in thinking that randomized experimental designs are best for demonstrating causation. Interestingly, this latter connection holds whether individuals are assumed deterministic or stochastic.

2. Theories and Causal Systems

In the logical empiricist tradition, theories are axiom systems formulated in a particular interpreted formal language. It was never claimed that scientists ever formulate theories in this way; only that this is how we should view theories for philosophical purposes. As it happened, it was convenient to take the first order predicate calculus with identity as the underlying language, if not for actually reconstructing particular theories, then at least for meta-discussions about theories. In this language it is natural to represent scientific laws as universal generalizations of the form $(x)\,(Fx \rightarrow Gx)$. If x

ranges over only actual objects, then logical empiricism remains faithful to the classical empiricism of Mill and Hume. Popper, who has claimed to be a critic of logical empiricism, has based his whole philosophy on the identification of scientific laws with universal generalizations.

Axioms in a formalized language provide what is sometimes called an *intrinsic* characterization of a set of models, i.e., interpretations that make the axioms true. Now it is arguable that from a scientific viewpoint all that matters is the set of models, indeed, often only one model. That this set of models is picked out by certain axioms in a particular formal language is of interest only to logicians. It is thus of considerable interest that the set of models may also be characterized *extrinsically*, by a suitable definition formulated in any language whatsoever, e.g., scientific English. If we identify theories with such definitions, then the general form of a theory, e.g., Newtonian Mechanics, is:

X is a Newtonian Particle System if and only if
  1.
  2., etc.

Some who advocate this view of scientific theories have insisted that the right-hand side of the definition be formulated solely in the language of set theory. So theories are set-theoretical predicates. Others are less restrictive. But this dispute among advocates of a semantic approach to theories need not concern us here. What is important here is that on this view, the fundamental form of an empirical claim is an application of a definition to a *particular* real system. For example:

Such-and-such real system is a Newtonian Particle System.

One may of course generalize such claims, as did Laplace when he claimed that every natural system is a Newtonian Particle System. But generalization is not the essence of science. Scientific laws are not generalizations, but statements governing the behaviour of particular kinds of systems.[1]

---

[1] Among the earliest contemporary advocates of a semantic approach to theories was P. Suppes, *Introduction to Logic* (1957), and 'What is a Scientific Theory?' in S. Morganberger (ed.), *Philosophy of Science To-day* (1967). He has until recently been most insistent that set theory be the canonical language of science. Other more recent advocates include Bas C. van Fraassen, 'On the Extension of Beth's Semantics of Physical Theories', *Phil. of Sci.* 37 (1970), 325–39, and 'A Formal Approach to the Philosophy of Science' in R. G. Colodny (ed.), *Paradigms and Paradoxes* (1972); J. D. Sneed, *The Logical Structure of Mathematical Physics* (1971); F. Suppe, 'Theories, Their Formulations and the Operational Imperative', *Synthese* 25 (1973), 129–64; and W. Stegmüller, *The Structure and Dynamics of Theories* (1976).

At this point we might proceed to develop an account of how such empirical claims are tested. But that is not our task here.[2] Rather, we shall leave behind detailed questions about the structure and testing of theoretical claims and focus on simple claims about highly simplified types of systems, i.e., *discrete state systems*.

3. *Discrete State Systems*

For present purposes it is sufficient to consider only a single transition, which reduces a discrete state system to a simple input-output system. Such a system is characterized by a set of inputs, I, and a set of outputs, O. For the moment assume that both are finite. Also, we will avoid questions about the direction of causation and simply assume that the output comes a finite time after the input. Following standard practice, we will call sets of outcomes 'events', and let $F = \{X_i\}$ be the set of all possible final events, including O and the null set. The basic structure of such a system is pictured in Figure 2. Such systems are further characterized by the nature of the relationship between initial (input) states and final (output) states. In principle there are three possibilities. Systems may be deterministic or indeterministic; and if indeterministic, then either stochastic or non-stochastic. Since there is no standard view of what an indeterministic but non-stochastic system would be like, we are left with two possibilities.

A. *Deterministic Systems.* Formally speaking, a deterministic system is characterized by the existence of a function, L, from I onto O. Thus, for any input, A, there is a unique output, o, where $L(A) = o$. Similarly, if $o \in X$, then $L(A) \in X$, where X is an event.

Such a system might be constructed by fitting a vertical cylinder

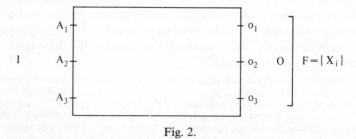

Fig. 2.

---

[2] For an account of theory testing that presupposes a semantic conception of theories, see R. N. Giere, 'Testing vs. Information Models of Statistical Inference', in R. N. Colodny (ed.), *Logic, Laws and Life: Pittsburgh Series in the Philosophy of Science*, vol. 6 (1977), especially section 5.3.

with a piston equipped with an electromagnet which in turn holds a steel ball. Assume that the piston can be set at only three different heights, q_1, q_2, and q_3. If the system is set in motion by turning the magnet off, then $I = \{(0, q)\}$ and $O = \{(p, 0)\}$, where p has three possible values which one could calculate using Newtonian physics.

The chief philosophical question has always been, How are we to interpret the function, L? Or, more precisely, what are the truth-conditions for statements of the form, $L(A) = o$?

The standard positivist answer to this question has been that $L(A) = o$ is true just in case *every* trial that has initial state A results in final state o. Or, if X is an event containing o, and t is a variable ranging over trials of the system, then $L(A) \in X$ if and only if (t) $(At \rightarrow Xt)$. This is often called the 'regularity view' of laws.

If the expression 'every trial' is taken to mean every *actual* trial, then the implausibility of this analysis becomes apparent if we consider systems that are never tried, or that are tried only a small number of times. If there are no trials, then any system law of the appropriate form would be vacuously true. If there were exactly one trial per input, then the system would have to be deterministic and the system law would be given by whatever outputs resulted on those trials. Is it just our imagination, perhaps aided by association with other systems, that leads us to think $L(A) = o$ might be *factually* false for a system that is never tried? It takes a steadfast Humean will to answer, Yes.

Even advocates of a regularity view must feel uncomfortable interpreting deterministic laws as *de facto* universal association. This is why the view is often stated counterfactually – though the counterfactual nature of the claim may be tacit. It is not just that every trial beginning with input A ends with output event X. Any trial that *were* to begin with A *would* end with X. But when formulated this way, it is clear that some further interpretation is needed. What are the truth conditions for such counterfactual statements? Thus 'The Problem of Counterfactual Conditionals'. It is significant that this problem was never adequately resolved within the positivist framework. Accounts of counterfactuals that use laws in the analysis are of course no good if the original problem is to give an account of laws that goes beyond *de facto* universal association.

In the analysis of scientific laws, the main alternative to regularity has always been some type of 'necessary connection'. The problem has been to say what type. Here one must be careful not to allow the assumption that any satisfactory account of causal necessity must be given solely in terms of actual regularities. Granting this assumption puts one squarely within the positivist framework. Whatever one does, it must be insisted that causal necessity is *not* reducible to universal regularity.

As indicated in the introduction, no systematic account of causal necessity will be attempted here. Only the most general features of causal necessity will be utilized in developing an analysis of simple causal hypotheses like, 'Smoking causes lung cancer'. So we shall say simply that $L(A) = o$ is true of a particular system, at some particular time, if, and only if, any trial with input A that might be made at that time must result in output o. Or, it is not physically possible that any output other than o result from a trial with input A. It is intended that such statements be factual, so that they are contingently true or false of a particular system at some particular time.

Asking anyone to accept such a notion would be asking a lot if the conceptual payoff for so doing were not great. But there is considerable payoff. One immediate dividend is an unambiguous rendering of counterfactual statements. First, we restrict the antecedent of any counterfactual to descriptions of possible initial states. For any initial state the system laws unambiguously determine the final state that must result. Thus we can automatically determine the truth value of any counterfactual of the form: If the system were tried with input A, the result would be output o. It is an open question whether one can extend this account to cover counterfactuals in which the antecedent ranges over variables other than system inputs. So much for deterministic systems.

B. *Stochastic Systems.* For stochastic systems there is no function relating unique outputs to each input. Rather, for each input there is a probability distribution, $\Pr_A (X)$, over all possible output events. A hydrogen atom constrained to a finite set of excited states would be an example of such a system. Let the atom be in one of its excited states at an arbitrary starting time, t_0. Let the final state be defined as the state at a later time, $t_0 + T$. Then each possible final state has a definite probability of being the state of the atom at $t_0 + T$. Considering all possible initial excited states, the 'law' for this system may be represented by a matrix giving all the transition probabilities for the time interval, T.

The *philosophical* problem of interpreting the probability distribution, $\Pr_A (X)$, for stochastic systems is exactly parallel to the problem of interpreting the function $L(A)$ for deterministic systems. The parallel answer in the positivist framework would be to make $Pr_A (X)$ the actual relative frequency of trials with output event X among trials with input A. In point of fact, however, almost no one has been willing to defend a *finite frequency interpretation* of probability. It makes probability values too arbitrary. It restricts probabilities to *rational* values. It is indeed a hard view to defend.

Since Venn the remedy for these defects has been to interpret probability in terms of the *limiting* relative frequency in an *infinite* sequence of trials. But this manoeuvre creates at least as many difficulties as it removes. First is the often overlooked fact that no statement of the form $Pr_A (X) = r$ has a truth value, simply because no real system ever undergoes an infinite number of trials. One should not be misled by the fact that limiting relative frequencies are *mathematically* well-defined. That is no guarantee that the notion makes sense applied to real systems. Only after one has granted this dubious step do the usual sorts of objections come into play, e.g., that the limiting relative frequency depends on the *order* of the trials. Infinite sequences can be rearranged so as to yield any relative frequencies whatsoever. This is why some frequency theorists insist that the sequences which define probabilities be 'random'. But there is no reason why real systems should generate sequences satisfying any of the various definitions of a random sequence – even granting an infinite sequence of trials.

As in the case of deterministic laws, positivist philosophers slip easily into a counterfactual mode – '$Pr_A (X) = r$' is true if and only if the relative frequency of X events for trials with input A *would be r* if the system *were to* undergo an infinite sequence of trials. But the needed truth-conditions for such counterfactuals are at least as difficult to specify as those for ordinary counterfactuals – and this problem has rarely even been recognized, let alone studied.[3] Lacking an adequate solution to this problem, the limiting relative frequency interpretation simply fails to apply to stochastic systems.

The alternative is to embrace a notion of *causal propensity* parallel to the notion of causal necessity. Stochastic systems, particularly micro-systems, possess inherent tendencies toward different outputs on *individual trials*. These causal tendencies have the formal structure of probabilities. So $Pr_A (X) = r$ means that the system in initial state A has a propensity with strength r for reaching final event X.

As before there is an immediate payoff in the interpretation of counterfactuals. What would happen if the system were to be run n

[3] For a recent attempt to deal seriously with this problem, and others, see Bas C. van Fraassen, 'Relative Frequencies', *Synthese* 34 (1977), pp. 133–66.

times with input A and constant propensity $Pr_A(X)$? Answer: There is a propensity distribution over the $n+1$ possible relative frequencies of the output event X. This distribution is given by standard formulae for independent trials with constant probability. And one does not have to go through elaborate additional explanations of what such single-case probability assertions mean.[4]

C. *Necessity and Propensity*. In terms of the immediate aim of the paper, the present section is a digression. But it contributes to the broader aim in that developing relations between the two notions, causal necessity and causal propensity, contributes to an understanding of both.[5]

Until fairly recently, the terms 'causality' and 'determinism' were synonymous. Quantum theory was said to herald the breakdown of causality. Today philosophers with many different viewpoints recommend expanding the concept of causality to include probabilistic causality as well.[6] Thus quantum theory is now regarded as indeterministic, but not acausal. The problem now is systematically to incorporate this expanded notion of causality into an overall philosophy of science.

A pleasingly simple solution is to make causal necessity a *limiting case* of causal propensity. This means identifying $L(A) = X$ with $Pr_A(X) = 1$. Utilizing concepts more common to logical or subjective probability, this means that propensities are *regular* and that propensity distributions are not only coherent, but *strictly* coherent as well. The reasons for imposing regularity on propensities, however, are different from those usually given for similarly restricting logical or subjective probability distributions.[7]

To put the identification in a somewhat broader context, we begin by defining a more general notion, *system necessity*, both for deterministic and stochastic systems. For *deterministic* systems the definition is:

(SND)   Nec $(X) = Df. (A)L(A) \in X.$

---

[4] A model for interpreting the propensities generated by sequences of trials of individual systems is developed in Part III of R. N. Giere, 'A Laplacean Formal Semantics for Single Case Propensities', *J. Phil. Log.* 5 (1976), 321–53.

[5] The points in this section are developed at greater length in R. N. Giere, 'Propensity and Necessity', forthcoming in *Synthese* 40 (1979).

[6] See, for example, P. Suppes, *A Probabilistic Theory of Causality* (1970), and W. C. Salmon, *Statistical Explanation and Statistical Relevance* (1971).

[7] Sections 7 and 8 of R. Carnap, 'A Basic System of Inductive Logic, Part I' in R. Carnap and R. Jeffrey (eds.), *Studies in Inductive Logic and Probability* (1971), contain a brief introduction to the concepts of regularity and coherence as well as further references.

Informally, an output event is system necessary if it is the deterministic result of every input. Viewing the inputs of a system as defining the 'possible worlds' in which it may operate, an output event is necessary for that system if it results in every possible world. The corresponding definition for *stochastic* systems is:

(SNS) $\qquad\qquad \text{Nec}(X) = Df. (A) \text{Pr}_A (X) = 1.$

Informally, an output event of a stochastic system is necessary if it has unit propensity for all inputs. The way systems are standardly defined, there is in general one and only one necessary event for either type of system, namely, the whole output set, O.

More interesting are the definitions of *system possibility*. Assuming that $\text{Pos} (X) = Df.$ Not Nec (Not X), the corresponding definition for *deterministic* systems is:

(SPD) $\qquad\qquad \text{Pos} (X) = (EA)L(A) \in X.$

The corresponding conversion for *stochastic* systems is:

(SPS) $\qquad\qquad \text{Pos} (X) = (EA) \text{Pr}_A (X) > 0.$

Informally, an output event is possible in a deterministic system if there is some input that leads deterministically to that event. An output event is possible in a stochastic system if there is some input for which that event has merely positive propensity. Metaphorically speaking, possibility for stochastic systems is a much weaker thing.

So long as the output set is *finite*, the identification of causal necessity with unit propensity poses no difficulties. Even when the output set is infinite but countable, the identification is plausible. Serious difficulties arise only if the output set is continuous. Infinite sequences provide a natural context for exploring these difficulties since the number of possible sequences is of the order of the continuum.

Imagine a simple binomial process with output events S and F, where $\text{Pr} (S) = \text{Pr} (F) = 1/2$. In the limit, of course, *every* possible sequence has probability zero. Thus according to SPS, no infinite sequence is physically possible. On the other hand, assuming that propensities are defined over all possible sequences, this total set has probability one. So by SNS, it is physically necessary that some sequence occur. There arises the paradox that it is physically necessary that some physically impossible sequence occur.

In this form, the paradox is easily avoided simply by insisting that one need never consider infinite sequences. They are a mathematical fiction. Neither the content nor the methods of science require consideration of infinite sequences of trials. And for finite sequences, no matter how long, the paradox does not arise.

But there are other important contexts which naturally give rise to continuous output spaces. In the theory of radioactive decay, for example, time is treated as a continuous variable. Standard measure theory assigns zero probability to each instant but probability one to the total integral from zero to infinity. By SPS and SNS, then, it is physically necessary that decay occur at some physically impossible instant. This paradox is not so easily avoided.

Maintaining the parallel between physical necessity and unit propensity seems to require a fairly drastic revision in our understanding either of physics, or of mathematics, or both. For example, it could be argued that there are no really continuous processes in nature and that the use of continuous mathematics is merely a convenience. It might also be argued that adopting a non-standard measure theory avoids the paradox. It remains to be seen whether either resolution is satisfactory.

Concluding this digression, recall that the positivist framework allows no easy identification of universal law with unit probability. Universal association implies unit relative frequency, but the converse fails. And as for transfinite outcome sets, limiting relative frequencies are not in general even countably additive – as de Finetti has long insisted.[8]

4. *Simple Causal Hypotheses*

We are now prepared to offer an analysis of simple causal hypotheses like 'Smoking causes lung cancer', as these are commonly understood, e.g., by public health officials. The first task is to decide whether these are (i) primarily statements about *individuals;* (ii) *generalizations* over individuals; or (iii) primarily statements about a *population.* The first possibility is easily disposed of. When the office of the Surgeon General issues a statement saying that smoking causes lung cancer, no particular individuals are singled out as the subjects of this statement. But neither does the statement seem to be a generalization covering all individuals in some group. It is certainly not being claimed that everyone who smokes will get lung cancer – that is patently false. Nor can it be saying that everyone who smokes thereby increases their chances of getting lung cancer. That is also pretty clearly false, though less obviously so. So it looks like it must be a statement about a population.

[8] See, for example, B. de Finetti, *Theory of Probability*, vol. 1 (1974), pp. 116–33; and also Bas C. van Fraassen, 'Relative Frequencies', loc. cit.

The next question is whether the population at issue is *finite* or *infinite*. Frequency theorists and R. A. Fisher would want to insist that the population is infinite, or at least potentially so. However, it is difficult to attribute such intentions to public health officials. Furthermore, if we can develop an adequate analysis assuming only a finite population, that is surely to be preferred. Infinite populations always create technical difficulties that are often irrelevant to the problem at hand. As for just which finite population is intended, that need not be of any concern here.

Our problem now is to analyse what is being claimed about the intended finite population. Moreover, the analysis is to be done using the notions of necessity and propensity developed above – notions which apply to individual systems, not populations. Fortunately we need not decide whether the individual systems that make up the population are deterministic or stochastic. We can simply do two analyses, one for each assumption.[9] As will become clear later, it makes little practical or methodological difference which analysis one adopts.

A. *Deterministic Analysis.* We now assume that all the individuals in the intended population are *deterministic systems*. It follows immediately that these individuals must differ in causally relevant respects. In all cases of interest, some members of the population will have the cause but not the effect. For example, not all smokers get lung cancer. If they were all the same, then all would exhibit the effect. Let us now develop a more precise statement of this obvious fact.

Given that individuals in any given population may differ both internally and in the inputs to which they are subjected (their environment), let us just assume that every individual is as it in fact is. We need only add that both the suspected cause (C) and its absence ($\bar{C}$) are possible inputs for every system. Similarly, both the suspected effect (E) and its absence ($\bar{E}$) are possible outputs for every system. We can now give a preliminary analysis of the claim:

(SCH) C causes E (in population U).

The analysis is:

(DA-1)   There is at least one member of U for which the system law, $L(C) = E$, is true.

___

[9] It is possible, of course, that a population contains both types of individuals. Worrying about this possibility seems not worth the effort since most populations one would ever encounter would be all of the same type.

Now of course no public health official would ever in practice make a statement as weak as this one. They are interested only in causes that might be operative in enough cases to be a public health problem, or at least generate enough cases of the effect to show up in health statistics. But these are practical concerns that it would be unwise to attempt to build into an analysis of the conditions under which a simple causal hypothesis *is true.* Later we will define another notion, the *effectiveness* of a causal factor, to express this sort of concern. Let us take (DA-1) as expressing the minimal condition under which (SCH) is true.

It is crucial to the understanding of (DA-1) that application of the system law, $L(C) = E$, may have to be counterfactual. Every member of the actual population either has C as input, or not. If the only members of the population for which the system law is true are systems which in fact have $\bar{C}$ as input, then C does not in fact produce any cases of E. But it would if some of those members did have C as input. That is what (DA-1) asserts.

To develop the analysis further, let us look more closely at a population, U, consisting of N individual deterministic systems. At any given moment the members of U fall into four categories: those with C and E; those with C but without E; those without C but with E; and those with neither C nor E. Let $\#CE$ represent the actual *number* of systems with both C and E; $\#C\bar{E}$ the number that have C but not E; and so on. The population is pictured in Figure 3. In purely *qualitative* terms, E *is positively correlated with* C if and only if the percentage of individuals with E is *greater* among individuals with C than among individuals without. Note that this is a statement about a particular existing population at a given time. In terms of actual numbers, positive correlation (also non-correlation and negative correlation respectively) is defined by the following relationship:

$$(\text{COR } E - C) \qquad \frac{\#CE}{\#C} \gtreqqless \frac{\#\bar{C}E}{\#\bar{C}}$$

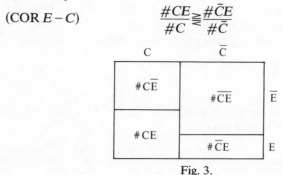

Fig. 3.

Turning Figure 2 on its side, one can easily write down the corresponding relationship for the qualitative expression, *C is positively correlated with E*. This is:

(COR $C - E$) $$\frac{\#EC}{\#E} \gtreqless \frac{\#\bar{E}C}{\#\bar{E}}$$

One sees immediately that (COR $E - C$) may be obtained from (COR $C - E$), and vice versa, simply by interchanging the letters 'C' and 'E'. This means that correlation is a *symmetrical* relationship. Since causation is not necessarily symmetrical, we have proof of the old adage that correlation is not the same as causation.

Recent attempts to define a causal relation within a positivist framework do not identify simple causal hypotheses with correlations. Instead they introduce additional related correlations which make possible a characterization of causation as a non-symmetrical relationship.[10] But all such attempts seem doomed to fail simply because any set of relative frequencies may exist by accident in an actual finite population. Thus the asymmetric conditions may be in fact satisfied in cases where a causal relation is extremely implausible. Similarly, the conditions may fail to be satisfied in the actual population even though it is obvious that there should be causal relation. But this is not the place to pursue such criticisms in detail.

The fact that our individuals are themselves deterministic systems, and that counterfactual statements for such individual systems are well-defined, means that we can consider counterfactual counterparts of the given population. This is done simply by considering each individual counterfactually. Actually our analysis will require introduction of *two* such counterfactual counterparts of the given actual population. One is the population that results if we assume, counterfactually, that every member has input C. The other results from the supposition that every member has input $\bar{C}$.

Now in the actual population, U, any designated effect will exhibit some definite relative frequency, $\#E/N$. Since finite relative frequencies have the formal properties of finite probabilities, we may call this quantity $P(E)$. But note that $P(E)$ is not a propensity. It is merely a relative frequency in an actual, finite population. Similarly, since for each individual system the law, $L(C) = E$, is either true or

---

[10] Salmon, op. cit., for example, introduces a condition called 'screening off'. P. Suppes, op. cit., introduces a concept of 'spurious causes' to do a similar job. The comments that follow apply to Suppes' treatment only if his probabilities are interpreted as relative frequencies. He himself remains uncommitted as to the proper interpretation of probability in this context.

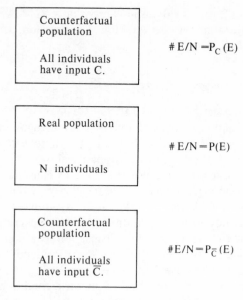

Fig. 4.

false, the number of systems that would develop E is well-defined for both counterfactual counterparts of the given population. Call these quantities $P_C(E)$ and $P_{\bar{C}}(E)$ respectively. Note that in general $P_{\bar{C}}(E)$ will not be zero because E may result from some *other* cause than C. All these various populations and quantities are represented in Figure 4.

Only a few minor refinements in terminology are necessary before we can state the final analysis. Instead of simply saying 'C causes E' we adopt the more cumbersome expression 'C is a causal factor for E in U'. This leaves open the possibility that C may be either a *positive* or a *negative* causal factor, where a negative causal factor for E is the same as a positive causal factor for $\bar{E}$. Now the analysis is:

(DA-2) C is a positive causal factor for E in U if and only if:
$P_C(E) > P_{\bar{C}}(E)$.

Reversing the inequality gives the definition for negative causal factors. Equality means that C is causally irrelevant to E in U.

As noted above, (DA-1) may be satisfied if there is but one individual in a very large population for whom C leads deterministically to E. The same is true of (DA-2).[11] In such a case the truth of the causal hypothesis would be uninteresting even if it were detectable. Public health officials are concerned not merely with the truth of causal hypotheses, but even more so with how *effective* the supposed causal input is. Now there are many ways one might define effectiveness, and pharmacologists have developed sophisticated *probabilistic* measures. For present purposes the following measure is convenient and useful:

(EFF) $\qquad Ef(C, E) = Df. \ P_C(E) - P_{\bar{C}}(E).$

For $Ef(C, E)$ read: The effectiveness of C for E in population U. The notation suppresses the reference to the population.

This definition has the consequence that C will have zero effectiveness for E in U if there is some *other* causal input, C', that produces E in every individual, independently of C. This suggests that one might try defining effectiveness simply as $P_C(E)$, with the proviso that there are no other causes of E present, so that $P_{\bar{C}}(E) = 0$. But this definition refers to a different population, or perhaps the same set of individuals in a different environment. It is not the population under investigation. And in general one will not know what all the other possible causes of E might be. So the suggested change is not very useful. We shall see shortly that effectiveness as defined by (EFF) plays a crucial role in standard methods for *testing* causal hypotheses. That is an added reason for sticking with (EFF).

B. *Stochastic Analysis.* We will now develop a second analysis of simple causal hypotheses, this time assuming that the members of our finite population are themselves *stochastic systems*. The interesting thing about stochastic systems is that we can speak of positive and negative causal factors for *individual systems* and not just for

---

[11] The compatibility of (DA-1) with (DA-2) requires one further assumption. The population must not contain equal numbers of individuals for which $L(C) = E$ and $L(C) = \bar{E}$, respectively are true, the one group in fact not having E and the other in fact having E. Otherwise (DA-1) would apply, but $P_C(E)$ and $P_{\bar{C}}(E)$ would be equal, the contrary effects of C in different individuals exactly cancelling out in the two counterfactual populations. Such a situation is unlikely, but possible. In that case one would have to abandon (DA-1) as merely a rough first approximation and stick with (DA-2) as the analysis. This means that C could be a deterministic cause for some systems in the population, but not be a causal factor in the population itself. This sounds funny, but is not a contradiction because deterministic laws refer to *individuals* and simple causal hypotheses to *populations*. In any case, the appropriate *methodological* response is clear. Look for some *other* factor that distinguishes these two subpopulations.

populations. The obvious definition is:

(CFIS)   *C* is a positive causal factor for *E* in *S* if and only if:
$\Pr_C (E) > \Pr_{\bar{C}} (E)$.

Again, reversing the inequality gives a definition of a negative causal factor, and equality means causal irrelevance.

Note that one side of the inequality in (CFIS) will have to be understood counterfactually since any individual will in fact either have *C* as input or not. If it has *C*, then the propensity on the right side of the inequality is the propensity the system would have if it did not have *C* as input. And vice versa.

Turning to populations of individuals, the counterpart to (DA-1) for stochastic individuals is:

(SA-1)   *C* is a positive causal factor for *E* in *U* (i.e., *C* causes *E*) if and only if there is at least one individual system *S* in *U* such that for *S*, $\Pr_C (E) > \Pr_{\bar{C}} (E)$.

As in the deterministic case, we can extend this analysis by considering two counterfactual populations, one which would result if every member of *U* had *C* as input, and one if every member of *U* had $\bar{C}$. The present case, however, is complicated by the fact that the relative number of *E*'s in each counterfactual population, i.e., $P_C(E)$ and $P_{\bar{C}}(E)$, are not determined by the respective counterfactual assumptions. All that is determined is a *distribution of propensities* over possible effect rates. However, the *mean values* of these distributions, μ_c and $\mu_{\bar{c}}$, provide a convenient measure of the causal influence of *C* in the population. Utilizing this measure we have the desired counterpart to (DA-2):[12]

(SA-2)   *C* is a positive causal factor for *E* in *U* if and only if
$\mu_c > \mu_{\bar{c}}$.

Once again, reversing the inequality yields an analysis of negative causal factors, and equality defines causal irrelevance. All the ingredients of this analysis are pictured in Figure 5.

As in the deterministic case, we need to distinguish between the simple fact that *C* is a causal factor for *E* in *U*, and its *effectiveness* as a causal factor. Following the discussion of effectiveness in the deterministic case, the suggested measure would be:

(EFF-*S*) $\mathrm{Ef}\,(C, E) = Df.\ \mu_c - \mu_{\bar{c}}$.

---

[12] The same sort of problem discussed in n.11 arises here as well. The response would be similar.

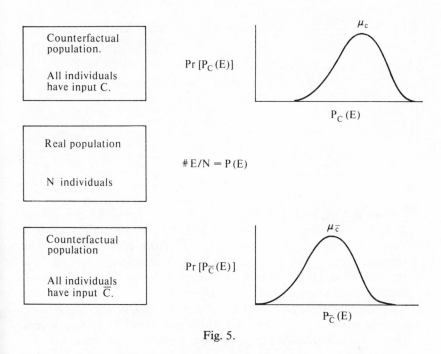

Fig. 5.

As before, this quantity appears in a natural way in standard accounts of how causal hypotheses are tested empirically, and is thus a natural measure to consider.

5. *Simple Causal Hypotheses and Experimental Design*

It is almost universally agreed among scientists that the best way to test a causal hypothesis is to employ a *randomized experimental design*. Such designs are commonly used in biology, the bio-medical sciences, and psychology. Sociologists and other social scientists regularly lament the fact that such designs are not generally possible in their fields. The analyses of simple causal hypotheses presented above explain why randomized experimental designs have this unique status.

In outline, a randomized design proceeds as follows: One first obtains a random sample from the population restricted to members which exhibit neither the cause nor the effect. This sample is randomly divided into two groups. One group, the *experimental* group is manipulated so that each has C as an input. The other group, the *control* group, is treated as much like the first group as possible, except that none are allowed to have C as an input. Then

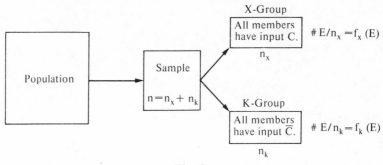

Fig. 6.

one waits an appropriate length of time and records the incidence of E in both groups. The important datum is the difference between these two fractions, $d = f_x(E) - f_k(E)$, or some convenient function thereof. Here f_x and f_k are the relative frequencies of the effect in the experimental group and control group respectively. The structure of this design is pictured in Figure 6.

Comparing Figure 6 with Figures 4 and 5 reveals why randomized experimental designs are uniquely appropriate to testing simple causal hypotheses. The experimental group may be regarded as a sample from the counterfactual population in which all members are supposed to have C. If you want to know how many cases of E you would get if every member of U had C, take a random sample of members of U that do not have C, and give it to them. Similarly for $\bar{C}$. So a randomized experimental design proceeds by sampling the counterfactual populations that, on the above analysis, serve to define the corresponding simple causal hypothesis. No more direct test can be imagined. Nor is one needed.

Of course there is a methodological problem due to the fact that we cannot in general examine the whole counterfactual population, only a sample. But this is just the problem that inferential statistics was designed to handle. And everyone knows, at least in outline, how the standard methods work. One begins by formulating the *null hypothesis*, H_0, that the mean value of the distribution for the difference, $d = f_x - f_k$, is zero. One then tests H_0 against the alternatives, H, that $\mu_d > 0$ (one tailed test), or that $\mu_d \neq 0$ (two tailed test). One then looks at the probability distribution for d assuming H_0 is true. If the *observed* value of d lies in the upper 5 per cent of this distribution (one tailed test), or in the upper or lower $2\frac{1}{2}$ per cent (two tailed test), one *rejects* the null hypothesis. Presumably, though this is *controversial*, one thereby *accepts* the alternative, H.

Strictly speaking, one is testing the *statistical* hypothesis, H_0, against *statistical* alternatives, H. But the test is rightly taken to be a test of the *causal* hypothesis as well. H_0 is a logical consequence of the statement that the *effectiveness* of C for E in U is zero, i.e., $\text{Ef}(C, E) = 0$. H is a logical consequence of the statement that $\text{Ef}(C, E) \neq 0$ (two tailed test). So to reject the null hypothesis is to reject the causal hypothesis that C is causally irrelevant to E. And that presumably means accepting the causal hypothesis that C is causally relevant to E.

Note, finally that $\text{Ef}(C, E) = 0$ implies H_0 on *both* the deterministic and the stochastic analysis. Thus from the scientists' point of view it makes no difference whether one assumes that the individual systems are deterministic or stochastic. One will end up accepting or rejecting the causal hypothesis on the observed data in exactly the same cases no matter which analysis one assumes.

If the above analyses of simple causal hypotheses show why randomized experimental designs are most appropriate for testing causal hypotheses, they also explain why *other* designs are less good. To take just one example, consider designs that are prospective, but *non*-experimental. This is the type of design used in the classic studies of tobacco smoking and health. One cannot take a sample of young non-smokers and force half of them to smoke for forty years. One can only compare subjects that are in fact smokers with others that are not. Thus one is only sampling the real population. One is not creating samples from the counterfactual populations that define the causal hypothesis. Thus, for example, there could be a much higher incidence of heart disease among smokers than among non-smokers even though smoking is causally irrelevant to heart disease. This could happen if there were some other input, e.g., drinking alcohol, that is for purely sociological reasons positively correlated with smoking, and does cause heart disease. Of course people who do such studies try to *control* for other inputs as well, e.g., by having equal numbers of drinkers and non-drinkers in each group. But the number of factors one can control for is much smaller than the number that might be causally relevant to the effect. So one is forced to use other arguments to buttress the causal conclusion. With *experimental* designs there is no such gap to be filled.

6. Conclusion

The proposed analyses of simple causal hypotheses do fit together well with widely accepted methods of testing causal hypotheses. This provides some reason for thinking that these analyses are on the right track. And this in turn provides some reason for taking seriously the notions of causal necessity and causal propensity on which these analyses are based, and for developing further a philosophical framework incorporating such notions. But hopefully even those committed to other frameworks will find the analyses themselves interesting – and challenging.

§17. JON DORLING

A Personalist's Analysis of Statistical Hypotheses and Some Other Rejoinders to Giere's Anti-Positivist Metaphysics

In addition to a few more minor comments on Giere's 'Causal Systems and Statistical Hypotheses' this reply sketches a partly novel explanation of why *de facto* universal generalizations can license counterfactual conditionals, and gives an apparently new personalist analysis of statistical hypotheses. I claim of counterfactuals that they follow by tense logic from conditional predictions, and that the latter contain provably non-material conditionals but nevertheless can be proved to follow from non-empty universal generalizations containing only material conditionals. The proofs use subjective probability theory. I reject the attempt to provide a non-circular semantics for statistical hypotheses in terms of truth conditions, but try to provide a semantics in terms of belief conditions, by trying to prove that a person's distribution of degrees of belief over all possible statistical hypotheses concerning the probability of a specified type of event is uniquely determined by his subjective probability assignments to finite sequences of outcomes of that type of event, i.e., to a set of statements already provided with definite truth-conditions and hence directly bettable upon. This reductive personalist analysis denies that the probabilities which occur in statistical hypotheses are identical with personal probabilities, yet nevertheless explains how they arise. It ought to be fully acceptable to the positivist, for whom statistical hypotheses are otherwise something of an embarrassment.

There are several things that I find congenial in Giere's paper. I approve of his attempt to eliminate hypothetical infinite populations; I accept his use of counterfactuals in the analysis of some of his examples; I agree that it does not, and should not, make any practical difference whether one's underlying model is deterministic or stochastic. I have three minor rejoinders to offer and three more major ones, the last of which will present my own personalist analysis of the semantics of statistical hypotheses.

Minor Reservations

1. *Simple Causal Hypotheses.* I am uneasy about the conception of 'simple causal hypotheses' which Giere takes as his starting-point. Does 'causes' mean the same in 'smoking causes lung cancer' and in 'saccharin causes bladder cancer'? My doubt is caused by the fact that I think that the first statement would be held to be misleading unless smoking *significantly* increased a person's chances of getting lung cancer, whereas the second statement seems only to require

that the use of saccharin *slightly* increases a person's chances of getting bladder cancer (at any rate if one pronounces the claim with the right emphases). This difference is connected with the fact that the first statement is apparently designed to deter consumers, and the second to deter manufacturers. But does this wholly explain why we do not, as naturally, say 'tobacco causes lung cancer', 'taking saccharin causes bladder cancer'? I have an uneasy feeling that all examples of 'simple causal hypotheses' will turn out to be statements intended essentially for lay consumption and not scientific hypotheses at all: by that I mean that they would not feature any longer in any fully-worked-out scientific explanation of the facts. Since semantic content cannot, in the lay non-scientific case, be separated readily, if at all, from Gricean pragmatic conversational implicatures, there will then be no clear criteria of adequacy for Giere's analyses.

2. *Stochastic Systems.* Here I want to make a cautionary remark about physics. Current quantum mechanics is not a stochastic theory. The hydrogen atom in an excited state is not a stochastic system. The proof goes as follows: (1) The Schrödinger, or Dirac, Equation, or the quantum electrodynamical Evolution Operator, describes a deterministic evolution of states, not a stochastic one. Giere's system of an atom in a vacuum state radiation field evolves, according to any such equation, into a unique superposition of states. (2) We cannot reinterpret this as a stochastic evolution of 'hidden' states, because the no-hidden-variables theorems show that there are no hidden states (my own no-partial-hidden-variables result, which provides essentially a completeness theorem for the Copenhagen interpretation, and uses more of Gleason's theorem than do other no-hidden-variables results, is the most relevant here). (3) But could we not still say that the evolution of states according to quantum mechanics is non-stochastic between measurements but stochastic at moments of measurement? No, because all realistic measurement interactions not only take time, but strictly speaking have neither a beginning nor an end. (4) Could we not superpose a stochastic process, whose contribution depended on the amount of measurement interaction, on the deterministic temporal evolution provided by the Schrödinger Equation and its analogues? No, because one cannot characterize measurement interactions in a way which would make them different in principle from other interactions, many of which are known experimentally not to lead to

a degeneration of superpositions into mixtures. (5) Could we regard quantum mechanics, not as a stochastic theory of the evolution of purely physical systems, but as a stochastic theory of the evolution of physical systems plus sentient observers? No, because, so long as such a theory contained more than one observer, it could not be Lorentz invariant. Quantum mechanics could admittedly still be interpreted as a Lorentz covariant stochastic theory of the evolution of physical systems plus von Neumann, and after von Neumann's death Wigner, but no physicist other than von Neumann and Wigner has ever believed this, and with good reason, because this interpretation is refuted every time any other physicist observes the result of a measurement.

So, as far as we know at the moment, there are no fundamental stochastic laws or processes in nature. Furthermore, it is extremely plausible that, for any genuinely stochastic theory, all its predictions could be reproduced with arbitrary accuracy by a hypothetical underlying deterministic theory, so that one could never give any no-hidden-variables proof for such a theory. So it is not clear that, if physicists did have any fundamental stochastic theories, that they would remain content with them. So do not let us get too excited about such theories and erect a whole philosophy around them.

3. *Randomized Experimental Designs.* In section 5 of Giere's paper, randomized experimental designs are just pulled out of a hat, with an argument for experimental, as opposed to non-experimental, designs, but no argument for random sampling or random division of samples. I hold that such procedures are pernicious and that in practice the best scientists always renege on them, when, as often happens, they give manifestly absurd results. What happens if our randomization procedure happens to yield substantially more alcoholics in the experimental than in the control group? Surely the right procedure is not random selection of a sample and random assignment to groups, but to match the members of the experimental and control groups in every additional factor which one considers at all likely to be causally relevant? Random selection will not in general achieve this, and where it doesn't it will not be as effective as systematic matching. This is, of course, just Savage's personalist objection to randomization procedures, but it seems to me devastating. Of course I still accept, for substantially the same reasons as Giere, the superiority of experimental over non-experimental designs in many instances.

Major Reservations

4. *'Syntactic' and 'Semantic' Approaches to Scientific Theories.* I think this distinction of Giere's is terminologically misleading since, if anything, it is the first approach (that of the logical empiricists) which is the more preoccupied with semantic issues; but, more seriously, I think his distinction conflates a number of logically independent issues: (i) whether we adopt an analytical or a holistic approach to scientific theories, (ii) whether we are ambitious or unambitious about the kind of statements we hope to make about the universe, (iii) whether we prefer to formulate theories within predicate logic or set theory, (iv) whether we are positivists or realists. It seems to me that there are evidently 2^4 possible philosophical positions we could adopt here, not 2 as Giere seems to think.

All Giere really seems committed to in the sequel, is unambitiousness about the sort of claims which scientific theories are expected to make about the universe; he thinks such claims will only be about particular finite systems and will not include more general laws. In fact Giere's degree of unambitiousness seems to lead him into metaphysical absurdities, for example into the suggestion that his counterfactual statements could be true or false of his particular system without their truth or falsity having to follow from more general laws with more than purely counterfactual content.

5. *Counterfactual Conditionals and de facto Universal Generalizations.* I accept Giere's use of counterfactuals in his examples (except for the absurdity just mentioned) but reject his conceptions of causal and physical necessity. (I shall later also reject his notion of propensity.) My position is that there are at least two perfectly good Humean analyses of the way purely *de facto* universal generalizations can entail counterfactuals.

The first is a simple metaphysically innocent kind of possible worlds construction. Take any set of *de facto* universal generalizations which one has chosen to call fundamental laws, and define the physically possible worlds to be all logically consistent structures in which those *de facto* generalizations are satisfied. Define a counterfactual to be true if its consequent is then true in every physically possible world in which its antecedent is true. On this analysis all and only what we have called the fundamental laws, and their consequences, come out as physically necessary, and all and only these license counterfactuals. Every counterfactual is physically necessary, but this is no kind of *de re* metaphysical necessity. Nor do

I need to give any *deep* explanation of why I have not included any of the 'accidental generalizations' in the philosophical literature in the set of what I choose to call the fundamental laws. For any distinction between 'accidental generalizations' and 'laws' will do in order to make this a well-defined language game, providing an acceptable semantics for counterfactual conditionals. *Why* we play this game – and it may be for purely mathematical enjoyment which would not be enhanced by adding to the 'fundamental laws' statements about the life-span of Dodos – is a question of pragmatics which need not be answered in order to show that the playing of such a language game has no metaphysical implications.

My second Humean analysis shows not merely that a Humean *can* consider most universal laws to entail counterfactual conditionals, but that he *must* do so.[1] First I argue that non-empty *de facto* universal generalizations entail conditional predictions which cannot be interpreted as material conditionals, even if the generalizations which entail them are interpreted as over material conditionals. I have in mind predictions like 'if that object is a raven, it will be black'. Such a conditional prediction cannot express a material conditional because the degree of belief in it cannot be the same as the degree of belief in a material conditional, because a bet on such a conditional prediction has a quite different pay-off matrix from a bet on a material conditional. In the event of the falsity of the antecedent, no money changes hands in the former bet, but the latter bet is won. The conditional prediction is actually stronger than the material conditional, because it is easy to show that, on pain of incoherence, the degree of belief in the latter must always be larger than the degree of belief in the former. However, and this is the interesting point, if we consider any n-ary conjunction of material conditionals, where it is known that the antecedent of at least one of them is true, then this conjunction must get exactly the same degree of belief as the corresponding, conjoint, conditional prediction. (For the pay-off conditions now become identical.) Hence if, as is usual, we define the degree of belief in a universal generalization as the limit of the degrees of belief in n-ary conjunctions of its instances, as n goes to infinity in such a way as to exhaust all instances of the generalization, then it follows that anyone who believes in a non-empty universal generalization, even over material conditionals, must assign at least as high a degree of belief to each particular conditional prediction which is related to that generalization. It

[1] My argument here is essentially merely a rather eclectic selection from theses previously argued for by Jeffrey, Adams, Mackie, and others.

follows that anyone who believes that all ravens are black must believe that if that object is a raven, it will be black. However, from the truth *now* of the non-material conditional 'if that object is a raven, it will be black', there follows, by ordinary tense logic, the truth *in future* of 'if that object had been a raven, it would have been black'. That is to say, counterfactual conditionals can be generated simply as past-tense versions of those conditional predictions whose antecedents have failed to materialize: They are, in such cases, trivially licensed by universal generalizations, even when the latter contain only material implications: or, at any rate, by such (non-empty) universal generalizations as there is at some time reason to believe in a potentially predictive context.

So that is my second reason for thinking that a Humean and a positivist can be happy with Giere's use of counterfactuals in his examples.[2]

6. *The Semantics of Statistical Hypotheses.* I don't agree with Giere that counterfactuals constitute a serious problem for positivists, but I do agree with him that statistical, as opposed to non-statistical, hypotheses constitute a problem for positivists (that is to say for those few brave souls who still insist on being provided with explanations of meaning which are not viciously circular). For statistical hypotheses cannot be provided with non-circular truth conditions. Von Mises's account, had it stuck to actual infinite sequences occurring in nature, would have been non-circular,[3] but it becomes circular as soon as we enquire into the meaning of the hypothetical infinite sequences we need whenever we do not believe in the actual infinite sequences, since the only law which would license the required counterfactual would be the original statistical one. Accounts in terms of finite, rather than infinite, sequences are either circular because they smuggle in probabilities, or fail to satisfy obvious conditions of adequacy. Accounts in terms of physical propensities trivially fail to provide truth-conditions which are not viciously circular, whatever else they may be trying to do.

I shall solve this problem by providing an acceptable semantics for statistical hypotheses, but one which is not truth-conditional but

---

[2] Giere's counterfactuals are, or had better be, licensed by *both* my analyses. Some counterfactuals, though, are licensed by the second analysis but not by the first: in this case we say that such a counterfactual is true in one sense but not in another. Some accidental generalizations in fact license counterfactuals of this kind.

[3] Though, even then, von Mises's account totally fails to explain our expectations about finite subsequences, or the evidential value we take these to have, and hence fails to meet reasonable conditions of adequacy.

belief-conditional. That is to say, I shall not assign a definite meaning to the statement that a statistical hypothesis is true, but I shall assign a quite definite meaning to the statement that somebody believes it to be true, with any definite degree of belief. The whole point of verificationism was to show that statements like 'God exists' were not such that anyone could intelligibly believe or disbelieve them. I shall show that statistical hypotheses are such that one can intelligibly believe or disbelieve them, in spite of their lack of non-circular truth-conditions.

It might at first seem that if one can only give belief-conditions, and not truth-conditions, for a statement, it cannot be regarded as stating anything objective about the real world. But suppose, as will be so here, that the belief-conditions are such that hard facts could force one to adopt any desired degree of belief or disbelief, short of 1 or 0, in the statement. Then I say the statement is indeed an objective statement about the real world, in spite of the only non-circular semantics it can be given being in terms of belief conditions.

I shall represent degrees of belief in statistical hypotheses by probabilities which satisfy the usual probability axioms. My task is to give a meaning to such probability assignments. I shall do this by showing that all such assignments are in fact uniquely determined by the subject's ordinary de Finetti-type betting odds degrees of belief in decidable propositions. So I shall explain what it is to believe in p, by reducing it to what it is to believe in q (which is something already understood), but without reducing p to q. In fact we are discussing three kinds of probabilities, those in statistical laws, those (subjectively) assigned to statistical laws, and those associated with (subjective) betting odds on decidable propositions. The first two kinds of probabilities, which are puzzling, will end up being totally explained in terms of the third kind of probability, but without thereby becoming, in any sense, identical with it.

Consider a type of event, like the tossing of a particular coin, with only two possible outcomes. (It will not matter whether you think this is ultimately to be regarded as a deterministic or as a stochastic system.) I shall consider statistical hypotheses like 'the coin has a three per cent bias towards heads'. I shall presently consider all possible statistical hypotheses about the degree of bias, and all possible distributions of degree of belief over this set. (The restriction to only two outcomes is also done without loss of generality, as I shall point out later.)

Consider first some specifiable *finite* set of hypotheses about the degree of bias. I shall show that any subject's distribution of degrees of belief over these is uniquely determined by $n-1$ betting odds degrees of belief in $n-1$ decidable propositions, whenever there are only n different hypotheses, about the degree of bias, at issue.

Let the hypotheses correspond to probabilities of the coin landing heads equal to $\alpha_1, \ldots, \alpha_n$. Let us call the degrees of belief in these $p_1, \ldots, p_n$, where $p_1 + p_2 + \cdots + p_n = 1$. Then the subjective probability, $P(H)$, of the coin landing heads on a first toss, is evidently

$$P(H) = \alpha_1 p_1 + \alpha_2 p_2 + \cdots + \alpha_n p_n.$$

This subjective probability is associated with a decidable proposition and therefore has a well-defined interpretation in terms of betting odds. The subjective probability of the coin landing heads on the first two tosses, $P(2H)$, is evidently given by

$$P(2H) = \alpha_1^2 p_1 + \alpha_2^2 p_2 + \cdots + \alpha_n^2 p_n$$

Similarly, for n heads

$$P(nH) = \alpha_1^n p_1 + \alpha_2^n p_2 + \cdots + \alpha_n^n p_n$$

The subjective probabilities on the left all have well-defined interpretations in terms of betting odds. Now I claim that if we know the row of numbers on the left, and the α's are prescribed for us, then this system of equations, indeed the first $n-1$ of them together with the condition that $\sum_{i=1,\ldots,n} p_i = 1$, uniquely determines all of the p_i.

This is a system of n linear equations in n unknowns. In matrix form it is $Mp = P$, where M is the matrix

$$M = \begin{pmatrix} 1 \ 1 \cdots\cdots\cdots 1 \\ \alpha_1 \alpha_2 \cdots\cdots\cdots \alpha_n \\ \cdots\cdots\cdots\cdots \\ \alpha_1^{n-1} \alpha_2^{n-1} \cdots \alpha_n^{n-1} \end{pmatrix}$$

We can solve it by operating with the inverse of M on the two sides, thus $p = M^{-1}Mp = M^{-1}P$, and so obtain the p_i (uniquely), provided M has, indeed, an inverse. It is a necessary and sufficient condition for the existence of an inverse that the determinant of the matrix M doesn't vanish. Now by very good fortune the determinant of this particular matrix can be shown, by a bit of algebra, to be expressible, up to a sign, simply as the product of all terms of the form $(\alpha_i - \alpha_k)$, where $k > i$ and i and k range over $1, \ldots, n$. But such a product can only vanish if one of its terms does, that is to say if two of the α's are equal to one another. But of course we've set up the problem so that these are all different, hence the determinant cannot vanish and the solution for the p's is unique.[4]

What does this mean philosophically? It means that provided we restrict ourselves to a finite number (however large) of possible statistical hypotheses, then our degrees of belief in these statistical hypotheses are uniquely determined by our subjective probability assignments to a finite (indeed smaller) set of decidable propositions. The latter subjective probabilities are already respectable even for arch-positivists like de Finetti, since they can be operationally defined directly in terms of bets. Hence I claim that this mathematical result makes the degrees of belief in statistical hypotheses equally respectable, although the interpretation in terms of bets is now more indirect. I claim I have provided an acceptable semantics both for statistical hypotheses and for degrees of belief in statistical hypotheses, for to provide a non-circular belief-conditional semantics for the former it is sufficient to provide a non-circular truth-conditional semantics for the latter, which I have just done (so far only for the finite case).

(The argument is not really restricted to the case of types of event with only two possible outcomes, for a statistical hypothesis specifying the probabilities for each of j outcomes is trivially equivalent to $j-1$ statistical hypotheses specifying the probabilities for associated events with two outcomes.)

Before considering the infinite case, it is worth remarking that the construction given almost certainly shows that statistical hypotheses are *objective* in the following sense. Events in the real world can force a subject to revise his personal probability distribution over statistical hypotheses concerning a particular type of event from any given initial probability distribution to any given final distribution, on pain of Dutch books over time being made against him. I shall not attempt to prove this, but the point is that Bayesian conditionalization over the direct betting-odds-interpretable subjective probabilities will automatically, by this construction, induce corresponding changes in the degrees of belief assigned to the statistical hypotheses, and any systematic departure on average from Bayesian conditionalization in the former case will (by a generalization of the

---

[4] The way I have set up the problem, it would be a muddle to suppose that there is a separate problem about the uniqueness of the α's. To determine the p's is to determine which α's have which p's, and the order we list them in is arbitrary. If a different set of n α's solved the equations for the prescribed P's, and with the same or different p's, this would, for me, be a problem with $2n$ α's, which would again possess a unique solution when $(2n-1)P$'s were given as data.

Putnam–Lewis–Teller argument) lay the subject open to money being won off him on average by a bookie with no better information than he has.

Now let me try to solve the problem of the infinite case, where all possible statistical hypotheses are considered. The argument I have given for the finite case cannot be directly generalized to the infinite case, so it is necessary to proceed somewhat differently. Consider any two distinct distributions of degrees of belief over the set of all possible statistical hypotheses about some type of repeatable event with two outcomes. I shall try to prove that these must dictate different subjective probability assignments to finite sequences of decidable propositions. It would then follow again that the totality of betting-odds-interpretable subjective probabilities must uniquely determine the distribution of degrees of belief over all possible statistical hypotheses. Suppose that the two distinct distributions of belief disagree over the degree of belief to be assigned to at least one statistical hypothesis which assigns a *rational* degree of bias α to a coin. Then I can argue as follows:

Suppose the denominator of this rational α is k. Consider some particular sequence of heads and tails with nk members (n an integer) and which contains the precise proportion α of heads. The degree of belief p in the hypothesis of bias α, contributes a term $p_\alpha \alpha^{nk\alpha}(1-\alpha)^{nk(1-\alpha)}$ to the betting odds subjective probability of this particular sequence. (Let the rival distribution of degrees of belief replace p_α by p'_α.) Now any other degree of bias β' contributes to the probability of this same sequence a term $p_\beta \beta^{nk\alpha}(1-\beta)^{nk(1-\alpha)}$ (with p_β replaced by p'_β for the rival distribution of degrees of belief). Now I say that the ratio

$$\alpha^\alpha(1-\alpha)^{(1-\alpha)}/\beta^\alpha(1-\beta)^{(1-\alpha)}$$

is always greater than 1 for all $\beta \neq \alpha$. (β need not of course be rational.) Proof: (part of the proof of Boltzmann's H-theorem): The logarithm of this ratio is clearly equal to 0 for $\beta = \alpha$. The first derivative w.r.t. α of the logarithm also vanishes if $\beta = \alpha$. The second derivative is just $1/\alpha + 1/(1-\alpha)$, which, since α is less than 1 and positive, is positive. Hence, considered as a function of α, this function (the logarithm of the original ratio) is concave upwards for all values of β; hence $\beta = \alpha$ yields an absolute minimum, and hence the value of the ratio in question is always greater than 1. Now what I want to prove is that, for n large enough, the part of the difference in the probability of such a sequence, *due* to the difference between p_α and p'_α, cannot be cancelled out by the difference between the various p_β and p'_β. Now if we consider a small enough range $(\alpha \pm \epsilon)$ surrounding α we can make the *total* degree of belief in all the hypotheses corresponding to points in this range, other than α, as small as we like. Hence this range can be chosen so that all those taken together can cancel out less than half the difference between p_α and p'_α. There is also an upper bound on the total probability associated with statistical hypotheses corresponding to points outside this range. Hence, by now choosing n large enough, we can ensure that

$$(p'_\alpha - p_\alpha)\alpha^{nk\alpha}(1-\alpha)^{nk(1-\alpha)} > 2 \sum_\beta (p_\beta - p'_\beta)\beta^{nk\alpha}(1-\beta)^{nk(1-\alpha)}$$

where the sum is over all β differing from α by more than ϵ. It follows that the two belief distributions must, for such a value of n, differ in the betting odds subjective probability that they assign to the sequence $nk\alpha$ heads and $nk(1-\alpha)$ tails. This proves the result required.

In the case where the two rival distributions agree over all degrees of belief assigned to rational values of α but disagree over some degrees of belief assigned to irrational values of α it seems to be substantially more difficult to prove the theorem and I do not know how to prove the result by a similarly direct argument. However the result is well-known,[5] being made use of in de Finetti's proof of his representation theorem. But, unlike de Finetti, I am using it not to show that in practice we can, or should, do without statistical hypotheses and probability assignments to them (which I would deny), but to give these semantic respectability.

[5] A convenient reference is vol. 2 of W. Feller's *Introduction to Probability Theory and its Applications* (1964). De Finetti's theorem is proved on p. 225. But the result I need already follows easily from Theorem 1 on p. 223, bearing in mind that Feller's 'distribution function' is defined (on p. 127) as a *cumulative* function and hence (without loss of generality) is everywhere right continuous.

§18. Comments and Replies
the Giere–Dorling Session

AGAZZI: The treatment of the causal relation presented in the paper, though ingenious and elegant, fails to be convincing for essentially two reasons. The first is that Giere is not right in claiming that 'scientific laws are not generalizations, but statements governing the behaviour of particular kinds of systems'. Indeed, in speaking of 'particular *kinds* of systems' and not of 'particular systems', he is committed to consider *all* systems of a given kind and this already calls generalization into play. This affects the subsequent analysis of the causal relation provided in the paper, which is aimed at taking into account individual systems instead of classes of systems, and in particular Giere's distinction between deterministic and stochastic systems.

My claim is that causal statements *are general* and that the distinction between deterministic and stochastic causation may be better restated on different grounds. The basic claim seems justified by the very fact that when asking, e.g., whether 'smoking causes lung cancer', we do not intend to refer this question to *one particular* smoker, but to smokers *in general.* but now we must distinguish the case in which a universal statement (i.e., a statement concerning a plurality or a class of individuals) is meant in a *distributive* sense and the case in which it is meant in a *collective* sense. This has far-reaching consequences on the way the statement may concern individuals. An example of distributive generalization is 'Men are mortal', because the predicate 'mortal' is meant to apply to (to distribute over) every single man. A trivial example of a collective generalization is 'Men are more numerous than women', where it is clear that it does not make sense to say that every man is 'more numerous' than every woman. A less trivial example might be 'Men are taller than women', where it is clear that the predicate of 'being taller' is not meant to apply distributively to every man compared with every woman, but rather to apply 'collectively' to the class of men compared with the class of women.

Now, what is called 'deterministic causality' may be interpreted as a causality expressible by a general 'distributive' sentence (like 'Decapitation causes death'), which *hence* can be translated into a sentence concerning individuals ('Every decapitated man dies'). On the contrary, 'stochastic causality' may be interpreted as a causality expressible by a general 'collective' sentence (like 'smoking causes lung cancer'), which expresses a property of a class and cannot immediately apply to single individuals. Let us now suppose that this sentence is true if at least a certain percentage p of smokers, within a given population, are affected by lung cancer (in comparison with the percentage of lung cancer in non-smokers). It follows that we require a *deterministic* relation between smoking and p, which is a property of the *class* of smokers detectable by means of relative frequency tests; and this does not involve any judgement about any single individual. It is only as a *façon de parler* that we say that a *given* individual has a probability p of getting lung cancer and this is simply a way of expressing our *subjective rational expectation* of his getting a cancer based on the information of his belonging to that class. It seems quite unjustified to move from an epistemic conception of the question to an ontological one – about an individual *propensity* – not only because this commits us to an engaging metaphysical assumption, which we can never test *by considering the individual*, but especially because all the payoff we may get from this assumption can be suitably restated by resorting to what we actually have at our disposal: information about classes and deterministic causal claims concerning classes. Stochastic causality is therefore only a special case of deterministic causality, involving non-distributive generalizations.

LEVI: According to Giere, the 'standard positivist' interpretation of the function L characterizing a deterministic input-output system asserts that $L(A) = o$ just in case every trial having initial state A results in final state o. Carnap explicitly rejected such an analysis in 'Testability and Meaning'. He denied that '$L(A) = o$' is a statement of law at least by implication; for, on his view in that essay, it is a singular statement predicating of a 'system' the disposition to respond in manner o given stimulus-condition A.

Whether Carnap was a 'standard positivist' or not, Giere's remarks contain no discussion of his thesis that disposition predicates are semantic primitives relative to descriptions of test behaviour. Like Dorling, I believe that subjunctive conditionals present no problems for positivists provided they are construed epistemically (as they should be whether one is a 'standard positivist' or not); but so construed they cannot be used to specify satisfaction conditions for disposition predicates which are not epistemically construed.

Dorling is also right about chances. There is no clear and noncircular way to specify satisfaction conditions for chance predicates in terms of descriptions of test behaviour. Nor can we look to reduction sentences for useful specifications of necessary or of sufficient conditions. We need to look to epistemic constraints linking judgements about chances with judgements about test behaviour.

None the less, I think Dorling is mistaken in his account of these epistemic constraints.

Let X know that the chance of coin a landing heads on a toss is either $\alpha_1, \alpha_2, \ldots,$ or α_n. Suppose X knows also that coin a is tossed, that the toss took place at time t, at place p, and by agent Y with apparatus A.

Dorling thinks it is 'evident' that X should assign subjective probability $P(H) = \Sigma \, p_j \alpha_j$ to the hypothesis H that the coin will land heads where p_j is X's credal or subjective probability that the chance of coin a landing heads on a toss is α_j.

Dorling's 'evident' thesis holds if X knows that the chance of coin a landing heads on a toss by Y with apparatus A at time t and place p is equal to the chance of coin a landing heads on a toss.

On the other hand, if X lacks this knowledge, Dorling's equation can run into trouble.

It is downright wrong if X knows that the extra information is 'stochastically relevant' – i.e., that the chance of a's landing heads on a toss by Y with A at t and p is different from the chance of a's landing heads on a toss. And if X is in doubt as to whether the extra information is relevant or irrelevant stochastically, the issue may not be clear. There is controversy concerning the conditions under which information about trials not known to be stochastically irrelevant may be ignored. Kyburg thinks that if one does not know one way or another whether the additional information is stochastically irrelevant, the extra information may be ignored. Only when X knows the extra information to be stochastically relevant should it be taken into account. This view leads to conflict with conditionalizing arguments (a point which does not disturb Kyburg but should disturb the Bayesian Dorling). For this reason, I favour an alternative view according to which such information can be ignored only when it is known to be stochastically irrelevant.

According to this latter position, in order to endorse the equation Dorling thinks evident, X will be obliged to know a great deal about chances as part of his background information. No sceptic concerning chances will be mollified, therefore, by Dorling's stochastic realism.

The point has far reaching implications. De Finetti claimed that statistical hypotheses are functionally replaceable by judgements of credal probability concerning test behaviour. His arguments invoke mathematical considerations similar to Dorling's and they fail for substantially the same reason. De Finnetti's construal of the presystematic connection between judgements of chance and judgements of test behaviour is in far too simplistic a manner.

We could dismiss chance as I construe it as metaphysical moonshine. Dorling wisely refuses to follow de Finetti down this path. He is also right to see the important analytical task to be clarifying the epistemological dependencies between judgements of chance and judgements of test behaviour. They are, however, more problematic than he has imagined.

KYBURG: 1. A short remark on a supposed revolutionary paradigm shift seems called for. Giere claims that theories are interpreted in 'the logical empiricist tradition' (which he seems to identify with positivism) as axiom systems in an *interpreted* formal language. (p. 252 above) He contrasts this with the modernistic view of theories as predicates. (He does not even demand that they be set-theoretical predicates.) A predicate is not a theory, though it may embody a theoretical structure. An axiom system, similarly, is not generally thought of as *fully* interpreted, but rather as embodying a theoretical structure applicable to certain domains. It is fairly evident that the two approaches are perfectly equivalent, modulo some relatively abstract and sophisticated matters of axiomatizability. One may prefer one to the other for a specified purpose, but this hardly seems to warrant talk of paradigms and revolutions.

2. Randomized designs have their uses and advantages, but the arguments from tradition and authority offered by Giere (pp. 267–9) do not seem overwhelming. In particular, randomization is neither necessary nor sufficient for an adequate test of a simple causal hypothesis on Giere's own account. Suppose that one *could* take a sample of young non-smokers, and force half of them to smoke for forty years. A certain number of members of the population under investigation (U) will turn out not only to drink alcohol, but to become alcoholics. If the sampling is properly randomized, it will produce samples in which *all* of the experimental subjects turn out to be alcoholics, and *all* of the control group turn out to be teetotalers. But according to Giere such a result, if obtained without randomization, would vitiate the conclusions of the study. Surely such a sample would be equally useless were it obtained by means of randomization. Such sampling results are rare, of course, but if we insist on randomization we must face the fact that they will occur with their appropriate low frequency in the studies we perform. Note in particular that in a properly randomized study, we have no motivation for stratification: i.e., considering frequencies in

various subclasses of *U*. It seems obvious that if the association of drinking and smoking in the prospective non-experimental design vitiates the causal conclusion, it should equally vitiate the causal conclusion in a prospective experimental design having the same characteristic. I conclude that randomization is not sufficient for the soundness of the conclusion. That randomization is not necessary is trivial: if we infer a conclusion from the finite frequencies in an experimental and a control group selected by some 'chance mechanism', and, contrary to our belief, this mechanism is deterministic, that inference is not thereby vitiated. If we learn that roulette wheels are in fact Newtonian Systems, not subject to quantum perturbations, we are not going to burn the reports resulting from studies in which randomization was carried out by means of roulette wheels.

MARGALIT: In talking about the effects of vaccination, say vaccination against polio, we should often be able to say:
  (a) The vaccination caused a drop in the dispersion of the disease.
  (b) The vaccination brought about the disease in some of those who were vaccinated (who would not have had the disease otherwise).
Both (a) and (b) may be true. Giere's analysis of causation can at best accommodate (a) but by no means (b). Hence the analysis is defective.

GIERE: For reasons that are quite understandable, though hardly worth discussing, I reinterpreted the proposed topic as being about the nature of probabilities *used in* statistical hypotheses. My view has always been that *scientific* inference does not require probabilities *applied to* statistical hypotheses. Indeed, I think introducing probabilities of hypotheses leads to a mistaken view of scientific inference and of scientific inquiry in general. Having argued for a theory of statistical inference not employing probabilities of hypotheses in several recent papers (e.g., 'Testing versus Information Models of Statistical Inference'), I sought in this paper to say something new about statistical hypotheses themselves. In keeping with the focus on *applications* of inductive logic, I concentrated on the nature of simple causal hypotheses of the type used in biomedicine and public health, e.g., smoking causes lung cancer.

Kyburg objects to my talk of competing paradigms in the philosophy of science. Except for some 'relatively abstract and sophisticated matters of axiomatizability', he says, the 'semantic' and 'syntactic' approaches to theories are 'perfectly equivalent'. As a technical point, this is correct. My reason for introducing the semantic view, however, was not so narrow. It was that the semantic view makes it natural to take the basic empirical claims in science to be about *individual systems,* not qualities, types of events, etc. To this I added the doctrine that 'system laws' are to be understood as describing physical necessities or physical propensities operating during particular trials of a system. My overall strategy was to show that by *assuming* individual necessities or propensities, one can generate an illuminating analysis of simple causal hypotheses like 'Smoking causes cancer'. This is the best way I know to argue for basic philosophical theses, e.g., that there are natural necessities and/or propensities. The standard response to such a strategy would be to point out ways in which the resulting analysis is *not* illuminating, thus undercutting the claim that the concept of a single case propensity or necessity helps us to understand science and the world. Except for Margalit's brief remarks, however, most of the comments on the paper do not take this form. They are mainly claims that statistical hypotheses and causal hypotheses are to be understood in some other way. That is the kind of response to be expected when fundamentally different approaches (I'm willing to drop the word 'paradigm') are at issue.

Dorling argues that *de facto* universal generalizations can and must entail counterfactual conditionals. He then proceeds to develop a 'belief-conditional' semantics for statistical hypotheses. Levi similarly insists that counterfactuals and chance hypotheses can be understood in terms of actual objects or events together with 'epistemic constraints'. And Agazzi analyses the difference between 'deterministic causality' and 'stochastic causality' in terms of the distinction between 'distributive' and 'collective' statements about a given population. I believe that each of these analyses is subject to the sorts of objections I raised against traditional 'regularity' analyses of causality. But the purpose of the paper was not so much to criticize 'actualist' analyses of causality as to exhibit the advantages of an alternative based on a notion of physical possibility, necessity, and propensity. Nor does the space allotted to this reply permit a detailed examination of the proposals advanced by Dorling, Levi, and Agazzi. The most I can attempt is to clear up several more localized disagreements and misunderstandings that have arisen.

Regarding the semantic view of theories, Dorling says that I am merely being 'unambitious' about the kinds of claims scientists can make using theories. He says I think 'such claims will only be about particular finite systems and will not include more general laws'. I said no such thing. On the semantic construal of theories, a scientist can be as ambitious as is appropriate or desirable. Using this view of theories, one has no difficulty interpreting Laplace's claim that every system in the whole universe is a Newtonian particle system – and what could be more ambitious than that? Thus the semantic account of theories does not restrict generalization. But neither does it make generalization the essence of science. It thus avoids the sterile debates over whether biology, geology, sociology, or history could be sciences because they deal only with a particular region of space and time – the earth.

In a similar vein, Agazzi says that by mentioning *kinds* of systems I am 'committed to consider *all* systems of a given kind and this already calls generalization into play'. The generalization involved, however, is merely logical and not empirical. In framing a definition one automatically defines a kind of system – all systems that fit the definition are systems of this kind. But that is a logical truism. On the other hand, one may formulate a definition without a commitment to there being any pretheoretically designated kind of system which fits the definition. Whether there are any such systems is always an empirical question. Of course scientists frame theories with particular types of systems in mind, and generality is often desired. But these obvious facts pose no difficulties for the semantic view.

Margalit's vaccination example does raise an interesting question for my analysis of simple causal hypotheses. Overall, however, it exhibits the virtues of taking the basic units of causality to be the propensities or necessities of *individual* systems. This conception of causality permits us to state the facts of the example in the natural way Margalit presented it. There are many individuals in the general population for whom vaccination prevents polio (or greatly reduces the propensity of its occurrence). However, there is a much smaller number of individuals for whom vaccination itself leads, with causal necessity, to polio (or increases the propensity of its occurrence). Looking at the whole population, there would be many fewer cases of polio if everyone were vaccinated than if no one were. On my analysis this means that vaccination is a negative causal factor for polio. The fact that it is also a positive causal factor for some subpopulation seems to be lost.

Stating the example clearly in terms of individuals in the population suggests how the apparent puzzle is to be resolved. Simple causal hypotheses, on my analysis, are relative to a *given population.* Taking the overall population as given, vaccination is a negative causal factor for polio – for that population. This, however, is compatible with there being some *other* population for which the reverse is true. And indeed, that other population might be a subgroup of the original. The real problem is not a problem for the logic of my analysis but for scientific methodology. How do we discover that there is such a subpopulation? And, how do we isolate its members? I think that an 'objective' approach to experimental design and the testing of causal hypotheses can provide answers to these questions, but that is another story.

Both Dorling and Kyburg object to the use of randomization in experimental design and accuse me of introducing randomized designs into the discussion without arguing for their legitimacy or usefulness. I agree completely that the use of randomization requires justification. Indeed, the very concept of random selection needs clarification. But neither justification nor clarification is required by my references to randomized experimental designs in this paper. All I claimed is that my analysis of simple causal hypotheses explains why *experimental* designs should be thought superior to *non-experimental* designs for testing causal hypotheses. This seems to me to provide an argument for the correctness of my analysis and, indirectly, for the notions of propensity or necessity on which it is based. The fact that randomization is standardly used, or thought to be used, in such designs is irrelevant to those claims.

As a completely independent point, I do think that taking individual propensities and necessities as basic provides the groundwork for an adequate justification of randomized procedures. The objection that a random sample might be obviously unrepresentative of the population makes tacit appeal to a relative frequency interpretation of the error probabilities in classical testing procedures. What happens in any particular inference is irrelevant to the long run frequency of successful inferences. However, if the data from any particular test are produced by the propensities or necessities of individuals, then one may justify concern about the particular inference at hand and introduce appropriate methodological rules. For example: stratify with respect to factors that might be relevant and ignore obviously skew samples. Developing this line of argument is a topic for another paper.

Finally, whether there are in the world any genuinely stochastic systems is a question I am quite willing to leave to those working on the foundation of quantum theory. Dorling has his views and others have theirs. Nevertheless, it does seem to me worth considering the *possibility* that there are such systems and exploring the consequences of this possibility for our conceptions of probability and statistical inference. The existence of some sort of single case propensity is one such consequence. Moreover, even if we should decide that all systems are really deterministic after all, it might still be useful to think of some systems *as if* they were stochastic when their detailed structure is unknown. This is one way of justifying the use of roulette wheels to construct random samples.

In the end, of course, I must agree with Dorling that one should not construct a whole philosophy of science on the possibility that there are genuinely stochastic systems in the world. This is why I was concerned to show that my analysis of simple causal hypotheses can be done either way, that is, with either stochastic or deterministic individuals. The fact that both versions of the analysis fit equally well with standard methods for testing causal hypotheses is thus a welcome bonus.

7

Properties and Inductive Projectibility

§19. SYDNEY SHOEMAKER
Properties, Causation, and Projectibility

The central contention of the paper is that the projectibility of predicates is rooted in the causal nature of properties. Both the regularity theory of causality and the traditional formulations of the problem of induction presuppose that a distinction can be drawn between 'real', 'genuine', or 'intrinsic' properties (changes, similarities, regularities) and what, appropriating a term of Peter Geach's, we might call 'mere-Cambridge' properties (changes, etc). Being 'grue', in Goodman's sense, is a good example of a mere-Cambridge property. The paper suggests that the essential nature of a genuine property consists in its potential for contributing to the causal powers of the things that have it and that properties are identical just in case they make, in all possible circumstances, the same contribution to causal powers. This, it is argued, helps to explain how enumerative induction can be (as Harman has suggested) a special case of 'inference to the best explanation', and why we are entitled to 'project' certain predicates (or certain regularities) and not others. Roughly, the 'projectible' predicates are those that stand for genuine, rather than 'mere-Cambridge', properties. The defense of this involves a discussion, and attempted rebuttal, of Reginald Jackson's recent claim that all predicates are projectible. The paper concludes by arguing that if we are entitled to regard any of our predicates as having determinate meanings and extensions, we are entitled to regard certain of them as being projectible (in the sense of standing for genuine properties).

1.

In his book *God and the Soul* Peter Geach posed the problem of how genuine changes are to be distinguished from what he called 'mere "Cambridge" changes', such as the change undergone by Socrates when he became shorter than Theaetetus.[1] Something undergoes a Cambridge change whenever some predicate comes to be true of it or ceases to be true of it, and something undergoes a *mere* Cambridge change whenever it undergoes a Cambridge change which, intuitively, is not a genuine change. The problem Geach poses is a special case of a more general one. Borrowing his term, we can also speak of Cambridge properties, Cambridge kinds, Cambridge resemblances, and Cambridge regularities. Every set will be a Cambridge kind, every well-defined predicate will stand for a

[1] Peter Geach, *God and the Soul* (1969), pp. 71–2.

Cambridge property, the sharing of Cambridge properties (or the co-membership in Cambridge kinds) will yield Cambridge resemblances, and a Cambridge regularity will exist whenever the instantiation of one Cambridge property (or kind) is 'constantly conjoined' with the instantiation of another. And the problem of distinguishing genuine changes from mere-Cambridge ones is equally the problem of distinguishing what is genuine from what is mere-Cambridge in the realms of properties, kinds, similarities, and regularities. A good example of a mere-Cambridge property is being grue, in Goodman's sense, and a good example of a mere-Cambridge similarity is the similarity that holds between an examined green thing and an unexamined blue thing 'in virtue of' their both being grue.

As a preliminary step towards clarifying the notion of a genuine, or 'instrinsic', property, one can say that such a property must be a 'differential property' in Michael Slote's sense, that is, must be such that if anything has it then anything exactly similar to that thing must have it.[2] Intuitively, this rules out being grue as a genuine property, since presumably an unexamined green emerald could be exactly similar to an examined green emerald, and so a non-grue one could be exactly similar to a grue one. But of course this relies on the still unclarified notion of genuine, as opposed to mere-Cambridge, similarity. If we had available only the notion of Cambridge similarity, it would make no sense to speak of two different things being exactly similar; for this would require two different things to belong to all of the same sets, which is an impossibility.

The problem of distinguishing genuine from mere-Cambridge properties, changes, similarities, etc. has an important bearing on two of David Hume's philosophical progeny, the regularity theory of causation and the problem of induction. Its bearing on the former comes out in the following passage from Quine's essay 'Natural Kinds'.

What does it mean to say that the kicking over of a lamp in Mrs. Leary's [*sic*] barn caused the Chicago fire? It cannot mean merely that the event at Mrs. Leary's belongs to a set, and the Chicago fire belongs to a set, such that there is an invariable succession between the two sets: every member of the one set is followed by a member of the other. This paraphrase is trivially true and too weak. Always, if one event happens to be followed by another, the two belong to *certain* sets between which there is invariable succession. We can rig the sets arbitrarily. Just put any arbitrary events in the first set, including the first of the two events in the first set; and then in

---

[2] Michael Slote, *Reason and Scepticism* (1970), p. 140.

the other set put the second of those two events, together with other events that happen to have occurred just after the other members of the first set.[3]

Plainly it has to be genuine regularities, not mere-Cambridge ones of the sort Quine here gives us a recipe for finding in abundance, which the regularity theorist holds to be constitutive of causality. And unless the regularity theorist is willing that his analysis be circular, he must hold that the genuine/mere-Cambridge distinction can be drawn in a way that does not involve making essential use of the notion of causality. As will be seen, I think that this view is mistaken.

The problem of induction is sometimes put by asking how we are justified in taking the fact that a regularity has held in observed cases as evidence that it holds more generally. To put it more briefly, how are we justified in 'projecting' observed regularities. But of course, if 'regularity' means 'Cambridge regularity', we are not in general justified in projecting observed regularities. This is one of the lessons Goodman's 'grue' has taught us. We might reformulate the problem by asking how we are justified in projecting genuine regularities. But this leaves the problem no clearer than the genuine/mere-Cambridge distinction. And it is arguable that the solution of the problem and the clarification of that distinction are much the same task.

Goodman remarks that 'the entrenchment of classes is some measure of their genuineness as kinds; roughly speaking, two things are the more akin as there is a more specific and better entrenched predicate that applies to both.'[4] Since for Goodman entrenchment is the primary measure of inductive projectibility, he seems to be asserting here a close connection between a predicate's being projectible and its extension's being a natural or genuine kind. The same connection is more explicitly asserted by Quine, who says that 'a projectible predicate is one that is true of all and only things of a kind'.[5] As these remarks suggest, there is a close match between intuitions about the inductive projectibility, or otherwise, of predicates, on the one hand, and intuitions about the genuineness, or otherwise, of properties and kinds, on the other. If someone proposed an account of the genuine/mere-Cambridge distinction which left it mysterious that genuine regularities should be the ones that are inductively projectible, this would be a good reason for concluding

---

[3] W. V. O. Quine, 'Natural Kinds', in *Ontological Relativity and Other Essays* (1969), pp. 132–3.

[4] Nelson Goodman, *Fact, Fiction and Forecast*, 3rd ed. (1973), p. 123.

[5] Quine, 'Natural Kinds', p. 116.

that he had mischaracterized the distinction. But a satisfactory elucidation of this distinction will have to do more than render intelligible the linkage between genuineness of property (sort, regularity, and so on) and inductive projectibility – for if only that were required, we could directly define genuineness in terms of projectibility, saying that a property is genuine just in case predicates standing for it are projectible. Another thing which a satisfactory account should make intelligible is our ability to detect genuine properties and genuine similarities in the world. And while there are these epistemological requirements that an acceptable account of the distinction must satisfy, the distinction itself is a metaphysical one, and calls for explanation in metaphysical terms. What all of this points to, I believe, is an explanation of the distinction in terms of the notion of causality.

2.

I shall focus mainly on the notion of a property, and hope that it will be fairly clear how what I say applies to such related notions as that of similarity and that of a regularity. Briefly put, my account of properties says that the identity of a genuine, or intrinsic, property is constituted by its potentialities for contributing to the causal powers of the things that have it.[6] For now I shall take the notion of a causal power as primitive. While I am prepared to count powers among properties, as a special case, I do not regard all genuine properties as powers. What is true is that any genuine property will give rise to certain powers if that property is combined with, i.e., coinstantiated with, certain combinations of other properties. Consider, for example, the property of being knife-shaped. Being a shape property, this is a Lockean primary quality. And it is not itself a causal power; for since knife-shaped things can be made of any of a variety of materials, ranging from steel to water vapour, there would seem to be no causal power they all have in common. But if combined with the property of being made of wood, this property yields the power of cutting butter and various other substances. If combined with the property of being made of steel, it yields a larger set of cutting powers. If combined with the property of being red, it yields the power of producing certain sorts of visual appearances or sense-impressions. And so on. Every genuine property has such a set of causal potentialities. What I claim is that the causal poten-

---

[6] This account is presented in more detail, and with considerably more supporting argument, in my paper 'Causality and Properties', forthcoming in Peter van Inwagen, ed., *Time and Cause: Essays Presented to Richard Taylor.*

tialities a property has are essential to it, that properties are identical just in case they have the same causal potentialities, and that what distinguishes genuine properties like green from mere-Cambridge properties like grue is that their possession makes a determinate contribution to causal powers.

I think that many people will be prepared to admit that at least some of the causal potentialities of a property are essential to it – that there could not be a world in which, for example, the property of being red had none of the causal potentialities it has in the actual world and had instead the causal potentialities which in the actual world characterize some other property, e.g., being spherical. Although I need not insist on this for my purposes in the present paper, my own view is that *all* of the causal potentialities of a property are essential to it. Thus to assert that a certain property makes a certain sort of causal contribution is, if the contribution is specified in purely general terms, to say something that is necessarily true if it is true at all. This permits us to deny that causally necessary truths are necessary in a different *sense* than logically necessary truths. We can say if we like that there are different kinds of necessity, of which causal necessity is only one. But these different kinds of necessity will correspond to different sorts of reasons why sentences express necessary truths, and not to different senses of the word 'necessary'. A sentence may express a necessary truth, and so be true in all possible worlds, because of its logical form, because of the meanings of non-logical expressions in it, or because of the essential natures of the referents of expressions in it. This gives us, respectively, logical necessity, analytic necessity, and metaphysical necessity. Causal necessity is metaphysical necessity; and like the metaphysically necessary truths recently discussed by Kripke, causally necessary truths are generally known *a posteriori*. Our knowledge of the causal potentialities of properties is largely empirical, despite the fact that the general propositions describing these potentialities are, when true, necessarily true.

But for present purposes I am less concerned to insist on the claim that all of the causal potentialities of a property are essential to it than I am to deny that the identity of a property consists in something that is independent of its causal potentialities. I deny, first of all, that there could be genuine properties having no causal potentialities whatever. It is perhaps an adequate reason for rejecting the possibility of there being such properties that this would make it impossible for us to know judgements of relative overall similarity. For if these were genuine properties the sharing of them would have to contribute to similarity; yet since detection, including perception, is a causal matter, the presence or absence of these properties would be undetectable in principle. I also deny that it is possible for two different properties to share all of the same causal potentialities. If that were possible, it would be impossible to know, or even have good reason for believing, that a single property is shared by two different things. For we know things' properties by their effects, including, importantly, their effects on our sensory states, and properties which shared all of their causal potentialities would be indistinguishable by any possible method of detection. Finally, I deny that the causal potentialities of a genuine property can change over time. To allow that such change is possible would be to preclude the possibility of our having the sorts of grounds we do have, or any other sort of grounds, for thinking that a property instantiated at one time is, or is not, the same as a property instantiated at another time.

There is, to be sure, a sense in which the causal potentialities of the property of redness, say, could change over time; its effect on human observers could change as the result of a change in human sense organs, or a change in the Earth's atmosphere and a resultant change in 'standard' lighting conditions. This would be a change in what E. M. Curley has called 'individual powers', i.e., powers to affect particular objects in certain ways.[7] Curley distinguishes these from what he calls 'sortal powers', i.e., powers to affect things of a certain (intrinsically characterized) kind in certain ways. It is the contribution of a property to sortal powers that cannot change over time, or vary from place to place. Even if the sense organs of human beings change, it will remain true that red things have the power to affect as they do now creatures of the sort we now are in circumstances of the sort that now prevail; this will remain true whether or not creatures of this sort and circumstances of this sort continue to exist. At any rate, this is true if redness is a genuine property (or 'sortal power') rather than an individual power.

This account could be extended to cover relations as well as properties. The laws that specify the causal potentialities of properties will frequently say what happens when things having certain properties are put in certain relations to one another; so these laws can be thought of as specifying the causal potentialities of these relations as well as the causal potentialities of the properties. Moreover, the considerations that indicate that the causal poten-

[7] E. M. Curley, 'Locke, Boyle and the Distinction Between Primary and Secondary Qualities', *Phil. Rev.* 71 (1972), 438–64.

tialities of properties are essential to them would indicate that the same is true of the causal potentialities of relations; it is as true of relations as it is of properties that it is by their effects that we know them. Finally, there is the same need for a genuine/mere-Cambridge distinction in the case of relations as there is in the case of properties. It is possible, for example, to define a relational predicate that stands to 'five feet away from' and 'ten feet away from' as Goodman's 'grue' stands to 'green' and 'blue'. While such a relational predicate would have as its extension a set of ordered pairs, the causal criterion would classify it as a mere-Cambridge relation; for the effects of the holding of this relation would vary even when the relata were exactly alike with respect to their (genuine) properties, and also stood in the same (genuine) relations otherwise.

I have expressed my view by saying that the essential nature of a property consists in its potentialities for contributing to the causal powers of the things that have it. This emphasizes the role of properties as causes or factors in causation. But properties play an equally central role on the effect side of the cause-effect relationship. An effect will consist in a change in the properties or relations of one or more things. And it is just as true on the effect side of the causal relation as it is on the cause side that the involvement of properties is in the first instance the involvement of genuine rather than mere-Cambridge properties and relations. For example, if something is caused to be grue, this will be in virtue of its being caused to be green or its being caused to be blue. And the identity of genuine properties consists just as much in what sorts of things cause them to be instantiated as it does in what sorts of things their instantiations cause or help to cause. Indeed, if after completing the impossible job of specifying the causal potentialities of all properties, i.e., specifying for each property all of the ways in which it can contribute to causal powers, we went on to specify for each property what all of its possible causes are, we would have done the same thing twice over.

It will no doubt have been noticed that in presenting my account of the notion of a genuine property I have repeatedly made use of the very notion being explained. The mark of a genuine property is that it necessarily gives rise to certain causal powers when combined with certain other properties – and the word 'properties' here has to mean 'genuine properties'. There are also more subtle circularities in the account, which I leave it to the reader to find. I believe that such circularity is unavoidable in the elucidation of fundamental concepts, including the notion of causality itself. What is wrong with the regularity theory of causality is not, in my opinion, its claim that singular causal statements are in some way 'implicitly general', but its attempt to give a reductive analysis of the notion of causality in terms of the notion of regularity and the related notions of property, kind, and similarity. As I have already hinted, I think that such an attempt to give a reductive analysis of the notion of causality is doomed to failure precisely because the genuine/mere-Cambridge distinction calls for elucidation (but not reductive analysis) in causal terms.

3.

Let us now see how this account applies to the problem of induction. To begin with, I follow Gilbert Harman in holding that enumerative induction is not 'a warranted form of nondeductive inference in its own right', but is rather a special case of what he calls 'inference to the best explanation'.[8] When we observe a regularity or correlation, and infer that it will continue into the future, or that it holds generally, we are justified in doing so, if we are, because given the rest of what we know the most plausible explanation of that regularity holding in observed cases is that there exist causal laws and antecedent conditions which together imply that the regularity holds in cases in which it has been observed to hold and in the cases into which we 'project' it. Sometimes the most plausible hypothesis will involve the claim that the uniformity holds universally, but usually the range of our generalizations is tacitly restricted in some way; I assume that we do not really think it is reasonable to predict, simply on the basis of the appearance of ravens so far examined, that ravens will not undergo mutations which will eventually result in there being substantial numbers of non-black ones.

If there is an explanation of an observed correlation or uniformity, this will consist in some set of causal facts. The explanation may be that the correlated items are themselves directly causally connected, as cause and effect or as joint effects of a common cause. More commonly, however, the causal connection will be less direct. We do not think that having the shape and other identifying features of ravens (exclusive of colour) itself causes something to be black. Nor, for that matter, do we think that the presence of the genes for those other features causes the presence of the gene for black colour. The explanation of such a correlation will involve such

[8] Gilbert Harman, 'The Inference to the Best Explanation', *Phil. Rev.* 74 (1965), 88–95.

things as the existence at some point in the past of conditions which gave black colour survival value for ravens, the genetic mechanisms by which colour, along with other traits, is transmitted from parent to offspring, and, if we press our demands for explanation far enough, the evolutionary process by which these genetic mechanisms developed. In other cases the explanation will be of quite a different kind. That copper conducts electricity is determined by features of its atomic structure, and it is in virtue of other features of that same atomic structure that it is ductile, malleable, reddish in colour, and so on – i.e., has the characteristic identifying properties of copper that were initially found to be correlated with electrical conductivity. If we ask why these different features go together, the answer will be in terms of atomic theory. Ultimately, any of these explanations would, if we could spell it out completely, terminate in laws that describe the causal potentialities of the properties and relations of things and their constituent parts. When we engage in enumerative induction, we typically do not have any specific explanation of this sort in mind. Often we project an observed regularity while being completely baffled as to why it exists. But in so far as we are entitiled to project an observed regularity, this is because we are entitled to think that there is an explanation of it which is 'projection-entitling', i.e., such as to imply, on reasonable assumptions, that the regularity extends beyond the cases in which it has been observed to hold. In other words, we are entitled to project the regularity, if we are, because we are entitled to believe that there is a set of causal factors that produced it and that the regularity we have observed is only part of a more extensive regularity produced by those factors.

How is this account of inductive inference helped by the acceptance of the sort of causal theory of properties I have suggested? To begin with, it is a consequence of this theory that from the very existence of properties it follows that there are causal laws governing the instantiation of these properties – these will be the laws that spell out the causal potentialities that constitute the essential natures of the properties. We can dismiss *a priori* the account of the world, call it the the 'null account', which says that there are no laws of nature, and that all regularities, genuine and mere-Cambridge alike, are equally accidental. We can also dismiss *a priori* the supposition that there may occur occasionally a 'change in the course of nature' which is due to a change in the laws themselves, i.e., to some of them simply ceasing to hold or being replaced by others. At any rate, we can dismiss the possibility that this might happen in the case of the laws which specify the causal potentialities which are essential to the various properties and relations that are instantiated in the world (and I suspect that these are all the laws there are). This does not mean that we know *a priori* that every event has a cause, and still less does it mean that we are assured *a priori* that regularities that have held in the past can always or generally be counted on to hold in the future. But it does, I think, make the reasonableness of induction seem less mysterious than philosophers in the Humean tradition have typically viewed it as being; for it helps to explain how we are entitled, when we are, to believe that observed uniformities have explanations that are projection-entitling.

We often speak of regularities as 'calling out' for explanation; and when a regularity calls out for explanation, it usually calls out for one that is projection-entitling. It cannot be true in general of Cambridge regularities that they call out for projection-entitling explanations – since for every Cambridge regularity which holds in our evidence class and also holds in some class of cases into which we might consider projecting it, there are infinitely many Cambridge regularities that hold in the evidence class and do not hold in that class of cases. It is primarily genuine regularities that call out for projection-entitling explanations; and as we shall see in the next section, the explanation of a mere-Cambridge regularity is always in the first instance the explanation of a related genuine one. It can happen that a genuine regularity lacks an explanation, and that it is sheer coincidence that it holds in observed cases. And sometimes what seem to be the only possible explanations will be so far fetched that it will seem more reasonable to ascribe the regularity to coincidence than to suppose that it has a projection-entitling explanation. So it will be if the observed regularity consists in the fact that the first five people I meet on my morning walk are all left-handed. But given the causal nature of properties, the more extensive an observed regularity is, the less likely it is that it holds coincidentally, and the more likely it is that the causal factors that produced it are such that it will continue for some time into the future. After passing fifty consecutive people who are left-handed, I will be willing to bet money on the next one being so.

In order to dispel any appearance that I am claiming to have solved the problem of induction, I should mention a few of the questions I have had to leave unanswered, partly from lack of space but largely from lack of competence. To begin with, there is the question of what exactly it means to say that the existence of a regularity in observed cases is a 'coincidence', and why it is that in certain cases we are entitled to rule out the supposition that an observed regularity is coincidental in favour of the hypothesis that it has some causal explanation or other. To put it otherwise, what is the basis of the belief that certain observed regularities (primarily 'genuine' ones) are highly improbable *except* on the supposition that there are causal explanations of them? Moreover, given that an observed regularity has some causal explanation or other, why are we usually justified in believing that the explanation is projection-entitling, e.g., such as to imply that the regularity will continue into the immediate future? The explanation of this cannot consist entirely in the fact that we are entitled to believe that genuine properties do not change their causal potentialities; for in particular cases we will have to be entitled as well to believe that particular things will not lose certain of the properties they possessed during the period in which the regularity was observed to hold, namely those whose causal potentialities played a role in the production of the regularity. In general, causal explanations of observed regularities will be projection-entitling only on the supposition that things tend to retain their properties, and so their causal powers, unless subjected to causal influences from outside them. And so we need to know how we are justified in making this supposition. And supposing we knew this, we would still have the job of explaining how we are justified in believing (when we are) that the things whose properties and relations account for a regularity that has existed until now in observed cases will not be subjected in the immediate future to causal factors that will change some of those properties and relations, and so terminate the regularity. To explain this we would have to explain, among other things, what entitles us to discount the possibility that things are subject to certain sorts of 'action at a distance' (either spatial, temporal, or both), and to take certain observations as entitling us to believe that something is, and will remain for some time, a relatively isolated causal system. I think that an elaboration of the causal theory of properties can throw light on some of these questions, but I lack an account which gives a comprehensive answer to all of them.

Before I end this section, I would like to suggest a way of viewing induction which is complementary to, rather than in competition with, the view of it as a special case of inference to the best explanation, which is the view I have just sketched. One can think of induction as the process of learning about universals by considering their instantiations. It is hardly a radical thesis that whatever intrinsic features a universal has at one time and place it has at all times and places; this is simply a consequence of what is meant by 'intrinsic' and 'universal'. Properties are universals; and what the causal theory of properties says is simply that the causal potentialities of a property are intrinsic features of it. What we observe in particular cases has to be the manifestation of the causal potentialities of the various properties and relations instantiated in those cases. There is much that is problematic about induction. But what is not problematic about it, if the causal theory is right, is the assumption that whatever we learn about the causal potentialities of a property by considering particular instantiations of it is true of it *qua* universal, and so will be true of it whenever and wherever it is instantiated.

4.

I have been assuming that there is a distinction to be drawn between 'projectible' and 'non-projectible' predicates, and have tried to link this distinction with the distinction between 'genuine' and 'mere-Cambridge' properties. But the assumption that there is such a distinction has been forcefully challenged by Frank Jackson in a recent paper.[9] Jackson argues that '*all* (consistent) predicates are projectible and that there is no paradox resulting from "grue" and like predicates'.[10] At the heart of his case is the claim that certain inductions involving 'grue' and similar predicates are illegitimate, not because the predicates themselves are inherently non-projectible, but because the inductions violate a condition which any legitimate application of the 'Straight Rule' of induction must satisfy. The condition is what he calls the 'counterfactual condition'; it says that if we wish to conclude on the basis of certain F's being G that certain other F's are G, we can legitimately do so on the basis of the Straight Rule only if there is no property H such that (a) H belongs to the F's in our evidence class, (b) H does not belong to the 'certain other F's' (those our conclusion says are G), or, at least we are uncertain whether H belongs to those other F's, and do not want to make it part of our inductive conclusion that it does, and (c) we know that if the F's in our evidence class had not been H, they would not have been G.[11] One of Jackson's examples

[9] Frank Jackson, 'Grue', *J. Phil.* 71 (1975), 113–30.
[10] Jackson, 'Grue', p. 114.
[11] I have slightly modified Jackson's formulation, the main change being the addition of the second clause in (b). Further modifications would be needed to rule out other unacceptable inferences discussed by Goodman, e.g., one to the conclusion that emerires not examined before T, like those examined before T, are green.

of a Straight Rule induction which violates this condition involves
someone concluding from the fact that all of the lobsters he has seen
have been red to the conclusion that the next uncooked lobster he
sees will be red, knowing that it is cooking (and presumably only
cooking) that makes lobsters red. Jackson regards the illegitimacy of
this induction as comparable with that of the induction from the fact
that all emeralds so far examined have been grue to the conclusion
that certain unexamined emeralds are grue, where it is known that
the emeralds so far examined would not have been grue if they had
not been examined. We would not conclude from the illegitimacy of
the first induction that the predicate 'red' is inherently non-
projectible, and Jackson thinks that there is no more reason to
conclude from the illegitimacy of the second that the predicate
'grue' is inherently non-projectible. In some cases an application of
the Straight Rule to an observed regularity involving 'grue' will not
violate the counterfactual condition. For example, if I conclude from
the fact that the emeralds in my evidence class are all grue to the
conclusion that the emeralds in the nearest jewellery store are grue
(where I can assume that the latter have all been examined), there
will be no predicate '*H*' true of the former emeralds but not of the
latter such that I know that if the emeralds in my evidence class had
not been *H*, they would not have been grue. In such a case Jackson
regards the induction as legitimate, and the predicate 'grue' as
projectible.

I certainly do not want to dispute the claim that the legitimacy of
Straight Rule induction requires the satisfaction of the counterfactual condition. But it is worth asking why this is. The answer is fairly
straightforward, and underlines the point, made earlier, that
enumerative induction is a special case of inference to the best
explanation. If the counterfactual condition is not satisfied, then the
causal facts which explain a correlation or regularity holding in the
evidence class do not imply that the same correlation or regularity
holds in the class of cases into which the conclusion projects it. For
example, given that the lobsters in the evidence class would not
have been red if they had not been cooked, the explanation of all of
the lobsters being red involves their having been cooked, and so
does not license a projection to the case of lobsters that are not
cooked. In short, the satisfaction of the counterfactual condition is a
necessary condition of our being entitled to believe that the explanation of the observed regularity is appropriately projection-
entitling.

But now suppose that I conclude from the fact that all of the emeralds in my evidence class are grue that the next emerald I examine before T will be grue, where T is the time mentioned in Goodman's definition of 'grue' (which I interpret as saying that something is grue at a time if and only if the thing is green at that time and the thing is (was, will be) first examined before T or the thing is blue at that time and is not (was not, will not be) examined before T). Is the counterfactual condition satisfied? Let T' be a time immediately after the last time at which I examined an emerald. Then all of the emeralds in my evidence class have the property 'examined at T' or before', and we can suppose that the next emerald I will examine lacks this property (and that I know that it does). Now in this case I might well know that if the emeralds in my evidence class had not had this property they would not have been grue – for I might know that, owing perhaps to an explosion in the emerald mine at T', if they had not been examined prior to T' it would be impossible for them to be examined before T. In that case the counterfactual condition would not be satisfied. Yet surely it is reasonable all the same for me to predict that the next emerald I examine before T will be grue. The reason, of course, is that the emeralds in my evidence class are green as well as grue, that this entitles me to believe that the next emerald I examine before T will be green (the inference to this conclusion does satisfy the counterfactual condition), and that it follows from something's being green and examined before T that it is grue. This is a case of what I will call *pseudo-projectibility*; although a projection involving a certain predicate ('grue') is illegitimate, we can legitimately get from its 'premiss' to its conclusion via two definitionally based deductions and a legitimate induction involving the projection of a different predicate ('green').

Now let us consider again the induction in which I conclude from the fact that the emeralds in my evidence class are all grue to the conclusion that the emeralds in the nearest jewellery store are grue. It is certainly true that if I know that the emeralds in my evidence class are all grue, I am entitled to infer that the emeralds in the nearest jewellery store are all grue. And in this case we can grant that the counterfactual condition is satisfied. But it can hardly be said that it is *because* the counterfactual condition is satisfied that I am justified in concluding that the emeralds in the jewellery store are grue. For here, as in the case of pseudo-projectibility just considered, we can get to the conclusion by way of a projection of 'green' and a definitionally based deduction; given that the emeralds in the jewellery store have been examined (which we can view as the conclusion of another induction) and that the time is before T, it follows from their being green that they are grue. Nor could it plausibly be maintained that the legitimacy of our conclusion is overdetermined – that it is guaranteed *both* by the availability of a Straight Rule induction involving 'grue' which satisfies the counterfactual condition *and* by the availability of the more complicated line of inference involving 'green'. It could hardly be said, for example, that our conclusion in this case is supported by two different inductions, and so is better supported than our conclusion in the case of pseudo-projectibility considered earlier.

I have already remarked that the requirement that the counterfactual condition be satisfied by Straight Rule inductions is explicable on the view, and I think only on the view, that enumerative induction is a special case of inference to the best explanation. Now on this view, I am entitled to make an inductive projection just in case I am entitled to think that whatever set of factors produced the regularity that holds in my evidence class must be such that they could not have produced that regularity without producing a more extensive regularity that extends into the cases into which I project it in making my induction. So let us see how this applies to the induction of 'grue' in my last example. The explanation of the fact that the emeralds in my evidence class are all grue must at least include the explanation of the fact that they are all green. And if there is anything more to it than that, this will not be any additional causal facts, but will be simply the fact that the time is before T and the analytic truths that (a) being in the evidence class involves having been examined, and (b) being green and examined before T entails being grue. So if the explanation is such as to be projection-entitling, what in the first instance it entitles the projection of is the correlation between being an emerald and being green. The explanation, if we had it in full, would invoke a lawlike connection between certain properties of emeralds and the property of being green (this following from the essential natures of these properties), and would say how emeralds acquired these green-making properties and why they are retained once acquired. It will be because we are entitled to think that the correct explanation, whatever it is, entitles the projection of 'green' in this case, together with our independent knowledge that any gems in a jewellery store will have been examined, that we will be entitled to conclude that the emeralds in the jewellery store are grue.

But now let us consider another case, which seems at first to be significantly different from this one. Suppose that there is a kind of objects, call them 'emerexes', which are naturally blue but are such that examining them causes them to become green. To give this a faint semblance of plausibility, let us suppose that emerexes can only be examined by the use of special instruments (to view them with the naked eye is fatal), and that it is the application to them of those special instruments that causes them to be green. Now suppose that I examine a set of emerexes (the only ones I have so far examined) and find them all to be green, and so grue (the time being before T). And suppose I know of the emerexes in this set that they were caused to be green by being examined, and that if they had not been examined they would be blue. Then if I were to conclude on the basis of their being green that the emerexe nearest the summit of Mt. Everest is green, not knowing whether that emerexe will be examined before T or not, my induction would violate Jackson's counterfactual condition. But let us suppose that I know that, if the emerexes in my evidence class had not been examined when they were, they would not be examined before T. Then I also know if they had not been examined they would still have been grue. For if they had not been examined they would have been, and would now be, blue; and being blue, together with not being examined before T, entails being grue. So it would seem that I would not violate Jackson's counterfactual condition if I inferred from the fact that the emeralds in my evidence class are grue to the conclusion that the emerexe nearest the summit of Mt. Everest is grue – where, again, I do not know whether that emerexe will be examined before T. Moreover, it seems that the conclusion of this induction is one that I would in fact be justified in accepting. It might seem, then, that we have a counterexample to the suggestion, which I implicitly made in discussing the previous example, that where a Straight Rule induction involving 'grue' is in conformity to the counterfactual condition, there is always a line of reasoning involving a projection of 'green' that will get us to the same conclusion, and that it is the availability of the latter that makes the conclusion justified.

But this is not a counterexample to that claim. Note first that if I know that the emerexes in my evidence class were caused to be green by being examined and would have been blue if not examined, then there are the following two generalizations which I know to be true of the emerexes in my evidence class: (1) emerexes are caused to be green by being examined, and (2) emerexes that are not examined are blue. Now I am to consider the emerexe closest to the summit of Mt. Everest, in total ignorance as to whether it has been examined or will be examined before T. To simplify matters we can lay it down that my inference is being made just before T, so that in it 'grue' amounts to 'green and examined or blue and not examined'. I know, as a matter of logic, that the emerexe in question has either been examined or not. Projecting generalization (1) to it implies that it is green on the supposition that it has been examined. Projecting generalization (2) to it implies that it is blue on the supposition that it has not been examined. Since these two suppositions exhaust the possibilities, I know that either it is examined and green or unexamined and blue – and given that we are at T, this amounts to the conclusion that it is grue. So again we find that where we have a seemingly legitimate induction involving 'grue', we can get to its conclusion by a line of argument that does not involve the projection of any predicates that would not ordinarily be counted as projectible.

Moreover, if we consider the explanations of why, in this example, the various generalizations hold in the evidence class, we see that here, as in the previous case, it is explanations of genuine regularities that are in the first instance projection-entitling. To be sure, the explanation of the fact that the emerexes in the evidence class are all green does not entitle us to project *that* regularity. What it entitles us to project is the regularity which consists in the fact that all of the *examined* emerexes in the evidence class were green. It is true that the explanation of the fact that all of the emerexes in the evidence class were grue, and of the fact that the counterfactual condition is satisfied by the 'grue' projection, is an explanation that implies that certain other emerexes are grue, and so is in that sense projection-entitling. But this explanation consists in the explanation of certain regularities involving greenness, blueness, being an emerald, and the operation of being examined in a certain way, namely regularities described by generalizations (1) and (2) above: emerexes are caused to be green by being examined, and emerexes that are not examined are blue.

Finally, a slight modification of this example gives us a case in which a Straight Rule induction involving a projection of 'grue' satisfies Jackson's counterfactual condition but is nevertheless illegitimate. For suppose I conclude on the basis of the fact that all of the emerexes I examined before T were grue to the conclusion that emerexes first examined after T will then (at the time of examination) be grue. Given what I have been assuming about emerexes, this conclusion is false; the first examination of these emerexes will cause them to be green, and since the examination will occur after T, this will render them non-grue (bleen, in fact). And this is of course the conclusion we will draw if we project the fact that generalizations (1) and (2) hold in our evidence class. Yet it seems that the inference to the contrary conclusion, that these emerexes will be grue, could satisfy the counterfactual condition if the projection of 'grue' in the original version of the example could do so. And if there is a possible case in which this inference does satisfy the condition, but is nevertheless illegitimate, then the inadmissibility of projections of 'grue' does not always consist, as Jackson apparently thinks, in violations of the counterfactual condition.

Earlier I described a case of what I called 'pseudo-projectibility'. What I have tried to bring out in my subsequent discussion is the similarity between that case and cases in which 'grue' might seem to be projectible and in which the projection of it would not violate the counterfactual condition. My inclination is to say that in these latter cases too the projectibility of 'grue' is pseudo-projectibility. But the main point I want to make is that where there is legitimate induction, the conclusion can be arrived at via inductions involving only predicates standing for 'genuine' properties and relations, those having essential natures consisting in sets of causal potentialities, and that what makes such an induction legitimate is the fact that observed regularities involving such properties and relations call for projection-entitling explanations in terms of their causal potentialities and, usually, the causal potentialities of other genuine properties and relations as well. I shall use the term 'projectible' to characterize predicates of this sort.

5.

I have been suggesting that the projectibility of predicates is rooted in the causal natures of genuine properties. But this suggestion would be of no help in dealing with the problem of induction if it were impossible for us to know whether particular properties, and particular regularities that have held in observed cases, are genuine or mere-Cambridge. Goodman's problem of projectibility is sometimes represented (but not, I think, by Goodman himself) as the problem of how we know, or are justified in believing, that the predicates we actually project are genuinely projectible–e.g., how we know that 'green' is projectible and 'grue' not. And this problem, if problem it is, seems much the same as the problem of how we know, or are justified in believing, that these predicates stand for genuine rather than mere-Cambridge properties.

I have argued elsewhere that we cannot make sense of the supposition that another person systematically projects predicates that are 'grue'-like relative to predicates we project, or that the predicates we project are 'grue'-like relative to predicates that are genuinely projectible.[12] I cannot repeat my arguments here. But underlying them is a point that has an immediate application to our present problem. In many cases our belief that a predicate has a meaning and an extension is inseparable from our belief that we, or at any rate someone, can reliably detect cases in which that predicate applies.[13] This is true of colour predicates and other predicates that are typically learned by ostension rather than by verbal definition and the like. Now the notion of detection is a causal notion. And in so far as one is committed to believing that the presence of the property a predicate stands for can be detected by the fact that in certain circumstances it produces a certain sort of effect, e.g., a reading on an instrument or a sensory state in an observer, one is committed to believing also that there is a 'lawlike connection' between the instantiation of that property and the occurrence of that sort of effect. But Goodman makes the occurrence in lawlike generalizations a mark of projectibility; and this fits with my suggestion that projectible predicates are those that stand for genuine properties, where genuineness of property is to be explained, as I have suggested, in causal terms. So believing that such a predicate has a meaning and extension, and that there is even the possibility of its being true or false of anything, involves believing that its applicability is detectable in certain ways, which in turn involves believing that it is projectible. But the non-linguistic counterpart of a projectible predicate is a genuine property. So we can also put this by saying that in thinking that there is a property such a predicate stands for, one is at the same time committed to thinking that this property is genuine.

This needs to be qualified, but the qualification will help to make the point. There could be a detector that detects instances of a non-projectible predicate, or (in other words) of a mere-Cambridge property. Goodman has said that 'we can readily construct a machine that will apply "grue" correctly upon being shown an object in good light.'[14] I doubt if this is true if we use the definition of 'grue' which Goodman himself gave in *Fact, Fiction and Forecast*, according to which it applies to things examined before T just in

---

[12] See my 'On Projecting the Unprojectible', *Phil. Rev.* 84 (1975), 178–219.

[13] I have included the qualifying phrase 'or at any rate someone' so as to allow for what Hilary Putnam has called the 'division of linguistic labor', and to cover such cases as the use of colour words by the congenitally blind. See Putnam's 'The Meaning of "Meaning"' in his *Mind, Language and Reality* (1975) vol. 2, pp. 215–71.

[14] Nelson Goodman, *Problems and Projects* (1972), p. 409.

case they are green but to other things just in case they are blue. For how is the machine to tell, after *T*, whether an object it is examining was examined before *T*? But Goodman's claim is no doubt true if we use the definition of 'grue' made current by Barker and Achinstein, according to which 'grue' is true of a thing at a time if and only if either the thing is green and the time is before *T*, or the thing is blue and the time is *T* or afterwards.[15] All we need is a machine that can detect green and blue, and which also can tell (say from a calendar-clock which is built into it) whether the time is before or after *T*. But here the working of the machine would depend on lawlike connections involving genuine properties (green and blue) in terms of which the mere-Cambridge property can be defined, and in the working of the machine the detection of genuine properties would be epistemologically prior to the detection of the mere-Cambridge property grue – just as it is in the case of the man who detects grueness by detecting green or blue and checking his watch and calendar.

It might be suggested, however, that since there can be devices that detect mere-Cambridge properties, we have to reckon with the possibility that we ourselves are unwittingly detecting such properties on just the occasions on which we think we are detecting genuine ones. But a little reflection shows that this is not a possibility. Suppose that the evil genius has built calendar-clocks into our brains, and has so constructed us that beginning in the year 2000 we will spontaneously begin applying the word 'green' to blue things and the word 'blue' to green things, believing all the while that we are using these words in accordance with our past usage of them. It is true that the evil genius could use us as unwitting grue detectors; knowing our construction, he could know that what we call 'green', whether before or after the year 2000, is grue (in the Barker–Achinstein sense). But it does not follow, and would not be true, that in calling something green we would unknowingly be ascribing to it the mere-Cambridge property of being grue, rather than the genuine property of being green. Up until the year 2000 we would be correctly ascribing the property of being green. After that we would either be mistakenly ascribing this property, or else correctly ascribing the property of being blue under the misapprehension that the word 'green' is the word we have all along been using to ascribe it. To achieve the effect we have imagined, the evil genius would have had to have designed us so that beginning in the year 2000

[15] See S. F. Barker and P. Achinstein, 'On the New Riddle of Induction', *Phil. Rev.* 69 (1960), 511–22.

either (1) the way certain colours look to us would be different than before (green things looking the way blue things used to look, and vice versa), or (2) our memory of how green and blue things formerly looked is systematically mistaken (these colours having been, as it were, interchanged in our memories), or (3) (if this is a different possibility than (1) and (2)) we systematically misremember what we formerly meant by 'green' and 'blue'. But whichever of these things he did, he would not thereby have brought it about that in our language the word 'green' is a nonprojectible predicate whose extension is a mere-Cambridge kind.

This is not to deny that an expression which we take to stand for a genuine property might fail to do so; for such an expression might fail to stand for any property whatever, genuine or mere-Cambridge. The evil genius might trick us into thinking mistakenly that there was a property we were able to detect by having certain sense-impressions, and so into thinking mistakenly that one of our predicate expressions stood for such a property. What is not possible is for what we take to be a sensible predicate to latch on to the wrong sort of property, a mere-Cambridge one, and to have the wrong sort of extension, a non-projectible one like that of 'grue'. And while I have not the space to argue this at any length, I think that this sort of mistake is impossible in the case of non-sensible predicates as well. Words for non-sensible properties and relationships have to be introduced into the language, and have their meanings and references explained to particular speakers, by the use of other words, including words for sensible properties. Typically such explanations will assert causal connections between the property the word stands for and other properties, and the success of the word's introduction will depend on there actually being such connections. When this is so there can be no question of the word's standing for a mere-Cambridge property; it stands for a real property or for nothing. Indeed, I think we can go further and say that in so far as the speakers of a language regard a predicate as projectible, this limits its possible referents to genuine properties. Consider the predicate 'condulates electricity', which Barker and Achinstein define as being true of a thing at a time 'if and only if the thing then conducts electricity and the time is prior to 2000 A.D. or the thing is then an electrical insulator and the time is not prior to 2000 A.D.'[16] If at some future time people forget the origin of this term, and come to regard it as inductively projectible, it will have changed its sense and reference, and will no longer have the

[16] 'On the New Riddle of Induction', pp. 521–2.

extension which the Barker–Achinstein definition gives it. Suppose, for example, that a philosophy graduate student working in a printshop replaces 'conducts' with 'condulates' in a standard encyclopedia, and that this initiates a process whereby 'condulates' gradually comes to be used in place of 'conducts'. In this case, surely, 'condulates' would take over the sense, reference, and extension now possessed by 'conducts', and would become a projectible predicate. In Goodman's terminology, a term becomes projectible in becoming 'entrenched' in the projective practices of the speakers of the language. But the relevant sort of entrenchment does not require an actual history of projection on the part of the projectible term; if overnight the evil genius switches 'condulates' and 'conducts' in the memories and linguistic habits of all speakers of English, then 'condulates' will become projectible, despite having had no history of projection.[17]

The upshot of all this is that the inductive sceptic cannot pose his problem by suggesting that it may be, for all we know, that the predicates we project are all unprojectible predicates standing for mere-Cambridge properties (e.g., that perhaps it is 'grue' rather than 'green' that stands for a genuine property). He can suggest, for all I have argued, that the predicates we project may stand for no properties at all, and may lack the potentiality of being true or false of anything. But if the purpose of this suggestion is to call all induction into question, then the suggestion will have to apply to the predicates used to describe subjective states, e.g., sensory experiences, as well as to other descriptive predicates. For it is as true of predicates like 'looks green' as it is of predicates like 'green' that in regarding them as having sense and reference one is committed to regarding them as inductively projectible.[18] So scepticism about induction, if it takes the form of scepticism about the projectibility of predicates (or the genuineness of properties), reduces to an extreme form of scepticism that threatens to call into question the very meaningfulness of the language in which it is expressed. I shall not attempt here to show that such scepticism is incoherent. I shall content myself with pointing out that in so far as we are entitled to think that our descriptive predicates do have sense and reference, that they have the potentiality of being true or false of anything, we are entitled to think that those of them we project stand for genuine properties and so are genuinely projectible.

[17] This does not conflict with Goodman's theory of entrenchment. See *Fact, Fiction and Forecast*, p. 95.

[18] See my 'Phenomenal Similarity', *Critica* 7 (1975), especially section IV (pp. 17–25).

Properties, Causation, and Projectibility:
Reply to Shoemaker

Shoemaker argues for two theses. His weak thesis is that whatever justification we may have for projecting properties depends on beliefs about the
explanation of those properties being instantiated. This I accept. The strong
thesis is that all the genuine properties of things (e.g., being green as
opposed to being grue) are nothing but 'potentialities for contributing to the
causal powers of things'. This I reject. The only arguments which
Shoemaker gives for this thesis are of a verificationist character – e.g., that if
there were more to properties than such potentialities, we would never have
good reason for believing that two things shared a common property. But
even if that were so, the things might share a common property all the
same – and it is not so; the principle of simplicity can give us the requisite
good reason. The strong thesis must be false; because the only good
grounds for attributing causal powers to objects are in terms of the effects
which objects typically produce. Such effects can only be recognized if
properties can be recognized. But if properties are nothing but potentialities
to contribute to causal powers, one will only have good reason for attributing
them to objects if their effects can be recognized. This leads to a vicious
infinite regress. The regress is broken if we suppose that there is more to
properties (e.g., to being square or red) than their potentialities to contribute to causal powers, something which enables us to recognize their
presence or absence independently of their subsequent effects. This is not to
deny that our judgements about whether an object has some property are
corrigible in the light of effects, and that *some* properties can only be
attributed to objects in the light of effects.

Shoemaker argues for two claims about the connection between the
properties of things and their causal powers, a weak thesis and a
strong thesis. I shall argue that the weak thesis is correct, but that
the strong thesis is not. The weak thesis is that whatever justification
we may have for projecting properties depends on beliefs about the
explanation of those properties' being instantiated. In Shoemaker's
words – 'when we observe a regularity or correlation, and infer that
it will continue into the future, or that it holds generally, we are
justified in doing so, if we are, because given the rest of what we
know the most plausible explanation of that regularity holding in
observed cases is that there exist causal laws and antecedent conditions which together imply that the regularity holds in cases in which
it has been observed to hold and in the cases into which we project
it' (p. 298 above). This is undoubtedly so, and there is a simple

reason for it. Our beliefs about what will happen in future depend on our beliefs about what are the laws of nature, for in so far as the behaviour of objects is necessitated and therefore predictable, it is laws of nature which necessitate it, and so it is knowledge of them which enables us to predict that behaviour. Having observed many A's in the past to have been B, and none to have been not-B, I can only reach a conclusion about whether the next A will be B if I have some belief about the nature of the laws operative in this field. I may come to believe that it is a law of nature or a consequence thereof that all A's are B; in which case of course I will project B. Or I may come to believe that it is a consequence of laws of nature that A's are B, but only under certain circumstances. In that case there will be an explanation in terms of 'causal laws and antecedent conditions' of it holding under those circumstances, and so I will only project b if I have some reason to believe that those circumstances hold for the A's into which I project B. Or I may come to believe that A's being B is not a regular matter at all; it is only a coincidence that the A's which I have observed have been B. In that case I will not project B at all. So I fully agree with Shoemaker's weak thesis, and with his more detailed account of inductive practice which springs from it. My point is simply that there is adequate justification for this thesis which does not depend on Shoemaker's strong thesis.

The strong thesis is that all the genuine properties of things (e.g., being green, or being square, as opposed to being grue) simply are causal powers; or, more carefully, are 'potentialities for contributing to the causal powers of the things' which have them, in the way which Shoemaker spells out on p. 294. There is nothing more to a thing having all the (genuine) properties which it does than that it has certain causal powers, powers to produce effects. From this thesis there follow other narrower claims – that there could not be 'genuine properties having no causal potentialities whatever' (p. 295) 'that at least some of the causal potentialities of a property are essential to it' (ibid.), and that things are 'exactly similar', 'just in case they have the same causal powers' (ibid.). As far as this paper is concerned, Shoemaker is prepared to allow that there might be causal potentialities of a property other than those essential to it – e.g., objects which are green might be more restful on the eye than objects which are red without this being of the essence of greeness. He admits, however, to believing the even stronger thesis that 'all of the causal potentialities of a property are essential to it', but he does not press this on us today. I must point out however that the claim (ibid.) that the causal potentialities of a genuine property cannot change over time does not follow from the strong thesis, but only follows from the even stronger thesis. For even if there is nothing more to a property than certain causal potentialities, there might still be causal potentialities linked to it only accidentally (e.g., being more restful) and these might change with time. So long as we had some ground for distinguishing between the causal potentialities of a property which were essential to it and those which were not, the reason which Shoemaker gives for holding that the causal potentialities of a genuine property cannot change over time would not apply; for we could pick out a property by its essential potentialities.

Having made these distinctions, the rest of what I have to say is concerned only with the strong thesis. What arguments does Shoemaker give in its favour? There is the argument that it provides a justification for the weak thesis; but I have argued that there is a perfectly adequate justification of that thesis which makes no appeal to the strong thesis. Shoemaker's other arguments for his thesis are those on p. 296 of his paper. These seem to me to have a strongly verificationist flavour, and to be mistaken. Thus Shoemaker argues that if two different properties could share all the same causal potentialities 'it would be impossible to know, or even have good reason for believing, that a single property is shared by two different things' (p. 296). The argument is that if two different properties could have the same causal potentialities, which lead objects possessing them to bring about various effects in various circumstances, we could never know whether objects which produced those effects in those circumstances did so in virtue of the same property or of different properties; and as, Shoemaker supposes, we can only recognize properties by their effects, we could never know whether two objects had the same or different properties. Now maybe it would be impossible to know this infallibly, beyond the possibility of error – but after all, all inferences from the observed to the unobserved have a certain fallibility about them. But a basic principle of all inductive inference is the principle of simplicity – postulate the simplest explanation of phenomena. The simplest explanation is more probably true than a more complex one. An obvious application of the principle of simplicity is Occam's razor for predicates – do not multiply predicates beyond necessity. It is simpler to suppose that two objects producing a certain set of effects in certain circumstances do so in virtue of possessing a common property than that they do so in virtue of possessing two different properties, between the effects of which there are no observable differences. Simplicity is evidence of truth, and so we do have 'good reason for believing' that a single property 'is shared by two different things'.[1] A similar criticism applies to Shoemaker's argument in favour of his claim that there could not be 'genuine properties having no causal potentialities whatever'. Given the principle of simplicity, we would never have any reason for believing in the existence of such properties. But, even so, there might (logically) be such properties. It may well be that the world has more mysterious features than man or any other rational being has the power to discover. The only reason for denying this is the dogma of verificationism – that a sentence is meaningful if and only if it can to some degree in some way be verified or falsified; but I do not believe that that dogma has ever been supported by any good reasons.[2]

It seems to me that not merely is Shoemaker's strong thesis inadequately supported by argument, but that it must be false – oddly enough for reasons very similar to those which he gives for supposing it true. For if he is right, we could never come to know or even have a reasonable belief about what properties objects have – and often we do have reasonable beliefs about this. For Shoemaker's claim is that any property simply is its potentiality for contributing to the casual powers of objects which possess it. Now what are these casual powers, powers to produce what? Presumably powers to produce changes in the properties or relations of objects, or to bring about the existence or non-existence of objects. All change is change in objects (e.g., something turning green) or in the relations between objects (e.g., one object getting more distant from another) or of objects (viz., their coming to exist, or ceasing to exist). One can recognize that objects have powers only if one can recognize when such changes have occurred, viz., if one can recognize that an object has changed its properties or

---

[1] In 'Causality and Properties' (forthcoming in P. van Inwagen (ed.), *Time and Cause:* (see p. 15 f.) Shoemaker has an argument against this suggestion. He cites one example where in using the criterion of simplicity to decide between two hypotheses, we already presuppose that properties remain constant in their causal potentialities. But it seems a contingent feature of the example which Shoemaker constructs that this presupposition is made; and, I cannot see that it has any tendency to show that we do not use the criterion of simplicity to provide our normal grounds for supposing that in general properties do remain constant in their causal potentialities, nor to show that in this example we cannot use it to justify the making of the presupposition. The widespread use of the criterion to rule out hypotheses which are odd in various ways suggests that we do use the criterion for the former purpose.

[2] I have argued this in one or two places – e.g., my *The Coherence of Theism* (1977), pp. 22–9.

relations to other objects or come to exist or ceased to exist. But objects are never naked; we recognize their presence by their properties – you see that I have brought a rabbit into existence by seeing that I have brought into existence an object of such and such shape, colour, furriness, etc. So to recognize that change has occurred, one has to recognize properties. But if properties are nothing but potentialities for contributing to causal powers, we have a vicious infinite regress.

For although one might be able on some one occasion to recognize straight off (without doing tests or observing effects) that an object had a certain causal power, one would only be justified in attributing the casual power to the object if one knew of the effects typically produced by similar objects on other occasions. One would only have grounds for saying that a liquid had the power to dissolve iron if it had been observed to dissolve iron in the past, or similar liquids had been observed to dissolve similar objects (e.g., metals) in the past, or some such thing. Claims to recognize powers and so potentialities to contribute to powers, need justification in terms of the effects which objects typically produce, and that involves justification in terms of the presence or absence of properties. But if properties are nothing but potentialities to contribute to powers, one could only justifiably attribute such properties to objects if one had observed their effects. And so ad infinitum. The regress is vicious.[3] Whereas if some properties have more to them than powers to bring about future effects, one may have some justification for attributing them to objects other than in terms of future effects, and so the regress can be broken. Maybe all judgements about the possession of properties are corrigible in the light of what happens in future, but we must have grounds for making them independent of future effects, if we are ever justifiably to start making them. There cannot be powers to produce things, unless there are things, other than powers which they produce – and no one can have any grounds for supposing that there are such, unless properties have more to them than powers.

But what more is there to properties than powers? In some cases we can see straight off what more there is. Which cases we judge these to be will depend on how phenomenalistically minded we are. There is quite a strain of phenomenalism in Shoemaker. He writes of our knowing 'properties by their effects, including, importantly, their effects on our sensory states' (p. 296) – as though one knew, as

[3] Contrary to what Shoemaker argues in his 'Causality and Properties', loc. cit, pp. 19 ff.

it were indirectly, that a thing was red, by its effects on our sensory states, which effects we are presumably aware of straight away. But in that case our sensory state being red (or us being in a state of being appeared to redly, or however one wishes to describe the situation) is not just a matter of it having been caused in a certain way (e.g., by an object reflecting light of such and such wavelength) or having certain effects (e.g., causing me to say that it is 'red'). For if I had an inverted spectrum (viz., if blue things looked to me the way red things look to most people, and conversely), the property would be different and yet the causes and effects could remain the same. True, as Shoemaker has argued elsewhere,[4] our subsequent judgements about whether a sensory experience was red will depend on its effects (e.g. on our memory); and our ability to recognize redness may depend in part on its having lawlike connections with other properties; but the nature of the property does not consist in such potentialities – as we can see by reflecting on it where we are aware or it; and as we can also see by reflecting on the infinite regress which results if we suppose that this holds for red and other observable properties, and by reflecting that there is no reason for supposing that it holds for red and nor for other observable properties.

For myself I do not hold that in any sense we often observe straight off the properties of our sensations, and certainly I do not hold that that is all we observe. What normally stares me in the face is not that something looks red, but that it is red; not that it feels square but that it is. So the redness and squareness of objects are among the properties which we observe straight off. I do not wish to argue here exactly which objects we observe straight off, but clearly we observe some objects straight off; and since one cannot observe anything without observing some of its properties, there are some properties which we observe straight off. If these are the redness and squareness of physical objects, rather than properties of sensations, we can see just by looking what more there is to such properties than the causes which produce them and the effects to which they give rise. That there is something more we can see by the fact that the world would be a different world if all the blue objects were red and all the red objects blue, and if the causal relations of redness became those of blueness, and conversely (e.g., blue objects reflected light of the wavelength currently reflected by red objects, and conversely). Once again, I do not wish to deny the points which

---

[4] 'Phenomenal Similarity', *Critica* 7 (1975), 3–34.

Shoemaker makes that our judgements about which properties objects have depend in part on their observed effects. To take a case most favourable to Shoemaker – I may initially judge that an object is square, but if I put it on a gentle slope and, apparently, it rolls downhill, I argue that surely it cannot have been square. Our judgement about whether the object is square is very much at the mercy of subsequent events. Yes, but how do I know that it rolled downhill? 'I saw it'; 'other people saw it'; we 'could not have been mistaken.' But then we affirm our judgement, that it did roll downhill because we are highly confident of our recognition of it rolling downhill, and that involves confidence that we recognize its distinguishing properties (in an object at the top of the hill and then in an object at the bottom of the hill) straight off. One judgement that I immediately observe some property is corrected by another, and that indeed can happen if my initial confidence in the latter is greater than my initial confidence in the former. But I only give up one judgement about properties on the basis of effects if I have greater confidence in another judgement about properties not based on effects. (And if I had great and equal confidence in both judgements in my example, I would have to claim that the object had changed its shape before being put on the slope.) The fact that our judgements about properties are corrigible in the light of subsequent developments does not mean that talk about properties is talk about those subsequent developments – as, once again, we can see from my example and from reflecting on the infinite regress which results if we suppose otherwise. Nor again do I wish to deny that we might not recognize properties which do not have lawlike connections – but again that does not mean that such properties do not exist, nor that talk about properties is always just talk about those lawlike connections. Nor of course do I wish to deny that things have causal powers, and that *some* properties involve causal powers.

How has Shoemaker come to adopt his dubious thesis? I do not know. But I have a suspicion that he would like an account of the world which makes the regularity of the behaviour of things a less mysterious matter. As he says on p. 299, his account has the consequence that from the very existence of properties it follows that there are causal laws. 'We can dismiss *a priori* the account of the world, call it the "null account" which says that there are no laws of nature.' But he is wrong if he is saying that a null or chaotic world is not a logically possible world. Indeed, almost all logically possible worlds are chaotic worlds. It is true that we could have virtually no knowledge of the world unless there were causal regularities, through knowledge of which we can check particular knowledge-claims and extend our knowledge beyond the immediately observable. Indeed, we could not exist as embodied beings unless there were such laws; our bodies would rapidly disintegrate. But all that follows from this is that if we exist in embodied form and have knowledge, there are causal laws linking property-instantiations with each other. And so given that we know that we have bodies and knowledge we can dismiss *a priori* the suggestion that our world is a chaotic world. But it remains no less mysterious that it is an ordered world, in which properties are instantiated in accord with logically contingent regularities; and no less mysterious that induction is ever successful.

Shoemaker is not the only writer to have argued that properties are simply causal potentialities. Achinstein has argued for this thesis, although with very much greater hesitation.[5] The thesis is one of very general interest. For example, if true, it would justify some of the often unargued intuitions of mind–brain identity theorists – e.g., that having a blue after-image is the same property as having certain c-fibres firing. It is in consequence of general importance to realize that it is false, and that the 'intuitions' remain unsupported by plausible theory.

[5] Peter Achinstein, 'The Identity of Properties', *Amer. Phil. Q.* 11 (1974), 257–75.

§21. Comments and Replies
The Shoemaker–Swinburne Session

MACKIE: Shoemaker has expressed his view by saying that the essential nature of a genuine property consists in its potentialities for contributing to the causal powers of the things that have it. This could mean either (A) that a property *just is* such a cluster of potentialities, or (B) that while a property is something more than this, there is a synthetic but necessary connection between the something more and the potentialities, so that each property must have just those potentialities which it has, and two properties never have exactly the same cluster of potentialities. Swinburne takes Shoemaker to be putting forward view A, and criticizes both this view and the rather verificationist arguments which support it. I agree with these criticisms, but I also want to argue that even if we accept A it would not do the work that Shoemaker wants it to do of taking some of the mystery out of induction, by showing that there could not be an utterly chaotic world. This would amount to some (fairly weak) form of the principle of the uniformity of nature, and I agree that something of this sort is needed as an intermediate step in the justification of induction. But view A will not achieve this. It makes it analytic that each property has such and such potentialities for contributing to causal powers, and that the same collection of properties cannot have different effects on different occasions, but in making this analytic, it makes it trivial and all but empty. The important, synthetic, and surely contingent truths are now located elsewhere – that things have properties in this sense, that a thing tends to go on having the same properties, and in particular that there are limits which there conceivably might not be on the actual instantiation of properties. For the world could still be chaotic, in that potentialities for contributing to causal powers might be collected in all logically possible combinations. Suppose that some property P is the cluster of potentialities a, b, c, d, and suppose that we find some instance of a, b, c, together. If d is also there, this will be an instance of P; if d is not there, it will be an instance of some other property, say Q. But will the co-occurrence of a, b, c, be any guarantee, or even indication, that d is there too? Not if P and Q are equally able and likely to occur. To ensure that there is more regularity in the world, what we need is not just that there are instances of properties in this sense, but that some of the logically possible clusters of potentialities do not occur – say, that if P occurs, Q does not – or at least that some of the possible clusters are markedly less frequent than others–say, that *P* occurs much more often than *Q*. In another paper, 'Causality and Properties',[1] Shoemaker has, indeed, considered a related objection to his thesis that causal laws are logically necessary. He examines but rejects the suggestion that, when propositions describing the causal potentialities of properties are, if true, logically necessary, there are also lawlike but contingent connections between 'conditional powers', that is, between the potentialities mentioned above. I can only say that so far as I understand his argument I find it quite unconvincing. It seems to me that it will be particularly these synthetic connections between different potentialities that will, on view *A*, constitute order as opposed to chaos, and there is nothing in *A* itself to ensure that there are such connections. It is contingent both that there are any such connections, and that there are the particular connections that there are, though it is, of course, plausible to argue that if there were no such connections we should not be able to recognize properties: we could not acquire knowledge of an utterly chaotic world.

The alternative view, *B*, is plainly not verificationist. It agrees with our ordinary assumption that powers and potentialities are grounded in intrinsic properties. (Again in 'Causality and Properties' Shoemaker claims that his view accommodates this belief, but again I find this claim unconvincing.) The 'necessity' of the connection between the intrinsic part of each property and its potentialities is now not logical, but is simply whatever causal necessity turns out to be. If there were an intrinsic feature on which the various potentialities rested, this would give some reason for expecting potentialities to cluster in the way required to make the world not utterly chaotic; conversely, finding such clustering provides some confirmation of the presence of such intrinsic features. The thesis that each intrinsic property and its potentialities are connected as *B* asserts is, indeed, a partial statement of causal determinism. If it holds, it holds contingently, and that it does hold will be an empirical discovery, for which we need and may be able to get supporting evidence, and which can then be used to bolster ordinary inductive reasoning. Altogether, then, I find view *B* much more attractive than view *A*. But I think Swinburne is right in taking *A* to be Shoemaker's view.

SHOEMAKER: 1. Swinburne and Mackie charge that my arguments for my theory of properties are 'verificationist'. They appear to have

[1] Loc. cit.

forgotten what verificationism is. What they here call verificationist are epistemological arguments of the form: (1) we know (or can know) facts of sort *F*; (2) if metaphysical thesis *M* were not true, it would be impossible to know facts of sort *F*; therefore (3) metaphysical thesis *M* is true. Arguments of this sort are often sound. And when they are not, this is not because they commit one to a verificationist theory of meaning, which they never do, but because they rest (as I think mine do not) on mistaken views about what is required for knowledge.

2. Swinburne's claim that there is 'quite a strain of phenomenalism' in my paper seems to be based mainly on his reading of my remark that 'we know things' properties by their effects, including, importantly, their effects on our sensory states', which he takes to imply that it is sensory states, and only sensory states, that we are aware of 'straight away'. But that implication certainly was not intended, and I am sorry if my use of 'know . . . by their effects' was misleading. As I intended that to be understood, knowing of a property-instantiation by knowing of (certain of) its effects is only one case of knowing a property 'by its effects'; another is that in which the causal chain by which a property-instantiation produces knowledge of its occurrence does not include the production of knowledge of something else from which its occurrence is inferred – and no doubt perceptual knowledge is often of this sort. I quite agree with Swinburne that 'the redness and squareness of objects are among the properties which we observe straight off'; but this is perfectly compatible with my account of properties, unless 'observing straight off' is taken to connote something which seems to me strictly impossible, namely an access to objects which is independent of their causal powers. Swinburne says that 'we can see just by looking what more there is to such properties [as redness and squareness] than the causes which produce them and the effects to which they give rise'. But I should have thought it obvious that any aspect of these properties that varied independently of their propensities to influence our sense-impressions, i.e., independently of how the objects look, feel, etc., to us, could not be revealed to us in sense perception. This is, of course, not to say that we know about such properties by *knowing* about our sense-impressions.

3. Swinburne's charge that my view gives rise to an infinite vicious regress is based on the misunderstanding just noted, i.e., his taking me to hold that knowledge of a property instantiation is in every case based on knowledge of its effects.

4. Swinburne invokes a version of Occam's razor, namely 'do not

multiply predicates beyond necessity', to refute my epistemological argument in favour of my theory of properties. He thinks that if we suppose, contrary to my theory, that it is not a necessary truth that properties having all the same causal potentialities are identical, it is still possible to explain how we can be justified in ascribing the same property to different things; this is to be done by appealing to considerations of simplicity. But it is worth noting that Swinburne's version of Occam's razor does not do for him what he thinks it does. Let us suppose, contrary to my view, that it is logically possible for different properties to share all of their causal potentialities. Swinburne's version of Occam's razor does not tell us to favour the view that this logical possibility is in fact not realized. What it tells us, in effect, is so to interpret our predicates that it makes no difference whether the possibility is realized or not. We can do this, for example, by viewing predicates as assigned to equivalence classes of properties (each consisting of properties which share all of their causal potentialities) rather than to individual properties, a predicate being true of a thing just in case the thing has any of the properties in the associated equivalence class. Given the supposition, this is eminently reasonable; but so interpreted Occam's razor does not serve as a guide for deciding how the world is, but rather as a guide for the semantic interpretation of our theories. And this leaves us with the question of how we know what we certainly think we know, and what we must know if we are ever to be in a position to know that a single property is shared by two or more things (or is retained by a thing over time), namely that properties that share all of their causal potentialities are identical. I do not see how any reasonable principle of simplicity can be used to answer this question once it has been allowed to arise – i.e., once it is held to be a logical possibility that we believe is false. But it seems evident to me that in fact we do not have any notion of difference of property that allows this question to arise, i.e., that allows that properties having the same causal potentialities may be different.

5. As best I can understand Mackie's *A* and *B*, neither of these views is my own. My view is not *B* if in claiming that a property is 'something more' than a cluster of potentialities it denies my claim that properties are identical (whether in the same possible world or in different ones) just in case they share all of the same causal potentialities. My view is not *A*, for Mackie makes it part of *A* that it is 'analytic that each property has such and such potentialities for contributing to causal powers', whereas on my view the necessity of the connection between being a certain property and having a

certain set of causal potentialities is *de re* necessity, and so of course not analytic. I am, however, willing to say that it is analytic that a property necessarily has the causal potentialities it has – as long as it is understood that the 'necessarily' in that statement is not to be explained in terms of analyticity. Mackie apparently thinks that in making this latter claim analytic my view makes it trivial. But this is a mistake; whether a claim is trivial has to do with its relation to what is already known, and has nothing to do with its logical status. What Mackie goes on to say, about the contingency of the ways in which causal potentialities cluster together, is something I argue to be false in my paper 'Causality and Properties', to which Mackie refers. Mackie says that he finds my argument unconvincing; but he gives no counter-argument, and I have not the space to repeat the argument.

SWINBURNE: I do not think that Shoemaker has avoided the basic point of my infinite regress argument by his claim that the necessity that the property has the essential causal potentialities which it has, is necessity *de re*. The point is that if we are to have grounds for saying that the same property P is instantiated, this will be because we can detect non-inferentially some property Q which is connected with P. We must have grounds for saying that Q is instantiated other than grounds in terms of other properties connected with Q (e.g., properties of effects). Otherwise we could never begin to ascribe properties. But we could not have such grounds unless there were more to properties than their causal potentialities.

Shoemaker asks whether I think that there could be a world in which the properties which figure in laws are grue-like relative to the properties which figure in laws in the actual world. I believe that 'grue' is intrinsically a positional predicate (see my *An Introduction to Confirmation Theory* (1973), p. 105). If laws must contain only qualitative predicates, the answer is No. But if laws may contain positional predicates, the answer is Yes. In that case however before the crucial time (e.g., A.D. 2000), we would have reasons of simplicity, (qualitative predicates are simpler than positional ones), for believing that the laws were not grue-like. The essential positionality of 'grue' is a perfectly adequate reason for not projecting 'grue'. We do not need Shoemaker's strong thesis.

I am glad that all that Shoemaker meant by (p. 296) 'we know things' properties by their effects' was 'we know the properties of things by knowing their effects.' Ordinary language would suggest a different interpretation – see 'by their fruits ye shall know them' or

'I knew that he was at home by the light in the window,' etc. I was not wishing to deny the evident truth of Shoemaker's remark under the former interpretation. Hence the fact that we know about properties because they have effects on our sense impressions in no way casts doubt on the truth of my remark that 'we can see just by looking what more there is to such properties [as redness and squareness] than the causes which produce them and the effects to which they give rise'. What we see no doubt we see because we are caused to see, but what we see is not that we are caused to see.

SHOEMAKER: In his further remarks Swinburne replies to a question I raised (at the conference) by saying that we can explain the unprojectibility of 'grue' by the fact that it is 'intrinsically' a positional predicate, and so do not need my 'strong thesis' to explain this. Now as Goodman has pointed out, on one criterion of positionality 'grue' is not positional (no time indicator occurs in it), while on another criterion every predicate is positional (every predicate has a definitional expansion in which a temporal indicator occurs). I do agree with Swinburne that there is a deeper sense in which 'grue' is positional and 'green' is not, and such that being positional in that sense counts against projectibility; but I think that being positional in that sense is just being 'grue'-like relative to predicates that stand for properties that are genuine in my sense. If Swinburne denies the latter claim, he must apparently allow the possibility of worlds – call them 'grue-worlds' – in which it is the positional rather than the nonpositional predicates that figure in laws (in which, for example, the roles *vis à vis* laws of 'grue' and 'green' are switched). Would the denizens of such a world be able to identify the positional predicates as such? It is hard to see how they could, since, among other things, in such a world it is positional rather than non-positional predicates that would be ostensively teachable and learnable. Or would the denizens of grue-worlds mistake positional predicates for non-positional ones, thereby dooming themselves to a history of successful projection of unprojectible (because positional) predicates? But if a 'mistake' of the latter sort is possible, what makes Swinburne so sure that *we* do not regularly make one? The answer can't be that it is 'simpler' to suppose that we don't.

MELLOR: Shoemaker's causal theory of the genuine properties of changeable things (i.e., substances in one standard sense, as opposed to events) offers to help with induction by supplying a basis for projecting predicates that name them and indeed assuring us that the predicates we project name such properties if they name any at all. I think the theory fails; its appearance of success stemming from the crucial respect in which it differs from a dispositional theory of the same properties which I gave in my 'In Defense of Dispositions', *Phil. Rev.* (1974). I argued there that only dispositional predicates of things are (or can be) used to describe properties, and that the identities of properties are given by theories saying what may or may not be invoked in causal explanation. Thus Newtonian inertial mass is one property, despite its conjoining an infinity of dispositions to accelerate under forces infinitely diverse in strength and direction, because the theory proscribes invoking a change in some of these dispositions to explain a change in others. Trivial matters of terminology apart, Shoemaker's theory only really differs from this in that he takes predicates like 'mass' to designate properties rigidly *à la* Kripke, whereas I take them to describe these properties more or less completely and hold a 'cluster' version of the description theory of property names. (My grounds for rejecting Kripke's account of property names are in my 'Natural Kinds', *Brit. J. Phil. Sci.* (1977); here I want not to pursue the dispute but to note its present relevance.) The immediately relevant consequence is that, for Shoemaker but not for me, genuine properties necessarily have the potentialities they do have to contribute to the causal powers of the things that have them. Hence predicates that rigidly designate such properties are projectible; those that don't aren't. For me, by contrast, projectibility depends on laws linking applications of dispositional predicates, and there is no necessity in that. Something has a Newtonian mass of m Kg only if for all positive real n a force of n Newton in any direction would accelerate it in that direction at n/m metres/sec². Now there is no more necessity either in or asserted by that conditional than there is in or asserted by one saying that any philosopher crossing the Atlantic these days would fly. Even if true, these conditionals don't claim that things and philosophers couldn't move about otherwise, merely that they wouldn't; and even if true, they're not necesarily true.

In saying this, I haven't overlooked Shoemaker's Kripkean concept of laws as being, if true, metaphysically necessary; I deny it. That a given mass can't change its inertial consequences follows from mass being a property and thus a universal, not from the laws involved being necessary. The laws involved, being already indifferent to time, can't change in truth-value, though they can turn out false, with counter-examples only cropping up after the year 2000. It doesn't follow from this truism that laws if true are necessary; any more than my inability to change the place of my birth shows I couldn't have been born somewhere else.

In particular, the inertial laws of Newton's theory could hold of something at one time, and enough of them fail at another for no mass predicate to apply to it. That is, a thing could have some Newtonian mass or other at one time and, at another, fail entirely to have any such mass (not even zero). That mass is a property which all things have at all times, and that change in this property has causal consequences, follows merely from the truth of natural laws and the way we group them together for explanatory purposes: laws such as the ones I cited, and others linking inertial mass to other, e.g. electrical or gravitational, phenomena. But the lawlikeness of such generalizations is a consequence (or restatement) of the projectibility of the predicate 'mass' (and others). So, on my view of these matters, it is lawlikeness and projectibility which provide the basis for distinguishing genuinely causal properties and changes from 'mere Cambridge' ones; not the other way round.

SHOEMAKER: Mellor apparently agrees with me that the causal potentialities of genuine properties cannot change over time, but rejects my 'Kripkean' contention that the causal potentialities are essential to it (and hence that causal laws are, when true, metaphysically necessary). He correctly senses that I would like to argue from the immutability of the causal potentialities of a property to their essentiality, and objects (in effect) that the former no more implies the latter than 'my inability to change the place of my birth shows I couldn't have been born somewhere else.' But let us consider the claim that I could have been born somewhere else. It seems clear that our acceptance, and understanding, of this claim depends on our being able to conceive of a possible history which branches off from my actual history at some point before my birth and includes my being, at the time of birth, at a place different from that at which I was in fact born – e.g., a possible history in which my parents moved to Montana between the time of my conception and the time of my birth. To say that I might have been an existentialist is to envisage other possible histories branching off my actual history – here, perhaps, the branching could be postnatal. What is important here is that there is a close linkage between identity across time and identity across possible worlds; the ways in which a given sort of thing can be different in different possible worlds depend on the ways in which such a thing can be different at different times within a single world. While nothing can of course undergo change with respect to such historical properties as having been born in Idaho, the fact that some of the historical properties of a thing could have been different (are different in different possible worlds) depends on the fact that change with respect to certain other properties (in this case location) is possible. Now let's move from the case of particulars to the case of properties. A property can vary across time, and so across possible worlds, with respect to such 'extrinsic' features as being Johnny's favorite colour, or being the colour of the sky. But if, as I hold and Mellor apparently agrees, a property cannot vary across time with respect to its causal potentialities, this at least strongly suggests that a property cannot have different causal potentialities in different possible worlds. However, this argument needs to be supplemented by an argument against the view that for each property there is a proper subset of its causal potentialities that constitutes an 'individual essence' of it, i.e., is such that the having of the causal potentialities in that subset is, in any possible world, necessary and sufficient for being that property, and that there are causal potentialities of the property which do not belong to that proper subset and are not essential to the property. I argue against the latter view in 'Casuality and Properties'; the argument is a close relative of the one Mackie found unconvincing.

HESSE: Shoemaker proposes to make a 'metaphysical' distinction between 'genuine' and 'mere Cambridge' properties etc. Metaphysics, unlike 'induction', is obviously now a clean word among philosophers of science. But the power of the conclusions drawn from its exploitation is enough to take an unreconstructed empiricist's breath away. Shoemaker recognizes, as we all do, the need for frameworks or principles other than the empirical in order to make sense of scientific inference. He argues, and I would follow him here too, that the modalities of cause, law, necessity, natural kind, 'genuine property', etc., are interdefinable and not reducible to non-modal concepts. But I would ask whether the task cannot be much more economically performed without talk of 'metaphysics', by openly recognizing that the distinctions to be drawn are distinctions defined *within some scientific theory-framework or other*, and are not analytically independent of all science. For example, Shoemaker apparently has an intuition that knife-shaped things do not have any causal power in common, and uses this to show that 'knife-shaped' is not a single 'genuine property' (p. 294). But how can he possibly *know* there is no causal power in common here except relative to some particular ontology of matter which lists all the fundamental entities and properties and their powers? Such fundamental ontologies are notoriously subject to change with changing scientific theories. Again, Shoemaker lists a number of still outstanding problems (pp. 300–2), including criteria for distinguishing coincidentality from causality, and for excluding the possibility of spatial or temporal action at a distance, and confesses that he lacks an account which gives a comprehensive answer to all of these problems. But how could a philosopher as such possibly have such an account? For all such problems are greatly in dispute as between different fundamental scientific theories. The theories are decidable, if at all, on empirical and regulative grounds which are far from arm-chair metaphysics.

Shoemaker does indeed accept the view that causality is relative to the 'best explanation', that is to previously accepted hypotheses and laws. As an account of induction this is either blatantly circular or a withdrawal to a much more modest view of the modalities as relative to our science, together with the more controversial belief that our science is, by and large, 'genuine' knowledge. The dispute might now move to the issue of whether our *theoretical* science (as opposed to instrumental pragmatics) is in its essence permanent and true, or whether it is subject to conceptual revolutions of the kind science has been through in the past. I will not pursue this dispute now. But if this *is* the real issue, it is astounding that Shoemaker makes much stronger claims for his modalities at the end of the paper, namely, if I have understood him, that there can be no language with sense and reference unless its predicate terms are 'genuine', with all the necessary and analytic overtones he has argued that this has. If I am right this claim would have to be made out, and the types of causal modality specifically identified, in relation to each specific framework, including its natural language. Shoemaker has given no argument whatsoever for believing that it can be shown a priori for every natural language as such.

SHOEMAKER: Hesse misunderstood what I said about 'knife-shaped'. Far from denying that this is a 'genuine' property, I offered it as a paradigm of one. Nor was my claim that there is no causal power a thing has simply in virtue of being knife-shaped offered as something known *a priori*. It is not even essential for me to insist on its truth. My purpose was simply to make the point that often a thing has a causal power in virtue of having a combination of different properties, each making its distinctive contribution to the having of the power; this was with a view to introducing the notion of a causal potentiality of a property (the potentiality of making such a contribution) and the claim that the causal potentialities of a property constitute its essential nature. Another misunderstanding is reflected in Hesse's saying that I 'accept the view that causality is relative to the "best explanation", that is to previously accepted hypotheses and laws'; I did claim that induction involves inference to the best explanation, but this was not any sort of relativity claim, and certainly not one about causality. As for the central theme of her remarks, while I am inclined to deny that the distinctions I was concerned with in my paper are 'defined *within some scientific theory-framework or other*, and are not analytically independent of all science', I think it is in fact not at all clear what this means.

MARGALIT: Let us imagine a community of Grue native speakers in which Professor Gruemaker advocates a distinction between genuine properties and pseudo-properties ('mere-Cambridge' ones). Grue, he claims, is a property; Green a mere-Cambridge property.

Shoemaker's response to our thought experiment is that in another paper he has shown that there cannot exist a community of native speakers of Grue. Had Professor Shoemaker indeed succeeded in showing that, he would be very much in the position of the officer who started to list a hundred reasons why his soldiers had not fired. First: they had no ammunition; Second: well, if you have no ammunition that's reason enough. Likewise if there are 'logical reasons' why a Gruese-speaking community cannot coherently be imagined to exist then that settles it. In such a case the notion of genuine property is parasitic on the notion of the genuine projectibility of the appropriate predicate.

But this is not Shoemaker's line. His explanation why his Doppelgänger Gruemaker can't talk Gruese coherently is based on the way language works, and this in turn is based on considerations which have to do with causality, not with logic. The way I understand his argument is that some predicates (observational perhaps) acquire meaning and reference only to the extent that there are 'reliably detectable cases' in which these predicates apply. But then clear cases (detectable cases) are such because there are causal relations between a property, say green, and its effect on the observer. So the impossibility of a native Gruese-speaking community is ultimately an outcome of the distinction between genuine properties and mere-Cambridge ones. That seems to be Professor Shoemaker's line.

I have two reactions to the above argument. First, the principle of 'reliably detectable cases' seems to be unreliable as far as meanings (intensions) of predicates are concerned. This I think has become amply clear from the literature against the Paradigm-Case-Argument. However, supposing that Shoemaker's defence will be that his principle is confined only to observational predicates (colour terms), I shall grant him his principle with this limited applicability, and shall move into my second claim. There are, I submit, clear cases for the application of 'grue' *today*. They are the reliably detected cases of green (from a Green-speaking community's point of view). Moreover I am not clear as to the reasons why 'grue' does not have a 'determinate contribution to causal powers', especially when the issue is presented from Gruemaker's point of view.

I find Professor Shoemaker's paper genuinely interesting, not mere-Cambridgely so. But if the claim that Gruemaker cannot coherently be supposed to talk Gruese has been argued and supported in another place, then – at least as far as the issue of projectibility goes – there is a sense in which one may say that Professor Shoemaker has presented us not so much with a paper which is wrong but rather with the wrong paper.

SHOEMAKER: Margalit suggests that I presented the conference 'not so much with a paper which is wrong but rather with the wrong paper'. Perhaps so; but in order to give what he would regard as the 'right paper' I would have had to repeat the arguments of a paper already in print ('On Projecting the Unprojectible' – see footnote 12 on page 309 of my paper in the present volume), and I assumed that that was not what I had been invited to do.

8

Computer Programs for Inductive Reasoning

§22. TERRY WINOGRAD
Extended Inference Modes in Reasoning by Computer Systems

This paper describes and discusses some computer reasoning systems which have been the result of research in Artificial Intelligence. It analyses their formal properties in the context of deductive logic, demonstrating the ways in which they embody systems of 'extended inference'. In such a system, the form and activity of the reasoning process plays an explicit role in the characterization of the possible inferences. This self-referential semantics leads to systems which have quite different properties from standard logical systems, and which offer new directions in understanding the problems of reasoning with ill-specified or informally defined information.

Introduction

One view of formal logic is that it is an attempt to answer the question '*What formal systems can we construct that operate in a well-defined way to carry out reasoning of the sort we observe in people?*' In artificial intelligence research, we build programs which in some interesting way duplicate the function of human intelligence. In doing so, we are not bound to follow any of the standard logical formalisms, and in fact we are interested in modelling the kinds of informal, imprecise, and possibly inconsistent reasoning which characterize human thought. We do so by building systems which are not abstract formal systems, but computer programs for carrying out reasoning in limited domains. Viewed as computational mechanisms, they operate according to precise computational rules and can be studied within the theory of computation. However, they can also be viewed at a different level of analysis as carrying out forms of inference which do not fit within the truth-theoretic semantics of deductive logic.

Inductive logic, in its various forms, has also dealt with non-deductive inference, considering evidence for conclusions which cannot be derived with deductive certainty. It has tended to concentrate on techniques which apply best to situations where more and more evidence can be accumulated, and the formal system can guarantee convergence to correct hypotheses in the limit. In general, the various forms of inductive logic (including Bayesian statistical reasoning, and enumerative induction) are applied to reasoning situations in which the sets of alternatives (and perhaps the prior probabilities) are given before the method is applied. The question of how a situation is broken up into distinct features or alternatives lies beyond (or perhaps before) the questions which are dealt with in the formal theory. Inductive logic has also not traditionally dealt with the problem of the acceptance of a conclusion which is not certain. In a practical situation, it is often necessary to act as if a particular conclusion were true, even though the formal rules of evidence can do no more than assign it a plausibility or demonstrate that it has not yet been falsified.

In artificial intelligence, we are faced with situations in which the demands of problem analysis and practical decision-making are quite different from those of careful scientific induction which are the typical inspiration for inductive logic. We are faced with problems of common-sense reasoning, rather than the rational investigations of high science in which experiments can be carefully controlled and repeated. Our goal is to design systems which are 'rational' in some sense of that word, even though they operate with ill-defined or informally defined information, and must choose actions without the luxury of unlimited information-seeking.

This characterization does not apply to all artificial intelligence programs. There are some such as the MYCIN program[1] which implement a formal calculus of evidence and belief much like those discussed by Cohen in this volume. Others (such as much of the classical work on medical diagnosis) fit squarely within the Bayesian tradition, and still others (such as Mitchell's work on hypothesis formation in chemistry) are pure 'Popperians' in their emphasis on the deductive falsification of hypotheses. However, there is a large class of programs which are directed at the kinds of problems suggested in the paragraphs above. They operate in a domain of common-sense reasoning, and emphasize the problems of choosing actions in a situation of partial knowledge. For the most part, these programs operate without benefit of formal clarity. They use *ad hoc* techniques which work for selected cases, but which are not amenable to a formal semantic analysis.

This paper describes and discusses some of these computer reasoning systems, looking at the formal assumptions implicit in them, in an attempt to formulate a broader perspective on what they are doing. On careful analysis, they can be viewed as implementing a kind of 'extended inference', in which the form and activity of the

[1] E. Shortliffe and B. G. Buchanan, 'A Model of Approximate Reasoning in Medicine', *Math. Biosciences* 23 (1975), 351–79.

reasoning process play an explicit role in the characterization of the inferences which can be made. This self-referential semantics leads to systems which have quite different properties from standard logical systems. A thorough understanding of these extensions will have to come through further research into the semantics of active inferential systems.

The Axiomatization of Action and Situations

An important part of the background for most of the systems described here is *situation calculus* for axiomatizing sequences of actions and their effects. This formalism was proposed by Green[2] and developed in its best known form by McCarthy and Hayes.[3] The central idea is to include *situations* in the ontological basis for the axiomatization (along with the physical objects, locations, etc. needed for the particular domain). For example, the fact that object $\underline{A}$ is at location $\underline{L}$ is represented $At(\underline{A}, \underline{L}, \underline{S})$ where $\underline{S}$ is a constant standing for a situation. Actions are expressed in terms of a finite set of primitive *operators*. An operator is a function one of whose arguments is a situation and whose value is a situation. The domain of an operator is limited to the set of situations that meet its *preconditions*. The set of all situations is a subset of the free algebra generated by the operators on a unique initial situation S_0. In a typical robot planning system, there would be operators such as MOVE(object, newLocation, situation) with axioms[4] such as:

$$\forall \text{obj},\text{loc},\text{sit At(obj, loc, MOVE(obj, loc, sit))} \tag{1}$$

$$\forall \text{obj}_1,\text{obj}_2,\text{loc}_1,\text{loc}_2,\text{sit} \tag{2}$$
$$\text{At(obj}_1, \text{loc}_1, \text{sit)} \land \neg \text{ obj}_1 = \text{obj}_2 \supset$$
$$\text{At(obj}_1, \text{loc}_1, \text{MOVE(obj}_2, \text{loc}_2, \text{sit))}$$

For each operator, there is a set of *frame axioms*, which characterize the *frame* that remains fixed while an action takes place

---

[2] Cordell Green, 'Application of Theorem Proving to Problem Solving', *Proceedings of the First International Joint Conference on Artificial Intelligence* (1969).

[3] J. McCarthy and P. J. Hayes, 'Some Philosophical Problems from the Standpoint of Artificial Intelligence'. In Meltzer and Michie (eds.), *Machine Intelligence* 4 (1969), 463–502.

[4] Those unfamiliar with artificial intellegence formalisms may be a bit uncomfortable with the ways in which the problems are mapped on to axiomatic logic. In order to make deductions based on knowledge about a world (e.g. the physical world of objects and motions of a robot) the system must start with a large body of axioms expressing its 'knowledge of the world'. These include not only the general laws, but also all of the specific facts. The criteria of simplicity and orthogonality that are applied to sets of axioms in mathematics are relevant only weakly if at all. One thinks in terms of systems with hundreds or thousands (for a broadly intelligent system, possibly millions) of axioms.

within it. Axiom (2), for example, states that an action which does not explicitly move an object leaves that object in its original place. The need for these axioms leads to the *frame problem* for systems that use the situation calculus for planning. Roughly, the problem is that to establish any proposition of the form P(obj, sit), it is necessary to prove (using the frame axioms) that it is true in the situation sit by chaining back through the entire set of operators that generated the situation, regardless of whether they had anything to do with obj or not. In many computer systems which use uniform deduction methods, the computational effort needed to produce a proof is exponentially related to its length, making the planning of all but the shortest sequences of operators impractical.

There are many issues that can be raised about this style of axiomatization. Note, for example, that two situations are identical if and only if they were produced by the exact sequence of operators (in the same order). Also, there is no simple way to talk about continuous changes, changes that take place over time (e.g. that overlap other changes), or to deal with simultaneous actions by multiple actors. However, it is not the intent of this paper to argue the merits of different schemes for axiomatizing action. This particular one is described because of its wide use in AI, in particular in the systems described here.

The STRIPS Formalism – Explicit Manipulation of Propositions

One of the first systems to combine formal logic with extended inference modes in a systematic way was STRIPS.[5] A STRIPS problem domain (such as the physical world of a particular kind of robot) is represented by a combination of general axioms for dealing with the properties of objects, space, etc. and specific axioms representing an initial situation. A subset of the specific axioms are stored in a *data base*[6] – a set of formulas satisfying:

> *One and only one situation constant appears in the formula. It may appear more than once (i.e., in several different terms).*

> *There are no variables appearing as situation arguments.*

[5] R. Fikes and N. Nilsson, 'STRIPS: A New Approach to the Application of Theorem Proving to Problem Solving', *Artificial Intelligence* 2 (1971), 189–208

[6] In any inferential system it is necessary to distinguish between those things that are 'true' in the domain it describes, and those that are 'provable' according to its rules of inference. In dealing with a computational reasoning system, it is useful to distinguish further between a 'knowledge base' (the set of formulas explicitly available in memory) and a 'data base' (a subset of these formulas treated specially, in that the inference procedures may explicitly depend on the presence or absence of formulas).

Because of these restrictions, each formula in the data base can be thought of as saying something about a particular situation. Formulas which quantify over situations, or which include two different situation constants are not allowed.[7] In general, the inferences required of the system involve a single situation.

Instead of having axioms like (1) and (2) above, the STRIPS formalism has associated with each operator, a *precondition list*, an *add list*, and a *delete list*. Each of these lists is a conjunction of formulas each of which contains free variables corresponding to the arguments of the operator, a single free variable corresponding to a situation, and (in the case of the delete list) arbitrary free variables not used as situation arguments. An operator can be applied to a set of arguments (one of which is a situation, called the starting situation) only when its preconditions are all provable when instantiated with those arguments. If it is applicable, there is a new situation generated by the operator (called the *resulting situation*), and new propositions are added to the data base:

For each formula in the add list, add to the data base an instantiation, with the resulting situation instantiating its situation variable.

For each formula in the data base that has the starting situation as an argument, create a new proposition, substituting the resulting situation for it. If this new proposition is an instantiation of a term on the delete list (with any assignments for the free variables that were not arguments to the operator) then ignore it. Otherwise, add it to the data base.

In a typical STRIPS application, there might be a primitive operator like that of (3):

Operator: $\underline{\text{MOVE(obj, loc, sit)}}$ (3)
Preconditions: $\underline{\text{HasControl(robot, obj, sit)} \wedge \text{InRange(robot, loc, sit)}}$
Add list: $\underline{\text{At(obj, loc, sit)} \wedge \text{At(robot, loc, sit)}}$
Delete list: $\underline{\text{At(obj, x, sit)} \wedge \text{At(robot, y, sit)}}$.

---

[7] In fact, the system does not store a complete explicit data base of this form. Since each formula refers to exactly one situation, and since situations are related by the sequence of operators being built into a plan, the system maintains a data base for only one situation at a time (the current farthest step of its plan). The situation variable is implicit in the state of the computation rather than explicitly stated in the memory structure corresponding to the formulas. This, together with appropriate information for regenerating the data bases corresponding to other situations as needed, greatly reduces the storage needs. Much of the computational advantage of STRIPS and similar systems comes from the use of a computation state as an implicit situation variable. In this paper I have suppressed discussion of this device, since it does not affect the logical properties of the system in terms of the set of inferences it will draw.

The activity associated with the add and delete lists cannot be formalized in first-order logic, since it depends on quantification over the formulas in the data. There is a crucial distinction between formulas in the data base, and those derivable from it. Given appropriate axioms and the locations of obj_1 and obj_2 in a situation sit, we might derive $LeftOf(obj_1, obj_2, sit)$. If OP is an operator whose preconditions are satisfied by sit, we cannot infer $LeftOf(obj_1, obj_2, OP(sit))$ from the fact that the delete list associated with OP does not contain a term with the predicate $LeftOf$. The logical consistency of the system depends on the fact that the data base can only include formulas that are in the initial data base (given as part of the axiomatization) or that are explicitly included in an add list. In general, this has been managed by keeping only simple terms in the data base. In most applications, the only predicates in the data base are the *primitives* (such as locations) from which other predicates (such as physical support relationships) can be derived.[8]

Micro Planner

MicroPlanner[9] is based on Hewitt's[10] Planner formalism, and has been widely used in robot planning.[11] A MicroPlanner system uses a data base which is similar to that of STRIPS, but restricted to single-term propositions. A program includes subroutines, called 'theorems',[12] of three classes, called *antecedent, erasing,* and *consequent*. Each theorem is associated with a *pattern*, a term containing arbitrary free variables. The body of each theorem is a piece of program code, which can use the primitives ASSERT and ERASE to add and remove propositions from the data base.

From a formal point of view, little can be said about the conclusions that the system draws, since arbitrary calculations can be

---

[8] See R. Fikes, 'Knowledge Representation in Automatic Planning Systems', in Anita Jones (ed.), *Perspectives on Computer Science* (1977), for further discussion of these issues.

[9] G. Sussman, T. Winograd, and E. Charniak, *Micro-Planner Reference Manual* (AIM-203) (1970).

[10] C. Hewitt, 'Description and Theoretical Analysis (using schemata) of PLANNER: A Language for Proving Theorems and Manipulating Models in a Robot'. Ph.D. Thesis (June 1971) (Reprinted in AI-TR-258 MIT-AI Laboratory, April 1972.)

[11] e.g. T. Winograd, *Understanding Natural Language* (1972).

[12] This terminology is unfortunate, since MicroPlanner theorems are quite different from the objects of formal logic, and if anything are closer to being specialized inferences rules than to being theorems. I have used the original terminology here, since it is standard in discussions of these programs, but have enclosed the word 'theorem' in quotes to remind the reader that it is being used in a non-standard way.

included that are not based on systematic rules of inference.[13] In practice, theorems have been used in limited ways that can be understood in terms of extended inference rules related to those of STRIPS. The standard uses are:

(1) *Consequent 'theorems' corresponding to inferences.* The Micro-Planner system does not have a general inference mechanism that applies inference rules to formulas to generate new formulas. Instead, the programmer provides a 'theorem' for each inference to be done. Formally, we can view the system as having only single-term formulas, and having a multitude of separate specialized inference rules. The fact that *'All French or English crows are black'* might be represented (in a simplified version of the original MicroPlanner syntax):

$$\text{(CONSEQUENT (Black ?}x) \qquad\qquad (4)$$
$$\text{(GOAL (Crow ?}x))$$
$$\text{(OR (GOAL (French ?}x))$$
$$\text{(GOAL (English ?}x))))$$

This 'theorem' is interpreted as the inference procedure: *'In order to prove that X is black, first prove that it is a crow. If that succeeds, then try to prove that it is French, and if that fails try to prove that it is English.'*[14] Although the notation resembles formal logic, (with some special syntactic conventions, such as marking variables with the prefix '?', and expressing conjunction implicitly by the inclusion of a sequence of formulas), it differs in that the order of the terms is significant. A theorem is specific to a direction of inference, and cannot be used by the system for other inferences (e.g., in this case, to prove that a non-black crow is not English). In addition to the

---

[13] Critics such as P. J. Hayes, 'In Defense of Logic', *Proceedings of the Fifth International Joint Conference on Artificial Intelligence* (1977), pp. 559–65, have pointed out the weakness of MicroPlanner and similar systems in not having a well-specified semantics. It is clear that MicroPlanner is quite *ad hoc* and its reasoning hard to specify precisely. This presentation is not intended to justify the details of the system, but to point out some of the issues it raised. In fact, the description here is a cleaned up version that ignores many of the complexities. I have avoided issues that do not bear on the fundamental questions of inference with which this paper is concerned.

[14] The use of these 'theorems' is recursive – e.g., there might be others that tell how to infer that something is a crow. There are many complexities in the language for specifying the sequencing of steps in a 'theorem'. They include the ability to write more than one 'theorem' for a given predicate and to call these in non-deterministic programs (i.e. ones that involve making arbitrary choices). The possible inference chains are explored through a mechanism known as *backtracking*, which is a method for systematically exhaustively exploring the possible combination of choices.

direction of reasoning, the specific order in which sub-parts are attempted follows the order of the theorem. Much of the debate about AI reasoning systems has centered around the advantages and disadvantages of explicit procedural specification of inferences.[15] The ability to include specific inference processes avoids many of the combinatorial problems of general deductive engines, but at the cost of limiting the set of inferences that can be made. As with other issues mentioned above, this one need not concern us here. In most uses, each theorem corresponds to an inference that could be made with standard inference rules and a formula corresponding to the body of the 'theorem' by straightforward translation. The key point is that the system can perform only some of the inferences which we would expect given the corresponding formulas and standard inference rules.

(2) *Consequent theorems corresponding to operators.* A second use of consequent theorems is to represent primitive operators of the type described in the section above. The preconditions, add list, and delete list of an operator are concatenated into a 'theorem' such as:

$$(\underline{\text{CONSEQUENT (MOVE ?obj ?loc)}} \qquad (5)$$
$$\underline{\text{(EXISTS (?x ?y)}}$$
$$\underline{\text{(GOAL (HasControl Robot ?obj))}}$$
$$\underline{\text{(GOAL (InRange Robot ?loc))}}$$
$$\underline{\text{(GOAL (At Robot ?x))}}$$
$$\underline{\text{(GOAL (At ?obj ?y))}}$$
$$\underline{\text{(ERASE (At Robot ?x))}}$$
$$\underline{\text{(ERASE (At ?obj ?y))}}$$
$$\underline{\text{(ASSERT (At Robot ?loc))}}$$
$$\underline{\text{(ASSERT (At ?obj ?loc))))}}$$

The sequential nature of MicroPlanner means that none of the actions on the data base specified in (5) would be executed unless the initial GOAL conditions are met. The net result is like the data base manipulations of STRIPS. The situation is not mentioned explicitly in the propositions, but is implicit in the computational structure. The state of the data base at any point in the computation

---

[15] See, for example, the discussion in T. Winograd, 'Frames and the Declarative-Procedural Controversy', in D. Bobrow and A. Collins (eds.), *Representation and Understanding* (1978), and in P. J. Hayes, op. cit.

corresponds to some situation.[16] Any proposition in the data base corresponding to a given situation remains in the data base following the application of a theorem of this sort (unless explicitly erased), and is taken as applying to the situation resulting from the corresponding operator.

(3) *Antecedent and erasing theorems used to manipulate the data base.* An extended use of data base manipulation is made possible by theorems that are explicitly triggered by changes in the data base, and in turn make other changes. A typical pair of theorems are:

$$
\text{(ANTECEDENT (At ?obj ?loc)} \tag{6}
$$

  (EXISTS (?x ?y)
    (GOAL (AT ?x ?y))
    (GOAL (ImmediatelyBelow ?y ?loc))
    (ASSERT (Supports ?x ?obj))))

$$
\text{(ERASING (At ?obj ?loc)} \tag{7}
$$

  (EXISTS (?x)
    (GOAL (Supports ?x ?obj))
    (ERASE (Supports ?x ?obj))))

Theorem (6) says that whenever a proposition matching the pattern (that an object obj is At some location loc) is added to the data base, the system should see if it can find an object whose location is directly below loc, and if so to add the proposition that it supports obj. Theorem (7) states that whenever an At proposition is erased, the corresponding Supports proposition (if one exists) should be erased. As with theorems corresponding to operations, there is an implicit situation variable in these assertions. The newly asserted and erased propositions correspond to the new situation. Typically, a single operator triggers a flurry of activity by theorems like these, since each assertion or erasure can in turn trigger other theorems recursively. During this activity, the data base may be inconsistent,

---

[16] The MicroPlanner formalism does not distinguish a 'theorem' to prove something in the current situation, from one which takes actions that will make it true in a new situation. The backtracking mechanism also intermixes in a somewhat confusing way the use of process state to represent situation, and its use to represent alternative choices in the making of inferences. These confusions are discussed in G. Sussman and D. McDermott, 'From PLANNER to CONNIVER: A Genetic Approach', *Fall Joint Computer Conference* (1972).

but once it has all been completed, it corresponds to the new situation.

There are many issues that arise in coordinating these procedures. They must be paired so the erasures keep pace with the assertions, and must be limited so as not to generate infinite numbers of assertions (e.g., one could not have an antecedent theorem that was invoked for assertions of the form 'X is even' and in turn asserted 'X + 2 is even'). They must be written so that their ordering will not lead to inconsistencies (e.g., a theorem using data that is inconsistent because another chain of theorems is still in the midst of making changes to the data base). In practical use, these problems lead to some difficulties in debugging the inference process, but do not create fundamental obstacles. The procedures that a programmer writes can be controlled to perform consistent inferences (albeit incomplete with respect to a standard set of inference rules).

THNOT – the Introduction of Provability into Reasoning

The features of MicroPlanner described so far are more elaborate than those of STRIPS, but were not generally used to produce inferences which went beyond what could be understood as normal (if limited) application of standard rules. MicroPlanner has an additional important feature in its treatment of logical connectives. As mentioned above, it contains no way of applying general inference rules to complex formulas. The propositions in the data base are not only quantifier free, but contain no connectives. Theorems have procedural analogues of connectives (labelled THAND, THOR, and THNOT).[17] The procedures for THAND and THOR are incomplete but consistent forms of the corresponding logical operators. THOR of two goals, for example, is a procedure that involves trying to establish the first, then if that fails, trying to establish the second. (THOR A B) will succeed only in cases where a more standard axiomatic system could prove (OR A B), but may fail in some such cases (e.g., where neither A nor B is provable, but A is provable given NOT B).

THNOT, on the other hand, has significantly different properties. The procedure for the form (THNOT A) can be paraphrased: '*Try to prove A. If you fail, then* (THNOT A) *is proved*'. The success of the THNOT does not depend on being able to prove NOT A, but

[17] One of the simplifications in the syntax used for examples in this paper is the omission of the prefix TH- which was part of every MicroPlanner key word (e.g., THGOAL, THCONSEQUENT, etc.) I have preserved it in THNOT in order to emphasize that it is significantly different from the logical NOT.)

on the failure to find a proof of $\underline{A}$. A typical use of THNOT would be in theorem (8) for determing whether an object has a clear top surface:

(CONSEQUENT (HasClearSurface ?*x*)   (8)

  (THNOT (EXISTS (?*y*) (GOAL (Supports ?*x* ?*y*)))))

The system attempts (using the procedural means it has for proving existentials) to find an object *y* supported by $\underline{x}$. If this fails, it infers that $\underline{x}$ has a clear surface. Of course, this is only meaningful in a system, such as MicroPlanner, for which there is a finite (and in fact reasonably small) limit to the set of inferences that will be tried for a given proof.

There is no necessary connection between the use of explicit data bases and the ability to have a THNOT inference. Typically only systems with explicit control of data bases (and in fact systems operating in finite domains) will have the appropriate properties of limited deductive processing. But more generally, the mechanism can be applied to any system in which an attempted proof can terminate without succeeding. It is not necessary that all proofs terminate, since the system can fail to establish a THNOT just as it can fail to converge on any other proof. Reiter[18] discusses a particular formalization of this kind of reasoning, which he calls 'default reasoning'. He equates the intuitive characterization '*In the absence of any information to the contrary, assume . . .*' with a formal inference rule '*If certain information cannot be deduced from the given knowledge base, then conclude . . .*'. As we will discuss below, this is an overly restrictive definition. However, it clearly applied to THNOT as implemented in MicroPlanner. Reiter expresses a theorem like (8) as an inference rule, using the symbol $/\vdash$ to stand for "fail to deduce", as:

$$(\forall x/\text{PhysicalObject}) \frac{/\vdash (\exists y/\text{PhysicalObject}) \ \text{Support}(x, y)}{\text{HasClearSurface}(x)} \qquad (9)$$

Inconsistency and the Ordering of Inferences

The use of THNOT depends on the finiteness of the inference process, but not on the details of its operation. Another form of reasoning that has been used since the earliest AI programs[19]

---

[18] R. Reiter, 'On Reasoning by Default', *Theoretical Issues in Natural Language Processing* – 2, (1978), pp. 210–18.

[19] e.g. B. Raphael, 'SIR: A Computer Program for Semantic Information Retrieval', in M. Minsky (ed), *Semantic Information Processing* (1967), pp. 33–145.

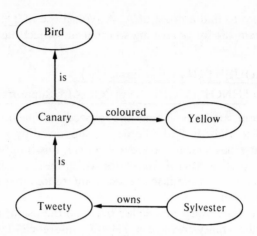

Fig. 7. Simple semantic network.

appears in MicroPlanner, and has been further developed in semantic networks.[20] It is based on explicit constraints on the order in
which inferences will be attempted by the system. In a typical
semantic network, propositions are stored in three different ways,
shown in Figures 7 and 8. The graphical notation of semantic nets is
widespread but not essential – the logical properties of these systems
could be duplicated precisely in a system that manipulated ordinary
predicate-calculus formulas.

First, there are single term variable-free propositions, such as
'*Tweety is a canary*' and '*Sylvester owns Tweety*'. These are rep-

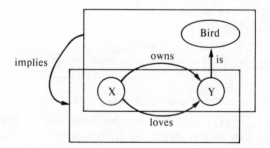

Fig. 8. Partitioned semantic network.

[20] e.g. G. G. Hendrix, 'Expanding the Utility of Semantic Networks through
Partioning', *Advance Papers of the Fourth International Joint Conference on Artificial
Intelligence*, (1975), pp. 115–21.

resented by *links* between *nodes* that correspond to constants and predicates.[21]

Second, there are implicitly quantified statements that depend on the basic structure of the network. *'All canaries are yellow'* is expressed with a link from the node representing the predicate Canary (or in the set-theoretic formulation, representing the set of canaries) to the constant Yellow. The system contains inference procedures that can combine the information from this link with the one linking Tweety to Canary in order to infer that *'Tweety is yellow'*. These inference procedures are stated in terms of following links, but can be easily understood as inference rules for dealing with quantification.

The third type of proposition is one containing connectives or nested quantifiers. In early semantic networks, such information could not be represented. In more recent ones (Figure 8 is based on Hendrix's work[22]) there are ways of representing all of the first-order predicate calculus. Figure 8 expresses *'Everyone who owns a bird loves that bird'*. It could be used in conjunction with the network of Figure 7 to infer that Sylvester loves Tweety.[23]

In most semantic network systems, the rules for drawing conclusions from configurations of links and nodes correspond directly to standard rules of inference. However, there is a critical difference in that there is a fixed order in which inferences will be tried. For example, propositions of the first type will be used before those of the second, and propositions of the second type before those of the third. This allows the network to operate consistently with inconsistent information. The most typical case is that illustrated in Figure 9. *'All canaries are yellow'*, *'Sam is green'*, and *'Sam is a canary'* are all in the network. Asked to find Sam's colour, the system will answer *'Green'* without ever finding the contradiction. This ability to

---

[21] The details of the mapping from the node and link notation onto the syntactic structures of predicate calculus leave much room for variation. The assignment of predicates, individual constants, and sets to node labels and link labels has been somewhat *ad hoc* in many systems. Recent work such as that of W. A. Woods, 'What's in a Link?', in D. C. Bobrow and A. Collins (eds.), *Representation and Understanding*, (1975) *pp.* 35–82; and L. K. Schubert, 'Extending the Expressive Power of Semantic Networks', *Artificial Intelligence* 7:2 (1976), 163–98, has been concerned with ensuring that it is well-specified. Here, we illustrate typical uses without carefully justifying their form.

[22] Op. cit.

[23] It should be clear that many details of the inference-rules are being omitted in this brief description. For a more systematic exposition, see Richard E. Fikes and Gary Hendrix, 'A Network-based Knowledge Representation and its Natural Deduction System', *Preprints of the Fifth International Joint Conference on Artificial Intelligence* (1977), pp. 235–46.

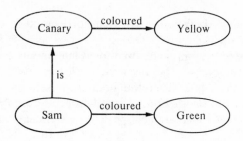

Fig. 9. Semantic network with contradiction.

reason from *default information* (information that is true in general but can be over-ridden by more specific knowledge) has been noted as an aspect of ordinary reasoning that does not fit into standard logic.

There are problems in trying to go beyond the simple cases for which this kind of system was developed. In trying, for example, to prove (or disprove) '*Sam is yellow*', it is not clear whether the logic of mutual exclusion of colours would be used early enough in the process to override verification of the statement from the generalization about canaries. Most systems do not have carefully developed overall ordering constraints. They have simple rules that produce the desired results for simple cases and leave the more complex ones under-specified. In general, the more limited the inferential powers of a system, the easier it is to specify clear ordering constraints. In MicroPlanner, for example, the rule is limited but clear: use propositions from the data base before executing any theorems.

Like THNOT, the success of this mechanism depends on the incompleteness of the inference mechanisms. Given a network containing inconsistent propositions, the system does not collapse under the weight of contradiction, because it lacks the inferential processes that would enable it to derive arbitrary nonsense from the contradictions.

Resource Limitation and Competing Processes

The two mechanisms described above are attempts to duplicate human reasoning in drawing conclusions from the failure to find information to the contrary. In MicroPlanner and Reiter's formalism, the system uses inference rules of the form '*If you are (completely) unable to prove X then infer...*'. In semantic networks, they are of the form '*If you are completely unable to prove X using inferences of type Y (e.g., specific instantiated propositions) then infer...'*. In both cases, it is the total failure of a proof process which enables the inference.

Another interesting property of human reasoning is that a given inference process can be tried for a limited amount of time, then abandoned or superseded by something else. Given something to prove (or remember, or answer) a person may fail to do so for some amount of time, then finally succeed. If during the interim, it becomes necessary to act (or to go on to something else), a negative inference may be drawn – '*If I haven't been able to prove it yet, it must be false.*' A person may well come to a conclusion, then arrive at a contrary one on further reflection.

Some recent artificial intelligence systems[24] are based on the explicit allocation of finite resources to inferential processes. These systems are structured not as a single inferential process, but many competing ones. These may be actually run simultaneously on different machines, or *time-shared*[25] on a single processor. A given computation can proceed for a limited amount of time and then be superseded by other computations, including one that observes the state that the first one reached. Such systems can have inference procedures that can be roughly paraphrased '*Try to prove X until you run out of resources, and if you have not yet succeeded, then infer that it is false*'. This kind of inference rule is context-dependent. Given identical bodies of propositions and the same inference task, two systems may come to different conclusions, depending on the resource demands and availabilities.

This organization captures some of our intuitions about common sense reasoning – the fact that reasoning varies with context and attention. It is related to known properties of human perception[26] in which the finiteness of processing power plays a crucial role. The major problem in building or understanding a system using resource-limited inference is in developing an appropriate measure for resources. If arbitrary measures are used (depending, for example, on irrelevant details of a computer implementation), then there is no reason to expect that the inferences made by such a system will be systematic or useful. One of the major lines of research in this

[24] e.g. D. G. Bobrow and T. Winograd, 'An Overview of KRL, a Knowledge Representation Language', *Cognitive Science* 1:1 (1977), 3–46.

[25] Time sharing is a standard computing technique in which a single processor alternates among a number of tasks, much like a chess expert playing simultaneous exhibition games.

[26] See D. A. Norman and D. G. Bobrow, 'On Data-Limited and Resource-Limited Processes', *Cognitive Psychology* 7 (1975), 44–64.

area is on the formal properties of memory structure and computational complexity that can be used as a theoretical basis for resource allocation.

On particular line of development recognizes different levels of organization in a knowledge base, each relevant to resources in its own way. The KRL-0 system developed by Bobrow and Winograd[27] distinguishes memory organization from logical organization. Propositions are grouped into *units,* which serve as memory chunks. These chunks correspond loosely to the *frames* proposed by Minsky,[28] and the intuitions surrounding frames (as discussed by Boden in this volume) were one of the major motivations for the KRL formalism. Whereas Minsky emphasizes the structuring of frames to correspond to natural groupings in the external world, Bobrow and Winograd emphasize their role in the logical organization of the reasoning system.

In KRL, each proposition (or *'description'*, as they are called) is *anchored* to a particular place in memory. *'Sylvester owns Tweety'* can be anchored in the unit for Sylvester, the unit for Tweety, or both. In measuring resources, the operation of following a link (called a *'coreference'*) to a new unit is taken as a larger step than that of using propositions embedded within a single unit.[29]

Canary [self: A Bird][colour: A Colour][owner: A Person]   (10)

Tweety [self: A Canary with colour = Yellow

owner = Sylvester]

The formulas of (10) represent the same information as Figure 7, but with some additional structure. It implies that colour and ownership are specially relevant properties of canaries, (indicated by having *slots* for them in the unit for Canary. This enables them to be anchored more closely to the unit for Tweety. The formulas of (11) represent the same basic facts, but organize them differently. Colour is listed as a property of birds in general, and ownership is expressed as an independent relation, anchored to neither of its arguments.

Canary [self: A Bird]   (11)

Bird [self: An Animal][colour; A Colour]

[27] Op. cit.

[28] M. Minsky, 'A Framework for Representing Knowledge', in P. Winston (ed.), *The Psychology of Computer Vision* (1975).

[29] As with the other systems above, this presentation of the KRL system is oversimplified. There are many issues relating to classical logical problems (such as the distinction between extensional and intensional forms) that play a role in the formalism, but are not directly relevant to the problems discussed here.

Ownership [self: A Relation][owner: A Person][owned: A Thing]
Tweety [self: A Canary
        A Bird with colour = Yellow
        The owned from an Ownership with owner
                                    = Sylvester]

The formulas of (12) are an alternative to the final one of (11) in which the relationship of ownership between Sylvester and Tweety is put into a separate unit, rather than being included as part of the description of Tweety. The details of how all of these variations affect the amount of resources needed to draw various conclusions are beyond the scope of this explanation. The illustrations are included to give some sense that what is being provided is an *additional* level of structuring laid on top of the basic propositional content, which provides structure for deciding what inferences to try in what order, and when to stop trying.

Tweety [self: A Canary
        A Bird with colour = Yellow   (12)
        The owned from an Ownership thatIs Ownership
                                         17]
Ownership 17[self: An Ownership with owner = Sylvester owned
                                     = Tweety]

Levels of Organization within an Inference System.

KRL violates the simplicity criteria that normally guide the development of logical formalisms. It provides distinct alternatives for stating a proposition, when from a strict logical point of view they all have exactly the same content. This complicates the statement of inference rules, since they must deal with the complexities of access as well as the standard issues of quantification, connectives, etc. In early versions, the inference process was specified in an *ad hoc* way similar to semantic networks. More recently, Smith[30] has been studying systems like KRL and Brachman's[31] semantic networks from a more formal standpoint, developing a *knowledge representation semantics*. He distinguishes five *levels* of organization of a formal representation as used in a computational reasoning system. Each level has its own structure, and is systematically related to

[30] B. Smith, unpublished Master's thesis (to be issued as a technical report in the Artificial Intelligence Laboratory), MIT (1978).
[31] R. J. Brachman, 'What's in a Concept: Structural Foundations for semantic Networks', *Int. J. Man-Machine Studies* 9 (1977), 127–52.

those above and below. Smith's levels are:

(1) Superficial notation: The organization as sequences of primitive symbols. In most languages (including KRL and predicate calculus) it is based on conventions for linear sequences of individual tokens (strings of letters separated by spaces or punctuation marks). In others (such as semantic nets) one uses more complex two-dimensional notations involving lines, nodes, boxes, etc.

(2) Syntax: The structure underlying the notation. We do not understand a predicate calculus formula, for example, as a linear string of tokens, but as a structured formula built up according to a syntax with rules for prediction, connectives, etc.

(3) Memory: In a physical computational system (such as a computer), there is a physical embodiment of the knowledge base. It can be described in terms of the structures of the machine – its memory organization.

(4) Belief: The inference processes of a system are based on an interpretation of the memory structures as corresponding to forms that are the basis for inference. The classification of these forms need not correspond exactly to the storage form in memory or the syntax of the notation. The examples from KRL above illustrate a diversity of syntactic (and memory) structures that are to be treated as having the same underlying belief structure.

(5) World: The structures of a formal system can be understood in terms of some world or model external to the system, which they represent.

For one familiar with formal logic but not with computer reasoning systems, it may not be clear why it is useful to draw all of these distinctions. Some of them are obvious. For example, it is straightforward to see that superficial notation is distinct. We could imagine representing predicate calculus formulas in a graphical notation quite different in appearance from the standard use of words and parentheses. In fact, in the history of formal logic there are many examples of the perspicuity that new notational conventions can provide. It is also clear that what Smith calls 'world' is distinct. It is the model, not the formal system. Tarski's recognition of this critical distinction underlies our modern understanding of logical systems.

However, from the traditional logical standpoint, the middle three levels are not distinct. The syntax of a formal system corresponds in a trivial way to the potential for inference – inference-rules are stated directly in terms of the syntactic forms. Memory is not an issue at all in considering an abstract formal system, since there is no sense in which formulas are 'stored'. In computer systems these levels are often differently organized. Considerations of efficiency call for an internal memory representation quite different from the external syntax. As knowledge is 'read into memory', a conversion is done, which can include reduction to canonical forms, cross-indexing, and modularization. In a similar way, the stored form may not be the most effective for specifying inferences, and there is a process of 'reading out' the contents of memory for use in the inference process, which can involve translation to yet another form.

In some systems, the relationships between these different forms are *ad hoc* or incompletely specified. However, it is possible to provide full consistent specifications for the different levels. One approach has been to maintain a strong uniformity among levels, for example by storing knowledge as a list of propositions in predicate calculus form, and using standard inference rules on them. The disadvantage of this approach is that it does not allow for the additional organization needed for the kinds of reasoning discussed above. If the inferential process makes use of special distinctions in deciding what inferences to try, or if we are to measure the resources they used in a systematic way, then the appropriate organization must provide means to express differences. The memory organization that is relevant to processing and resources is not implicit in the underlying logical organization. All of the extended inference modes depend on the 'extra-logical' information which is represented at other levels of organization.

The tools of model theory cannot be applied without major modification. Loosely stated, the insight of model theory is that for an appropriately well-behaved deductive system, there is a formal object (the model) that can be specified independently of the specific linguistic forms and inference rules, and in terms of which the meaning of the formulas can be understood. The systems described above are ill-behaved in exactly the way that violates this. The inferences they draw are founded in an essential and unavoidable way on the details of the memory forms and inferential processes with which they work. A model that attempts to be independent of this will no longer have the appropriate correspondence to the inferences that are drawn.

There have been some attempts by logicians within the field of artificial intelligence to deal with these problems. McCarthy[32] argues

[32] J. McCarthy, 'Circumscription Induction: a Way of Jumping to Conclusions', unpublished report, Stanford AI Project (1978), on line as (SU-A) MINIMA(s77, jmc).

that formal notions of *minimal entailment* and *minimal inference* can capture many of the phenomena of human plausible reasoning. Reiter[33] makes a simple first attempt to provide a formalization of default reasoning. Both of these projects share with Hayes[34] the belief that it will be possible to add a formalization of extended inference modes on top of a system in which model-theoretic semantics apply to the underlying representation language. Hayes is emphatic in maintaining the separation[35] between the *epistemological adequacy* of a system (its well-formedness with respect to truth-theoretic semantics) and the *heuristic adequacy* (the ability of its inferential procedures to arrive at desired conclusions in a reasonable amount of time). He argues:

The metatheory of logic is a collection of mathematical tools for analyzing representational languages... What these tools analyze is not the behaviour of an interpreter, or the structure of processes in some running system, but rather, the extensional meaning of expressions of a language, when these are taken to be making claims about some external world... Logical meaning justifies *inferences. A running system* performs *inferences: some of its preocesses are the making of inferences... The inference structure of the language used by a system does not depend on the process structure.*

It is my belief that this approach will not prove adequate. A statement like '*If you don't know something has moved, assume it is in the same place*' or '*Canaries are generally yellow*' does not have a meaning in any semantic system that fails to deal explicitly with the reasoning process. The issues of inference as a process, and of knowledge bases as physical systems with resource implications, will have to be dealt with in some kind of semantic theory that does not first assume a process-free semantics for the formulas in the system.

Motivations for Extended Forms of Inference

At this point let us review the reasons for developing inferential systems with extended modes of inference. The additional complexities and problems are justified by concerns of two sorts: efficiency of inference, and the ability to do plausible reasoning.

Many of the programs that use extended inference modes do not draw any conclusions that would not have been drawn in a more standard system. However, they operate in a way that shortcuts a complex process, or allows for a more economical axiomatization. In STRIPS, the use of explicit data base manipulation to deal with the

[33] Op. cit.
[34] Op. cit.
[35] Originally discussed in J. McCarthy and P. J. Hayes, op. cit.

frame problem makes it possible to avoid the explicit statement of frame axioms for all those things that remain unchanged, and, in conjunction with the implicit specification of situations, provides an efficient way to maintain consistency. A simple robot manipulator, or an airline-schedule question-answerer can use what Reiter[36] calls *closed-world reasoning*. In a domain for which the system is complete, the failure to find an object fitting a given predicate is equivalent to a proof that no such object exists. A system could instead contain explicit axioms that enumerate the closed sets, such as:

$$\forall x \ (\text{Flight}(x) \bigwedge \text{Connect}(x, \text{San Francisco, London})) \supset \qquad (13)$$
$$(x = \text{Flight } 254 \bigvee x = \text{Flight } 394 \bigvee \cdots \bigvee x = \text{Flight } 987)$$

In the closed-world case, the use of failure-to-prove (e.g. with THNOT) in the appropriate cases does not extend the range of inferences, but can be much more efficient than using enumerations.

If efficiency were the only issue, then the whole enterprise would be of far less interest, and indeed might well be tackled from a different direction – that of providing a second-order overlay to a normal inference system. This has been advocated by Hayes[37] and explored in the AMORD system at M.I.T.,[38] which is described as providing 'a set of conventions by which the explicit control assertions are used to restrict the application of sound but otherwise explosive rules'. Indeed, this approach may well provide important clarifications of extended inference systems in general.

The more interesting uses, though, are those in which the system is enabled to do reasoning of a sort we would informally describe as based on plausibility rather than deduction. We have mentioned the use of non-provability (either total, or with resource limitation) as a basis for using *default values*, which are assumed true in general but can be overruled in a specific case. Sandewall[39] has proposed an approach to the frame problem using a logical operator he calls UNLESS (essentially equivalent to THNOT). Instead of providing a frame axiom for each thing that remains unchanged through an operation, he has axioms for each source of change, and a general inference schema that can be loosely paraphrased '*If you can't prove*

---

[36] Op. cit.
[37] Op. cit.
[38] J. de Kleer, J. Doyle, G. L. Steel Jr., and G. J. Sussman, 'Explicit Control of Reasoning', MIT AI Laboratory Memo 427 (June 1977).
[39] E. Sandewall, 'An Approach to the Frame Problem, and its Implementation', in B. Meltzer and D. Michie (eds.), *Machine Intelligence* 7 (1972), 167–94.

that the operations changed something, then assume that it is the same'. The burden of consistency then rests on guaranteeing that, if anything is changed, that fact will indeed be provable. This approach corresponds to the kind of reasoning a person will do if asked a question like *'Where do your parents live?'* In most circumstances, one has no way of proving that they have not moved their residence in the last few moments, but in the absence of proof to the contrary, we are content to act as though things remain as they were.

Inference based on lack of immediate knowledge to the contrary has more subtle dimensions that have been explored by Collins[40] and his co-workers.[41] In examining the problems of geography tutoring, they observed many cases of reasoning in which a kind of second-order criterion is applied involving the 'importance' of a fact. If asked *'Is the Mekong River longer than the Amazon?'*, a student reasons: *'I don't know of its length. If it were longer than the Amazon, it would be important and I would have heard of it, and therefore it must not be.'* The key element is in deciding that the length of a river is important with respect to the amount of knowledge the student has of geography. If asked *'Does the Mekong river have any major tributaries?'*, the absence of information cannot be taken as a negative answer, since the fact is not important enough for its truth to assure the student's knowledge. Similar reasoning can be applied in answering a question like *'Were any U.S. Presidents women?'* while it would fail to answer on the basis of lack of knowledge the similar questions *'Have any governors of U.S. states been women?'*, or *'Were any U.S. presidents natives of Indiana?'*

Another interesting related use is Pople's[42] *abductive reasoning* in a medical diagnosis system. Given a set of symptoms, the program generates hypotheses for the likely causes. Rather than following a straightforward Bayesian approach, Pople's system makes use of a network of associations between symptoms and diseases which includes distinct relations <u>Manifests(Disease, Symptom)</u> and

---

[40] A. Collins, 'Fragments of a Theory of Human Plausible Reasoning', *Theoretical Issues in Natural Language Processing – 2*, (1978), pp. 194–201.

[41] A. M. Collins, E. Warnock, N. Aiello, and M. Miller, 'Reasoning from Incomplete Knowledge', in D. G. Bobrow and A. Collins (eds.), *Representation and Understanding* (1975), pp. 383–416. The present discussion includes only one of the many forms of plausible reasoning discussed by Collins.

[42] H. Pople, J. Meyers, and R. Miller, 'DIALOG, a model of Diagnostic Logic for Internal Medicine', *Advanced Papers of the Fourth International Joint Conference on Artificial Intelligence* (1975), pp. 848–55.

Evokes(Symptom, Disease). Every symptom which could be caused by a disease is linked by a Manifests relation (along with a numerical strength of the association), but the reverse is not true. The set of diseases linked by the Evokes relation to a symptom are only those which an experienced doctor would think of as an explanation. In looking for the causes of a set of symptoms, the only diseases considered are those which the symptoms evoke. This incompleteness with respect to the set of all possible causes makes it possible for the program to limit its search and come up quickly with highly valued hypotheses.

Current Exploration

In recent discussions[43] it has been argued that the properties of extended inference systems make them suitable for building formal reasoning systems that have many of the properties of natural language and natural reasoning that resist traditional semantic analyses. One of the most discussed problems has been the 'family resemblance' discussed by Wittgenstein. Many words (such as 'game') cannot be precisely defined in terms of more primitive semantic features since the set of objects or situations to which they apply does not have a common core. Any attempt at precise definition will lead either to an unending enumeration of cases or to a sense of the word that is artifically limited.

In defining a term within a computer system, the most obvious method corresponds in a straightforward way to logical definition. Corresponding to each predicate the system will contain an expansion (either a formula or a program) whose elements are based on other predicates, which in turn can be expanded until at the base there is some set of *primitives* that can be directly evaluated. There has been much discussion about the nature of this evaluation,[44] and the fact that in a procedural formalism, it can be an effective test (using perception) rather than a formal primitive. However in either case, the effective means of applying a complex predicate is through recursive reduction to primitives of some sort.

In systems based on extended inference modes, it is feasible to have definitions that are not based on reduction. The initial step is the same – corresponding to a predicate, there is an expansion (or a set of alternative expansions) in the form of formulas or programs

---

[43] e.g., T. Winograd, 'Towards a Procedural Understanding of Semantics', *Revue Internationale de Philosophie* (1976), fasc. 3–4, pp. 117–18.
[44] See e.g., G. A. Miller and P. N. Johnson-Laird, *Language and Perception* (1976).

using other predicates in the system. These in turn have their own expansions. However, there need not be any ultimate *grounding* in primitives. Definitions can be circular in the sense that a predicate can be defined in terms of other predicates that in turn are defined in terms of the original one. Such a definition, if used in a standard proof procedure, would lead to non-termination, and could never be demonstrated to apply to anything. In an extended inference system, on the other hand, it can be applied in a form of depth-dependent reasoning.

At the first levels, the expansions are used fully – in order to decide whether a prediction is true, its expansion is invoked. As the process proceeds, extended inference modes can be applied to the sub-problems it generates. They can be accepted as true if no immediate evidence demonstrates their falsity. The notion of 'immediate' can be changed by context and depth of reasoning.[45] Also, the system need not be thought of as testing the truth of a single isolated prediction. In general, the problem can be thought of as one of *best match* among a finite set of alternatives. For example, in choosing an English word to apply to an observed object, we select among a finite vocabulary, and can quickly reduce the problem to a small set of choices. In such a context, even a direct contradiction need not eliminate the possibility of using a word. Given some kind of measure of how much contradictory information is found (in a resource-limited inference process), the system may accept a prediction on the basis that is the most highly valued among the choices, even though there are specific parts of the definition which (at the depth of inferencing done for them) seem to be contradicted.

The net effect of such a system is that a predication will be 'believed' ('proved' is a somewhat questionable word in this context) in cases where there is only a partial fit between the definition and the object to which it is applied.[46] Of course, this can generate nonsense unless the system carefully controls the use of the extended inferences. The ability to accept contradiction and to jump to conclusions on the lack of evidence makes sense only in a context where memory organization and resource allocation have been

[45] The ways in which current context and focus affect understanding have not been well understood or studied in the context of logical formalisms. The possibility suggested here is that their effects should be analysed in terms of the resource limitation and ordering of inferential processes.

[46] This is not the only kind of system which allows for partial match. One can, for example, base a system on complete reduction to primitive features, then decide on how well two things match by counting the number of features in which they agree and disagree. The approach here is different in that it does not depend on descriptions 'bottoming out' on atomic features.

thoroughly and carefully designed. No one has yet demonstrated a system that operates in this fashion for anything but isolated examples, but the notion of reasoning by *partial match* has long intrigued artificial intelligence researchers[47] and continues to be a source of technical ideas. If formal systems of this type can be built and understood, we will have a significantly different basis for describing meaning than the atomistic reductionistic semantics of standard logic and computer programming.

Conclusion

Computer systems for carrying out reasoning have been built using a mixture of deductive logic and extended inference processes that are not formalizable in standard truth-theoretic terms. They allow for inferences based on the ability or inability to prove things that fall into several categories:

1. Explicit presence or absence of formulas in memory.
2. The failure of a finite deductive process to prove something. Actually the first case is a special instance of this, in which the deductive process has no inference rules at all.
3. The order in which different inferences are tried.
4. The failure of a resource-limited inferential process to prove something, in a given context with a given allocation of resources.

The systems that result do not have many of the standard properties that make formalization seem tractable. They are not consistent in the standard sense (although they are mechanistic, so that the result of any specific inferential process is uniquely determinable). The set of provable theorems in such a system is not recursively enumerable[48] and they are clearly not monotonic, in the sense that there will be propositions $\underline{A}$, $\underline{B}$, and $\underline{C}$ such that $\underline{B}$ will be inferred from $\underline{A}$, but $-\underline{B}$ from $\underline{A} \wedge \underline{C}$. However, it is possible systematically to describe the activity of such systems in terms of the different levels of organization they impose on the reasoning process. Through careful examination of the properties of different memory representations and accessing strategies, we may be able to find useful formal characterizations of non-deductive inference modes.

This paper does not address problems of inductive logic as they are normally formulated. However, the systems it describes can be viewed as filling in the other end of a spectrum of rationality. At the

[47] See e.g., J. Moore and A. Newell, 'How Can MERLIN Understand?' in L. Gregg (ed.), *Knowledge and Cognition* (1973); M. Minsky, op. cit; and D. G. Bobrow and T. Winograd, op. cit.

[48] See R. Reiter, op. cit, for a discussion of this point.

end more typically treated in inductive logics, one is dealing with a situation with a high degree of recurrence. Factors are controllable, multiple experiments can be carried out, and no conclusion need be drawn until sufficient information is gathered. In dealing with common sense reasoning, we are at the other end. Situations are unique, different along many dimensions whose relevance cannot be determined ahead of time. The pragmatic necessities of action often preclude the careful contemplation which lends itself to the sifting of evidence. The sets of alternatives to be considered must be generated as an essential part of the reasoning process, and may depend on the confluence of many contextual factors.

I suggest that the mechanisms of resource limited reasoning described above are well suited for dealing with the kinds of non-deductive reasoning which make up a large part of human thought. This can only be established by a good deal of further exploration, which this paper is an attempt to provoke.

§23. Margaret A. Boden
§23. Margaret A. Boden
Real-world Reasoning

Traditional logic has not taken account of the computational constraints on finite systems engaged in processes of reasoning, but has considered instead the idealized justification of the results of idealized reasoning. But rationality cannot in practice do without the processes of natural reasoning. Computational concepts and computer implementations of learning offer a vocabulary that is more adequate to the richness of these processes than is familiar logic, though no less rigorous. Real-world reasoning often makes intelligent use of specific content, of examples taken to be representative of a class, and of errors intelligently arrived at in the first place. It also employs a great deal of prior knowledge and inferential competence in order to learn from experience. Computational analyses of inductive learning can throw light on the structure and dynamics of real reasoning in science and everyday life.

1. *Introduction*

Unlikely though this conference is to attract a visitation from the local Porn Squad, its organizers might be accused of publishing a dirty word. 'Induction' carries overtones of the loose, the shoddy, and the impure, if not of the positively indecent. Even those, like Russell, who defend induction clearly regard it as the poor man's deduction. While as for psychologism, *that* is not fit even for chickens. In the eyes of his peers, the logician who falls prey to psychologism has been seduced by a temptress of disreputably easy virtue. Truly rational reasoning is less easy (though more virtuous) than the common-sense variety, and must satisfy rigorous canons of philosophical respectability. In sum, if induction is to be invited into the logician's parlour at all, it must be strictly chaperoned by formal measures of confirmability; and psychologism cannot be so invited, since it has no acceptable epistemological pedigree.

I see the prime message of Terry Winograd's paper[1] to be that these attitudes on the part of the typical logician betray an excess of zeal, if not an epistemological prurience. Traditional logic has not taken account of the computational constraints on finite systems engaged in processes of reasoning, but has considered instead the idealized justification of the results of idealized reasoning. And, as in so many areas of human endeavour, the ideal may be much less complex than the reality. Artificial intelligence ('AI') offers a methodology that is well suited to the exploration of formal models

[1] Terry Winograd, 'Extended Inference Modes in Reasoning by Computer Systems', above, pp. 333 ff.

of rational, albeit fallible, thinking. In particular, it can illuminate the dynamic interaction of principles of inference and background knowledge, and clarify some of the psychological subtleties of everyday reasoning that the more traditional methods tend to neglect.

In this paper I shall mention some psychological and computational examples that support Winograd's stress on the importance of stereotypical world-knowledge and semantic content in reasoning, and his insistence on the computational inevitability of error in intelligent induction.

2. The Content of Reasoning

Logicians traditionally conceive of reasoning in terms of its abstract logical form, rather than its concrete content. Thus arguments are classified, and their validity assessed, in terms of abstract inferential schemata such as the Aristotelian figures of the syllogism, BARBARA and her syllogistic sisters – or her more modern granddaughters of propositional and predicate logic. It follows that amusingly absurd content can be given to a logician's arguments without in any way affecting their force as valid arguments. Lewis Carroll's *Sorites* are a case in point. These logical puzzles involve sets of individually incredible and collectively hilarious propositions, such as 'A fish that cannot dance a minuet is contemptible', and 'No shark ever doubts that it is well fitted out', and they may give obviously false conclusions, such as 'Rainbows are not worth writing odes to'. The tacit assumption is that the content has no *rational* importance: at most, it fulfils a motivating function, by sugaring the pill of logical rigour with a coating of entertainment.

Some psychologists, too, analyse everyday reasoning in 'logical' terms, stressing the contribution of formal structures but ignoring the effect of concrete content. Piaget is a case in point. His theoretical account of 'formal operations' implies that once this stage of intelligence has been achieved in adolescence, its hypothetico-deductive abstractions can be used irrespective of specific context by the adult.[2] But psychological experiments have shown that this is not so. Two problems of identical logical form may be easy or difficult, depending respectively on whether they do or do not tap familiar situations prompting common-sense reasoning.

For example, it is extremely difficult for people (including professors of logic) to guess which of four cards (showing the symbols *A*, *D*, 4, and 7 on their uppermost faces) would need to be turned over

[2] Barbel Inhelder and Jean Piaget, *The Growth of Logical Thinking from Childhood to Adolescence* (1958).

to determine the truth-value of a sentence expressing an abstract and arbitrary rule like 'If there is a vowel on one side of a card, then there is an even number on the other side'.[3]

But most adults have no difficulty at all with problems of identical logical form if they are given envelopes (not cards) and rules like, 'If an envelope is marked PRINTED MATTER REDUCED RATE, then it must be left open.' Specifically, a mere 19.3 per cent success rate on the abstract task rises to a staggering 98 per cent in the realistic situation. If 'sensible' rules like the one about PRINTED MATTER REDUCED RATE are applied in a less realistic experimental setting (cards being substituted for actual envelopes), the success rate is 87 per cent.

Experiments like these support the emphasis on stereotypical 'frames' that is characteristic of much current work in AI, such as that described by Winograd.[4] Presumably, the subjects in these psychological experiments had enough knowledge of our postal system to know that, generally speaking, printed matter goes at a reduced rate in envelopes left open for inspection. And presumably, too, the experimenter's rule about PRINTED MATTER RE-DUCED RATE implying openness was able to access this everyday knowledge, or frame, because of the closeness of verbal and semantic match between the two. The drop from 98 per cent to 87 per cent success when cards were substituted for actual envelopes in the experiment suggests that perceptual matching may also be important in accessing and moving inferentially within this 'postal frame'. It would be interesting to see what would happen to the success rate if all the envelopes marked PRINTED MATTER were very tiny and daintily decorated, like those used for gift-cards, whereas only huge ones made of brown paper were marked INTERFLORA MESSAGE or MERRY CHRISTMAS FROM . . . (assuming of course that additional rules linked the latter markings with sealed envelopes).

In real-life thinking it is useful to have a specific inference stored, to the effect that if you are mailing printed matter you should not lick the envelope-flap. (Is this psychologically equivalent to the advice that in these circumstances you should leave the envelope open? Almost certainly not, even in a world where all envelopes are lickably stickable. Brain-damaged patients may be well aware that

[3] P. C. Wason, 'The Theory of Formal Operations; A Critique', in B. A. Geber (ed.), *Piaget and Knowing: Studies in Genetic Epistemology* (1977), pp. 119–35.

[4] M. L. Minsky, 'A Framework for Representing Knowledge', in P. H. Winston (ed.), *The Psychology of Computer Vision* (1975), pp. 211–77. See also chapter 11 of M. A. Boden, *Artificial Intelligence and Natural Man*. (1977).

an envelope should or should not be left open, without being clear as to how licking a part of it–which part?–relates to its open or closed state. Logically, however, the two forms of advice are equivalent in the world hypothesized.) This is useful in real life because if the pattern 'printed matter' (or, as in the experiment, the mark PRINTED MATTER) can access this specific inference or procedural advice quickly, then appropriate action can be taken more swiftly than if it had to be deduced by general inference-rules from axiomatically represented information about envelopes and printed matter.

I am assuming here, as do many AI workers including those that were the focus of Winograd's paper, that the hardware of the brain does not function fast enough to make a general theorem-proving procedure feasible. Proponents of the 'theorem-proving' approach in AI dispute this assumption, and attribute their own lack of success in dealing with any but relatively trivial problems to the primitive state of current computer technology.

Because the creator of the PLANNER programming language shared this assumption, he designed PLANNER so as to enable the programmer to allow for information to be used in this 'sensible' fashion.[5] Indeed, in PLANNER any given item of knowledge can be stored in four forms: as a declarative statement that A implies B, which can be accessed by general inferential processes of the sort described by deductive logic; as an erasing theorem that is itself a procedure telling the system to erase A, if B is erased (as it might be, for example, if the system finds that B is false); as an antecedent theorem (procedure) instructing the system to infer B, if given A; and as a consequent theorem (procedure) advising that if you want to prove B one method is to try to establish A.

Supposing that someone wants to know whether an envelope should be left open, her friend (or an inner voice) might say impatiently, 'Well, it contains printed matter, doesn't it!' A PLAN-NER program could respond in essentially the same way, drawing the correct conclusion quickly, provided its data base contained two items. First, it needs to have stored (perhaps as a result of recent perceptual investigation) the fact that the envelope contains printed matter, expressed either as a purely declarative item or as an antecedent theorem about the envelope. Second, it needs a conse-

---

[5] Carl Hewitt, *Description and Theoretical Analysis (Using Schemata) of PLAN-NER: A Language for Proving Theorems and Manipulating Models in a Robot.* AI-TR-258, MIT AI Lab. (1972).

quent theorem that would be written thus:

(CONSE (X) (SHOULDBELEFTOPEN $?X)
      (GOAL (CONTAINSPRINTEDMATTER $?X)))

The 'X' in this expression declares a local variable, bound in this instance to the envelope. The '$?X$' is a semi-open, pattern variable, which can be given a value in the pattern-matching process if it has not already got one.

This PLANNER theorem is logically equivalent to 'All envelopes containing printed matter should be left open', or 'If it contains printed matter, then it should be left open', or 'Containing printed matter implies needing to be left open'. But instead of being stored as an axiom in the conventional sense, it is a mini-program that explicitly advises the system to try first to establish that something contains printed matter, should it wish to know whether it must be left open. Provided that it is quickly accessible (by way of the indexing scheme for selecting patterns and the subsequent pattern-matching processes) this domain-specific procedure, and its PLAN-NER cousins, will be computationally more economical than unin-dexed lists of facts (such as the arbitrary rules given to the experi-mental subjects mentioned above) that have to be manipulated by general deductive procedures. That is, the advice 'If you know it contains printed matter, then assume it must be left open' is often more helpful than the syllogistic knowledge, 'This envelope contains printed matter, and all envelopes containing printed matter are to be left open'.

(Strictly, PLANNER leaves it ambiguous whether the envelope is left open or is to be left open, for PLANNER cannot represent the difference between proving that B and bringing it about that B. POPLER, a language essentially similar to PLANNER, disting-uishes INFER procedures from ACHIEVE procedures.[6] So the POPLER programmer can express the difference between an en-velope's having been left open and its having to be left open, the program selecting one or other as appropriate. However, because of its inadequate indexing mechanisms, POPLER programs tend to be slow unless special indexing structures are written by the program-mer.)

The example of PLANNER suggests that learning that envelopes containing printed matter are left open is not a matter of merely

---

[6] D. J. M. Davies, *POPLER* 1.5 *Reference Manual*. TPU Report 1, Edinburgh Univ. AI Lab. (1973).

adding an isolated fact of the form 'All *A*'s are *B*'s' to one's memory. rather, it may involve such processes as representing this item of knowledge in 'antecedent', 'consequent', or 'erasing' form as well as in the form of a bare fact. Psychological experiments have confirmed what commonsense suggests, that on learning new facts people often erase previous beliefs–or at least make them (temporarily or permanently) inaccessible.[7] But the computational intricacies of such processes are still unclear. For instance, how is the need for deletion evaluated, especially in cases where there is no straightforward logical contradiction involved? (Should a biologist delete, amend, or retain–perhaps relabelling as 'myth'–her previous belief in Genesis?) And what systematic considerations are relevant to whether one generates an antecedent representation or a consequent one–or both? How does the learning system decide that one or other of these is likely to be needed?

Learning also (and correlatively) involves the integration of the new fact into a developing knowledge-structure that both relates it sensibly to other facts and makes it readily accessible in those contexts where it is likely to be needed. Winograd discussed such knowledge-structures under the heading of 'frames'. The contexts in which one first learns and later accesses such facts as the one about envelopes being left open for printed matter are psychologically, or computationally, rich in related facts, perceptual cues (such as size, colour, and label of envelope), motor actions (such as licking envelopes), and goal-structures. We know that printed matter tends to be of lesser importance and urgency than personally-penned letters, and that this is one reason (another being its commonly greater weight) why it goes at a reduced rate. For reduced postage rate implies reduced speed, and this is acceptable for printed matter generally. An experimental problem in which the PRINTED MATTER concerned a Government Health Warning about a raging cholera epidemic, and so needed to go in sealed envelopes carrying first-class postage, might show interestingly different patterns of inferential success.

In general, the specific and varied content of a frame has to be richly indexed during learning and development of the frame if it is to be maximally useful for access and inference in reasoning-tasks of varying types. Unlike traditional inductive logic, computational models of learning can in principle take these issues into account,

---

[7] P. C. Wason, 'On the Failure to Eliminate Hypotheses . . . : A Second Look', in P. N. Johnson-Laird and P. C. Wason (eds.), *Thinking: Readings in Cognitive Science* (1977), pp. 307–14.

since computational concepts have been developed specifically to characterize such features of the representation and use of knowledge. This is not to say that the problems have been solved or that learning is well understood. But work such as that described by Winograd is raising some of the relevant questions. The development of KRL, for instance, has been prompted by considerations of computational efficiency in the storage, indexing, and inferential use of frames. And its cousin KRS also explores how reasoning may be aided by computationally rich representations of semantic content.

Just as semantic content aids reasoning, so it can aid learning. A recent program written by R. J. D. Power and H. C. Longuet-Higgins provides a computational model of the inductive learning of the number-names (numerals) in various natural languages.[8] One of the general morals drawn by the authors is that language acquisition involves the use of semantic clues, even in order that the learner may come to distinguish well-formed from ill-formed sentences. The program is able to make intelligent guesses about the meaning of numeral expressions on the basis of syntactic analogy, and can intelligently reject incorrect or anomalous inputs presented to it in the attempt to catch it out (such as the suggestion that 'twenty and ten' means 37 or that the English numeral for 24 might be 'two dozen' rather than 'twenty-four'). Asked to explain 'Why?' it evaluates a numeral as a particular number, it displays the structure it assigned to the numeral and the schematic rules used to interpret that structure as the number concerned. The program learns to count in and interpret the numerals of languages as different as English, French, Japanese, Mixtec, Suppire, and Biblical Welsh. And it does this on the basis of no more input than a list of a few representative numerals, and the numbers for which they stand.

The semantic content upon which the program draws in order to do this (and which the authors suggest is intuitively used by adults learning numerals in a foreign language) involves the arithmetical notions of sum, product, difference, and (primitive) number. Primitive numbers are those directly named by single words in the lexicon of the language concerned (so a number may be primitive in one language but not in another: compare 'eighteen', 'dix-huit,' and 'duodeviginti'). These unstructured numerals have to be learnt by rote. (They are syntactically unstructured, being single words; they

---

[8] R. J. D. Power and H. C. Longuet-Higgins, 'Learning to Count: A Computational Model of Language Acquisition', *Proc. Royal Soc. London B* 200 (1978), 391–417.

may of course show semantically significant morphemic structure, as in 'sixteen' and less obviously in the French 'seize'.)

But the meanings of most numeral expressions consisting of more than one word are inductively learnt by generalizing from the evidence presented so far. Given the information, for example, that the numbers 20, 21, and 29 are named by the numerals 'twenty', 'twenty-one', and 'twenty-nine', the program induces that the number 25 will be named by the expression 'twenty-five' – and not, say, by 'five from thirty'. Moreover, on being next told that 30 is named 'thirty', it induces the correct numerals for all the numbers between 31 and 39. It is able to do this because it represents numeral expressions as structured instances generated by schematic formulae, and one and the same formula or rule can generate many series of numbers – as in the English expressions for 21–29, 31–39, ... 91–99.

The program is not misled by the French habit of naming 70 (non-primitively) as 'soixante-dix'. And this is not because the teacher is always kind enough to present this new numeral immediately after its predecessor representing 69: the teacher may 'skip' direct from 'soixante' to 'soixante-dix'. The program recognizes the new lexical item as a compound of 'soixante' and 'dix'. And it realizes, because of its grammatical knowledge about the syntax and semantics of numeral systems in general, that this must be the *sum* of 60 and 10 rather than their *product* – which is named 'six cent'. It recognizes 'quatre-vingt', on the other hand, as the product of 4 and 20, not their sum. For it knows that if a smaller number precedes a larger number, without a conjunction, then a *product* is in question: compare 'quatre-vingt,' 'four hundred', 'twenty-four' – and remember that there were four *and* twenty blackbirds baked in the pie. Arithmetical reasoning involving the concepts and operations of sum and product enable the program to reject evidence as spurious: if told that 'twenty-four hundred' means 420, the program refuses to accept this and prints 'SURELY NOT'.

The variety of superficially different parsings that the program can deal with is illustrated by its ability to learn to interpret the Mixtec numerals for 380 (literally: fifteen four score) and 799 (one four-hundred fifteen four score fifteen four) and the Biblical Welsh expressions for 59 (four on fifteen and two twenty) and 2,999 (subtract one five twenty and nine hundred and two of thousand). Numerals such as these make 'quatre-vingt dix-neuf' look simple indeed.

A less 'Baconian' program it would be difficult to imagine. The program might rather be termed Kantian – as might other AI models of learning such as those mentioned in Winograd's paper. Kant insisted that there must be some prior structures within the mind enabling one meaningfully to interpret and assimilate one's experience. As he put it, intuition without concepts is blind. Similarly, Chomsky has argued that natural language learning would be impossible without prior principles of structure in terms of which to generate and test hypotheses about the grammar of the linguistic input. But Chomsky, especially in his earlier work, underplayed the role of semantics in syntactic induction. Without its arithmetical knowledge and reasoning capacity, Longuet–Higgins' program could not learn to parse numerals as intelligently as it does. It also needs its two 'principles of induction', which the authors say seem to apply to all known numeral systems.

The first of these principles is the one that underlies the inductive jump from 'twenty-one' and 'twenty-nine' to 'twenty-five', and also to 'ninety-seven' once 'ninety' has been learnt by rote. It concerns expressions in which the (semantically) major term is a number rather than a product, and states that 'If two such expressions, having the same major term and the same arithmetical operation, are both realized by a given syntactic form, then any expression involving the same major term, the same operation, and an intermediate value of the minor term, is well-formed, and is also realized by that form'. The second inductive principle allows the program to induce the correct English expression for 513, having been told that the numeral for 113 is 'one hundred and thirteen'. This principle applies to the syntactic forms of sums and differences in which the (semantically) major term is not a constant but a product. It is: 'If a sum or difference has a product as its major term, then the syntactic form or forms by which it can be realized are left unchanged by replacing that product by any other product which is generated by the same formula'. One might think of these two inductive principles as expressing the universal 'deep grammar' of natural language numeral systems – but notice that they involve both semantic and syntactic considerations, and presuppose arithmetical reasoning ability in the language learner.

A person – or program – unaware of arithmetical concepts such as sum, product, and difference (and syntactic distinctions too) would be unable intelligently to induce a foreign numeral system from limited experience of it, but would have to learn it entirely by rote. Very young children, of course, do not immediately realize that 35 must be 'thirty-five' after they have learnt the numeral for 25; nor do they realize that 23 will be called 'twenty-three' on being told that 21 is 'twenty-one'. The sense in which they have *learnt* the English names for 21 or 25 is less well-structured than that in which they will as adults learn the French number names, although this is not to say that their knowledge should be represented as a passively-acquired list of items on the classical-empiricist model.[9] Among psychologists, Piaget has been outstanding for his Kantian emphasis on the role of prior structure in the assimilation of new experiences, and for his non-Kantian stress on the gradual development of these organizing structures in infancy.[10] Work on inductive learning in AI should help to illuminate the structures and processes involved.

3. *Errors in Reasoning*

Error has often had a bad press in the philosophical, and even the psychological, literature. The rationalist Spinoza was so metaphysically embarrassed by it that he denied its existence, saying that what appears as erroneous reasoning is instead the correct solving of a different problem. Psychologists too have often claimed that apparent errors are due not so much to errors *in* reasoning (faulty inference) as to errors *while* reasoning. For instance, experimental subjects may be wrong in their interpretation of what is required of them, they may misinterpret the premisses, they may forget essential information, or they may even not be motivated to solve the problem. That these sorts of processes may give rise to what is termed error is undeniable, as is shown by research like Mary Henle's on syllogistic reasoning[11] and Peter Bryant's on transitive inference in young children.[12] But it is true also that error may arise from inference – indeed, from intelligent inference from true premisses.

In the realm of deductive logic, of course, such a statement is absurd. Even Russell's paradox is not an error, but a paradox: a much more highly-regarded animal. The fact that inductive reasoning is prone to error is one of the reasons for its being held in such low esteem by many logical purists. But Winograd's discussion of resource-limited processing and partial matching, for example,

---

[9] Aaron Sloman, *The Computer Revolution in Philosophy: Philosophy, Science, and Models of Mind*, chapter entitled 'On Learning About Numbers', (1978).

[10] Jean Piaget, *The Psychology of Intelligence* (1950).

[11] Mary Henle, 'On the Relation Between Logic and Thinking', *Psychological Review*, 69 (1962), 366–78.

[12] Peter Bryant, *Perception and Understanding in Young Children: An Experimental Approach* (1974).

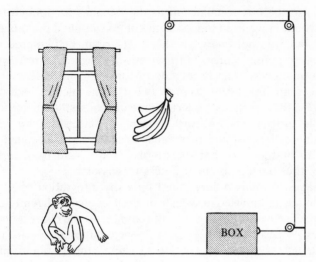

Fig. 10

showed how computational systems must lay themselves open to error if they are to function intelligently in a rich and largely unknown world.

As an example of what I mean by intelligent error, consider what happened when I showed my eight-year-old son the situation pictured in Figure 10, and asked him how the monkey would get the bananas. Without any prompting or comment from me, he immediately replied, 'Well, monkeys are intelligent, aren't they. So he'd know he was in a house because of the curtains, and houses always have scissors in them so he'd go and get some scissors and cut the string'. When I asked him at what point the monkey would cut the string, he said, 'Where it joins onto the box.'

Clearly, he made an error: monkeys are not *that* intelligent. But his error showed how an eight-year-old child (who if Piaget is right would not be able to follow, still less formulate, a solution of this problem expressed in the hypothetico-deductive terms associated with the theory of pulleys) can intelligently access and fruitfully integrate many varied items of world-knowledge in his reasoning.

It was clear from his answer to my second question that, whether or not he had realized the problem of compensatory movements posed by the pulley arrangement, he had noticed the functional relation between the bananas and the far-end of the supporting string. For otherwise, the scissors would have been used to cut the string by the bananas. (When I asked him whether the monkey could use the box to climb up to the bananas he pointed out that they would move even higher as the monkey pulled the box towards them: but I do not know whether that insight had entered into his original response – nor would I necessarily regard his retrospections on the matter as entirely reliable.) Moreover, he remembered that monkeys are intelligent animals (what if the picture had shown a sheep?), that curtains generally mean houses, that scissors are suitable instruments for cutting string, that scissors are generally available in houses, and that bananas cannot be suspended from a hook in mid-air – so that the monkey must have been *inside* the house, thus having potential access to scissors.

What is of interest here is not only the integration of zoological and domestic knowledge, which in itself is an intelligently creative matter since he normally thinks of monkeys in the context of zoos or jungles. What is of interest also is the recognition of specific items of knowledge as relevant. He knows other things about monkeys besides their being intelligent, other things about curtains than that they are usually found in houses, and other things about houses than that they have scissors in them. How were these specific items found and integrated so quickly?

Attempting to represent this reasoning in computational terms would help to sensitize one to the large variety of inferential patterns that might have underlain his verbal response. To take just one example, the main direction of access might have been from *curtains* through *house* to *scissors*, or from *scissors* through *house* to *curtains*. The former progression would have been initiated by a reasoning strategy that asked, 'What clues are there in the picture as to where the monkey is?', while the latter might have arisen from a strategy that asked, 'What needs to be done, what instrument could do it, and is it available?'

Winograd's discussion of frames is relevant again here. I personally find it much more plausible (both on computational and 'intuitive psychological' grounds) to postulate that my son was accessing a familiar 'house-frame' to get from *curtains* to *house* that that he was using a generalization of the form 'All curtains are found in houses'. This assumes, of course, that the house-frame is indexed in such a way that it is readily accessible by way of the cue *curtains*. In other words, I find a frame-explanation that posits an inference from an exemplary representation of a house more plausible than alternative explanations that would rely on universally quantified inductive generalizations about curtains and houses. The case is different, however, for the inference from *house* to *scissors* – and this for two reasons. First, even if his house-frame contained *scissors* as an item explicitly represented in it, the relevance of scissors would need to be established by some goal-directed instrumental reasoning such as that I identified as 'the second strategy' above. In addition, I find it much more difficult to believe that *scissors* are a feature of house-frames than that *curtains* are – even though he was certainly correct in saying that houses usually contain scissors. Outside this sort of problem-context (what sort?), one does not normally think of *scissors* as soon as one thinks of *house*. It is possible, however, that some process of the spreading of activations within an associative network (such as that implemented in AI terms by Quillian)[13] could establish a connection between *scissors* and *house* once these two items had been independently accessed.

Many other questions of this type would have to be faced if this common-sense reasoning were to be modelled in computational terms. For example, on the assumption that he had noticed the pulley, precisely how did this cause him to infer that what needs to be done is to cut the string (an inference without which scissors are irrelevant)? And is there a clear-cut distinction between reasoning by inductive generalizations of the form 'All *A*'s are *B*'s' and reasoning on the basis of an example, or frame? AI workers who favour frames often suggest that learning is a matter of selecting (how?) individual items – such as one's own house or body – to function as exemplars in reasoning. But it might be that information which was *learnt* in the form of inductive generalizations was *stored* and *used*, for reasons of computational efficiency, as a frame. On the likely assumption that both these types of learning (as well as others) occur, what determines which will take place when?

It is significant that adults shown Figure 10 sometimes just laugh (never thinking of scissors), and sometimes make the error of saying, 'Well, he'd push the box, of course, and climb on it.' Acquaintance with Kohler's exemplary (*sic*) work on *The Mentality of Apes* makes this 'unthinking' response rather more likely, and sometimes a person stops in mid-sentence as they belatedly realize the surprise: the pulley. A person thinking in these terms, and shown a picture with a rabbit instead of a monkey, might find the solution temporarily 'blocked' by their knowledge that rabbits are not strong enough to push boxes, at which point they might think up the alternative strategy of cutting (presumably, nibbling) the string. Or of course they might refuse to enter the game at all, pointing out that rabbits

[13] M. R. Quillian, 'Semantic Memory', in M. L. Minsky (ed.), *Semantic Information Processing* (1968), pp. 227–70.

are really dumb animals. (One friend pointed out that the bananas would come within the monkey's reach if the box were to be pushed closer to the wall.)

A number of computational models of the 'monkey and bananas' problem have in fact been produced within AI. Most of them employ 'theorem-proving' procedures which utilize general inferential processes, and bury 'common-sense' knowledge of the laws of physics inside their assumptions that on moving the box, *this* changes and *that* does not. (How might such contrasts be learnt in the first place, whether by programs, monkeys, or children?) One of the assumptions typically made by these programs is that on moving the box, the position of the bananas does not alter – and in the 'classic' version of this problem, *sans* pulley, this assumption is of course true. But none of these theorem-proving programs throws any light on how the picture can be intelligently interpreted as contradicting this assumption. The work on frames described by Winograd does not do so either; but it does suggest (which the theorem-proving approach does not) ways in which pulleys, curtains, houses, and scissors – and the IQ of monkeys – might be brought together in an intelligent (albeit mistaken) response to Figure 10.

It would be misleading to say (with Spinoza or Henle, perhaps) that my son did not really make an inferential error, since given his premises his solution was correct. For this implies that his premiss about monkey intelligence was simply mistaken, and should be replaced by another. But which other? That monkeys are not intelligent? Surely not. That monkeys are not as intelligent as humans? Well, he already knew that – and maybe it was readily accessible to him as soon as 'monkey's intelligence' was accessed. That monkeys do not know about curtains, and aren't bright enough to reason from *curtains* via *houses* to *scissors*? But this is an absurd suggestion: that they do not know these things or have this reasoning ability is very likely true, but to suggest that it be stored for use as a premiss in the problem-situation under discussion is computationally ridiculuous. For an indefinite number of similar pictures could be drawn, each requiring a separate premiss to be fished out of memory so as to prevent the wrong conclusion. Rather, one needs to be able to cross-check this suggested solution with one's general knowledge of the intelligence of monkeys, so as to decide whether the story told by my son is plausible or not. Plausible reasoning, involving partial matches between analogous cases, in conditions of incomplete knowledge, is required – and it is this type of reasoning which was highlighted by Winograd.

Some work in AI shows how error may be positively useful to an intelligent system, if it can be accurately diagnosed as due to a mistaken assumption or faulty strategy which can be modified accordingly. For example, the HACKER learning program is able to benefit from its mistakes so as to improve its own programs for building structures out of blocks.[14] For this 'inductive' learning from its experience of its mistakes, HACKER requires rich computational structures and ways of continually monitoring its own plans and performance. For example, it must be able to distinguish the different types of error, or bug, in its performance that are due to general classes of error in goal-seeking that arise because of the interactions between various actions (and preconditions for actions) within one overall plan. Its programmer has distinguished five such classes of error-generating bug, which he terms: PREREQUISITE-CONFLICT-BROTHERS; PREREQUISITE-MISSING; PRE-REQUISITE-CLOBBERS-BROTHER-GOAL; STRATEGY-CLOBBERS-BROTHER; and DIRECT-CONFLICT-BRO-THERS. These underlying bugs in the program's reasoned planning manifest themselves during the execution of its performance-programs in various ways, in the form of unsatisfied prerequisites, double moves, or failure to protect a condition that must continue to exist until a specific point in the plan.

HACKER is written in CONNIVER,[15] a programming language basically similar to PLANNER. Like KRL also, CONNIVER enables the programmer to set up 'demons'. Demons are active processes that can be relied on to monitor the data-base and make modifications or pass on messages to other processes as necessary, and which thus enable one to write relatively intelligent programs. Thus we saw in the previous section that PLANNER antecedent and consequent theorems indexed by general patterns can trigger the immediate inference of *B*, given *A*, or the attempt to establish *A* if *B* is what is required. Analogous facilities are used by HACKER in the form of CONNIVER 'if-added' and 'if-needed' methods. The language also has a useful feature called its 'context-mechanism'. This enables a computational system economically to store and make available contextual information that is shared by many different sub-processes, such as the processes aiming at successive sub-goals generated by one and the same higher-level goal, or the various moves of a box that leave the neighbouring bananas in the

---

[14] G. J. Sussman, *A Computer Model of Skill Acquisition* (1975).
[15] G. J. Sussman and D. V. McDermott, *Why Conniving is Better than Planning*. AI Memo 255a, MIT AI Lab. (1972).

same position. And a very short passage of program-code ensures that the reasons for doing something, the necessary preconditions, and the reasons for failure in execution will be automatically stored and passed to those computational processes that may have need of them. These computational facilities are crucial to HACKER's assessment of its success or failure in its activities, and to its reasoned self-corrections in light of its experience. And these abilities in turn depend on the program's structural diagnosis of the five different types of bug (so that the program illustrates the point made in section 2, that learning from one's experience presupposes prior knowledge and inferential competence).

HACKER may be described broadly as 'inductive' because it learns from experience. Unlike some of the programs described by Winograd, however, its reasoning processes are strictly deductive in nature: it identifies and patches bugs by deduction from its initial premises and its (deductively arrived-at) plan-CRITICS. But novel CRITICS are generated as a result of experience, and this is why the program's performance and planning abilities improve. (In an equally broad sense of 'deduction', it is sometimes said that all computation is deductive. For example, 'probabilistic' reasoning deduces that X is probable, given Y.)

If one considers the sort of inductive (though non-'Baconian') reasoning that is involved in the planning or interpretation of experiments, it is clear that interactions between the various experimental parameters, and between these and the background conditions, must continually be taken into account if the 'correct' interpretation is to be reached and the 'predictable' outcome observed. Just as there are significantly different types of bug affecting plan and/or execution (of which five have been identified by HACKER's programmer), so there are analogously distinct ways in which an experimental prediction may fail or a scientific hypothesis be falsified (or appear to be falsified). A plan that can be criticized by HACKER before being run and patched so as to remove the bug, or a hitch in execution that HACKER can notice and remedy so as to rerun the plan in corrected form, are analogous to a hypothesis that can be amended and so saved or an experiment that can be discounted. And a program like PLANEX,[16] which (unlike HACKER) can remedy faults during execution and go on from where it left off, reminds one of the way in which a scientist may tinker with an experiment in progress, so as to avoid having to start afresh. Parallels such as these

[16] R. E. Fikes, P. E. Hart, and N. J. Nilsson, 'Learning and Executing Generalized Robot Plans', *Artificial Intelligence* 3 (1972), 251–88.

suggest that a computational analysis of the logic of induction would help to illuminate the structure of scientific reasoning and the way in which – as Popper has insisted – science progresses through (not just in spite of) its errors.

4. Conclusion

Inductive reasoning 'as she is spoke' is more worthy of epistemological respect than is commonly allowed by logicians. If one is to take into account the real computational constraints upon real computational systems, then the norms of real – or even artificial – thinking have at least as much right to be treated as normative as do the rules of deductive logic. For rationality cannot in practice do without them. Winograd described deductive logic as an approximation to a much richer set of natural reasoning processes. Philosophers in the past have tended to decry suggestions that rational thought be characterized in terms of these processes, rejecting such attempts as a 'psychologism' that need have nothing to do with the ideal even if it faithfully reflects the real. This attitude arose partly because of a rationalistic horror of error (although approaches such as Popper's fallibilism have commendably counteracted this general tendency), partly because of a failure to take sufficiently seriously the Kantian point that one needs a great deal of knowledge already if one is to be able to learn more, and partly because of the lack of any formal or theoretical vocabulary adequate to characterize the processes and content of the knowledge involved in inductive reasoning.

Computational concepts offer the promise and the beginnings of such a vocabulary. If we ask, 'How should computer-simulated learning be structured?' we soon come to see that the search for, evaluation, and acceptance of evidence has to be considerably richer (both in structure and content) than this:

'I know what you're thinking about,' said Tweedledum; 'but it isn't so, nohow.'

'Contrariwise,' continued Tweedledee, 'if it was so, it might be; and if it were so it would be; but as it isn't, it ain't. That's logic.'

§ Comments and Replies
The Winograd–Boden Session

KYBURG: 1. Both Boden and Winograd indicated that one of the purposes of computer representation of inductive reasoning might be to augment our ratiocinative powers, or to make clearer how we *ought* to reason inductively, but neither did more than offer rather vague endorsement-in-principle to this normative dimension. Many of the philosophers at the Conference have also suggested that their goal is only to understand and clarify how science progresses and how inductive arguments are evaluated.

2. I would like to suggest that what we should be concerned with as philosophers (rather than as psychologists or historians or sociologists) is not descriptions of scientific change or inductive argument, not merely understanding or clarifying or even rationally reconstructing induction, but rather with developing and explicating the standards to which inductive arguments ought to conform.

3. I lost track of the number of times the maxim, 'Ought implies can' was solemnly enunciated. Whatever its virtues in ethics, the maxim is false for logic. One ought to be consistent; one ought not to offer invalid deductive arguments. No one lives up to these norms; but they are valuable precisely because they can be approached; formal logic gives us standards by which we can measure our approach to them. We can tell when someone leaps to conclusions, or when he resists overwhelming evidence, or when he exhibits very inappropriate degrees of belief. There are as yet no generally accepted standards for this inductive sort of argument.

4. The task of inductive logic is to develop such standards. But the development of inductive norms cannot take place in a vacuum: they must be standards appropriate to human beings, not to angels and not to chimpanzees (though knowledge about the latter is more likely to provide useful information than knowledge about the former). This is one reason that computer simulation of inductive reasoning may very well yield important grist for the philosopher's mill.

5. But there is another reason for close co-operation between those who work in Artificial Intelligence and those who work in inductive logic, mentioned by neither of the speakers. Just as an arithmetic program does arithmetic the way people *ought* to do arithmetic, and not (thank goodness) the way people actually *do* do arithmetic, nor the way an omniscient deity would do arithmetic, so an inductive program should embody standards and norms reflecting the way people ought to argue inductively. These norms are little

understood, and inductive programs representing actual reasoning may contribute to our understanding of them. But, just as important if not more important, these norms are not totally unknown. Philosophers have thought about them for many years, and if they have not achieved agreement about what they are, they have achieved some agreement about what they are not. Philosophers therefore have much to contribute to the development of ideal inductive programs designed to reflect how people *should* reason inductively.

6. A corollary of this is that programmability might be taken as a criterion for a 'system' of inductive logic; and, even more important, that the results of constructing an inductive program incorporating certain proposed standards of rationality, feeding in an appropriate set of raw data, and observing the output, might well serve as an extremely useful test of those proposed standards. There is every reason, on both sides, for close co-operation between AI and inductive logic.

COHEN: Connections between inductive logic and artificial intelligence run in both directions.

First, it has to be recognized that laboratory experiments are not the only source of data for checking out the psychological reality of AI programmes. Evidence that human thinking actually functions in accordance with such a programme may also be sought from adequately based philosophical reconstructions. Indeed, where the thought-pattern involved is a fairly sophisticated one, and the programme's aim is to simulate human thinking at its best, philosophical reconstructions may well constitute a more fertile source of data than laboratory experiment. A prime example of such a source would be logical analyses of inductive reasoning-patterns that have actually been instantiated in the history of science. Hence, as Arthur Burks has pointed out, those inductive logics, like Baconian[1] ones, that stick closest to concrete examples of actual human reasoning, especially in the low sciences, will obviously have most to offer as a basis for computer simulation. But where, as in the Carnap–Hintikka school, inductive logic becomes more a matter of invention than of representation, and so choice between one system and another can no longer be supported by detailed analogies from

[1] I assume that Boden's use of this adjective in quotation-marks is intended to imply the features that Popper (e.g. *Conjectives and Refutations* 1963), pp. 12 ff.) mistakenly attributes to Bacon's inductive logic. Actually, of course, Bacon was well aware (as shown by his preference for what he called the method of the bee over that of the ant or the spider) of the importance of the conceptual apparatus with which an inductive investigation approaches its subject-matter.

the history or philosophy of science, inductive logicians have less to offer that is relevant to exercises in computer simulation.

Secondly, there is also an important connection that runs in the other direction: AI can contribute to the foundations of inductive logic. The opportunity for such a contribution arises in the following way. No criterion of inductive assessment can escape some kind of relativization to a particular sub-language. This is equally true for Carnapian range-measures, for Shackle–Levi measures of potential surprise, or for the Baconian method of relevant variables; and the 'grue' paradox confirms it. Anyone who proposes a particular type of criterion for inductive assessments is therefore obligated to disclose how he thinks the appropriate sub-language is, or should be, selected and under what circumstances it is, or should be, modified. Otherwise he offers only a partial representation of, or norm for, inductive reasoning. It is like telling people what to do with a machine when it is already built, but not telling anyone how to build it. Neither the Shackle school nor the Carnap one have taken this problem seriously. For example, Niiniluoto and Tuomela, in their book *Theoretical Concepts and Hypothetico-Inductive Inference* (1973) have talked about differences between assessments in richer and poorer sub-languages, but have said nothing about how we may, or should, decide which sub-language is safe to use for a particular task or when we need to modify or enrich the sub-language already in use. But, if one does try to work out a detailed solution of this problem, or of a part of it, as I have tried to do in *The Probable and the Provable* (1977) pp. 135 ff. for my concept of a list of relevant variables, one finds that the complexity of the issues involved defeats any easy confidence of correctness. One needs to set up a quasi-operational definition, according to which anyone who has built up his sub-language or list of relevant variables by such-and-such kinds of operation is assured of its appropriateness. But how can we test whether these kinds of operation have been fully specified? An appropriate AI programme might be the best way to do this. We may also hope thus for an eventual AI solution to the following problem: under what conditions can the syntax of human language (or some sufficiently important part of it) be learned by a Baconian inductive learning programme? Must such a programme incorporate *a priori* certain specifically grammatical constraints on its space of hypotheses, as Chomsky argued against me in his *Reflections on Language* (1976), pp. 204–14, or could the relevant constraints on admissible hypotheses be of a less specific nature, as suggested in my *The Probable and the Provable*, p. 262?

9

The Evaluation of Rival Inductive Logics

§25. JONATHAN E. ADLER

Criteria for a Good Inductive Logic

We critically examine Lakatos's 'Changes in the Problem of Inductive Logic'. While Lakatos's critique is specifically directed at Carnap's programme, we raise the question as to whether Lakatos has succeeded in showing that the recent development of alternative inductive logics is also part of a 'degenerating problem-shift'.

We first briefly summarize Lakatos's critique of Carnap's programme, and mention his few critical remarks with respect to more recent work in inductive logic. Second, we note some points at which more recent work is able to answer, *prima facie*, some of Lakatos's objections.

In our examination of Lakatos's critique, we apply it to two main influences in inductive logic: the 'subjectivist' theory of probability and decision-making, and 'localization'. We also look at problems and promises that arise for recent work, under these influences, that are somewhat independent of Lakatos's critique. We conclude that the evaluation of inductive logic is much more complex than Lakatos's critique allows, and so, whatever the merits of some of his (and others) criticisms, they do not foreclose the possibility that the research programmes in inductive logic will make important contributions to the major problems in empiricist theory of knowledge and philosophy of science.

1.

Imre Lakatos's 'Changes in the Problem of Inductive Logic'[1] is a sustained critique of Carnap's theory of inductive logic, developed within a novel framework. This framework combines an historical approach to the appraisal of Carnap's *programme*, with evaluative criteria that focus on *problem-shifts*. A problem-shift is *progressive* if it leads to a solution of a problem more interesting than the original

---

[1] I. Lakatos, 'Changes in the Problem of Inductive Logic' in I. Lakatos (ed.), *Inductive Logic* (1968), pp. 315–417.

one; and *degenerating* if it retreats to solving a less interesting problem than the original.[2]

Lakatos does not provide criteria for determining what is or is not a problem. This is not a serious inadequacy since we often have general agreement about which are the relevant problems for inductive logic. More serious is the fact that there are no criteria offered for assessing the relative merits of problems, and for evaluating the simplicity of assumptions introduced to solve these problems. Also, his criteria for progress (or degeneration) in problem-shifts should be extended, if his framework is to be used for a comprehensive evaluation. A progressive problem-shift, in this extension, is one in which the problems solved by a programme or theory are more interesting than those, within the purview of the programme, left unsolved or ignored. And a problem-shift is a degenerating one when the problems solved are less interesting than those, within the purview of the programme, that are unsolved or ignored. This seems to me an improvement because it broadens the basis for evaluation. In particular, we are now not restricted to appealing only to the *original* problems, nor to determining the relevant problems in terms only of the research programme under test. These emendations have a self-serving motivation in that they provide justification for our appeal to a wider class of problems than Lakatos himself considers.

One of the main reasons for characterizing Carnap's inductive logic as a *research programme* is, presumably, to remind us that it is capable of modification and development as it is applied and tested. So criticism will be more decisive if it is directed not just at the present formulation of the programme, but also at any reasonable alterations in the basic claims.[3] One question that my discussion of Lakatos's critique raises is this: to what extent are his criticisms of Carnap applicable to the recent developments not just in Carnap's

---

[2] See ibid., pp. 316–17. For a fuller treatment of his methodology see I. Lakatos, 'Falsification and the Methodology of Scientific Research Programmes' in I. Lakatos and A. Musgrave, *Criticism and the Growth of Knowledge* (1970), pp. 91–195. The discussion of his methodology is quite brief in I. Lakatos, 'Changes in the Problem of Inductive Logic' in I. Lakatos (ed.), *Inductive Logic*, pp. 315–417, and his views have their central application to scientific research programmes, though Lakatos certainly believed his theory of criticism has wider scope. See for example, I. Lakatos, 'Falsification and the Methodology of Scientific Research Programmes', p. 180, n. 2. In this paper Lakatos connects the problem-shift criteria with the better-known concepts of 'content-increasing', 'content-decreasing', and '*ad hoc*' stratagems.

[3] See, for example, I. Lakatos, 'Changes in the Problem of Inductive Logic', p. 357, n. 2. In I. Lakatos, 'Falsification and the Methodology of Scientific Research Programmes', more explicit concern is given for alterations in programme by distinguishing between, say, 'heuristics of a theory' and 'the hard core'.

programme, some of which he alludes to,[4] but in the whole field of inductive logic generally? A cursory examination shows that many of Lakatos's criticisms appear answered by some of the more recent systems of inductive logic. It could be that these systems are sufficiently different from Carnap's that Lakatos would not have taken his criticisms to apply, and that a new line of attack (if any) was needed. Alternatively, he could have believed that these new systems represent a mere patching-up of the Carnapian programme, which ultimately can be seen as parts of the same degenerating problem-shift. The question raised here is being asked not just of the students of Lakatos: Nagel, Popper, Putnam,[5] and others have all provided, like Lakatos, important criticisms of Carnap's work. One gets a sense from reading these critics that the target was broader: almost anything that might be considered an inductive logic would be subject to some of their objections. The question then is this: are the recent developments in inductive logic vindications of Carnap's programme, which can answer the valid criticisms of the above philosophers, or are these new systems still vulnerable to objections analogous to those brought against Carnap? I cannot hope here to answer this question, although my discussion will constitute a small part of an answer. Rather, by seeing how Lakatos's critique fares with respect to more recent work (as well as with Carnap), and, more generally, by looking at the difficulties one faces in giving a comprehensive critique of the whole programme of inductive logic, I hope to elicit answers from others.

This paper will proceed as follows. First, we will briefly summarize Lakatos' critique of Carnap's programme, survey his few remarks about more recent advances in inductive logic, and note some points at which recent advances, *prima facie*, answer some of the criticisms leveled at Carnap. The second, and, along with the last sections, the major part of this paper, is concerned to explore two of the main influences on recent work: the 'subjective' (or 'personalist', or 'Bayesian') theory of probability and decision-making, and the 'localization' of inductive logic. We want to indicate problems and promises these influences hold out in addition to those that Lakatos

[4] See, for example, I. Lakatos, 'Changes in the Problem of Inductive Logic', pp. 360–1.

[5] E. Nagel, 'Carnap's Theory of Induction' in P. Schilpp (ed.), *The Philosophy of Rudolf Carnap* (1963); 'Principles of the Theory of Probability', *International Encyclopaedia of Unified Science* (1949); K. R. Popper, *The Logic of Scientific Discovery* (1959); H. Putnam, 'Degree of Confirmation and Inductive Logic' in P. Schilpp (ed.), *The Philosophy of Rudolf Carnap*. This is only a partial list of relevant works. For additional references see the Bibliography in H. E. Kyburg, 'Local and Global Induction' in R. Bogdan (ed.), *Local Induction* (1976).

and others have considered, as well as seeing how we can extend Lakatos's framework to these approaches. Finally, we will argue that the full evaluation of inductive logic is much too complex for the scheme that Lakatos envisages, although this 'defence' of inductive logic itself requires a number of concessions to Lakatos.

2.

Carnap's inductive logic, on Lakatos's reconstruction, aimed to solve the problem of the foundations of knowledge (the logic of justification) which was only one of the two main problems of neoclassical empiricism (the other being the logic of the growth of knowledge). He would solve the former problem by showing that problematic generalizations were partially provable on the basis of the unproblematic observational evidence. Carnap's programme was an attempt:

(1) to justify his claim that the degree of confirmation satisfies Kolmogorov's axioms of probability; (2) to find and justify further secondary requirements for the determination of the sought-for measure function; (3) to construct piecemeal a complete, perfect language of science in which all propositions can be expressed; and (4) to offer a definition of a measure function which would satisfy the conditions laid down in (1) and (2).[6]

At two points Lakatos summarizes in a brief way the kinds of problem-shifts that Carnap's programme underwent:

... [from] his original bold idea of an a priori, analytic inductive logic to his present caution about the epistemological nature of his theory; ... [from] the original problem of rational degree of belief in hypotheses (principally scientific theories) first to the problem of rational degree of belief in particular sentences, and finally, to the problem of the probabilistic consistency ('coherence') of systems of beliefs.[7]

... Carnap and his school shifted the original center of gravity of the problem of induction away from informality to formality, away from methodology to justification, away from genuine theories to particular propositions, away from evidential support to betting quotients.[8]

One of the most important problem-shifts, one clearly degenerating, is away from inductive logic, as providing the norms for the evaluation of the logic of various scientific judgements about empirical

[6] I. Lakatos, 'Changes in the Problem of Inductive Logic', p. 323.
[7] Ibid., p. 317.
[8] Ibid., p. 374.

support of hypotheses, to what Lakatos calls the 'abdication of the inductive judge'. Inductive logic then provides no more than a requirement that the set of beliefs be coherent.[9] Admittedly Lakatos ends the main section with a surprisingly weak conclusion: '... the historian of thought *may* have to record a "degenerating problem-shift"'.[10] But at the end of the essay we have a stronger, more characteristic summation, all in italics:

The programme of inductive logic or confirmation theory set out to construct a universal logical confirmation function with one absolute metric, which, in turn, is based on one distinguished touchstone theory. This *one* touchstone theory usually takes the form of a Laplacian proto-distribution over the sentences of a universal formal language. But this atheoretical (or, if you wish, monotheoretical) approach is useless, and the programme of an absolute, universal confirmation function is utopian.[11]

In his contribution to the Schilpp volume for Popper,[12] Lakatos writes:

The second prong of Popper's attack was directed against the programme of an a priori probabilistic inductive logic or confirmation theory ... In this campaign too Popper achieved a complete victory, although 'inductive logic', displaying all the characteristics of a degenerating research programme, is still – sociologically – a booming industry.[13]

Lakatos goes on to repeat a charge he also made in 'Changes':[14]

But the second prong of Popper's anti-inductivist campaign can be interpreted in an even stronger sense. It can be said to have been directed against *any* infallible a priori metaphysical inductive principle, whether probabilistic or nonprobabilistic, which would serve to assign a *proven* metric to the field of scientific statements.

Nonprobabilistic logics of confirmation are still being produced – some with great ingenuity – by philosophers of science who understood Popper's arguments against probability logic, but not this more general message.[15]

He adds as a footnote to this that 'Hintikka, L. J. Cohen, and, perhaps, Levi could be mentioned here'.[16]

(We want to put aside, as much as is possible, the Popperian critique of inductive logic and subsequent controversy. It is an issue

[9] Ibid., p. 373.
[10] Ibid. My emphasis.
[11] Ibid., p. 416.
[12] I. Lakatos, 'Popper on Demarcation and Induction' in P. Schilpp (ed.) *The Philosophy of Karl Popper* (1974).
[13] Ibid., p. 259.
[14] I. Lakatos, 'Changes in the Problem of Inductive Logic', p. 398.
[15] I. Lakatos, 'Popper on Demarcation and Induction', pp. 259–60.
[16] Ibid., p. 269, n. 107.

that may have dealt with, in detail, though often without fruitful communication.[17] Also, Popper himself has expressed serious doubts on Lakatos's work as giving an accurate portrayal of his views.)[18]

What then of Lakatos's own characterization and implicit criticism, of inductive logics as requiring an 'infallible *a priori* metaphysical principle'? In Levi's case the qualifier ('perhaps') is understandable: Levi disparages any attempt at the type of proof or justification that Lakatos takes as the motivation for adopting such principles.[19] Cohen's theory[20] can be construed as an attempt to uncover the logical structure of the concept of empirical support as used in on-going science. From this perspective Cohen accepts whatever principles of empirical support can be ascribed to scientists on the basis of the inferences they draw. His assumptions are no more infallible or *a priori* than theirs. Finally, in the case of Hintikka[21] (or even Carnap for that matter) one must distinguish between the question of the choice of the *c*-function from that of the framework of a probabilistic inductive logic within a certain regimented language. The choice of such a *c*-function is justified both *a priori* (e.g., as required for 'learning from experience') and *a posterori*, in terms of the agreement of the resultant theory with our intuitive judgements.[22] But neither Carnap nor Hintikka need claim that the set of admissible *c*-functions is adequate for all possible worlds (nor even that there is one *c*-function that is correct for all domains in this world). We can imagine a world in which whatever hypothesis is warranted on any of these *c*-functions later turns out false. A possible world in which nature was so antagonistic to us might be one where there could not be any 'learning from experience' and the only *c*-function that would be justified is $c\dagger$. Nor does the general framework itself involve infallible *a priori* principles. It is not

[17] See A. Michalos, *The Carnap–Popper Controversy* (1971).

[18] K. Popper, 'Replies to Critics' in P. Schilpp (ed.), *The Philosophy of Karl Popper* (1974), pp. 999–1013.

[19] I. Lakatos, 'Changes in the Problem of Inductive Logic', p. 398; I. Levi, *Gambling with Truth* (1967), pp. 3–6.

[20] L. J. Cohen, *The Implications of Induction* (1970).

[21] See, among others, J. Hintikka, 'Induction by Enumeration and Induction by Elimination' in I. Lakatos (ed.) *Inductive Logic*; J. Hintikka, 'Toward a Theory of Inductive Generalization' in Y. Bar-Hillel (ed.), *Logic Methodology and the Philosophy of Science* (1965).

[22] Carnap's view on the justification of the choice of a *c*-function have undergone changes. See R. Carnap, *Logical Foundations of Probability*, 2nd ed. (1962), especially pp. 564–7; R. Carnap, *The Continuum of Inductive Methods* (1952); and for his most recent views, R. Carnap, 'Inductive Logic and Inductive Intuition' in H. E. Kyburg and H. Smokler (eds.), *Studies in Subjective Probability* (1964); P. Schilpp (ed.), *The Philosophy of Rudolf Carnap*; and R. Carnap and R. Jeffrey (eds.), *Studies in Inductive Logic and Probability*, vol. 1 (1971).

falsifiable, just as Popper's methodology is not, but this is a reflection on its logical status, which does not entail any substantive claims about the world.[23]

Although there are other occasional references to recent inductive logics, Lakatos does not go any deeper than the level that the above quotations indicate.

3.

The central criticisms of Carnap's theory appear, *prima facie*, answered within with more recent work. These criticisms argued that the confirmation judgements from Carnap's theory were relevant only to unimportant parts of scientific inference and did not capture the really advanced and major types of scientific inference. Thus, for example, the Principle of Instantial Relevance is objected to because it allows confirmation to increase by '. . . completely mechanical repetition of the same experiment'.[24] Further, the irrelevance of theories to confirmation, typified by the result of 0-confirmation for universal hypotheses, seemed to commit inductive logic to giving scientific inference an overly instrumentalist interpretation. There were also objections that (seemingly) non-enumerative forms of inference, such as by elimination of competing hypotheses, and those that arise when the variety and analogy of the evidence are taken into account, cannot be adequately represented in Carnap's theory.[25]

The system of inductive logic due to Jaakko Hintikka and developed by his colleagues is both an extension of Carnap's system and yet one in which these difficulties appear to be met. The most obvious case is that universal hypotheses can receive greater than 0-confirmation.[26] Enumerative induction has a central place, but it is balanced by the dominance of an eliminative factor, when elimination is not complete. Finally, theories can play a very central role in confirmation in that they can provide direct support for hypotheses, and this gives weight to a realist view of theories and theoretical terms.[27]

[23] None the less again, like Popper's methodology, it is open to criticism.

[24] I. Lakatos, 'Changes in the Problem of Inductive Logic', p. 344.

[25] Apart from the references in footnote 5, see also P. Achinstein, 'Variety and Analogy in Confirmation Theory', *Philosophy of Science* (1963).

[26] See J. Hintikka, 'Induction by Enumeration and Induction by Elimination'; J. Hintikka, 'Toward a Theory of Inductive Generalization', and the recent symposium, 'Systems of Inductive Logic Where Generalizations Can Receive Non-Zero Probabilities' in F. Suppe and P. S. Asquith (eds.), *Proceedings of the Philosophy of Science Association Meetings* (1976), vol. 2.

[27] For important developments in Hintikka's approach to inductive logic see R. Hilpinen, *Rules of Acceptance and Inductive Logic* (Acta Philosophica Fennica, 22 (1968); and especially, I. Niiniluoto and R. Tuomela, *Theoretical Concepts and Hypothetico-Inductive Inference* (1973).

Other recent inductive logicians, though deviating further (than Hintikka) from Carnap's theory, are more sensitive to the relevance of history of science, and of current on-going science, in providing constraints on their systems. Here is just one example. Wesley Salmon has argued that the use of Bayesian ideas about prior probabilities in confirmation explains the relevance of the history of science to its rational reconstruction: we can use these prior probabilities as a measure of the plausibility of a newly proposed hypothesis and thus account for the fact that some hypotheses are not and, presumably, need not be given serious consideration (at a given time). Salmon's notion of 'plausibility' has also been invoked to give partial explanation for the importance of the 'consilience of inductions'[28] in the history of science.[29]

4.

Two of the major influences on recent work in inductive logic are the subjectivist theory of probability and second, the localization of judgements of empirical support (or acceptability) to specific contexts of enquiry.

Important features of the (normative) subjectivist theory[30] for inductive logic include their approach to the uncovering and structuring of partial beliefs in terms of betting behaviour. Subjective probability can be developed, as Savage does, on the basis of relatively weak axioms of preference. Secondly, the subjectives justify their type of quantification by showing that a system of beliefs is coherent (in their special sense) if and only if it conforms

[28] W. Salmon, 'Bayes's Theorem and the History of Science' in R. Stuewer (ed.), *Minnesota Studies in the Philosophy of Science*, vol. 5 (1974). See also R. Butts, 'The Consilience of Induction and the Problem of Conceptual Change in Science' in R. Colodny (ed.), *Logic, Laws, and Life*, Vol. 6 (1970). Although Salmon's use of Bayes's Theorem to capture the virtue of conservatism does account for a value of consilience, it should not be taken as telling the whole story. See here M. Hesse, 'Consilience of Inductions', in I. Lakatos (ed.), *Inductive Logic*; and M. Hesse, *The Structure of Scientific Inference* (1974), particularly pp. 205–17.

[29] The concept of acceptance, distinct from support, has come to play a more prominent role in inductive logic. Levi has urged that many of the criticisms of Carnap's work lose force in the context of acceptance. Thus, Levi argues even 0-confirmation need not be a barrier to acceptance. Levi conceives of his theory of acceptance as providing a meta-theory for evaluating theories of confirmation. See I. Levi, *Gambling With Truth* (1967).

[30] Classic sources for the subjectivist theory include: B. de Finetti, 'Foresight: Its Logical Laws, Its Subjective Sources' in H. E. Kyburg and H. Smokler (eds.), *Studies in Subjective Probability* (1967), pp. 93–158, and B. de Finetti, *Theory of Probability* (1974–5); F. Ramsey, 'Truth and Probability' in *The Foundation of Mathematics* (ed. Braithwaite), (1960); and L. J. Savage, *Foundations of Statistics* (1954). Richard Jeffrey's *The Logic of Decision* (1965), is an important recent contribution.

to the calculus of probability (Dutch Book Arguments).[31] Third, in addition to the 'static' condition of coherence, they argue that changes in probability, with additional evidence, should be made according to the rule of conditionalization (or Bayes's Rule).[32] Subjectivists argue that, under these and some other conditions, initial probability assignments are eventually 'swamped' by new evidence and analogously, that a convergence in probability assignments will take place.

Isaac Levi's *Gambling with Truth* is rightly considered '... a classic of local induction'.[33] The pragmatism that dominates local induction, particularly as Levi envisages it, takes justification as appropriate only where there is a legitimate doubt, and takes as input to settle this doubt all that is unquestioned within the specific enquiry. (Roughly, doubt is illegitmate if it could be raised in any enquiry, e.g., Humean scepticism). The approach is progressive; Levi writes:

Human knowledge is subject to change. In scientific inquiry, men seek to change their knowledge for the better. The central problem of epistemology ought to be, therefore, to provide a systematic account of criteria for the improvement of knowledge. Alternatively stated, the problem is to offer a systematic characterization of conditions under which alterations in a corpus of knowledge are legitimate or are justified.[34]

Localization is obviously a matter of degree, dependent upon how much one takes as unproblematic input, but the goals of all local theories are similar, namely to shift from concern with the defense of the rationality of induction to the formulation of the criteria by which induction does or should proceed. It is an activity within the more manageable 'new riddle of induction', i.e., within the task of explicating valid inductive inferences.[35]

Let me sketch here what I take to be one way in which the

---

[31] For an analysis of the subjectivist approach and particularly the Dutch Book Arguments see D. H. Mellor, *The Matter of Chance* (1971), chapters 1 and 2. Mellor argues for the thesis that personalism and the objective propensity theory are compatible.

[32] The latter requires the 'dynamic assumption' connecting '... conditional probability with probability given'. The terminology and quotes are from I. Hacking, 'Slightly More Realistic Personal Probabilities', *Phil. Sci.* 34 (1967). Paul Teller in 'Conditionalization and Observation', *Synthèse* 25 (1973), attempts to provide a justification for the rule of conditionalization through Dutch Book Arguments.

[33] Bogdan makes this remark in his Preface to the book he edited, *Local Induction* (1976). Bogdan's Bibliography contains references to other recent systems of local inductive logic.

[34] I. Levi, 'Acceptance Revisited' in R. Bogdan (ed.), *Local Induction*, p. 1.

[35] This is the task that Goodman sets for inductive logic in N. Goodman, *Fact, Fiction and Forecast*, 2nd ed. (1965) (e.g. pp. 97–9).

subjectivist theory and local inductive logics could each contribute to progress on the kind of epistemological issues that Lakatos takes as fundamental. The controversy over the nature and degree of objectivity in the growth of scientific knowledge is one that inductive logic must participate in if it is to justify its claims to general philosophical interest. One can distinguish three tasks which, if they can be met, would go quite far in providing the defence of the objectivity of scientific change that is needed. First, one has to explicate the inferences occurring in scientific reasoning and offer criteria (or justification) for distinguishing these inferences from other 'invalid' forms (e.g., counter-inductive policies). Second, one must justify both the explication and the criteria by showing how they maximize certain goals of science (e.g., truth, or explanatory power) and contribute to science's progress. Finally, if one can show that the assumptions needed to meet the basic standards of rationality (parts of which are determined by the first two tasks) are minimal, inductive logicians can justify the plausibility of these standards as providing normative constraints on science (without *detailed* historical evidence). The first task is one that local inductive logics have already given much effort to. By determining judgements of empirical support within well-defined enquiries they have been able to give more realistic representations of the 'consilience of inductions', of the role of theories in inference, of the importance of the variety and analogy of evidence in increasing confirmation, of eliminative induction, and of the weight of evidence (to mention some well-known problem-areas for Carnap's programme). Work relating to the second task includes not only traditional off-shoots of the justification of induction (e.g., connecting empirical support with increased probability, falsification, and self-correcting methods), but more recently, in approaching acceptance by way of epistemic utilities, it is argued that meeting the particular criteria for acceptance will maximize certain cognitive values.[36] (From the subjectivists' side, attempts have been made to extend the Dutch Book Arguments to provide a justification not just of the 'static' condition of synchronic rationality, but also the 'dynamic' condition for changes in probability judgements.)[37] The third task is one which subjectivists have much to offer because a crucial aspect of their theory is the minimal input and constraints they impose, and the strong output they claim to get: namely, *a posteriori* probabilities that are objective, in that they arise from alterations in judgements

[36] See here I. Levi, *Gambling with Truth*; and K. Lehrer, 'Induction, Consensus, and Catastrophe' in R. Bogdan (ed.), *Local Induction*.
[37] See footnote 32.

as the evidence accumulates and exhibit a pattern similar to the 'convergence of opinion', which many philosophers, following Peirce, have taken as a hallmark of objectivity. (Additionally, in Jeffrey's model there can be evidence without certainty and this improves upon the empiricist picture because it allows knowledge without the strong assumptions of certainty or foundations.)[38]

In mentioning some ways these two approaches can contribute to the controversy over the growth of scientific knowledge, I do not mean to accept uncritically all of their claims and arguments. We will see that Lakatos has important criticisms of both approaches. The subjectivist theory has been subject to extensive criticism in the literature. For example, the subjectivist has frequently been charged with starting with such arbitrary judgements (while maintaining a scepticism about imposing any stronger constraints than coherence) that he must leave us quite uninformed about actual scientific reasoning. Moreover, so the critics continue, any enquiry, explicated on the subjectivist model, is threatened with having its conclusions appear unfounded, even if consistent.[39]

The central question that arises for local inductive logics is this: has their pragmatism pushed aside all the important philosophical issues? Localization is a matter of the additional input that one uses to derive one's judgements of inductive support. This input is not questioned within the particular context in which it is used. To give a few examples: In Levi such input comes in with choice of ultimate partition; for Abner Shimony[40] in the choice of competing hypotheses and assigning them non-trivial probabilities; in Hintikka in the weighting of certain parameters; and in Cohen in the choice of relevant variables and judgements of the material similarity of hypotheses. But no simple ordering is possible because the aims are not all the same. Some of these theories are meant to be more normative (e.g., Levi's) and some more descriptive (e.g., Cohen's). Clearly, localization is a matter of degree depending upon how

[38] See R. Jeffrey, 'Probable Knowledge' in I. Lakatos (ed.), *Inductive Logic*; and R. Jeffrey, *The Logic of Decision*.

[39] *If* the subjectivist theory is epistemologically relevant in the way suggested, then these 'charges' become virtues of the theory. The point is that, if objectivity can be shown to arise from the most minimal basis (namely, arbitrary subjective judgements), then one can be much more secure about science being, to a very high degree, objective since its initial judgements are so much better founded. For this specific task of justifying the imputation of objectivity to scientific change, there is no need to commit oneself to the view that the subjectivists provide the correct model for all inference in science. See also M. Hesse, *The Structure of Scientific Inference*; and J. Dorling, 'Review: Mary Hesse, *The Structure of Scientific Inference*', *Brit. J. Phil.* 26 (March 1975), 61–71.

[40] A. Shimony, 'Scientific Inference' in R. Colodny (ed.), *The Nature and Function of Scientific Theories* (1970).

much input is appealed to. Without arguing this point, we are still able to give more force and precision to our initial worry about local inductive logics.[41] The above question divides up into then two basic questions: First, to what degree are we giving up the important issues of epistemology by accepting more and more data as unproblematic? Second, by so relativizing induction to specific contexts haven't we, in effect, given up the hope of showing the objectivity of the growth of scientific knowledge? The second is a special case of the first, brought on by the worry over the fact that inductive logic is made to depend on scientific judgements for initial input rather than to provide the framework for evaluating the rationale of those judgements.[42] Let us explore one instance of this question.

5.

Local inductive theorists, to take the most obvious case, shift away from the grand problem of the justification of induction. Since the assumptions that Hume argued were unjustifiable are needed in any scientific enquiry (insofar as these are inductive), these assumptions will form part of the (unquestioned) input to local inductive logic. In this respect, global inductive logic is not much better off. When it comes to trying to give *a priori* justification for rejection of c-functions, like $c\dagger$, appeal is made to requirements of 'learning from experience'.[43] Such a requirement is just as much in need of

[41] Some of the themes in this paper are also discussed in J. E. Adler, 'Evaluating Global and Local Theories of Induction' in F. Suppe and P. S. Asquith, op. cit., pp. 212–23.

[42] Thus, H. E. Kyburg concludes his essay, 'Local and Global Induction' in R. Bogdan (ed), *Local Induction*, with the dilemma for local inductive logics that they are either 'irrelevant or impotent', p. 215.

[43] Carnap, of course, hoped eventually to find sets of principles as *a priori* valid as 'learning from experience' to narrow down the range of acceptable c-functions, and ultimately to show that '... induction, if properly formulated, can be shown to be valid by rational criteria'. (Carnap in R. Carnap and R. Jeffrey (eds.), *Studies in Inductive Logic and Probability*, Vol. 1, (1971), p. 31). In this hope he was greatly encouraged by the subjectivist theory and the principles, such as coherence, regularity and symmetry, which the subjectivist theory connected (via Dutch Book Arguments) to probabilities. But it is unlikely that more such principles can be found simply because there seem to be many plausible contexts for the remaining continuum of c-functions. In *The Continuum of Inductive Methods*, Carnap relates the choice of c-functions to well-known statistical methods, but now the inductive logic takes on more a local than a global look.

The grand problem of induction has also met with severe obstacles even in the more restricted goal of vindication. Hacking has shown that Salmon's attempt to vindicate the straight rule requires principles that many, including Salmon, do not find acceptable. See I. Hacking, 'One Problem About Induction' in I. Lakatos (ed.), *Inductive Logic*, which is a response to Salmon's 'The Justification of Inductive Rules of Inference', ibid. See also I. Levi, 'Hacking Salmon on Induction', *J. Phil.* 62 (1965), 481–7.

justification, when viewed from the Humean perspective (although not when viewed from most non-sceptical ones), as requirements that nature be uniform. A more significant shift is away from Goodman's 'new riddle of induction'. Local inductive logic goes along with Goodman, as I have said, in seeking to distinguish valid from invalid inductive inferences, without trying to provide any deeper justification for this than is offered by successful practice. But there has not been very much work done on trying to formulate the principles that can make the discriminations that Goodman takes to be necessary for distinguishing projectible from non-projectible hypotheses. Since projectibility is directly related to confirmability, and like the latter, a matter of degree, this a problem within the domain of local inductive logics.

One reason for the inability of local theories to solve Goodman's Paradox is simply an instance of the point made above: by taking as input what is given in an enquiry, they have already accepted (implicitly) a separation of hypotheses into projectible and non-projectible. But there are also additional difficulties, for if Goodman[44] is right the projectibility of predicates in a hypothesis is a relative matter. A hypothesis may change its status as projectible with new evidence or the introduction of new competing hypotheses. Thus no absolute distinction between say 'green' and 'grue' can be made, if Goodman is correct, on the basis of positionality, simplicity, qualitativeness, etc. One way Goodman has challenged such moves is by showing the symmetry of 'green' and 'grue' through interdefinability. Further, the discriminations and conclusions he draws, if directly abstracted for formalization, do not seem

---

[44] For Goodman's 'theory of projectibility' see the last chapter in his *Fact, Fiction, and Forecast*. See also N. Goodman, I. Scheffler, and R. Schwartz, 'An Improvement in the Theory of Projectibility', *J. Phil.* 67 (1970) pp. 605–8. A. Zabludowski and Goodman and Ullian have had a significant debate in *J. Phil.* (1974–8) stemming from Zabludowski's attempt at refutation of Goodman's theory.

One 'solution' due to Blackburn (*Reason and Prediction*, 1973) purports to show that an asymmetry can be created by going from state to structure descriptions. But Blackburn's argument fails if we use the interdefinability to redescribe the state and structure descriptions in terms of 'grue' and 'bleen'. One can then easily calculate that the confirmation for 'All emeralds are grue' is higher than for 'All emeralds are green' to the same degree that the reverse is the case in Blackburn's earlier presentation.

Mary Hesse's discussion, in *The Structure of Scientific Inference*, is quite complex, and I am not at all sure whether she ultimately wants to answer Goodman's paradox or accept it and work from there. Her account, for one thing, does not meet the relativization requirement, and it is unclear why her requirement *A* (that realistic testing of hypotheses be possible) is needed. Why isn't the more formal statement of conflict between hypotheses enough? See M. Hesse, *The Structure of Scientific Inference* (1974), ch. 3.

to fit well with the usual inductive logics. New evidence may increase a hypothesis's level of projectibility. This suggests that a situation could arise in which the confirmation of a hypothesis on two evidence-statements could be greater than the sum of the confirmations of the hypothesis on each evidence-statement alone. Goodman also makes discriminations of projectibility that are finer than that of logical equivalence, which is the minimal level for most inductive logics. Thus, in the 'solution' offered by Hintikka and his colleagues,[45] to take one example, we weight the parameter of the 'grue-world' less than that of the 'green-world' because it is less regular. This looks question-begging, but at least it has the merit of simplicity. It also has the virtue of not giving absolute judgements of projectibility, both in the sense that projectibility has its effect in degrees and also in the sense that a judgement of projectibility is not a once-and-for-all judgement. On the interpretation given to these parameters they represent conjectures about the degree of regularity in the world (of the specific enquiry). The problem is that at some level we will have to discriminate the projectibility of hypotheses that are logically equivalent, while the regularity of our world should not be affected by our choice of formulations.

With this brief look at the two major influences on recent work, together with some discussion of their distinctive promises and problems, we turn to a more detailed look at Lakatos's critique.

---

[45] See J. Hintikka, 'Inductive Independence and the Paradoxes of Confirmation' in N. Rescher (ed.), *Essays in Honor of Carl Hempel* (1969). The solution that I will discuss is the one in Niiniluoto and Tuomela, *Theoretical Concepts and Hypothetico-Inductive Inference*, which, though within the framework of Hintikka's system, delves further into the philosophical grounds for using the parameter to create the desired asymmetries.

Niiniluoto and Tuomela want to argue that the asymmetry between 'green' and 'grue' can be found in the fact that the hypothesis with the latter predicate requires two criteria for telling whether it is satisfied, whereas the hypothesis with the former predicate requires a *one*-membered subset of the 'grue' criteria (p. 190). Given this analysis and the assumption that there is an economy in man's conceptual system, they conclude that Mr Green and Mr Grue will agree that the parameter of grue is greater than for green, and consequently the green hypothesis will have greater probability than the grue one.

The obvious question is whether Mr Grue will agree that the green-hypothesis, as Grue construes it (i.e., as definable in terms of 'grue' and 'bleen') requires only one criterion, whereas grue requires two. Quite the contrary, I would have thought, on the basis of Goodman's arguments. In a footnote they seem to acknowledge that this might be a problem, but they do not at all solve it. (See p. 195, n. 8). It may nevertheless be interesting to conjecture whether or not, as they must assume, every category that we distinguish linguistically can be known to be satisfied by applying just one criterion. Why cannot two categories (as distinguished linguistically) be known only as a sort of Gestalt combination? And why cannot such a combination-category be simpler to know than its parts?

6.

A 'central dogma' of neoclassical empiricism, for Lakatos, is '*the dogma of the identity of: (1) probabilities, (2) degrees of evidential support (or confirmation), (3) degrees of rational belief and (4) rational betting quotients*'.[46] Because of the mutual support and justification each concept gives to the others, Carnap sought to maintain this identity. As it became clearer that the chain cannot be maintained, Carnap was forced into various problem-shifts. The most important being the '"*atheoretical*" *problem-shift*'.[47]

Lakatos wants to break this chain apart. Lakatos's success appears to depend on his showing that these concepts, when explicated, are not identical. A doubt arises, though, about the importance of such a result: surely explications can be mutually supportive without being identical. In large part, we will see, Lakatos's attack on this chain, even if successful, would only damage the programme under a too restrictive construal.

Equating degrees of rational belief with rational betting quotients is a premiss in the Dutch Book Argument which provides a crucial justification for having one's beliefs conform to the probability calculus. This argument itself, though, does not require all explications of scientific inferences in an inductive logic to be purely probabilistic, unless supplemented by the incredibly strong premiss that only one particular function can be correct. Thus, for example, in (tentatively) accepting a universal law, or assigning it a high degree of support, one needn't be willing to bet that there will never be a counter-instance.[48] One can recognize that the Paradoxes of Weight of Evidence (or Popper's Paradox of Ideal Evidence) show that different functions may be necessary to evaluate the support for a hypothesis under the different questions that might be asked.[49] Finally, Carnap can easily agree that degrees of rational belief are

---

[46] I. Lakatos, 'Changes in the Problem of Inductive Logic', pp. 349–50.

[47] Ibid., p. 351.

[48] See I. Levi, *Gambling With Truth*, ch. XIII, section 3. See also M. Hesse, *The Structure of Scientific Inference*, ch. 8.

[49] Lakatos's discussion of this problem in 'Changes in the Problem of Inductive Logic' is on p. 344–5 and again p. 365, n. 3. (There is a typographical error on p. 345, n. 3 which should refer the reader to p. 365, n. 3.) See below, pp. 402–3 for the discussion of Lakatos's use of the 'paradox of weight of evidence'. Popper's solution to his 'paradox of ideal evidence' simply takes evidence which asserts something about one's evidence as irrelevant to the objective probability but relevant to the *corroboration* of the hypothesis. See K. Popper, *The Logic of Scientific Discovery*, pp. 408–10. Second, Cohen has suggested the introduction of second-order confirmation functions (although for different purposes) in 'An Argument that Confirmation Functors for Consilience are Empirical Hypotheses' in I. Lakatos (ed.), *Inductive Logic*, pp. 247–50. Third, Levi in *Gambling with Truth*, ch. IX simply denies that there is any

not identical with degrees of evidential support if all this comes to is that the former is explicated by $p(h, e)$ and the latter requires a relevance concept such as $p(h, e) - p(h)$. Let us look more closely at this last point.

Lakatos takes it as a criticism of Carnap's theory that only the latter, $p(h, e) - p(h)$, does not imply the Consequence Condition, whereas the former concept, $p(h, e)$, both entails the Consequence Condition and is the only one supported by betting intuitions. To make this into a criticism, though, Lakatos has to establish that these differences arise from a conflict between the '... two rival and mutually inconsistent intuitions ... ', our betting and our evidential support intuitions. The former intuition certainly is that the weaker of two hypotheses cannot be riskier. The latter one is that it is possible for there to be some h and h' such that h entails h', and the evidential support that the evidence gives h is greater than that for h'. But if taken strictly this doesn't at all conflict with our betting intuitions. To say that evidence can have a greater positive relevance to one hypothesis than to the other does not entail that this hypothesis is thereby less risky. One is asking different questions and getting different answers. Admittedly this splits the identity between probability, rational degrees of belief, and evidential support, but it does not split it in an important way since the latter is still a significant function of the former.

If this point is accepted, then Lakatos's argument against the identity of rational betting quotients with probabilities will also be seen as less significant than it at first appears. He writes:

... if we assume, for the sake of the argument, that betting quotients do measure degrees of rational belief, but also that the only rational source of belief is evidential support, and finally that evidential support is not probabilistic, then what is the correct conclusion from the Ramsey-De Finetti theorem? The correct conclusion is that it is irrational to base our theory of rationality on the manichean assumption that if we do not arrange our bets (or degrees of belief) probabilistically an evil power will catch us by a shrewdly arranged system of bets.[50]

paradox since we are considering different bodies of evidence, and they will set different levels for acceptance. These approaches do not deny Popper's use of the paradox to reject the subjectivist assumption that '... degrees of the rationality of beliefs in the light of evidence exhibit a *linear order*'. K. Popper, *The Logic of Scientific Discovery*, p. 408. Richard Jeffrey does not accept this criticism. He argues that the subjectivist can reflect the differential effects of the evidence in that the earlier function will be indeterminate over a larger range of propositions than the later ones, which arise with increasing evidence. See R. Jeffrey, *The Logic of Decision*, pp. 183–5.

[50] I. Lakatos. 'Changes in the Problem of Inductive Logic', pp. 359–60.

First, the assumption of the Dutch Book Argument, about the opponent who arranges the bets, is surely no more than a common type of abstraction for the sake of a dominance argument. It allows us to examine a decision under the worst circumstances (without assuming this is the way the world is in all cases).[51] Second, Lakatos's conclusion that '. . . evidential support is not probabilistic', while it suggests a radical rejection of any probabilistic basis for evidential support, actually amounts to no more than that evidential support cannot be fully explicated as $p(h, e)$. Thus it leaves room for evidential support to be a significant function of probabilities. Lakatos accepts the latter (and, for similar reasons, Popperian measures of corroboration would also be, in this sense, probabilistic), so his argument is quite weak. One simply accepts the non-identity of rational belief with evidential support, while maintaining that the latter provides a crucial source for the evaluation of the rationality of beliefs.

7.

The central problem-shift of Carnap's programme for Lakatos is the one from the appraisal of universal propositions (e.g. theories, laws) to particular propositions. The motivation for this shift was the result of 0-confirmation for universal propositions.[52] This shift finally led to a '. . . "confirmation theory" (which (1) was *essentially concerned with betting on particular predictions . . . [and] (2) the rational betting quotient for any particular prediction was to be independent of the available scientific theories'.*[53] This Lakatos refers to as the 'weak atheoretical thesis' because it makes '. . . *theories dispensable in the logic of confirmation'.*[54] Lakatos's criticism of this thesis is relevant even to those inductive logics which may reject both the 0-confirmation result and the weak atheoretical thesis, because his criticism undermines key parts of the subjectivist theory and certain types of localization in inductive logic.

The 'weak atheoretical thesis' could only be maintained if confirmation theory displayed a type of linguistic invariance and if rational betting quotients (or empirical support) for particular proposi-

[51] For a discussion of the conditions for the Dutch Book Argument see D. H. Mellor, *The Matter of Chance* (1971), parts of chapters 1 and 2.
[52] But see C. Howson, 'Must the Logical Probability of Laws be Zero'? *Brit. J. Phil. Sci.* 24 (1973), pp. 153–63.
[53] I. Lakatos, 'Changes in the Problem of Inductive Logic', p. 337.
[54] Ibid.

tions are calculable independently of theoretical background.[55] Moreover, the thesis also requires that judgements of support on the evidence have a more general independence from the theories available in support of them.[56] Most recent inductive logicians would agree with Lakatos in rejecting such a strong independence between theoretical background and confirmation of hypotheses.[57] But it is not easy to explain how these theoretical inferences are supposed to influence confirmation without incurring either the problem of trivialization (e.g., deduction from some *ad hoc* manufactured theory) or language dependence.[58] Alternatively, the determination of choice of a correct language may be left to considerations external to the confirmation theory. Lakatos's conclusion is that ultimately Carnap cannot assume that the choice of a correct language is unproblematic and, in fact, such choice will require appeal to the '*Popperian problem of corroboration of theories*'.[59]

This conclusion is not that devastating in our broadened conception of the programme of inductive logic, which takes many of the apparently competing systems (including Popper's theory of corroboration) as all contributing to different parts of a complete reconstruction of scientific inference. But a more serious shift, presumably degenerating, results if Lakatos's final appraisal of Carnap's programme is roughly correct. This is his argument that ultimately there

[55] One example Lakatos gives to support his contention that this thesis is false is a situation in which bets are placed on predictions from Einsteinian versus Newtonian theory. We are to imagine that Einstein's theory has passed, whereas Newton's theory has been falsified by one crucial test, and now the question is how does the scientist compare with the inductive judge in respect of their bets on conflicting predictions. Lakatos claims that the scientist impressed by 'dramatic refutations' will offer a daring bet, whereas the inductive judge, who cannot assess theories, will offer only a very cautious bet. (I. Lakatos, 'Changes in the Problem of Inductive Logic', pp. 368–9). We should note, though, as Carnap repeats in this volume (R. Carnap, 'Inductive Logic and Inductive Intuition' in Imre Lakatos (ed.) *The Problem of Inductive Logic* (1968), pp. 258–67), that even the instance confirmation of Newton's theory, unlike Einstein's, would be 0. So it is not clear what the basis is for Lakatos's claim of a large asymmetry. Secondly, since the grounds for the bets would include the degree of similarity between the crucial test already decided and the predictions in question, there doesn't seem to be any general principle involved here to justify this bet, and further, therefore, the grounds for the bet obviously turn on factors outside those of degree of confirmation.

[56] These are some of the themes of I. Lakatos, 'Changes in the Problem of Inductive Logic', section 2.3.

[57] See, for example, M. Hesse, 'Consilience of Inductions'.

[58] I. Lakatos, 'Changes in the Problem of Inductive Logic', pp. 361–6. For an analysis of different requirements of linguistic invariance that an inductive logic may try to meet see Niiniluoto and Toumela, *Theoretical Concepts and Hypothetico-Inductive Inference*, ch. 10, section 1.

[59] I. Lakatos, 'Changes in the Problem of Inductive Logic', p. 364. See also Niiniluoto and Tuomela, *Theoretical Concepts and Hypothetico-Inductive Inference*, p. 194.

is an 'abdication of the inductive judge'. By this Lakatos means that inductive logic requires so much input from the scientist that the inductive logic can play only the most limited critical role in evaluating the rationality of decisions in science.[60] It is in 'revolutionary' science that Lakatos finds the greatest dependence of language on theory, and correspondingly it highlights the most serious abdication of the inductive judge.

The kind of radical 'conceptual change' in the growth of science that Lakatos urges against Carnap raise difficulties for Bayesian conditionalization too.[61] Conditionalization requires that one change ones probability assessments with new evidence by application of Bayes's Theorem. And this Lakatos argues, occurs only with cumulative growth (or 'normal-science'), but not with the more important radical changes brought on by acceptance of new theories in 'revolutionary science'.

One response to this type of criticism, which some philosophers of science have put forward, is to accept it and restrict inductive logic to normal science or to take the principles of inductive logic as culturally or historically relative.[62] This ploy does abdicate *a* role of the inductive judge and, perhaps, too great a role.

Since for such radical changes to raise problems for inductive logic we must have some independent grounds for asserting their rationality, and because for such cases to be 'radical' enough to make a difference there must be evidence to 'rationalize' it, Lakatos requires that such rational changes can occur without evidence. If the following meta-principle were true, this would justify 'Lakatos'

---

[60] I. Lakatos, 'Changes in the Problem of Inductive Logic', in pp. 364, 372. The dual, interrelated problems, of over-relativization of inductive logic, and language-dependence is a theme raised by critics of Levi. I. Hacking, 'Review: of I. Levi, *Gambling with Truth*', *Synthèse* 17 (1967) and R. Hilpinen, *Rules of Acceptance and Inductive Logic* (Acta Philosophica Fennica, 22 (1968), discuss examples where acceptance of a hypothesis according to Levi's rule A varies with different choices of ultimate partition. For Levi's response see his 'Acceptance Revisited' in R. Bogdan (ed.), *Local Induction*, pp. 62–7.

Localization also leads to greater limitations of cross-field comparisons: see Cohen's discussion in L. J. Cohen, *The Implications of Induction* (1970). Lakatos himself favours a greater relativization of judgements of support to specific contexts (e.g., where we have genuine competitors).

[61] I. Lakatos, 'Changes in the Problem of Inductive Logic', p. 347.

[62] See for example, R. Swinburne, *An Introduction to Confirmation Theory* (1973); A. Michalos, *The Carnap–Popper Controversy* (1971). See also I. Lakatos, 'Changes in the Problem of Inductive Logic', p. 387, and I. Lakatos, 'Falsification and the Methodology of Scientific Research Programmes', p. 151. Alan Musgrave's arguments in 'Logical Versus Historical Theories of Confirmation', *Brit. J. Phil. Sci.* 25 (1974), pp. 1–23, for a historical *rather than* a logical theory of confirmation seem to overstate the case. Since this point comes down to the need for relativization to background knowledge and not to the senselessness of comparisons of confirmation across some historical periods, it is not opposed to logical theories.

description: there are times in an enquiry when the rational thing is just completely to reassign our valuations to hypotheses or evidence. Whether such a principle is true or not, its application is quite limited. In the cases Lakatos has in mind there is all sorts of evidence around, e.g., anomalies for existing theories, that might rationalize the changes. It is a case by case question as to whether or not a revolutionary change in science can be accounted for in terms of anomalies for the existing theory and the relevant gains (e.g., boldness) promised by the new theory. It probably is the case, though, that there are interesting cases where radical conceptual reorganization comes about through the success of a new theory, without explicit statements at the time to justify the shift completely.

But arguments like Lakatos's concentrate on a successful change of theory, and its discontinuity with the past, without acknowledging that the inductive logician, in attempting to evaluate the rationality of such a shift, is not bound to take account of only that evidence, if any, that precipitates the shift.

This gives us an insight into how the inductive logician, particularly the 'localist', can begin to answer Lakatos without having to make strong denials of conceptual change. We have gone along with taking the 'input' to the inductive logic as beyond the inductive logic's ability to criticize, i.e., as representing steps in the abdication of the inductive judge. But this is not quite fair. For the inductive logic should be able to re-evaluate (perhaps in conjunction with other inductive logics) these inputs in the light of the output. Similarly, we may not be able to specify all the antecedents of change for which our confirmation function is defined, or can give reasonable values, but we can observe the consequences of such changes and use that as data to evaluate the shift. Conceptual change may be an important facet of scientific advance, but it is not itself above being considered a hypothesis or conjecture about the best course for progress. It can therefore be evaluated in the light of its consequences. Local inductive logics need not abdicate too much of their normative roles if they can show how there is a critical interaction between the input they take as given and the resultant conclusions about empirical support. The answer to the question of whether changing from theory T to T' was rational, may be that we have to wait and see what future experimentation will show. A bold theory which holds out great promise for progress may be acceptable for just that reason. The inductive logician, though, can wait to shift attention from that stage of decision to later ones where more of the implications and tests have been made. It is true then that he cannot account for *all* rational changes of belief; but then some changes can be rational in the light of factors which are external to inductive logic.

This point bears on Lakatos's and others use of the history of science as a basis to criticize inductive logics. A multitude of examples have been offered which in one way or another are supposed to refute some canon of inductive reasoning or some model of science, such as the hypothetico-deductive model. These examples seem to me greatly to underdetermine the conclusions drawn, simply because, however reasonable scientists are in making certain decisions (say about giving up one theory for another), these decisions will be motivated not just by (or sometimes not even by) logical or cognitive factors alone, (e.g., probability, excess content, falsification) but also by methodological ones (e.g., availability of alternative theories) and practical ones (e.g., availability of research grants). The conformity of the *overall* pattern of scientific development to one or another model of rationality will be the test for such reconstruction – not those particulars of the history for which it appears difficult (if not impossible) to separate decisions in the logic of justification from decisions in the logic of discovery. Thus, for example, a scientific community's rational decision to continue to use a theory in the face of a purported counter-example need not show a disregard for the hypothetico-deductive model, but may rather reflect the balancing of such considerations with those of the cost of investigation, or the lack of serious alternatives. So long as the cognitive factors can be construed as overriding in the long run (i.e., if the progress of a scientific enquiry, viewed from a long historical distance, follows the predictions, which are arrived at by taking the logic as depending only upon these factors), the scientific community will not have abdicated from having the achievement of comprehensive truth, and an understanding of the world, as a central aim. The canons of rationality of local inductive logic can be applicable and important in evaluation of scientific change without having to be everywhere operative in scientific research. Of course, a certain set of procedures must be operative in a broad way such as experimentation, observation, and replication of results, if inductive logic is to be applicable. But, I take it, it is not controversial that scientific enquiry, in at least a rough way, engages in such activity. The questions come in when we ask to what extent are the results of such activity determinate of scientific decisions. If these assumptions are met, and we can presume success with the tasks mentioned above, pp. 388–9, then the more general response to Lakatos's important arguments about 'abdication of the inductive judge' is a form of the pragmatic maxim that what is accepted as given at one stage of enquiry – and something must be – need not forever remain immune to revision.

8.

The original programme of inductive logic has gone through important changes. Some of the old problems are now ignored. Some new ones have been suggested. The rudiments of answers to some other problems have been proposed. New inductive logics have become more sensitive to the shortcomings in Carnap's programme with respect to what actual scientific inference and theorizing looks like. These gains have their costs in the additional input required for application.

I have tried to point up each of these situations. The assessment of these gains and losses, requisite for a comprehensive evaluation, is more complex than Lakatos's critique allows. Let me further support this point on two counts. First, there are hardly any *absolute* criteria about when to accept a theory or hypothesis. This is only partially a reflection on the many reasons and aims one can have in acceptance. It is also a reflection on the multiplicy of methodological and cognitive factors that are relevant to the acceptance of hypotheses. Since these factors may conflict one has either to ignore some of them or, more reasonably, to work out a balanced decision in choosing to accept or reject a hypothesis.[63] Second, the intuitive

---

[63] One of these factors, already mentioned, is conservatism. Here are two other cases where its relevance comes in. First, Lakatos, 'Changes in the Problem of Inductive Logic', pp. 400–1, takes Carnap's view of sampling from an urn as too restrictive (a '. . . poor model of science') because it allows only that the next selection may be of a certain colour ball, but not that one could '. . . equally well pull out a rabbit . . .'. Second, David Miller, 'Making Sense of Method: Comments on Richard Jeffrey', *Synthese* 30 (1975), 139–47, makes a very sharp contrast between Bayesians and Popperians. Miller imagines a situation in which since B is the bolder theory, $p(B) < p(A)$. For Popper B is preferred, and A is preferred only if B is undermined. For Bayesians, according to Miller, the situation is reversed. The choice is underdescribed, relative to normal contexts of decisions. Prefer for what purpose? While boldness is a major factor in evaluating the acceptability of a hypothesis, surely there are other factors as well, such as, crucially in this case, plausibility relative to background knowledge. Similarly, however, poor urn models are only a small fraction of those hypotheses consistent with the data that are serious candidates for investigation. If all possibilities must be considered at each stage of science, progress in inquiry would be blocked.

In general, there seem to be hardly any critical differences between the views of Popperians and inductive logicians in their sophisticated forms and in normal contexts of scientific decision-making. Most of the important epistemological and

principles or factors that are relevant to confirmation or empirical support are not always applicable at every level of enquiry.

Lakatos's critique of Carnap[64] invokes a number of absolute criteria. For example, if we may oversimplify somewhat, he claims that a test is only a test if it is the most severe possible, that one should always prefer the bolder hypothesis, that repetitions never increase support for a hypothesis, and that testing is only possible relative to a 'touchstone theory.' Firstly, though, in response, such alternatives are not always available. Frederick Schick[65] has an example where the alternative to accepting the hypothesis if it proves false is not belief in some alternative, but suspension of judgement. There was no genuine alternative, Schick claims, to George Miller's hypothesis that 7 ± 2 is the limit to the number of discriminations we are capable of making within any unidimensional category. Second, if one takes this absolute approach, one must throw away information. In between a most severe test and mere repetition there are data to be found. What is the reason for ignoring them? In Lakatos's example[66] he shows that evidence which is decisive between h and h^*, can be irrelevant *between h and h'*. But Lakatos is forced to ignore a third possibility that this same evidence may still be relevant, though not decisive, to our taking h' as a serious candidate.[67] If we use the history of science as Lakatos

methodological points that Popper has made have a firm place in inductive logics: e.g., importance of severity of tests, the greater weight to refutations, the relevance of boldness to acceptability. Further, no one need maintain the type of 'justificationism' that Popper objects to. There is no quest for certainty, nor reliable truth, in the way he objects to. That objection comes down only on those who would offer inductive principles that directly tie ampliative inferences to the way the world is. So long as the inductive logician does not allow his statements about 'good reasons', 'justification', or 'empirical support' to be directly falsifiable (or have direct implications for the way the world is), he does not run against Hume's arguments which are so important for Popper. So once we consider the balancing of all the relevant cognitive factors in scientific growth, and use the conclusions of inductive logic only as guides to action and decision (without any further certification by observation), I do not see that recent work is not broadly consonant with Popper's philosophy of science going further in the fineness of discriminations it can make (e.g., between two equally bold, equally corroborated theories, with one having greater number of observed positive instances).

Similarly, most probabilistic inductive logics incorporate severity of tests in the relation between antecedent likelihoods and resulting confirmation if the prediction holds. See I. Lakatos, 'Changes in the Problem of Inductive Logic', pp. 379–80 and 382.

[64] I. Lakatos, 'Changes in the Problem of Inductive Logic', for example pp. 344–5, 413, 415–16.

[65] F. Schick, 'Three Logics of Belief' in M. Swain (ed.), *Induction, Acceptance, and Rational Belief* (1970).

[66] I. Lakatos, 'Changes in the Problem of Inductive Logic', p. 417.

[67] Cf. the factor of conservatism discussed above in footnote 63.

wants, it is doubtful that one can find situations in which all factors, but one, are equal between hypotheses, so as to offer a crucial test. In lieu of this, since factors such as conservatism, boldness, severity of test, variety of evidence, theoretical background, etc. can be independently shown relevant to the search for comprehensive truth, the inductive logician should be sceptical of dictums of the form: one should always prefer the hypothesis with the greater 'amount' of any one particular factor.

9.

Lakatos's absolutes turn on taking a certain advanced stage of science as paradigmatic of all science. Here I want to develop a point of Mary Hesse's, '. . . that enumerative induction is more fundamental than eliminative'.[68] Eliminative induction requires, what Lakatos takes as the paradigm of experimentation, that there be a set of alternative hypotheses. This is obviously a correct characterization of sophisticated experimentation in science and it has been adopted in a number of recent inductive logics. Eliminative and enumerative induction need not be in conflict because the *genuine* alternative that the eliminativist needs for his methods to apply, ultimately presuppose the kinds of correlations that enumerative induction best evaluates.

Rejection of principles such as the Principle of Instantial Relevance, on the ground that they do not give adequate weight to theoretical influence on confirmation; or of 'betting intuitions' for 'empirical support'; or of enumerative for eliminative induction; ignore the fact that the latter concepts involve richer assumptions than the former. What is gained, in the way of closer representation of actual scientific inference, is at the cost of generality. Before we can have a single case prove a hypothesis we need grounds for taking the domain as quite 'regular'. These grounds must go back, if Hume is to be believed, to simple positive correlations.

Of course, even though Carnap considers it a major virtue of his program to have derived the Principle of Instantial Relevance from weak axioms, it does not follow that he is committed to advocating the mere mechanical repetition of tests as a way of increasing confirmation. This is not only because the methodological implications of his theory cannot be directly read off from the axioms. Carnap emphasized that in the application of inductive logic we should adopt the rule of maximizing expected utility and the total

[68] M. Hesse, *The Structure of Scientific Inference*, p. 173.

evidence requirement. If a test has been repeated many times, it thereby becomes more likely to turn out correctly. This diminishes its value for us, and this can be sufficient reason for not recommending continuous repetition.[69]

Different inductive logics sometimes apply better or worse at different stages of enquiry (from the pre-scientific to the most advanced scientific domains). Lakatos claims that in such pre-scientific domains the inductive judges' judgements are weakest because whereas he may give high *c*-values, the scientist may find the results quite unreliable. Now it is hard to know what to make of this objection since it is just to cover such cases that Carnap's introduction of a parameter is appropriate. In such cases the choice of a parameter would be a cautious one so that confirmation rises very slowly. (Admittedly, the flexibility afforded by the use of parameters such as λ, are at the cost of a greater abdication of the inductive judge.)

The claim that enumerative induction is the most general and basic type of inductive inference is not to be taken as claiming the reducibility of any given inductive inference to induction by simple enumeration. When alternative patterns of inference become available with increasingly rich background information it may be hardly possible or worthwhile to try to express this information. It would also tie us to the 'origins' of our knowledge in a way that does not permit the 'leaps' that come about with genuinely new and innovative theories. This point explains why quite a number of different principles of inference can co-exist, even when they *prima facie* conflict. Consider the Conjunction Principle: if $c(h, e) = r, c(i, e) = s$ and $1 > s > r > 0$ then $c(h \& i, e) < r$. A number of philosophers have suggested that there are cases in which inferences follow a pattern where $c(h \& i, e) = r$.[70] From one's betting intuitions the latter appears wrong: surely the risk involved in accepting a conjunction on given evidence is much greater than accepting either conjunct. On the other hand it can be argued, and it looks quite coherent, that if each of two hypotheses has passed a test at different levels, then in considering them together we need not repeat any test the least well-supported has passed. The point is that these explanations do not conflict because the latter is assuming as implicit background

[69] Lakatos makes this charge in 'Changes in the Problem of Inductive Logic', pp. 344–5. See, though, C. Howson, 'Why Once May Be Enough', *Australasian Journal of Philosophy* 55 (1977), 142–6.

[70] See L. J. Cohen, *The Implications of Induction* (1970), *The Probable and the Provable* (1977), and Levi's reconstruction of Shackle's views in I. Levi, *Gambling with Truth*, and this volume.

that the additional riskiness of a conjunction, that is the additional ways it can be falsified, are not serious possibilities in this enquiry. Although there are typically good reasons for such decisions, there is no reason that one should always be able to supply them. This provides partial justification for our denying Lakatos's narrow conception of the programme of inductive logic as the finding of the single correct c-function. Different systems of inductive logic, or methodologies may be more interestingly seen as offering accounts of different parts of scientific inference, and not necessarily rival ones.

10.

Lakatos's critique does not foreclose interesting new developments in inductive logic, and many of his particular criticisms of Carnap's programme rest on too rigid a conception of that programme. Lakatos does raise some major issues for the programme of inductive logic. In particular, he accurately points out the kinds of fundamental problems which should be the focus of attention. Nonetheless, ultimately his criticisms depend too heavily on a particular stage of the programme of inductive logic, and on a narrow construal of the goals of an inductive logic.[71]

Of course, in trying to undermine the strong negative conclusions that one may draw from Lakatos's critique, we have had to make some 'retreats' in the claims for an inductive logic. Thus we have taken inductive logic (as part of the logic of science) as not relevant to all aspects of the rationality of decisions; we have allowed that alternative inductive logics and methodologies may not be competing with one another; we have granted that none may be universally correct, and all may be complementary parts of a total picture of inductive or scientific reasoning. We have seen that *some* abdication of the inductive judge is needed to capture certain advanced types of scientific reasoning. These cannot be taken as decisive retreats. For example, the last one Lakatos himself believes is necessary

---

[71] Important recent work related to the development of finer and more sophisticated meta-criteria for inductive logics include W. Goosens, 'A Critique of Epistemic Utilities' in R. Bogdan (ed.), *Local Induction*; R. Hilpinen, *Rules of Acceptance and Inductive Logic*; H. E. Kyburg, 'Local and Global Induction' and *The Logical Foundations of Statistical Inference* (1974); I. Levi, *Gambling with Truth*; and I. Niiniluoto, 'Inquiries, Problems, and Questions: Remarks on Local Induction' in R. Bogdan (ed.) *Local Induction*.

(although the claim that such additional input is always required strikes us as too strong). A comprehensive evaluation of inductive logic, one that could answer my original question, though it must start from Lakatos's work, must then go beyond it, in developing and applying more complex and sophisticated criteria[72] for a good inductive logic.

---

[72] I want to thank Richard Burian and Catherine Elgin for helpful comments on an earlier draft.

§26. Radu J. Bogdan
Two Turns in Induction

My discussion of Adler's paper concentrates on two major turns in our search for a good inductive logic: the methodological and the conceptual turn. The methodological turn brings together a variety of recent concerns for statistical decision and testing, acceptance, epistemic utilities, local justification, etc. I take Adler's defence of recent developments in inductive logic and his constructive suggestions to reflect the methodological turn. But I point to some tensions in his discussion of local induction, subjectivist theories, and Carnap's programme.

In the second part of my reply I show that the latter can be reinterpreted as a form of conceptual modelling that produces a global probability model. This leads us to consider the conceptual turn in inductive logic. Unlike Adler, I think that Carnap's inductive logic fails to capture the logic of induction in science, and give some reasons for thinking so. I also try to show that this should not deter us from giving due attention to the stage of conceptual modelling in scientific theorizing. Our inductive strategies depend on, and therefore should reflect, that stage.

Jonathan Adler's decision to take Carnap's programme as a frame of reference, review Lakatos's critique of it, and see how and why some post-Carnapian developments can avoid this critique, sets a good framework for our discussion. While discussing some of Adler's claims I want to exploit this framework from a different perspective. Carnap's programme identifies two basic dimensions of an inductive logic, one conceptual and another methodological. Historically, they often appear as conflicting turns in the development of inductive logic. They need not be so if we are prepared to let induction cover more than just prediction or choice or acceptance or justification and thus incorporate both methodology and conceptual constructions. Beyond the details of my discussion of Adler on Lakatos on Carnap this is the view I want to advocate.

1. *The Methodological Turn*

Most criticisms of, and alternatives to, Carnap's programme indicate a definite turn toward (what Carnap called) the methodology of induction. Carnap's own list of methodological problems[1] anticipates most of these reactions as well as many recent concerns for statistical decisions and testing, acceptance and epistemic utilities, etc. Contrary to what Carnap believed, the methodology of induction turns out to be much more than just applying an inductive

---

[1] See his *Logical Foundations of Probability* (1950), secs. 44A, 48, and 49.

formalism. To many people it *is* induction or, rather, it characterizes a variety of ways of *doing* induction in which prior input of various sorts, contexts, theories, and conceptual commitments, different and often conflicting epistemic objectives (such as content, simplicity, etc.) and theoretical tasks (such as explanation, prediction, etc.) play an equally important role. For brevity, I will call this variety *methodological induction* and the ideology behind it the *methodological turn*.[2] These terms characterize no particular approach to induction and in fact lump (indiscriminately) many approaches together. My reason for introducing them is primarily dialectical: by sharpening the Carnapian contrast between formalism, conceptual framework, language, on the one hand, and use, application, real-life constraints, on the other hand, I want to probe some of its underlying assumptions and suggest a new interpretation. As far as this task goes, what is common to different methodological approaches is more important than what is not.

The methodological turn indicates a tendency to 'spread' inductive justification or support over a more extended, more complex and ramified sequence of steps of which evidential and theoretical support, informational content, parameters of epistemic caution and of conjectured regularities in the domain, etc. are only a part. The conceptual effort to capture these ingredients in one single (numerical or qualitative) measure should not obscure their initial diversity. It is the recognition of the latter that sets methodological induction apart from other approaches.

The methodological turn is also a sign of epistemological modesty. It tells us that in the process of reconstructing scientific knowledge a good inductive logic should apply later and to less by presupposing more – where the comparison is made with premethodological, typically globalist beliefs about what an induction-from-scratch can and should do. I take such modesty to reflect in many ways the locality inherent in methodological induction. To this extent, then, the methodological criteria for a good inductive logic should reflect the various ongoing concerns for localization and, as Adler put it, be less absolute and unidimensional and relativized to the means, tasks, values, and stages of an enquiry.

I take this view of methodological induction to be in some agreement with the final message of Adler's paper. Since, at this point, I do not find much interest in adding details to Adler's able

---

[2] The ideology is exemplified elsewhere as well. Popper's critique of inductive logic is an instance of it, and so is the recent historico-critical reconstruction of science. Lakatos's own view tries to bring all these together.

and informative survey, let me mention some areas where my reading of the methodological turn seems to differ from Adler's.

As a matter of philosophical strategy, Adler starts by granting the globalist, induction-from-scratch view too much. Generous as this strategy may be, it entails the risk of taking epistemology as being almost coextensive with a global and presuppositionless account of inductive knowledge. This should be resisted on both methodological and (as we shall see later) conceptual grounds. Indeed, I see this concession as conflicting with the spirit of the methodological turn.

One instance of this is when Adler worries that localization as either acceptance of unproblematic input or contextual relativization may undermine our epistemological ability to account for the objectivity of the growth of knowledge. This worry may be tactical since later in the paper Adler observes that any input and context can be criticized and revised. Still the worry itself is premethodological. Knowledge by induction simply *is* contextual and input-dependent and to this extent local, and so is its justification. It is the ways people *interpret* this locality that should concern us. For some it is linguistic (or conceptual) localization, for others the localization is initially subjective, for still others it is (intersubjectively) pragmatic or experiential or built into some background knowledge. We need more epistemological insight and research to sort these out but the fact of locality is as brute as any and to doubt or question it is reactionary.

Another instance concerns Adler's claim that the subjectivist theory of probability and induction explains and justifies the objectivity of the growth of knowledge. This is no longer a tactical claim but a conviction based on the familiar argument that the theory assumes very little, invokes only accumulation of data, and obtains objectivity as intersubjective agreement. There are well-known objections to this being an adequate model of inductive knowledge and I will not repeat them here. Instead, I will only emphasize the implicit equation of the growth of knowledge with a non-methodological induction governed solely by some priors, coherence, and conditionalization. The subjectivist's point is (or had better be) not that we induce this way, for there is no convincing psychological or social evidence that we do. Whether we should induce this way really depends on what we take, and want, our knowledge to be; but this requires another discussion. The real point behind Adler's claim is rather that we can retrospectively reduce our inductive feats to the model, and thus provide an adequate justification. It is a logical virtue of the subjectivist theory that this can often be accomplished. But the trouble with this theory is that it either takes induction to assume too little, which is quite unrealistic, or it is willing and able to incorporate many non-evidential factors and parameters but, as in a conditional proof, the latter get eventually dismissed as auxiliary premises, which goes against the methodological way of looking at inductive justification.

Finally, whereas I see methodological induction to be a radical departure from Carnap's inductive logic, Adler seems to contemplate a certain continuity. So, unlike Lakatos, he thinks that Carnap's program is not a degenerating one. If, as it seems, he has in mind Carnap's (pure) inductive logic designed to capture induction in science (the aim of the 1950–2 system), then I again disagree. I think that there are enough criticisms around, some well documented in Lakatos' essay, showing why Carnap's inductive logic fails to be a logic of scientific induction. I share the view that Carnap's later shift to a normative decision-theoretic position can be taken as a tacit admission of this failure.

If this is so, then what is the role of an inductive logic like Carnap's? And what exactly is inductive in such a logic? Let us consider these questions under a new angle, one which might also contribute to a better understanding of what makes induction possible.

2. *The Conceptual Turn*

The angle I am going to discuss now marks the *conceptual turn* in the design of a good inductive logic. The conceptual turn is intended to refer here to a crucial stage of scientific theorizing, a stage of rational ideality which enables us to deal conceptually and formally with an empirical reality. I will call it the stage of *conceptual modelling* when an abstract, idealized model of an empirical domain is posited. It attributes a neat, well structured 'ontology' (of ideal gases, or mass points, etc.) to an otherwise untidy, open-ended part of the empirical world. Such models are not the result of inductive experience, although the latter may test their adequacy and serviceability. Nor should they be confused with specific, empirical claims intended to account for what happens in the model-posited world. Nor, finally, are they to be regarded as outcomes of lucky guesses. In other words, they are independent of induction, discovery, and methodology, at least as currently viewed.

Naturally the models scientists cherish most are formal. In many sciences these are probability models. They define a space of possible events, and incorporate, or are associated with, certain probability distributions and certain general patterns of (in)dependence, (non)randomness, (a)symmetry, and the like, governing those distributions. Quite often statistical analysis starts from such models.

With this sketchy background consider now the following slow motion reconstruction of Carnap's enterprise. It starts by being an exercise in mathematical theorizing. Up to a point, to use Freudenthal's term, only the 'infrastructure' of first-order logic and its semantic representation distinguish it from what a pure probability theorist does. Nothing inductive so far. Beyond this point, however, we can take Carnap as constructing an implicit universal or *global probability model* whose posited ontology (regarded purely semantically) may be characterized as an 'urn ontology', i.e., a most abstract representation of a chance (or stochastic) set-up. There is (strictly speaking) nothing inductive about this stage either. Only some general assumptions about the ontology are made.

These two stages are clearly acknowledged by Carnap[3] in his discussion of the reasons for accepting the axioms of his inductive logic, in particular the 'general axioms'. He then considers, in a third stage, some 'special axioms' which are designed to capture some inductive constraints, basically learning from experience. But let us read the end result in a different way. Suppose we want to capture c^*-induction but take the axioms as so many constraints our model imposes on the world where this induction takes place. In other words, suppose that we look for a world that only Carnap c^*-model fits. Then ask yourself, somewhat transcendentally: What kind of world would make this supposition true? An answer that comes to mind is a certain statistical-mechanical universe. Another, suggested by Ian Hacking, is that of a metaphysical universe as envisaged by Leibniz. Be this as it may, the point is that in one form or another such an universe comes with associated assumptions concerning the probability distributions of its basic configurations and concerning patterns of (in)dependence, (non)randomness, etc., governing the former. It is this group of associated assumptions that enables the model to deliver the required logic of confirmation. But let us see if the model actually delivers the logic. Consider several important possibilities.

In the spirit of our earlier transcendental exercise, consider a world that instantiates Carnap's c^*-based model. Then one has either to accept the strong assumptions associated with such a

---

[3] Carnap, 'Replies and Systematic Expositions' in P. A. Schilpp (ed.), *The Philosophy of Rudolf Carnap* (1963), p. 977.

world,[4] which is a very stiff price to pay for an inductivist, particularly because there is very much prior input to rely on; or one has to face the serious objection that in such a world there may be no need for induction to begin with, and that probability deductions from the model may suffice. Then there is the conflict discussed by Salmon: If the degree of confirmation is designed to capture the basic Humean dimension of induction, namely the logical independence of the past/observed from the future/unobserved, and do so via partial entailment, then learning from experience is impossible. If, on the other hand, the degree of confirmation captures the latter, it fails to account for independence.[5]

In the statistical-mechanical version of the world that we are still contemplating there is a familiar illustration of these two sets of objections. Consider the latter. Carnap's $c\dagger$ corresponds to the Maxwell–Boltzmann statistics while his c^* to the Bose–Einstein one. The former treats individual particles as being (practically) independent whereas the latter does not. So far no particle has been found to obey the Maxwell–Boltzmann statistics. This may be an empirical accident, although there are people who think that this is no accident because the assumptions of independence and noninteraction underlying those statistics are simply wrong.[6] Be this as it may, we are left with the important and philosophically plausible suggestion that we should contemplate a natural connection between ontological dependence and interaction *and* the possibility of learning from experience. After all, this is why causation plays such a central role in induction (as Hume himself was so much aware) and why the acquisition of information is possible only when finding or positing structures in the domain under investigation. Consider now the former set of objections. A Bose–Einstein universe, for example, comes with so many (theoretical, empirical, stochastic) assumptions that either induction is no longer needed or its working in such ideal conditions is irrelevant to the rough world of the methodologist. In a sense, this explains Carnap's nonchalance toward, say, scientific laws or inductive acceptance. Indeed, in such an universe one does not look for laws; most lawful features are already contained in the assumptions. Nor does one need to accept anything, in any plausible sense of acceptance; one just makes the

[4] This is a position taken by Ian Hacking. See his *The Emergence of Probability* (1975), ch. 15. Carnap's view is that such assumptions are generally methodological.

[5] Wesley C. Salmon, 'Partial Entailment as a Basis for Inductive Logic' in N. Rescher *et al.* (eds.), *Essays in Honor of Carl G. Hempel*, (1969), pp. 47–82.

[6] Significantly, this is Harold Jeffreys's view in his *Theory of Probability* (1939), sec. 7.6.

required computations, and this is what Carnap meant by probability assignments. In other words, it is the strength of the assumptions that enables Carnap to concentrate on singular predictions only and to disregard acceptance.

But many people will disagree with this transcendental construal, so let us relax its requirements. Up to a point, I think, one can still make the same claim. Thus suppose that, locally, Carnap's model applies to a given empirical situation where a particular statistical probability (be it relative frequency or propensity) is known and reflected by a Carnapian inductive probability. Then, by Carnap's own admission,[7] the latter may as well be dispensable. If, on the other hand, that statistical probability (or a parameter) is unknown, then an estimate is required. Although the problem of estimation in Carnap's work is a tricky one, here are some possible objections. First, there is the objection that the estimate itself is a tentatively accepted conjecture,[8] which is a very un-Carnapian thought. Second, if this is not so, then estimation is again a purely formal computation and one falls back on the previous objections as to why this is possible in the first place. Finally, I see a potential and unilluminating regress in Carnap's notion of the reliability of an estimate.

Thus, no matter how looked at, Carnap's probability model fails to deliver a consistent logic of induction. This is where my perception of Carnap differs from Adler's. My distinction between model and logic, and the resulting reconstruction of Carnap's programme are not only heuristic. Mature scientific theorizing consists very much in empirically interpreting given conceptual models – when it is independently established or assumed that the empirical domain obeys the constraints of the model. This then guarantees the applicability of formal methods and calculi. Carnap's mistake was to believe that his global probability model can deliver the logic of evidential support, or confirmation, in science. The objections presented so far (as well as many others in the literature) have the feature of either breaking the connection between Carnap's logical probability (based on his model) and induction, or building so many assumptions into this connection that induction becomes a mere exercise in computation relative to a universe about which we already know a lot.

In addition to all this, there is more to induction than evidential support, and there is more to evidential support than a probability-

[7] R. Carnap, *Logical Foundations of Probability*, sec. 49B.

[8] See Jaakko Hintikka, 'Carnap versus Essler versus Inductive Generalization', *Erkenntnis* 9, (1975), 240–1.

model it may rely on. Then there are many contexts where no probability models are available or where different models are used, in which case there might be no conceptual grounds for support to be probabilistic. Even when support is probabilistic, and relies on an adequate model, the assumptions that a scientific theory associates with the model are going to make a lot of difference. This is what is going to distinguish the powerful models of mechanical statistics from those, say, of population statistics. To a large extent, the postcarnapian developments that Adler successfully defends against Lakatos's critique of Carnap reflect an awareness of these various circumstances. But they do so, I believe, by radically departing from Carnap's initial programme.

The Carnapian failure, however, should not obscure the crucial role conceptual models play in our understanding and design of a good inductive logic. Otherwise we would not only misrepresent or totally ignore a vital segment of scientific theorizing that has a bearing on our inductive strategies but, philosophically, concede too much both to the excessive methodologist and the radical subjectivist. Consider again our transcendental exercise. What it assumes, they would say, is that there is a structurally true story of the universe which fits a certain model. But in real life, they would go on, we do not *know* whether this is so or not. This is where empirical knowledge and induction come in, and where the methodological (or subjectivist) turn, or rather retreat, starts from. This may be correct in the long run but (remember Keynes's phrase?) at each stage, before so retreating, we had better make sure that we have an idea (model, projection) of what the domain of enquiry is structurally like, i.e. what configurations of entities, properties, and relations should we expect to find. This is precisely what models help us to do.

At issue here is also the problem of *in-formed* realism. It does no good to say, as many philosophers do, that scientific knowledge approaches a mysterious, formless truth. We had better have an anticipation of what this truth might be like – or else we might miss it altogether. First metaphysically, and then through modelling, this is how science operates.

Excessive methodologism misses this point. Here I would side with Adler against Lakatos. Thus, although aware that Carnap's inductive logic works when applied to 'closed games' or 'closed statistical problems',[9] Lakatos maintains that science is an 'open

---

[9] Imre Lakatos, 'Changes in the Problem of Inductive Logic' in I. Lakatos (ed.), *The Problem of Inductive Logic* (1968), pp. 373, 407.

game' and that 'urn games are poor models of science' on the (Popperian) evidence that the possible variety of the universe is not exhausted by urns and balls and that in fact 'you may equally well pull out a rabbit, or your hand may be caught in the urn, or the urn may explode ... '.[10] Possible as this may be, it still betrays a misunderstanding of modelling in science. Although, as we saw, Carnap's conflation of a probability model with the logic of confirmation may have contributed to this confusion, the closed (urn or statistical) games are certainly models *in*, and not *of*, science. It is precisely by positing a structurally idealized ontology associated with certain regularity patterns that such models have the serviceable virtue of not allowing urns to explode or contain rabbits or not letting us bother if they occasionally do. When this occurs more than occasionally we may be well advised to play a different game with different models.

The catastrophic view I am criticizing here squares not only with the un-in-formed and unanticipating view of truth discussed earlier but also with the (still widely shared and respected) Humean notion that ontological anarchy follows from the logical independence of individuals or events. To show that both the catastrophic view and the Humean notion are mistaken one has to examine the role theories play in induction and the many ways in which models, laws, and strategies of generating data conspire in detecting and/or imposing higher (such as invariance, conservation, etc.) and lower (i.e., pertaining to specific laws) regularity patterns in the empirical domain under investigation.[11] That such patterns may be wrong is no argument for their absence or dispensability. Fallibilism does not entail anarchy in knowledge. The problems of uniformity and projectibility, about which Adler has some interesting things to say, should be approached along these lines too.

3. *Concluding Remarks*

As I said in the beginning, the implicit view underlying this discussion is that induction is a multidimensional affair, and that most of these dimensions are not by themselves inductive. I take this to be the main lesson of the methodological turn. A strong prejudice that tends to obscure this lesson is that induction is a simple inference or computation. This is the rationalist ideal of the inductivist. In

---

[10] Lakatos, op. cit., p. 401.

[11] I have briefly dealt with this in 'Hume and the Problem of Local Induction' in R. J. Bogdan (ed.), *Local Induction* (1976). See also Roger Rosenkrantz, *Inference, Method, and Decision* (1977), ch. 4.

demolishing it Hume had perceptively shown what ontological assumptions, if independently vindicated, would bring us close to the ideal. Although still obsessed by the ideal, our inductive interests are more regional and dependent on the type, sophistication, temporal stage, and aims of a scientific enquiry. Even when so constrained, an inductive strategy relies on a prior model of the domain of that enquiry. I take this to be the main lesson of the conceptual turn. Such models will themselves be regional and dependent in the earlier sense, and in turn will make different inductive strategies possible. That the probability calculus applies or that statistics takes over completely is only a tribute to the strength of the model and of its associated assumptions. That, when this happens, we let either of them measure support, etc., and guide our degrees of belief, is not so much, or not primarily, an indication of rationality as it is a commitment to what made such measurement and guidance possible in the first place.

I do not want to conclude without mentioning that the tension between the conceptual and the methodological turn is an old story in the philosophy of induction. Jevons, for instance, was an optimistic conceptualist who based his reduction of induction to probability on a model according to which 'nature is to us like an infinite ballot box, the contents of which are being continually drawn, ball after ball, and exhibited to us'. The same model was contemplated by Peirce before seeing, somehow in the spirit or our earlier transcendental exercise, what assumptions go with it, and turning methodologist. And so on. The story did not change this century, both before and after Carnap. Are we then destined to go through the whole thing again and again? Yes, I am tempted to say, if we want either to capture induction in a probability model alone or to disregard such models altogether. Both positions are extreme and invite cyclical counterreactions. No, if we take a closer look at models, methodology and the various parameters of scientific theorizing and see a local interplay at work. The key to a good inductive logic may be found in the overall interaction of these elements rather than in any particular one.[12]

[12] Some of the ideas presented here were discussed with Ian Hacking, Jaakko Hintikka, and Paul Humphreys. Their reactions and suggestions were very helpful, and they will find here my warm thanks. I also want to thank Jonathan Adler for the excellent and stimulating interaction we had while I was preparing this paper.

§27. Comment and Replies
The Adler–Bogdan Session.

ROSENKRANTZ: I would like to add some remarks to Adler's on Lakatos's charge that inductive logicians cannot account for the introduction of novel concepts or for radical theory change. The Bayesian index of support (viz., average likelihood) illustrated in my contribution to this volume applies, as I emphasized, to any theory and is not confined to a previously given partition of hypotheses. I also stressed the possibility that by 'switching frameworks', inductive support (which reflects both accuracy and simplicity) can be made to increase more sharply than by further complicating an already complicated theory. If, for example, the accuracy gained by adding an epicycle to a geostatic model is slight, then its addition would actually reduce the support of the model. At the same time, even a highly inaccurate version of the heliostatic model based on coplanar, uniform circles, might conceivably be better supported than a much more accurate but vastly more complicated formulation of the geostatic theory.

In the discussion that prompted my comment, Adler also wondered what, if any, substantive differences divide Popperians from their opponents. The Bayesian criterion of progress that I defend in my paper holds that a modification of theory is 'progressive' just in case evidential support is increased. Lakatos propounded a far more stringent criterion, viz., that each modification issue in novel predictions, some of which are corroborated. Popper has proposed similar structures, requiring that theoretical refinements increase testability. While modifications of physical theory have often met these strong requirements, the successive complications Mendelian genetics has undergone – multiple alleles, polygenes, incomplete dominance, and the like – definitely have not. Each such complication reduced the testability of the theory in the straightforward sense of increasing the number of possible experimental findings which the theory could accommodate, and generally without issuing in novel predictions. (Indeed, polygenic inheritance and incomplete dominance allow one to reintroduce the 'intermediate' types characteristic of the blending theory of inheritance.) I submit, then, that if we take the pronouncements of Lakatos and Popper to heart, Mendelian genetics must be lumped with Ptolemaic astronomy as a 'degenerating research programme'. However, as I illustrate in my paper in connection with genetic linkage, the complications in question improved accuracy enough to offset the loss of simplicity and so increased the support of the simpler Mendelian models they replaced. By the lights of the far more liberal Bayesian criterion, these complications were solidly 'progressive'.

LEVI: Adler has offered us an able and provocative review of responses, which might be called 'inductivist' in some sense or other, to the anti-inductivist critique developed by Popper and restated and shaped in his own way by Lakatos. I have little in the way of criticism to make of the specific points made in Adler's discussion; but I do think he has conceded too much to a Popperocentric perspective. From the Popperian point of view, all non-Popperians look very much alike. Adler grants this by portraying the views he discusses as diverse 'problem-shifts' in the Carnapian 'research programme' for inductive logic. This portrayal is highly misleading.

The views Carnap and Popper shared in common are far more important than their differences. Both understood logic in an objectivist sense according to which it is a science of third world entities divorced from the aims and attitudes of human agents, social institutions and contingencies of their situations. Both stood opposed to psychologism, although they both tolerated what Carnap called 'qualified psychologism' – i.e., norms prescribing constraints on rational belief applicable to all agents regardless of their circumstances. They both stressed that scientific enquiry is under objective critical control in the narrow sense of 'objective' according to which principles of objectivist logic or qualified psychologistic logic are objective.

Both Popper and Carnap denied that the expansion of a body of propositions accepted as evidence via induction is subject to objective critical control and in various ways sought to deny that such inductive inference occurs in scientific enquiry. They both appealed to Hume in support of this anti-inductivist thesis.

Given these shared agreements, the differences in their outlook are far from overwhelming. Carnap thought that principles of an objectivist (or qualified psychologistic) inductive logic could be defended which (so he initially hoped) would be so powerful that, given agent X's corpus of knowledge or evidence, X would be obliged as a rational agent to adopt a definite state of credal probability judgement. Popper, on the other hand, thought there are no principles of inductive logic in this sense at all. Popper did not deny that agents make judgements of certainty and probability; but the propriety of such judgements is so heavily dependent on the situation of the agent that they cannot be subjected to any objective criticism – not even by appealing to a requirement of credal coherence demanding that probability judgements conform to the calculus of probabilities. Popper was and remains a more radical subjectivist concerning probability judgement than any member of the personalist camp! Because he, like Carnap, insisted on the objectivity of scientific inquiry, he was compelled to downgrade the importance of probability judgement in scientific enquiry just as both Popper and Carnap downgrade the importance of inductive expansion of a body of knowledge.

In his essay, Lakatos reviewed several difficulties confronting Carnap's original project – namely, the construction of an objectivist inductive logic powerful enough to obligate all rational agents sharing the same evidence to endorse the same credal state. Carnap subsequently abandoned the project himself.

None the less, like the personalist Bayesians, Carnap maintained that there are some context-independent constraints on credal probability judgement which may claim to be principles of inductive logic in the objectivist sense. Whereas Popper maintained that anything goes in probability judgement, Carnap, like the personalists, held that anything goes within very weak limits. The legitimate core of Lakatos's criticism of Carnap is that if anything goes within very weak limits in probability judgement and probability judgement is central to scientific activity, science is subjective to its core – counter to the common Carnap–Popper outlook.

Recall, however, that Lakatos, like Feyerabend, held that scientific enquiry as Popper saw it could be subject to objectivist critical control only within very weak limits. Feyerabend and Lakatos responded to this shared perspective on Popper in different ways. Ignoring relatively minor details, Feyerabend concluded that anything goes, whereas Lakatos did not. Lakatos contended that the extremely narrow standard for objectivity used by both Carnap and Popper should be modified by introducing critical standards which take contextual factors explicitly and systematically into account.

This contrast between the responses of Feyerabend and Lakatos to problems with objectivity in Popper's views is parallelled in the Bayesian camp. The self-styled 'tempered personalist' Shimony seeks to identify norms which constrain the adoption of states of credal probability judgement relative to the agent's body of knowledge and, in addition, to other contextual factors such as the problem investigated and the hypotheses seriously proposed as solutions to the problem. Whatever the merits of Shimony's proposals in detail might be, his approach resembles Lakatos's relativization of appraisals of hypotheses in enquiry to features of research programmes and to evaluations of problem shifts in such programs as degenerating or non-degenerating. If Shimony is a tempered personalist, Lakatos is a tempered Feyerabendian.

Thus, even from his own perspective, the breakdown of the Carnapian program for inductive logic should not have led Lakatos to despair of bringing probability judgement under critical control. The control would not be objective in the narrow sense which those suffering from the Curse of Frege crave; but it would be objective in the somewhat relaxed sense which allows contextual factors to be taken into account systematically and explicitly in norms of appraisal.

Once we have seen this far, we may well ask why Lakatos, Shimony, and other such contextualists do not concede that revisions of a body of knowledge or evidence via inductive expansion may also be brought under systematic critical control even though neither deductive nor inductive logic impose many constraints on such revision. Once Lakatos loosened the bonds of the Third World he should have been more open to ways and means of bringing both credal probability judgement and revisions of knowledge under critical control. I conjecture that his failure to do so is attributable in part to his tendency to divide the philosophical community into Popperian sheep and anti-Popperian goats.

Fortunately Adler has not been misled as Lakatos was by this dichotomy. Yet, to the extent that his exposition perpetuates the dichotomy, I fear it will be misleading.

ADLER: 1. On similar grounds both Bogdan and Levi find that I have too closely identified recent work in inductive logic with Carnap's programme. Bogdan takes local induction as characterized by a methodological turn, which he believes should be sharply distinguished from the Carnapian goal of a pure global inductive logic. Levi considers the crucial factor in local induction to be the rejection of the 'Curse of Frege' and the acceptance of an ideal of objective knowledge which allows contextual factors to be constitutive of our 'critical controls', but does not fall into subjectivism. Levi takes the dichotomy of formal logic or psychologism to be misconceived. He claims that Carnap (and Popper too, although here he and Bogdan are in disagreement) should be distinguished from local inductive logicians because it is just that sharp dichotomy which is crucial to Carnap's programme.

It is clear from my paper that I share with Bogdan and Levi the perspective which finds the progress and promise in inductive logic in the methodological turn, and the correlative acceptance of a broader conception of objectivity. On this score they may be right that even my limited commitment to recent work, as being broadly within the Carnapian programme, is wrong or misleading. But my criteria for such grouping were on the basis of their sharing a common set of critics and objections. Neither Levi nor Bogdan appears to question the grouping on the basis of those criteria.

2. Bogdan takes it that my use of the subjectivist theory makes an '... implicit equation of the growth of knowledge with a non-methodological induction governed only by some priors, coherence and conditionalization'. This is not my view, but I expect it is my fault that Bogdan has this idea, so I would like to expand my remarks on the subjectivist theory. I think these remarks will also provide at least partial answers to some of the objections to that theory that Bogdan alludes to.

There are two ways one may approach the controversy about the objectivity of scientific development. The main way has been as a dispute about certain general philosophical theses as applied to science (e.g., meaning invariance, the theory–observation distinction, conceptual relativism). But a much less canvassed way is as a philosophical prelude to the testing of alternative hypotheses to explain certain phenomena. The phenomena include the shift from disagreement to agreement over the acceptance of a scientific theory after investigation or criticism. This approach is interesting for a number of reasons. First, it begins the discussion from a more-or-less shared premiss. Kuhn and his opponents share this view of the phenomena to be explained. And Kuhn takes the view that the explanation will be irreducibly sociological (Feyerabend and Kuhn themselves disagree here about the extent of such agreement in the scientific community.) Second, starting from this point of agreement we can make the integral relation of the detailed histories of science that are offered in defence of the hypotheses more plausible than the purely philosophical debates allow. The latter can only take these as examples, whereas they are presented by both Kuhn and Feyerabend as more than just illustrative. Third, it leads to a whole range of testable hypotheses about the degree of independence of investigators, the nature of the agreement, or the relation of individual opinion to group behaviour. Fourth, and somewhat paradoxically, I think that by looking at these alternative hypotheses from the point of view of the subjectivist theory the Kuhnian hypothesis loses plausibility even before it has a detailed empirical test. If the phenomena are the resulting agreement about acceptance, and if we can establish that there was a high degree of independence among investigators, and that there were data that would justify the acceptance of the theory, then the subjectivist has a simple explanation of this phenomena: a convergence of opinion through Bayesian conditionalization. This is not going to be a very full explanation, and I do not think that at every level of science the subjectivist story is complete. Rather it provides an objective framework wherein other accounts (e.g. of methodological induction) can provide a better explication. So the subjectivist theory is meant only to apply to one problem: namely, it is a defence of science as meeting at least a minimal level of objectivity without which none of the richer types of inductive logic would be applicable. What makes the subjectivist explanation so plausible is the simplicity of the assumptions and the high degree of rationality it attributes to scientific activity without going beyond generally shared premises about scientific behaviour. The simplicity of the explanation can be attributed to its being a type of 'invisible hand explanation' in the sense that Robert Nozick gave to that expression. It is an explanation of a phenomenon (under a given description) which appears to require an intentional plan to have it occur without appeal to any such intentions. In particular, so long as one's system of beliefs is and remains coherent and one conditionalizes on new data, one can expect a convergence of opinion even with widely divergent prior probability judgements. Such has long been taken as a hallmark of objectivity. One simple reason is that unless the grounds for the change in probability judgements were the sharing of a common set of data (reflecting a 'common world') the resulting agreement appears as a massive coincidence. The public, self-corrective nature of science is what led Peirce to expect such convergence and even define the truth in terms of it. Since properties such as self-correctiveness are properties of the scientific enterprise viewed as a *whole*, we needn't worry too much about Bogdan's claim that the subjectivist theory seems false as a descriptive theory of *individual* behaviour. (But even that claim may be questioned. See here L. Jonathan Cohen's discussion[1] of the experiments of Tversky and Kahneman.)

I have not tried to make good my use of the subjectivist theory to vindicate a minimal type of objectivity in science. Rather I have suggested some further ways this thesis could be developed, along lines determined by Bogdan's criticisms. I do not have the space for additional discussion except to mention how a subjectivist's convergence may be relevant to the infinite regress argument in epistemology. Generally, foundationalism is seen as the only answer to

[1] *The Probable and the Provable*, pp. 258–64.

the regress argument by giving us a self-justifying starting point for knowledge. But the argument is broken if there is a starting point even if not justified. The response will be that this is no alternative because now no member higher up the chain will be justified. But if convergence of opinion does confer justification, by that very convergence (under the appropriate conditions), then I suggest we can reject the assumption that the *process* of justification cannot itself confer justification. Our starting-points may be arbitrary and radically corrigible but they can still give rise to highly justified systematic theories.

3. In his suggestive discussion of 'modelling' confirmation functions, Bogdan assumes an urn model whose statistics conform to Carnap's c^*. Given this model, Bogdan then goes on to confront Carnap with some dilemmas ultimately aimed at rejecting the Carnapian theory. The first one is that in such a world we must either 'accept the strong assumptions . . . ' or realize that '. . . there may be no need for induction to begin with, and that probability deductions from the model may suffice'. But as far as I can see both 'horns' are acceptable. If for c^* to hold, just as for the Bose–Einstein statistics to hold, certain descriptions must be true of that model, then (trivially) that is just what must be accepted if one believes the model is correct. If Bogdan could show us that some more minimal inductive logic (i.e., one with fewer assumptions) held whenever c^* does, that would lead us to reject c^* as superfluous. But for reasons I have given in the main text, this is unlikely. The second horn of the dilemma reflects the well-known fact that any inductive argument can be turned into a deductive one by supplying missing premisses of a corresponding enthymeme. Granted c^*, and given the empirical judgements of the sample, then it is itself central to Carnap's whole view that the confirmation equation would be analytic. The other dilemma is that, if confirmation is to capture the Humean situation of independence, then no learning from experience is possible. But, if learning from experience is possible, then we do not capture independence. The answer to this dilemma is that the possibility of learning from experience is a *defeasible a priori* assumption that we make for any inductive logic to get started. In making such an assumption we, of course, deny independence because this will lead to $c\dagger$, which is just that function which is appropriate when our assumption does not hold. This is a purely formal point.

When Bogdan concludes that there is no role for Carnap's probability logic '. . . that cannot be performed by conceptual modelling, deductive applications of the probability calculus ... and methodological induction ... ', he is not in fact giving a reason for rejecting that probability logic. First, his three components require more complex assumptions to apply. Second, and again as argued in the main text, methodological induction rests on, though is not reducible to, the kind of statistical urn models which are paradigmatic representations of Carnapian confirmation problems. Moreover, Bogdan is here assuming that the type of model is given, when the point of induction – and, in particular, an open parameter in Carnap's continuum – is just that we are trying to *discover* whether this model is accurate for our world. Bogdan holds that, before we can proceed to say which world we are in, we had better have '... an idea of what the domain of enquiry is structurally like ... '. This may well be, but from the epistemological or methodological point of view neither has priority. What we learn from induction by testing one conjectured model interacts with, and constantly leads us to revise, what we learn by testing other models.

List of Participants
at the Conference

E. W. Adams   Dept. of Philosophy, University of California, U.S.A.

J. Adler   Dept. of Philosophy, Brooklyn College, U.S.A.

E. Agazzi   Dept. of Philosophy, Genoa University, Italy.

F. Altrichter   MTA Filozofiai Intezete, Hungary.

S. Blackburn   Pembroke College and Sub-Faculty of Philosophy, Oxford University, U.K.

D. Bloor   Science Studies Unit, University of Edinburgh, U.K.

M. Boden   School of Social Sciences, Sussex University, U.K.

R. Bogdan   Dept. of Philosophy, Stanford University, U.S.A.

A. W. Burks   Dept. of Computer Science and Communication, University of Michigan, U.S.A.

L. J. Cohen   The Queen's College and Sub-Faculty of Philosophy, Oxford University, U.K.

J. Dorling   Dept. of Philosophy of Science, Chelsea College, University of London, U.K.

W. K. Essler   Philosophisches Seminar II, Munich University, West Germany.

R. N. Giere   Dept. of History and Philosophy of Science, Indiana University, U.S.A.

I. Hacking   Dept. of Philosophy, Stanford University, U.S.A.

M. B. Hesse   Dept. of History and Philosophy of Science, Cambridge University, U.K.

R. Hilpinen   Dept. of Philosophy, University of Turku, Finland.

S. Körner   Dept. of Philosophy, Bristol University, U.K.

T. Kuipers   Dept. of Philosophy, University of Groningen, Netherlands.

H. Kyburg	Dept. of Philosophy, Rochester University, U.S.A.
K. Lehrer	Dept. of Philosophy, Arizona University, U.S.A.
I. Levi	Dept. of Philosophy, Columbia University, U.S.A.
J. L. Mackie	University College and Sub-Faculty of Philosophy, Oxford University, U.K.
A. Margalit	Dept. of Philosophy, The Hebrew University, Israel.
H. Mellor	Faculty of Philosophy, Cambridge University, U.K.
B. Meltzer	Dept. of Artificial Intelligence, University of Edinburgh, U.K.
D. Miller	Dept. of Philosophy, Warwick University, U.K.
W. Newton-Smith	Balliol College and Sub-Faculty of Philosophy, Oxford University, U.K.
I. Niiniluoto	Inst. of Philosophy, University of Helsinki, Finland.
R. Rosenkrantz	Dept. of Philosophy, Virginia Polytechnic and State University, U.S.A.
W. Salmon	Dept. of Philosophy, Arizona University, U.S.A.
E. Scheibe	Dept. of Philosophy, University of Göttingen, West Germany.
S. Shoemaker	Dept. of Philosophy, Cornell University, U.S.A.
R. Swinburne	Dept. of Philosophy, Keele University, U.K.
P. Teller	Chicago Circle, University of Illinois, U.S.A.
R. Tuomela	Dept. of Philosophy, University of Helsinki, Finland.
B. Wojcicki	Polish Academy of Science, Wroclaw, Poland.
T. Winograd	Computer Science Dept., Stanford University, U.S.A.

INDEX